Victims of Nazi Persecution in the Channel Islands

Victims of Nazi Persecution in the Channel Islands

A Legitimate Heritage?

Gilly Carr

BLOOMSBURY ACADEMIC
LONDON • NEW YORK • OXFORD • NEW DELHI • SYDNEY

BLOOMSBURY ACADEMIC
Bloomsbury Publishing Plc
50 Bedford Square, London, WC1B 3DP, UK
1385 Broadway, New York, NY 10018, USA

BLOOMSBURY, BLOOMSBURY ACADEMIC and the Diana logo are trademarks of
Bloomsbury Publishing Plc

First published in Great Britain 2019
Paperback edition published 2021

Copyright © Gilly Carr, 2019

Gilly Carr has asserted her rights under the Copyright, Designs and Patents Act, 1988,
to be identified as Author of this work.

For legal purposes the Acknowledgements on p. x constitute an extension of this
copyright page.

Cover image © Gilly Carr

All rights reserved. No part of this publication may be reproduced or transmitted
in any form or by any means, electronic or mechanical, including photocopying,
recording, or any information storage or retrieval system, without prior
permission in writing from the publishers.

Bloomsbury Publishing Plc does not have any control over, or responsibility for,
any third-party websites referred to or in this book. All internet addresses given in this
book were correct at the time of going to press. The author and publisher regret any
inconvenience caused if addresses have changed or sites have ceased to exist,
but can accept no responsibility for any such changes.

A catalogue record for this book is available from the British Library.

A catalog record for this book is available from the Library of Congress.

ISBN: HB: 978-1-4742-4565-4
PB: 978-1-3501-9266-9
ePDF: 978-1-4742-4569-2
eBook: 978-1-4742-4567-8

Typeset by Deanta Global Publishing Services, Chennai, India

To find out more about our authors and books visit www.bloomsbury.com and
sign up for our newsletters

*This book is dedicated to Frank Falla and other victims of
Nazi persecution from the Channel Islands, who have been my constant
companions while writing this book.*

Contents

List of Illustrations	viii
Acknowledgements	x

Part One 1940–1946

1	Introduction	3
2	'Alone amongst a Crowd': The British Experience in Nazi Prisons and Concentration Camps	23
3	1945–1946: Cementing De-legitimization	49

Part Two 1945–1965

4	The Impact of PTSD on the Agency of Victims of Nazi Persecution	73
5	The Decades of Silence? 1945–1965	95
6	An 'Unofficial Official': The Role of Frank Falla	118

Part Three 1965–Present

7	Game-Changers and Incremental Memory Events	147
8	Acts of Repair, Acts of Rescue	170
9	Conclusion: A Legitimate Heritage?	195

Notes	209
Bibliography	234
Index	240

List of Illustrations

Figure 2.1	The entrance of Fort de Romainville today. Copyright: Roderick Miller / Tracing the Past e.V	26
Figure 2.2	Straubing Prison hospital today. Copyright: Gilly Carr	28
Figure 2.3	Fort de Villeneuve-Saint-Georges today. Copyright: Gilly Carr	31
Figure 2.4	The ruins of Zöschen labour camp today. Copyright: Gilly Carr	33
Figure 2.5	Newspaper article written by Frank Falla in July 1945. Copyright: Guernsey Press / Frank Falla Archive. Courtesy: Island Archives, Guernsey	43
Figure 3.1	Bailiff Alexander Coutanche in a cameo role in a still from the Crown Film Unit's production *The Channel Islands 1940–1945*, held at the Imperial War Museum, copyright expired	51
Figure 3.2	Graph showing number of incidences of themes in the CFU film, *The Channel Islands 1940–1945*	52
Figure 3.3a and b	Major John Manley and Major John L'Amy of the Jersey Loyalists. Courtesy: Jersey Heritage	60
Figure 4.1	Segment of the compensation testimony of John Draper. Copyright: The National Archives. Contains public sector information licensed under the Open Government Licence 3.0	85
Figure 5.1	Frank Tuck's Christmas card. Courtesy and copyright: Angela McAllister	99
Figure 5.2	Two of the children of Bill Symes holding his paperknife made in Buchenwald, and a postcard smuggled out of the camp. Courtesy and copyright: Gilly Carr	100
Figure 5.3	Frank Falla at a gathering of Europe's Maquis leaders, Belgium, 1946. Copyright: the Frank Falla Archive. Courtesy: Island Archives, Guernsey	104
Figure 6.1	Frank Falla's briefcase containing his correspondence. Copyright: Gilly Carr	119
Figure 6.2	Frank Falla and the 'Frankfurt / Naumburg Crooks' at their April reunion. Copyright: the Frank Falla Archive. Courtesy: the Island Archives, Guernsey	128
Figure 6.3	A V-sign badge made by Roy Machon. Copyright: Gilly Carr	133
Figure 6.4	The 1965 compensation celebration dinner for the 'ex-Belsen, ex-Buchenwald, ex-Frankfurt, ex-Naumburg Channel	

	Islands political prisoners of the Nazis'. Copyright: unknown. Courtesy: Rosie Jeffreys	141
Figure 6.5	Frank Falla typing *The Silent War*. Copyright: the Frank Falla Archive. Courtesy: the Island Archives, Guernsey	142
Figure 7.1	Joe Mière by Andrew Tift. Jersey Heritage Collections. Copyright: Andrew Tift	150
Figure 7.2	Philip Bailhache unveiling the political prisoners' memorial 1995. Copyright: *Jersey Evening Post*	152
Figure 7.3	Jewish Memorial in Guernsey after the brief HMD ceremony in 2012. The single small basket of flowers reflects the size of the crowd. Copyright: Gilly Carr	158
Figure 7.4	Peter Symes reading out his father's testimony about Buchenwald, HMD 2015, Guernsey. Copyright: Gilly Carr	161
Figure 7.5	The author speaking at HMD in Guernsey in 2016. Copyright: Gilly Carr	164
Figure 8.1	Diagram to show the relationship between an event, its legacy and its heritage. Copyright: Gilly Carr	171
Figure 8.2	Sidney Ashcroft's memorial plaque, Straubing, Germany. Copyright: Gilly Carr	180
Figure 8.3	The Resistance Memorial, 4 May 2015. Copyright: Gilly Carr	181
Figure 8.4	Jean at her father's grave in Halle. Copyright: Gilly Carr	184
Figure 8.5	Pat in Pšov, Czech Republic, at the place where her father was reburied in 1945. Copyright: Gilly Carr	185
Figure 8.6	Philip Machon by his grandfather's memorial in Hamelin. Copyright: Gilly Carr	186
Figure 8.7	The homepage of the Frank Falla Archive, www.frankfallaarchive.org Copyright: Gilly Carr	187
Figure 8.8	The Jersey resistance trail. Copyright: Jersey Heritage	191
Figure 9.1	Allied war cemetery with Maurice Gould's grave on the right, Howard Davis Park, St Helier. Copyright: Gilly Carr	201
Figures 9.2a, b and c	John Ingrouille's grave in 2010, 2015 and 2018. Copyrights: Gilly Carr (9.2a), Dave and Rosie Bradshaw (9.2b) and Molly Paul (9.2c)	202–4
Figure 9.3	The café of Jersey War Tunnels. Copyright: Gilly Carr	205

Acknowledgements

This book was written during two successive sabbaticals from the University of Cambridge in 2015 and 2018. My time during these periods has been split between my study in Cambridge and archives in London, Jersey, Guernsey and France. During the intervening period between my sabbaticals I have been fortunate enough to be able to pop over to St Helier or St Peter Port to commemorate Holocaust Memorial Days, or to be able to support or contribute to heritage projects, witness memorial unveilings, or speak at Liberation Day events. Much as I love Cambridge, regular trips to the Channel Islands have helped me survive the high-pressure environment of my university life.

During my many trips to Jersey and Guernsey, I have relied heavily on the kindness, generosity and companionship of many friends and colleagues. In no particular order I would like to thank the following people for their professionalism, friendship and kindness:

At Jersey Heritage: Jon Carter, Chris Addy, Lucy Layton, Louise Downie, Val Nelson and Doug Ford. At Jersey Archives: Stuart Nicolle (who has put up with almost daily and increasingly apologetic email requests from me during my sabbaticals), Linda Romeril and staff.

At the Island Archives, Guernsey, Nathan Coyde and Darryl Ogier have kindly helped with my incessant requests for them to trawl through the darker (but not necessarily the dustier) recesses of the archives; and the staff of the Priaulx Library, especially Sue Laker, has kindly allowed me scans of old issues of the Guernsey Press. I am grateful in particular to Jason Monaghan and Helen Glencross at Guernsey Museums and Art Gallery for being willing to support new memorial erections and exhibition ideas in the Island.

There are other Islanders who I would like to single out for my thanks: the late, great Michael Ginns and Josephine Ginns (for *everything*, including the cake); Freddie Cohen (for his insight into his work behind the scenes in promoting the memory of Jews in Jersey and for his interview on the opposition and support he encountered); Doug Ford (for his humour, appreciation of my limericks and interviews); Mark Lamerton (for his regular packages of Occupation news from the Jersey Press and his friendship); Gary Font (for his game-changing and example-setting work at the Slaveworkers' Memorial and for being one of the good guys); Paula Thelwell (for her dedication to the cause and love of a good story); and Elis Bebb (for being my HMD partner in crime, friend and dinner buddy, and for being willing to have the finer details of our work aired in public).

Although Michael Day, former director of Jersey Heritage, is no longer in Jersey, I would like to thank him for allowing me to interview him at length about his memories of his JHT years and the game-changing work he carried out there.

I would like to thank former Bailiffs Sir de Vic Carey and Sir Philip Bailhache for their interviews carried out a number of years ago now, but which were still relevant for my work here. I hope that neither man is too taken aback by my characterization of the power of the 'Carey effect' or the 'Bailhache effect'. Sir Philip was also kind enough to do me the honour of speaking at the opening night of my exhibition at the Wiener Library, for which I am extremely grateful. I would also like to thank him for sending me copies of many of his past speeches.

At the Wiener Library I would like to thank Barbara Warnock, Christine Schmidt, Mary Vrabecz and Elise Bath. These wonderful women have helped me find the records of Islanders in prisons and camps, and were a pleasure to work with on my exhibition *On British Soil: Victims of Nazism in the Channel Islands*.

I am especially pleased that I have been able to bring the Frank Falla Archive into this book. My first thanks for the origin of this project belongs to Sally Falla, who handed her father's archive into my safe keeping in 2010 so that I could study it. She and Tim Falla have been so helpful in sharing their memories of their father. Frank Falla is the one person above all others from the Occupation generation that I wish I could have met. I hope that the website dedicated to his memory will be a suitable testament to all Channel Islander victims of Nazi persecution. The members of the Frank Falla Archive team who have helped me with this project include Roderick Miller, who has done a better job than I ever could in researching the 125 (so far) prisons and camps to which Channel Islanders were sent. Susan Ilie has been an invaluable researcher and second pair of hands and eyes for me in Guernsey. Helen Gray from Jersey Heritage has also helped me greatly with her website know-how. Switch Digital are responsible for the handsome layout of the website, informed by Cord Pagenstecher at the Freie Universität in Berlin. None of it could have been possible without funding from the EVZ Foundation in Berlin, who were prepared to believe me when I told them that Channel Islanders had indeed been deported to Nazi prisons and concentration camps.

The 'acts of rescue' described in Chapter 8 have been high points of my life. I will never forget the trips made to Germany and the Czech Republic with Jean Harris and Pat Fisher, and I thank them for being willing to make the pilgrimage and for allowing me to come with them to find their fathers. I don't think I have ever got through so many tissues in a single week. Without Michael Viebig in Halle, Director of the Roter Ochse memorial, and Pavel Vařeka at the University of West Bohemia, the exact locations of the bodies of Joseph Gillingham and Joseph Tierney would not have been found. These men provided the final jigsaw piece and for this I will always be grateful for their help.

I am indebted, too, to Patrick Clahane at the BBC, who so expertly handled production of both documentaries, driving on the wrong side of the road in Germany, and coping with the over-enthusiastic roadside police in goodness-knows-where in the Czech Republic, about whom we will say no more. Thank you, too, to Chris Roberts for being game enough to come with me to Straubing to find his relative Sidney Ashcroft. More recently, the trip to Hamelin with Phil Machon and Diana Hill was a memorable and emotional one, and I was so grateful to have the opportunity to witness and be part of the ceremony in Am Wehl cemetery with them both. The exploration around the grounds of the prison and the dark heritage of the town and its surroundings was made so much more enjoyable through their company. We owe a debt of gratitude to

Bernhard Gelderblom for his hard work, fund-raising and activism in Hamelin, not to mention his hospitality during our visit.

Rachel O'Flynn and Mary Pring are the two wonderful women at the Foreign Office archives in Milton Keynes who helped me obtain testimonies of Channel Islander victims of Nazi persecution, and who have shown their support for these men and women by attending the memorial unveiling in Guernsey and the opening night of my exhibition at the Wiener Library. Wonderful women indeed!

Saving the best almost till last, the children and grandchildren of victims of Nazi persecution have enabled several chapters of this book to be written through their honesty, openness and willingness to trust me with their loved one's stories, their own experiences of growing up with a survivor in the family, their family documents, and even precious family artefacts which they lent to the Wiener Library for my exhibition *On British Soil*. While I have named Pat, Jean, Sally, Tim and Phil above, I would like to pass on my sincere thanks to Clare and Angela McAllister, who have shared with me their extensive and valuable archive, the contents of which have not yet been exhausted, Amanda Hibbs, Mark Fisher, Phil, Ian and Paul Domaille, Peter Creasey, Mary Bichard, Jean Gathercole, Peter Symes and Joan Hall, Bryan O'Meara, Karen McGee, Sally Nicolle, Kathleen O'Meara, Dawn Crowson, Rosie Jeffrey, Andy Le Maitre and Sidney Le Maitre, Rosie Bradshaw, Keith Friend, Andrew Hassall, Rose Short, Jill Robilliard and Colin Lainé, Audrey Bird, Howard Hacquoil, Jo, Andrew and Jean Duquemin, Gemma Green, and all members of the Facebook group *Channel Islander Victims of Nazi Persecution*. I hope you feel that I have done your loved ones justice and spoken for them in a way that they would have approved of.

A number of you have allowed me to use images of you and your loved ones in this monograph, and my greatest debt of gratitude here is to Sally Falla and the Frank Falla Archive. Other copyright holders include Roderick Miller, Rosie and Dave Bradshaw, Jersey Archives, Rosie Jeffrey and, last but not least, Andrew Tift, whose portrait of Joe Mière captures his life's work so well.

I'd like to thank Louise Willmot, friend and colleague, for giving me her thoughts on Chapter 6, a chapter which turned into an *homage* to Frank Falla and his work. My PhD student and fellow dark heritage scholar, Margaret Comer, kindly read through Chapter 8 and gave it her seal of approval. Ideas from Chapters 4 and 5 were presented to the British Association of Holocaust Studies in 2018 – my thanks to the audience for their thoughts. An earlier and shorter draft of Chapter 7 appeared as '"Have you been offended?" Holocaust memory in the Channel Islands at HMD 70' in *Holocaust Studies* 22(1): 44–64 in 2016. The journal's website can be found here: https://www.tandfonline.com/loi/rhos20.

My final thanks go to my husband Jon, who wrongly imagined that he might get to spend a little more time with me than normal during my sabbaticals. I'd like to thank him for his patience, his love and his support, as well as his occasional stint as anthropological informant.

Part One

1940–1946

1

Introduction

Introduction and narratives of Occupation

In May 2015, Sir Richard Collas, Bailiff of Guernsey, pulled aside a Guernsey flag to reveal the Resistance Memorial to a sizable crowd who had gathered to witness the historic occasion in which the acts of their parents and grandparents would be honoured for the first time. Just over two years previously, Collas had also unveiled a Blue Plaque to Marie Ozanne, one of those whose names also appeared on the Resistance Memorial. These were the first memorials ever erected in Guernsey to those who had been imprisoned, deported or who had died as a direct result of their offences against the Germans during the Occupation of 1940 to 1945. Similar memorials in the sister Channel Island of Jersey had been erected two decades earlier, but even these had taken fifty years to come into being.

This small snapshot into the memory and heritage of those who defied, resisted or protested against the occupiers, or otherwise offended against them, provides a suitable lens into understanding the central questions which frame this book. Why did it take so long for this group to be remembered through memorialization? Why were so many of the victims of Nazism who were imprisoned in or deported to Nazi-controlled prisons and camps on the continent excluded from the narrative of Occupation for so long? Why has there been a difference between the two largest Channel Islands of Jersey and Guernsey? And how and why do they fit into the British narrative of war or even the Holocaust, if at all, or are the Channel Islands and mainland Britain entirely disconnected, separate things? If so, should this continue to be the case? Is there a connection between the Holocaust and victims of Nazism in the Channel Islands and, if so, what is it?

These questions are by no means the only ones addressed in this volume, but they form its central building blocks and provide its inspiration and starting point. I also seek to explore the experiences of British victims of Nazism during the war and in its aftermath, and to use this to join the Channel Islands' narrative to that of the rest of the Britain. For too long have they been left on the margins, easily ignored or waved aside because of their small size. And yet, as the only part of the British Isles to be occupied during the war, they could play a larger part in supplementing or disputing current narratives. This has been difficult because, until recently, they have not been allowed to challenge the wartime narratives of even the Channel Islands themselves.

The evolution of the narrative of Channel Islands' war memory has passed through four phases, expressed through heritage in forms such as museum exhibitions, memorials and commemorative ceremonies.[1] While the 1940s and early 1950s were a period of celebrating military victory while mourning dead soldiers and 'cleansing' the Islands of the 'taint' of German military hardware, after this was complete most of the 1950s and 1960s was a period of self-imposed amnesia. This was a time of political and social necessity for people to focus on the future to rebuild their lives and the Islands' economies. In the later 1970s, when the post-war or second generation had reached adulthood, the Islands entered a phase of 'Occupation nostalgia', which has never entirely faded. In the face of the silence of the Occupation generation, their children discovered the Occupation for themselves through collecting militaria and restoring bunkers. This period has also focused on Liberation Day, which itself is a recurring leitmotif for the invocation of the more positive, 'exciting' parts of the Occupation and a repression of its more traumatic aspects. The fourth phase in memory has been visible only from 1995 onwards (and only in Jersey), when we see the beginnings of anamnesis, a 'remembering' of the victims of Nazism a whole generation later than in other parts of Western Europe.[2]

The late cause of the recognition of victims and the reach of the tendrils of the Holocaust to the Channel Islands is explored in this book, and is partially explained by the strong influence of the Churchillian paradigm, both in the Channel Islands and the UK. For historian Paul Sanders, this paradigm speaks of the 'blood, toil and tears' of 'sublime and unwavering steadfastness in the face of adversity'.[3] It is a narrative which states that 'the British were not a nation of victims, but of victors'.[4] John Ramsden has also identified this 'Churchillian interpretation' or myth of the war,[5] which Mark Connelly suggests may even have its roots in the Great War, when the key national traits were 'self-reliance, stoicism and self-sacrifice'.[6] But was this narrative somehow enforced upon the Channel Islands or did they choose it for themselves?

Paul Sanders' argument about the Churchillian paradigm presents an image of Islanders flailing around in 1945, searching for a way to talk about or frame the Occupation in its aftermath:

Still, with no place other to fit their war memory that the straightjacket of UK war memory – the Churchillian paradigm – islanders locked into the celebration of sublime heroism and unwavering steadfastness. The Occupation was stripped down to the dogma of 'political correctness' of the post-war period: 'our chaps' in the Channel Islands did a fantastic job in fighting their corner and defending the population. The Germans there didn't really behave too badly because they respected the British and, besides, were 'officer gentlemen', quite similar to the British themselves; evacuees and escapees participated directly in the 'British war', their brethren indirectly, by keeping on smiling, eluding the 'Gestapo' bloodhounds and following the Allied news.[7]

Cheryl Jorgensen-Earp has argued more recently that Islanders 'readily tapped into existing notions of British spirit that had bolstered the war since its advent' and explored 'their own feelings about England' in order to express a 'traditional patriotism' which formed a counter-ideology which was 'pitted against Nazi dogma during the

Occupation'. Such a resistance gave 'a sense of what life should be like, a common ideal of freedom and respect'. Jorgensen-Earp further argues that support for this patriotic counter-ideology was a form of resistance in itself, and that

> *the familiar images and catch-phrases of patriotism served as a shorthand, easily and quickly exchanged under the nose of the occupiers. As the Occupation ground on and conditions became increasingly wearing, the 'we can take it' attitude woven through Churchill's speeches and Londoners' response to the Blitz served as a barrier against both despair and numbed acquiescence to German control.*[8]

In other words, rather than 'locking' themselves into the Churchillian narrative after the war because they had no other allowable place for an experience that threatened to upset notions that Britain held about itself, Jorgensen-Earp argues that Islanders chose this particular patriotic narrative for themselves from the earliest days of the Occupation as an expression of resistance. An additional motivation for this, she argues, was because, with Channel Islands men fighting in the British armed forces, and with so many evacuated children living in the UK, their 'greatest treasure [was] under the custody of Great Britain'.[9]

The Churchillian narrative may have sustained Islanders both during and after the Occupation, but it could not sustain the Islanders whose experience fell outside its boundaries. Some of those who survived and returned from concentration camps were given a platform on which to tell their stories. It was perhaps not difficult for the story of high-profile returning victims of Nazism such as Harold Le Druillenec of Jersey, said to be the only British survivor of Bergen-Belsen at its liberation, to be viewed through a lens of stoic endurance until liberation (by the British). He had demonstrated both patriotism (in listening illicitly to the BBC) and self-sacrifice (in helping to shelter an escaped Russian forced labourer, which caused his own deportation and that of his sister, Louisa Gould, who died in Ravensbrück). He also spoke at several war crimes tribunals, and narrated his own story on the BBC.[10] Perhaps it is not surprising that he and his sister emerged as victims of Nazism par excellence after the Occupation, a rare glimpse of an allowable narrative that did not pause to dwell on the neighbours who informed upon them, nor to criticize the local authorities who did not do more to protect them. It also does not surprise us that they were both among the first batch of British 'Heroes of the Holocaust' honoured by the British government in 2010.

But in addition to those few returners whose stories were acceptable because of the patriotism of their original acts, there were many, many more whose offences lacked the nobility and glamour of patriotism, or who lacked school teacher Le Druillenec's public speaking skills, education and eloquence; part of this book explores their silencing and their stories. There were also survivors who would never speak of their experiences again, except through brief euphemistic allusions to 'what happened in Germany', or who were hampered by symptoms of post-traumatic stress disorder (PTSD) or lifelong physical disabilities caused by brutality, ill-treatment and forced labour. Then there were those who did not survive to speak of what they endured. Other former prisoners clearly found neither kudos nor post-war celebrity in discussing their brief sojourn in French prisons for acts of theft, even if it was of German property; their narratives rarely survive today and can be reconstructed only through surviving court and prison records. It is no coincidence that accounts which endure, and those which were included in the earliest books of the Occupation, belong to those who served prison sentences of often-undescribed severity for patriotic acts such as drawing up V-for-Victory signs, calling out '*Heil* Churchill', listening to the BBC on illicit radios, or collecting military information to share with the British government.[11] The narrative of resistance, in the form that it was allowed to emerge, did not much deviate from the Churchillian narrative, and focused more on the (patriotic) acts than on the details of the consequences of the acts, namely, suffering in Nazi prisons and camps.

Definitions: Who are we talking about?

Those imprisoned or deported for their acts against the occupiers form the core subject matter of this book. They and the perceived illegitimacy of their actions lie at the heart of this exploration into why they were excluded from Occupation narratives and heritage for so long. I use the term 'heritage' here in a double sense. On the one hand, I refer to heritage 'products' in the form of museum exhibitions and memorials, and the more recent digital heritage innovations which allow intervention where traditional forms of heritage are unwelcome or difficult. On the other hand, I also mean it in the wider sense of that which may be inherited. Within this I include personal and group histories and stories which can be handed down in a community or allowed to fade, depending on the degree to which it is valued and legitimized.

The people or group to whom I refer comprise several different categories of people, and in the main I refer to them collectively as 'victims of Nazi persecution' or 'victims of Nazism'. This has also inspired the title of this book, and is taken from the language used in a bilateral agreement between the British government and that of the Federal Republic of Germany.

On 24 July 1964 applications were invited from, or on behalf of, UK nationals who were victims of Nazi persecution, that is, 'persons who suffered detention in a concentration camp or comparable institution'[12] according to the poster advertising the compensation claims. This compensation was the outcome of a long-awaited agreement, the details of which were worded deliberately vaguely. It stated that one million pounds sterling had been given by West Germany for the benefit of 'United Kingdom nationals who were victims of Nationalist-Socialist measures of persecution and who, as a result of such measures, suffered loss of liberty or damage to their health, or, in the case of those who died in consequence of such measures, for the benefit of their dependents'.[13]

While the Channel Islands were and are not part of the United Kingdom, its citizens are British, and so the choice of words for the Anglo-German agreement was misleading; however, the Channel Islanders were to be eligible for compensation, as established by a former prisoner, Guernseyman Frank Falla, whose work deservedly forms a chapter of this book. These particular 'victims of Nazi persecution' form the subject matter discussed here.

While the compensation claims were open to a variety of people who fitted this description, there were two named groups who the Foreign Office had in their sights at the beginning of the process when estimating how many people of which group should receive compensation. The largest by far were the Jewish refugees who had come to the UK after the war and who had subsequently applied for British nationality. The second largest group were estimated to be Channel Islanders, although the Foreign Office factored into its calculations in the planning stages only those deported to civilian internment camps. Although earlier correspondence with the Islands' authorities had provided a gross underestimate of those deported for offences against the occupiers, this tiny number was not added to the Foreign Office's original sums.

It soon became clear that the West German government did not want either refugees or resistance workers to be named in any bilateral agreement as they were unwilling to compensate either group.[14] The refugees had not been British during the war, and resistance workers were perceived by them to be responsible for their own fate, which they had brought about through their own actions. Therefore the two governments concurred that the final agreement should omit the words 'refugee' or 'resistance' and was, instead, left vaguely worded. The Foreign Office was left to quietly administer the compensation as they saw fit.

In the event, the Foreign Office's early predictions about the categories of people who would eventually receive compensation were right, although the number of Channel Islanders who applied were far fewer than at first estimated once those held in internment camps were to be excluded, much to the disappointment of this group. This left only two classifications of eligible applicants from the Channel Islands: Jews and those deported for offences against the German occupiers.

Only two non-British Jews resident in the Channel Islands during the Occupation are known to have applied for compensation, and both had British nationality by the time of the bilateral agreement, but not during the war. Julia Brichta, who was Hungarian when she arrived in 1939, was sent to Ravensbrück for black market offences (her Jewish identity was never proven); and John Max Finkelstein, a Romanian Jew who retired to Jersey in the early 1930s but subsequently was sent to Buchenwald. Although three other Jewish women without British nationality died in Auschwitz after their deportation from Guernsey in 1942, no evidence has yet been found of applications for compensation from their families. This book is therefore not about the experience of Jews resident in or deported from the Channel Islands; the reader is referred elsewhere for information on this subject.[15] Nor does this book concern the subject of forced labourers in the Channel Islands; they were not part of the bilateral agreement of those to be compensated. However, much of the content of this book has relevance for other British victims of Nazism, even though it is specifically those deported for offences against the occupiers who are my subject of interest.

Some might take issue with my use of the term 'victim', as it implies those who did not survive and this book is about survivors just as much as those who died. For some, the word 'victim' also implies a certain passivity and powerlessness – a person without agency or the will to fight. This is not the case for those we examine here; many of the Channel Islanders under discussion would not have survived without the will to endure until their liberation. The Foreign Office included both the living and the dead in their use of the word 'victim', as do I.

Undeniably, 'British victim of Nazi persecution' is something of a mouthful to describe all of those deported from the Channel Islands for offences against the occupiers. Was there another term that they used to describe themselves? Indeed there was, and it was a term used by the German and Channel Islands' authorities during the Occupation to describe specifically those who offended against the Germans. This term was also adopted with pride as a badge of honour during and after the Occupation by those imprisoned: they were called 'political prisoners', and this term was espoused by Joe Mière, a guardian of memory for this group who we will meet later in this volume.

There is far greater evidence for the use of this term in Jersey, where a 'Political Prisoner log' was kept by the local authorities from August 1940 onwards.[16] While in Guernsey, the concept of a 'political prisoner' was used by prisoners to describe somebody who had been *deported* for offences against the Germans, in Jersey the nomenclature was also used among those kept in the local prison and who developed a 'political prisoner consciousness' from the autumn of 1944 onwards. This was because, from the summer of 1944 onwards, no more deportations to the continent could be carried out after the Allied invasion of France, and so the prison population was not regularly renewed and replaced. From the perspective of those with longer sentences, while the numbers in prison grew, the 'hard core' of inmates soon grew to know each other through the circulation of autograph books and, later, certificates, in which they self-identified as 'political prisoners'.[17] Therefore I also refer to the subjects within this book as 'political prisoners', because this is what they called themselves.

However, this term is not without its problems or critics. In the second edition of *The Ultimate Sacrifice*, which tells the story of the Jersey 21,[18] Paul Sanders rightly argues that many of the offences which were labelled 'political' were nothing of the sort. He argued that in order to keep control in the Channel Islands, the Germans had to introduce more and more regulations which turned ordinary non-criminal activities, such as listening to the BBC, into an offence. Further, many of the acts which transgressed the regulations were not political in intent, but merely acts of desperation or survival. Therefore, to call these acts 'political', and those imprisoned 'political prisoners', is to endorse the occupier's logic.[19] Warming to this theme in the third edition, Sanders further argues that the term 'political prisoner' should not be used because 'the value of the historian should lie precisely in his or her ability to provide nuance; and this does not include preferring certain essential categories over others for the sake of convenience'.[20] Sanders' preference is for the term 'victim of Nazi persecution', which accords with the Foreign Office's term that I adopt here myself.

There are further reasons for using this term, Sanders argues, and these include the fact that Nazi punishment – that is, suffering or death in prisons and camps – was out of all proportion to the offence committed. He also argues that 'victim of Nazism' is to be preferred to the term 'resister', because while all resisters who were deported were victims of Nazi persecution, not all victims of Nazi persecution were resisters.[21] Indeed, a number of those deported had committed no offence at all, or were falsely accused. Yet others were deported for 'economic offences that were ambiguous in character' and not necessarily conscious acts of resistance.[22] The Germans pillaged goods and property in the Channel Islands, and so theft of German property was considered to be 'fair game' and entirely legitimate, but was not necessarily an act of resistance. Indeed, 'resistance' is a slippery and problematic concept that comes with much baggage, but the reader is referred elsewhere for a full discussion on the subject in the Channel Islands' context.[23]

To conclude, Sanders' logic implies that both Joe Mière and Frank Falla, important characters in this book, were incorrect in referring to themselves and *all* of their colleagues as 'political prisoners', although he does concede that to use *only* 'victims of Nazi persecution' *all* of the time is odd, and that sometimes other terms are applicable.[24] This author concurs. However, because the epithet of 'political prisoner' was reclaimed (perhaps quite incorrectly on many occasions) by many of those deported to prisons and camps, and because the present volume has these people at its heart and discusses their experiences from their point of view, it takes a 'political-prisoner-centric' view. Therefore this volume uses 'political prisoner' and 'victims of Nazi persecution' or 'Nazi victim' interchangeably, and occasionally 'resister' where appropriate. The key thesis of this book is not about correct nomenclature of this group; rather it is about the legitimacy or otherwise of their actions, and how the perception of this has changed over time since 1940.

Legitimacy

The lens through which I examine victims of Nazi persecution in this volume is that of *legitimacy* – the legitimacy of their actions, their punishment and the right to have their stories told, remembered and incorporated into narratives of the Occupation. This applies to heritage projects, such as museum exhibitions, memorials and digital heritage, just as much as history books and formal education in schools. Legitimacy, as I use it in this volume, is tied up with *rights* just as much as with justification. Discussion of rights – indeed, human rights – is pertinent to most or many of the victims of Nazism discussed here, whose human rights were ignored and abused in Nazi prisons and camps. This abuse, which had a lifelong impact on the men and women involved, not to mention their families and the lives of the second generation, allows us to reassess the offences of those involved and to feel sympathy and empathy for their suffering. While these emotions are not difficult for an outsider, some inside the Channel Islands, who grew up with an Occupation narrative which considered these people as criminals who did the wrong thing, might struggle to react in this way.

The root of the word 'legitimation' comes from the Latin *legitimus*, meaning 'lawful'. Some of the offences against the occupiers – most notably, theft – would not have been considered lawful before the Occupation, and it is this which many might find challenging. And yet this theft against the Germans was often an attempt to redress the balance against the plundering of Channel Islanders' goods and resources which had been ongoing since the arrival of the occupiers. Yet when we pause to consider the consequences of that theft, are we still content that such 'thieves' should be denied rehabilitation today? Brian O'Meara, who stole a bicycle from a German when aged just sixteen, was sent to Buchenwald concentration camp. He was joined there by James Quick and Alfred Baker, all three deported from Guernsey for theft. Herbert Smith died in Augsburg Gestapo prison following brutal treatment in Neuoffingen labour camp. Sidney Ashcroft died in Straubing prison. Both of these men had stolen food from the Germans. While Ashcroft is 'fortunate' in that his name now appears on a new memorial in Guernsey (the family of Smith asked for his name to be omitted), such an honour means that he will probably be spoken of, in time, as a 'hero' of the Occupation, as has been the case for those listed on Jersey's equivalent memorial. And yet no such elevation in memory and rehabilitation is offered to the unnamed who survived.

The desire to divide the Occupation generation – and most especially those deported for offences against the authorities – into heroes and villains also has its problems. Just as it is harsh to characterize anyone who suffered in a concentration camp as a villain, so it is equally difficult to cast them all as heroes. Hungarian woman Julia Brichta is probably the clearest case in point. She was deported from Guernsey for black market offences and was sent to Ravensbrück concentration camp, where she became a kapo or prisoner functionary, a job which came with a truncheon and a whip and power over other prisoners. Julia was Jewish, although she denied her heritage, and maintained that she looked out for other British women in the camp. Despite her position of authority on the side of the perpetrators, her compensation claim of the mid-1960s showed that she was suffering from symptoms of PTSD as well as the physical ill-effects of being in a concentration camp.[25] She defies such easy categorization.

There were other Islanders whose stories are very different, such as Canon Clifford Cohu who called out the news from his bicycle, and during his rounds in the hospital in St Helier; or Marie Ozanne, who repeatedly wrote to the German *Feldkommandant* to criticize his actions towards Jews, forced labourers and others. Both Islanders acted according to their Christian consciences. Cohu died in Zöschen labour camp, while Marie Ozanne was let out of Guernsey prison in 1943 due to ill-health, dying soon afterwards of blood poisoning from a burst appendix. Their actions were more clearly heroic. Many other deported Islanders were ordinary people who listened to their radios illegally, or were innocent of the charges levelled at them. There was nothing particularly special about their actions, yet their suffering and sometimes death in a prison or camp raises their status in our eyes.

This book does not attempt to make heroes out of all of those who were deported. Such binary hero / villain categorizations of ordinary people does not help us to understand them or the Occupation any better; it sheds light, instead, on people's attitudes today. My aims are those of legitimation, rehabilitation, reconsideration and even redress using heritage projects as a means to achieve this, as the latter part of this book explores. This is not to say that former prisoners themselves were incapable of fighting for the same aims: a small number of them, and those who championed their cause, fought to overturn attitudes after liberation and continued their struggle for a legitimate place in the narrative of the Occupation.

This topic is an important one because the Channel Islands form something of an anomaly within Europe. Because those who had participated in the Resistance groups of Europe 'enjoyed an almost automatic legitimacy in the eyes of the nation',[26] the myth of the Resistance and their legitimacy played a vital role for post-war identities, rebuilding national self-esteem, and the construction of narratives of occupation in so many formerly occupied countries after the war. The Channel Islands, however, are the one place where the status and memory of such people were never elevated; instead they were, in the main, denigrated (or at least, not rehabilitated) by the local authorities in Jersey until the mid-1990s, and in Guernsey until the present day.

Within this large group are a range of different people who committed a range of diverse acts of protest, defiance and resistance. Some of these deeds were not intentionally resistant, as we have seen, but were simply about survival or trying to maintain some semblance of normal life. Many of these varied acts were controversial both at the time and now. Is there a case to be made for the legitimacy of buying or selling food on the black market which had originally been stolen or siphoned away from the Germans? Or the understandable verbal abuse or assault of the soldiers of occupation? Was theft from the Germans really fair game? As we've seen, some paid for such thefts either with their lives or long sentences in concentration camps. It is hard to maintain, in the face of such suffering, that these deeds were wholly illegitimate and that the deported deserved their fate. If we forgive – or at least seek to understand – the act, and condemn the resulting over-punishment, then the door begins to open for both sympathy and the legitimacy of honouring their memory.

If we cast aside the categorizations of hero and villain, we find other problematic categorizations of the conduct of victims of Nazism: opinions vary, for example, about the wisdom of certain acts. Were Clifford Cohu and Marie Ozanne foolish, brave or both? We might also consider those who escaped by boat – or who attempted to do so – from the Channel Islands. While the motivation of many was to join Allied forces, or their families in the UK, there were often minor repercussions for those left behind, such as restrictions on fishing and access to beaches.[27] Perhaps this might make us question the ethics of the escapers, and certainly it divided the opinion of Islanders left behind, although attitudes changed after D-Day.[28] Those who were caught in the act of escaping were imprisoned. The most famous trio of this description were Dennis Audrain (who drowned in the attempt), Maurice Gould and Peter Hassall. The latter two were deported as *Nacht und Nebel* prisoners and were brutally treated in Hinzert concentration camp and elsewhere. Gould died shortly afterwards in Wittlich prison from tuberculosis, his health fatally weakened by his treatment in the camp. Hassall survived, but battled with symptoms of PTSD afterwards.[29]

Offences against the occupiers varied over time in terms of their perceived bravery, patriotism, wisdom and benefit to the local community, depending on whom one asked.[30] Legitimacy was very much in the eye of the beholder. During the Occupation, those connected to the local administration were more likely to disapprove of any such 'resistant' actions than those without such connections.[31] What makes it harder to make any single statement about the legitimacy of the actions of the offenders is that while we may refer to them today – as we look back from a distance of seventy-five years – as a 'group' in the singular, they have never been any kind of unified entity and their actions during the Occupation varied greatly. Offences against the occupiers were also carried out by individuals, by families, or by very small numbers of people working together who did not broadcast what they were doing for reasons of personal safety. The highest number of any group tried for collective action in either Guernsey or Jersey was eighteen people,[32] although this was very much an exception and not the rule.

The 'troublemaker' epithet that became attached to the few who risked (or so it was imagined) bringing serious reprisals upon the entire community has become attached instead to the many. While the stories of a minority are recounted with pride – undisputed heroes such as Harold Le Druillenec or those of elevated memory such as the Jersey 21 – awareness of the majority has not yet been achieved in the consciousness of the public, let alone rehabilitation. This is principally a problem of a lack of names and associated stories. But how can one raise awareness about those who lack names, faces and stories?

In the last two chapters, my own attempts to rehabilitate Nazi victims through heritage projects are discussed. I have not been content to simply observe and commentate on the work that has been carried out by others. This book is not solely an exercise in archival research, nor a purely historical account, although it might fit this description for all but its last two substantive chapters. Here I switch academic discipline and voice and shift into an analysis of the heritage of victims of Nazism in Chapters 7 and 8. I also assess my own activism in this area: I have contributed to, created and instigated many heritage projects on victims of Nazism in the Channel Islands, and these chapters provide an opportunity to reflect on my own work, its motivations, its struggles and its successes.

Over the last decade I have interviewed and worked with many family members of victims of Nazism. I have accompanied a number of them on trips to Germany to find the graves of their loved ones. I have also been able to share archival documents with families and thus restore stories to them which their family members were never able to voice. My own curiosity about the 'lost' nature of graves, of archives and of stories which were not really lost at all, but simply undiscovered, uncollected and buried has made me wonder why they have not been found decades before. For example, Frank Falla's memoir *The Silent War* was published in 1967. In it he described his long fight for compensation for Channel Islands' victims of Nazism. Yet why had nobody thought to enquire about or track down his archive until 2010, when I took on this task? Why had the local authorities in Guernsey not located the bodies of Herbert Smith, Sidney Ashcroft, Charles Machon and Joseph Gillingham of the Guernsey Eight?[33] What assistance did they give the families, if any, and why did it take seventy years or more after their deaths to find them? Most puzzling of all – but explored in this volume – why did it take until 1996 in Jersey and 2015 in Guernsey to raise memorials to those who died in Nazi prisons and camps, and why were the numbers involved not finally established before these dates? Why is Herbert Smith's name omitted, at his family's request? These are all questions which I address, and all are connected with the legitimacy, perceived and otherwise, of the actions of those convicted of offences against the occupiers.

This legitimacy is related to Judith Butler's concept of 'grievability', which considers whose lives in war can be legitimately forfeited and not grieved over. Her words find particular and considerable resonance within the context of victims of Nazism in the Channel Islands and are worth quoting at length:

> Under contemporary conditions of war ... the shared conditions of precariousness leads not to reciprocal recognition, but to a specific exploitation of targeted populations, of lives that are not quite lives, cast as 'destructible' and 'ungrievable'. Such populations are 'lose-able', or can be forfeited, precisely because they are framed as being already lost or forfeited; they are cast as threats to human life as we know it

rather than as living populations in need of protection from illegitimate state violence, famine or pandemics. Consequently, when such lives are lost they are not grievable, since, in the twisted logic that rationalizes their death, the loss of such populations is deemed necessary to protect the lives of 'the living'.[34]

In the Channel Islands context, those who offended against the Germans were a threat to the rest of the population because they had the potential to provoke reprisals upon everybody else, as I have noted. Such reprisals were threatened but never carried out beyond temporary confiscation of radios or hostage-taking followed by release, although this wasn't the point. Those who planned to carry out acts of resistance were declared by the local authorities in Guernsey, days before the Occupation began, as their 'most bitter enemy'.[35] From the very start, resisters were an embarrassment, illegitimate and ungrievable; their lives were as good as forfeit. The rest of the population needed to be protected from them.

Having taken such a position from the start, one might ask the extent to which the local authorities in the Channel Islands were culpable for not protecting such people: not defending them adequately in court or demanding to do so, not intervening on their behalf, and not acting for their benefit behind the backs of the occupiers. Indeed, in some cases the local authorities acted as co-prosecutors with the Germans, albeit in separate courts.[36] Admittedly, local lawyers or advocates were not always allowed in German military courts, especially in the more serious cases.[37] Where they did so, their actions were often restricted to asking for mitigation of sentence.[38] The local authorities could also plead, after a period of imprisonment for the accused, for remission of sentence, especially if pressed into it by the families of those concerned. For example, John Ingrouille's parents in Guernsey visited Bailiff Victor Carey to entreat him to ask the Germans for a reduction of sentence for their son. He made such an appeal but it was rejected.[39] However, a more vigorous stance could have been taken. The local authorities could have made a stand and demanded to be able to defend accused Islanders. But, in the words of Frank Falla, they 'did not bother to insist on what, after all, was a common right of an accused person under international law'.[40]

Although writing about those in positions of authority who protested against the Nazis' antisemitic policies and those relating to euthanasia, lawyer Richard Weisberg has argued that 'direct protesters, standing alone, were not killed, punished or even professionally sanctioned' for doing so.[41] There is a popular assumption in the Channel Islands that if the local authorities had stood up to the Germans then they would have been shot or deported, and therefore should not be criticized for not having done so. This is demonstrably false as there are a number of instances of when they did so and were not sanctioned for it.[42]

By not protecting their own people, then, were the local authorities acting legitimately in framing offences against the occupiers – and therefore the lives of offenders – as illegitimate and therefore forfeit? Indeed, they were not, which happened to be unfortunate for those who were imprisoned and subsequently deported. While public speeches on this point have been made by Island leaders in Jersey since the mid-1990s, they have not in Guernsey, although opportunities have been provided – and missed – for such speeches. The inherited political climate there is such that such admissions would still be taboo.

Paul Sanders has discussed and criticized the operation and logic of the utilitarian arguments such as 'greater good' and 'restraint and influence' made by the Islands' leaders, whereby they were prepared to sacrifice the minority when the Germans demanded it while protecting the majority, depending on the 'in-groups' and 'out-groups' at the time. While the in-groups were Freemasons and former servicemen, for whom the local authorities were prepared to fight hard to prevent being deported, the out-groups comprised Jews and political prisoners – those who were to become victims of Nazism – in order to keep their powder dry for bigger battles which they considered would be more worth fighting for.[43] The victims of Nazism were simply ungrievable until around 1995.

The lack of honour or respect accorded to these people has indirectly led to a position whereby it has become extremely difficult for others, over the years, to quantify them, and to do more than simply publish anecdotes and interviews with the same individuals whose stories were clearly patriotic and legitimate. Perhaps the first person to begin to catalogue the stories of those imprisoned and deported was John Hamptonne L'Amy, a retired army major born in 1882 whose unpublished memoirs were probably compiled in Jersey in the immediate aftermath after the Occupation.[44] Different parts of his memoir are devoted to giving accounts of particular cases of imprisonment or deportation of Islanders, and divided into subheadings such as 'Dachau', 'Naumburg / Saale', 'Buchenwald' and 'Neuengamme', telling the story of those who survived such places in their own words. It details underground movements, political prisoners and details of escaped and sheltered slave workers. The majority of the work focuses on plight of political prisoners, although L'Amy makes no attempt to quantify them.

Ten years later, Alan and Mary Wood's 1955 volume, *Islands in Danger*, was published. They noted with some surprise a lack of a roll of honour of '*those who had died for their courage*', and '*found it hard even to get a complete list of islanders who had ended their lives in gaols and concentration camps, and to separate out the patriots from the thieves and Black Marketeers*'.[45] Such a separation would not be attempted or advocated today because of the murky waters which characterized the complex situation of the Occupation. Neither would we feel comfortable in condemning the 'thieves and Black Marketeers' from the Channel Islands who endured concentration camps such as Buchenwald, Dachau and Ravensbrück.

If stories of deportation and survival abounded in 1955, attempts after this date to compile lists had mixed results. In Chapter 5, we'll see the struggle of the local authorities in Jersey and Guernsey to account for even a fraction of those deported during their correspondence with the British government in the early stages of the compensation claims. Frank Falla's work, considered in Chapter 6, was focused on getting compensation for his friends and colleagues who he met in prison, and any other former political prisoner who he could help. There is no indication in his archives that he was keeping a roll of honour for posterity of all those deported from the Channel Islands.

There was a minor resurgence of interest in former political prisoners in the 1970s, no doubt triggered by twenty-fifth anniversary of liberation. In 1970, Channel TV screened *The Bitter Years*,[46] a forty-minute documentary which gave an overview of the entire Occupation. Only a few former political prisoners were given screen time or referred to: Harold Le Druillenec, Louisa Gould and Stanley Green – all high-profile Islanders with impeccable and patriotic reputations. The narrator, Roy McLoughlin, also described the five 'patriots' from Guernsey who ran GUNS,[47] and the voice of Frank Falla is heard, describing how five of them were deported and only three returned. However, none of these men was named.

In 1974, Jerseyman Richard Mayne published a short article in the *Channel Islands Occupation Review* about Jersey's 'forgotten Islanders'. He listed thirty-six people from Jersey who were arrested during the Occupation and sent to the continent to serve prison sentences, noting the '*complete lack of a record*' available. '*Every town and village in Britain and in France has, at least, a list of civil and military casualties in World War II*', he lamented. '*Jersey, to its shame, does not know the details of either*'.[48]

In his official history of the Occupation, published in 1975, Charles Cruickshank had nothing to say about the numbers or legitimacy of the deported, but instead offered accounts of anonymized deported Islanders. He described GUNS, as 'the most intelligent and effective form of resistance open to Islanders', and informers as 'despicable',[49] but otherwise neither condemned nor praised the efforts of those who were deported.

In 1979, Roger Harris of the Channel Islands Specialist Society (CISS)[50] wrote *Islanders Deported*, about the 2,200 Islanders sent to civilian internment camps in two waves of deportations, in September 1942 and February 1943. His book contained one chapter devoted to those sent to penal prisons and concentration camps, listing twenty-nine from Guernsey and forty-three from Jersey. The information connected with each person is scant in the extreme, fragmentary, and (in some cases) erroneous. '*In the minds of many people left in the Islands*', Harris wrote, '*These were the heroes of the Occupation ... while for some they were just fools who got caught. ... Other people were also sent to the Continent but as these were genuine undesirables and known criminals, over the passing years there has been even less interest in recording them.*'[51] While Harris did not comment on whether the lack of interest stemmed from members of the CISS, or whether it emanated from the Channel Islands, the still-dark cloud hovering over the names of 'heroes', 'fools', 'undesirables' and 'criminals' was clear to see.

Even by 1991, Peter King considered Roger Harris' research to have provided '*excellent coverage and the best list so far*'.[52] King himself provided information on those listed by Harris, using sources such as the Woods' *Islands in Danger* and Frank Falla's memoirs, and repeating earlier errors now known to be incorrect. He stated that '*somewhere between 70 and 100 Islanders served sentences in Europe*', a calculation that was unexplained.[53] After observing the lack of honours given to survivors, he reflected that it was true that '*some of the prisoners had been convicted of genuine offences, but others were clearly innocent*'.[54] It is not clear what constituted a 'genuine offence', but presumably King meant acts which would have been considered against the law in peacetime, such as theft from the Germans (given that people were not deported for 'civilian' offences such as burglary). This reveals a rather black and white approach to expectations of behaviour in the context of military occupation.

A shift in attitudes was occurring by the mid-1990s. Rather than reflecting on the criminality or otherwise of those deported, journalist Madeleine Bunting was more concerned by their lack of recognition or honours, or statues set up in their name. She argued that the history of the Islands' resistance (and, by extension, presumably the suffering of Islanders in prisons and camps) had been neglected for two reasons:

> *Firstly, the story of those men and women who sacrificed their lives is an embarrassment to the many islanders who could not match their courage. Secondly, many islanders who did make gestures of defiance paid dearly for them, and could not look to their government, for protection. Their stories show up the relationship the island governments had formed with the Germans, an integral part of which was that resistance would not be tolerated.*[55]

For all the criticism that has been levelled at Bunting, she was the first person in forty years to express surprise at the lack of recognition given to those who were deported; unlike the Woods, she did not try to separate out the heroes and villains. She believed that Islanders should be judged for their failure to '*remember and acknowledge those who were sacrificed to the islands' welfare*',[56] and argued that only when there are exhibits in '*all the islands' museums*' and '*well cared-for memorials and plaques in their memory*' would Islanders have begun to tell the whole story of the Occupation.[57] She recognized the importance, as do I, of the legitimacy of heritage to victims of Nazism.

To help redress this lacuna, Jersey Heritage Trust (as it was called at that time), led by far-sighted director Michael Day, helped to commission research into those from Jersey who died in Nazi prisons and camps. *The Ultimate Sacrifice* (a book now in its third edition) was written by Paul Sanders, a historian I characterize later in this book as a 'game-changer'. The first edition was published in 1998, and the Lighthouse Memorial in St Helier, erected in 1996, names those who died. This activism through publication and memorialization has now ensured that the Jersey 21 are perceived as heroes of the Occupation, regardless of the patriotism or legality of their acts. Those who sheltered slave workers rub shoulders with those who were caught with radios, those who committed larceny, and escapees. This significant act of heritage, which was slow to have been replicated by Guernsey, has successfully changed perceptions in Jersey.

Such research, however, did not involve the compilation of a master list of those who had been deported, although Sanders drew upon the research of Joe Mière, whose work we consider in Chapter 7. Mière was the first person who really began this work in earnest. He did not differentiate between those whose acts he perceived as legitimate, illegitimate, patriotic or unpatriotic. Numbers mattered just as much as or more than the offence, and all were treated as undifferentiated 'political prisoners'. He, himself, had been imprisoned for tarring the houses of the girlfriends of the heads of the German Secret Field Police and the Naval Harbour Police.[58] While Mière and his actions were firmly in the category labelled 'troublemaker' by other Islanders – those to whom Frank Falla referred (with pride) as the '*naughty lads who stepped out of line with the Germans*'[59] – they were equally firmly perceived as patriotic and therefore legitimate by Joe Mière.

When Mière tried to obtain information during the 1990s, when he was now in his seventies, about those who'd been sentenced during the Occupation, he was repeatedly denied access to the files. He offered to '*take an oath of secrecy … not to divulge any names or any details of individuals convicted of criminal offences*' and asked to '*compile these lists before I get too old to remember and before non-Jersey writers distort our occupation history*'.[60] He tried petitioning the Bailiff in 2001,[61] which led to correspondence with the Solicitor General, who denied him access to the records on the grounds that the names of political prisoners were mixed in with names of those who had committed '*criminal offences according to the ordinary law of Jersey such as theft*', and that '*some of the people who are named in these records may still be alive and living in Jersey*'.[62] Two years before he died, Mière begged local community leaders such as the chair of the Jersey Jewish Congregation, Freddie Cohen, to intervene on his behalf. '*Do I have to break a window or some other crime to get into the prison, and try to read these records, or do I have to break into the prison – it would be like the old days, breaking into German Army Quarters. I might be old now, but the spirit is still there.*'[63] Mière tried his best, but in the end had to rely, as he had done all his life, on oral testimony from former political prisoners who visited him in the Underground Hospital and told him their story.

At the time of his death in 2006, Mière's list of those deported stood at 563;[64] however, this list included those deported to internment camps in 1943 and some foreign workers of the Organization Todt who did not live in the Channel Islands before the Occupation.[65] It also included mistakes and some misspelled names. There is also no information about how his list was compiled although, as we have seen, there is a fairly extensive paper trail to show how Mière was repeatedly refused access to court records of the Occupation years still closed while he was alive. Because Mière was also a great source and collector of oral testimony, it seems likely that many on his list were included this way, with all of the problems inherent in such a method.

In 2003, three years before he passed away, he was chosen as Jersey Heritage Trust's Portrait of the Jersey Citizen for 2003. This painting shows Mière sitting in a concrete tunnel of the old underground hospital where he had once been curator. In the shadows around him are the faces of his fellow prisoners whose memory he worked so hard to preserve. A year later, his book on the story of Jersey's political prisoners, *Never to be Forgotten*, was published. True to the end to his prisoner friends and his own style of 'loyal Jersey patriotism', he wrote: '*Could you sleep peacefully, knowing you had not respected the memory of dear friends and fellow Channel Islanders who died under brutal conditions in German prisons or concentration camps?*'[66]

Because of the problems with Mière's list, and starting from scratch, in 2015 I calculated that the minimum number of those deported from the Channel Islands to Nazi prisons and camps on the continent must lie somewhere between 226 and 253 people. This estimate was based on a number assumptions made because of the incompleteness of the archival record.[67] Since then, with the advent of the Frank Falla Archive website (discussed in Chapter 8), which relies *only* on a list of verified names, the grand total of names currently listed lies at 215.[68] This is not assumed to be a final number. But why has it proved so difficult to compile a list, both now and since the end of the Occupation?

A large problem has been the scattered nature or loss of the relevant archival records. In Guernsey, then as now, the police logbooks which recorded notifications by the occupiers of every military court tribunal sentence[69] are not yet in the archives, but still in the police station. The copies of sentences passed by the military courts are patchy and not all survive; these are kept in the Island's archives. While at least some of the Guernsey prison records have survived, these do not record who was deported. Of the original German records from the prison and court-martials, nothing survives; it is assumed that these were destroyed towards the end of the Occupation. However, immediately after the Occupation, intelligence officers in Guernsey found a file of judicial records kept by the *Feldgendarmerie*.[70] This comprised a list of Islanders tried by German military courts. The intelligence officers copied only a sample of these names, dates, convictions and sentences, which do not match any extant records in the Island or in London archives, although some of the names are recognizable. Neither does the court case or prisoner number next to each name match that given in any other surviving records. Although it clearly survived the Occupation, the whereabouts of the original file of German judicial records is now unknown. The sample list is in the Imperial War Museum in London.

In Jersey the situation is much better, facilitated by the digitization and placing online of all charge sheets given to the local authorities by the occupiers, which recorded the outcome of military court tribunals (although, like in Guernsey, an unknown number were deported without trial or without notification of the authorities). The prison logbook also survives, and a note was made if a prisoner was 'transferred to France'. However, this book was kept by the local prison warders and recorded only the prisoners who were moved into their side of the prison after their trials. There is no extant record of prisoners kept in the German-controlled part of Jersey prison, where they awaited their trial. This is reputed to have been destroyed only in the 1970s, at the time of the demolition of the wartime prison.

There has not always been free access to these records; some Occupation-period files are still closed today. And yet, while the foregoing may explain the problems that researchers and even the local authorities have had in calculating the number of those deported, it does not explain why nobody in a position of authority made it their business to keep track of names and numbers during the Occupation itself, nor to tick off the names of those who returned, raising the alarm when people failed to reappear. One cannot help but wonder whether the explanation for this was that, regardless of the post-war chaos, such people, on the whole, did not matter; they were not 'grievable'; they were troublemakers and their actions had not been legitimate. Barring some notable examples such as Harold Le Druillenec, Louisa Gould and Canon Clifford Cohu, the rest were able to be dismissed as metaphorical or actual 'troublemakers, thieves or black marketeers'.

Sources

This volume has been inspired by and benefitted enormously from access to the applications for compensation written by Channel Islanders in the mid-1960s. My awareness of this resource came from the extensive personal archive of Frank Falla. In his memoir *The Silent War*, written in 1967, he referred to his central role in helping Channel Islanders get compensation for Nazi persecution. Guessing correctly that his family might have kept his papers, I appealed for them to get in touch with me, which they did in 2010. Falla's daughter gave me her father's briefcase and bags filled with his personal archive, comprising scrapbooks filled with his newspaper articles, correspondence with other former prisoners and copies of their testimonies, and letters to and from the Foreign Office, politician Airey Neave, and other people in positions of power and responsibility with regard to the compensation agreement and its administration. This book has its foundation in Falla's files, now partially digitized, and available on www.frankfallaarchive.org.

This archive alerted me not just to the Channel Islands' place in the compensation scheme, but to the nature and composition of the compensation claims, most especially the presence of detailed testimonies. My search for the applications of other Channel Islanders and people from the UK revealed that they still existed, but as closed Foreign Office files. Several years of continued discussions with the Foreign Office's archive team resulted in the eventual release of these to The National Archives in 2016.

The testimonies, coupled with the very few memoirs in existence written by deported Islanders, revealed to me the experience of Channel Islanders in Nazi prisons, labour and concentration camps. This was a narrative which dwelt on deliberate targeting of Islanders by guards, for most of the war, of bullying and ill-treatment because of their nationality, followed by preferential treatment coupled with speedy repatriation at the very end. It seems likely that this provides an insight into the wider experience of other British civilians in such places of incarceration.

In examining the construction of wartime and immediate post-war narratives, the archives in Guernsey and Jersey (including their newspaper archives) were invaluable in building up a picture. This was also informed by the files of Captain Dening of the intelligence service, held by the Imperial War Museum, as well as other Home Office, Foreign Office and intelligence service files held by The National Archives. In many cases, relevant conversations between the Channel Islands and London are spread between multiple non-consecutive files in the four archives today, and it is necessary to have sight of them all in order to fully understand the sequence of events, the accusations made, and the explanations and counter-accusations provided.

The correspondence in Falla's archive also allowed me to study precisely how Falla negotiated with the Foreign Office, not just to ensure that Channel Islanders were compensated, but also how he fought to make sure that those who he believed deserved compensation received it. His desire to push continuously yet always courteously for either compensation or satisfactory explanations of rejection allow us a privileged insight into the (at times faulty) logic of the decision-making process at the Foreign Office. This, coupled with the Foreign Office's marginalia and notes in the application form papers, proved revealing.

The children of victims of Nazi persecution are today scattered mostly between the Channel Islands and England, and locating them was achieved principally through the local newspapers, word of mouth, public lectures, and radio and TV appeals. While contact was first initiated for the purposes of locating families of the Guernsey Eight for the unveiling of a new resistance memorial in Guernsey, this soon spread organically to encompass other families. Around forty-five individuals were interviewed using semi-structured questionnaires in order to build up a picture of the extent to which experiences in prisons and camps were shared with the second generation, and how much that experience impacted the rest of the life of the victims of Nazism and, in turn, their families. I was particularly interested in symptoms of PTSD, their manifestation, the awareness of and sympathy towards mental health problems within the family, and the extent to which symptoms overshadowed the lives of those affected.

In researching the final section of the book, I moved away from archival study and towards more oral testimony collection and participant-observation-driven fieldwork. This included travelling with the children of victims of Nazism to various locations in Europe, and attending ceremonies which had at their heart the commemoration of victims of Nazism. This fieldwork has also had an activist stance, helping to organize those ceremonies, playing a part in memorial erection, and creating digital heritage to help raise awareness of victims of Nazism.

Book structure

This book is made up of three parts, each assessing a different time period. The first part, comprising Chapters 2 and 3, is set during the war and immediately after it. Chapters 4 and 5 deal broadly with the period 1945 to 1965, with Chapter 6 set in the period of the compensation claims of the mid-1960s. The third part, a more personal part of the book, comprises Chapters 7 and 8, with Chapter 7 covering 1965 to present and Chapter 8 focusing on the years 2015 to present. The book as a whole thus spans almost eighty years.

The aim is to build a historical picture to explain the long-term processes of silencing Channel Islander victims of Nazi persecution and marginalizing them from history, memory and heritage. To that end, the second chapter is set during the war, examining Islanders in camps and prisons, exploring what typified the British experience of Nazi persecution, and witnessing how friendship groups were created in these places of incarceration. I also explore the long-term impact of this friendship, which survived death, and examine how it motivated those who survived to come home to testify for those who died, fight for the legitimacy of their offences and resulting experiences in prisons and camps, and their right to be remembered.

In Chapter 3 I examine what happened in the Channel Islands immediately after the war, when the local authorities had to justify their actions to their citizens and to the British government. This was done in the face of local dissent by the first groups of Islanders to speak up for the dead and to call for the prosecution of those whose actions led to the death of their fellow Islanders. I ask whose actions, the local authorities or resisters, would be considered the more legitimate by history, what arguments were made, and who would be the final arbiter in this early post-war period.

Chapter 4 surveys the victims of Nazi persecution who came home, and the range of their mental and physical health conditions and symptoms. While their friends still in the Islands had had limited success in fighting for them and the legitimacy of their actions, to what extent was the ability of victims to act constrained by their impairments to body and mind? I ask whether and how the attitudes of the Channel Islands' authorities compounded their conditions, and whether this in turn decreased the number of people willing to speak out.

The fifth chapter assesses the first twenty years after the war to assess whether this was a period of silence and inaction on behalf of former political prisoners. Although this was not yet a period of the creation of monuments relating to victims of Nazism, was there any publicity about what they had experienced? We examine them in their own homes and witness the extent to which their families were aware of what happened to them. We also see champions beginning to emerge to fight battles with the local authorities over the legitimacy of their actions. But to what extent was the lack of legitimacy being compounded in a way that would affect them in the future?

Chapter 6 focuses on the work of Frank Falla, a guardian of memory from Guernsey for other victims of Nazism, as he fought for compensation for himself and his friends, both living and dead. It follows his correspondence with the Foreign Office and catalogues his successes in gaining compensation and victories in overturning rejected cases. I scrutinize his strategies for success, asking what the local authorities did to help or hinder his work. I also assess the repercussions of the compensation claims for the legitimacy of victims of Nazism in the Channel Islands.

Chapter 7 takes us into the final section of the book: the period from 1965 to the present day. It discusses the role of guardians of memory and those I call 'game-changers' in changing the narrative in Jersey from the late 1980s onwards. Characterizing their actions and the events that they orchestrated as 'incremental memory events', and using these as inspiration for what can be achieved, the chapter assesses whether incremental memory events can be carried out by would-be game-changers on Holocaust Memorial Day in Guernsey with the same result.

I examine, in Chapter 8, the potential for the scattered legacies of victims of Nazi persecution to be turned into a fragmented heritage which can be brought together in a digital heritage format. Drawing on the theoretical approach of the previous chapter, it assesses whether such interventions in the heritage arena can provide effective incremental memory events to change narratives of the past. Using the framework of 'reparative heritage' and 'acts of rescue' in the heritage arena, this chapter also asks whether such heritage can raise awareness, especially through social media, to establish a new baseline of legitimacy for victims of Nazi persecution.

In the final chapter I draw together the threads of arguments presented in the previous chapters to make a concluding statement about the legitimacy of victims of Nazi persecution. I also reflect upon the utility of the incremental memory event as a strategy within the field of heritage activism that can be used by others to facilitate change to long-held outdated narratives. I also consider those still left out of narratives: the informers, whose damaging actions led to the arrest of many of the victims of Nazism. To what extent will it be necessary, desirable, ethical or possible to name these characters in heritage presentation in the future, and will it help the Channel Islands move forwards in their *rapprochement* with the past? I also place the victims of Nazism within the conversation surrounding Britain and the Holocaust, and recent scholarship which seeks to draw attention to the myths surrounding Britain's role.

The roots of this book go back to 2010, when Frank Falla's family gave me his archive. Since then, I have been increasingly motivated to pick up the baton which he laid down in 1983, upon his death. Nearly three-quarters of a century has passed since the end of the Occupation, and still the repercussions of that period continue to reverberate in the

Channel Islands. Narratives change with each generation, but not without the actions of guardians of memory and game-changers. Memorials do not erect themselves, and heritage projects need supportive people to see them through. These need a body of scholarship on which to build in order to inform, justify or legitimate their presence. I hope that this book can contribute to that endeavour.

2

'Alone amongst a Crowd':
The British Experience in Nazi Prisons and Concentration Camps

Introduction and sources

The Channel Islander experience in Nazi prisons and concentration camps is a depressingly familiar litany of starvation, ill-treatment, forced labour, beatings, torture, disease, murder and even incineration in gas ovens.[1] But this list is not exclusive to Channel Islanders and could be applied to any of the peoples of occupied Europe who found themselves deported and imprisoned by the Nazis. This chapter, then, attempts to explore the specifically Channel Islander or British experience in Nazi prisons and camps. What, if anything, characterized their journey through the system? Was there anything that formed their common experience?

When Channel Islanders were deported to Nazi prisons and concentration camps, they often found themselves alone as the only British prisoner present. If they were very fortunate, they found other Channel Islanders, or British or American military personnel or civilians in their places of incarceration. For the most part, however, they found themselves surrounded by a cacophony of different languages and men or women of many different nations. This chapter explores not only the experience of being British in Nazi camps and prisons, but also the importance of friendship groups for the Islanders as they tried to negotiate the experience of disease, starvation, extreme cold and forced labour through support groups of those united by language and nationality.

Unfortunately and frustratingly, very few Islanders who experienced Nazi prisons and camps wrote memoirs; in fact, we can list just five published accounts.[2] A small handful of unpublished manuscripts also exist,[3] along with a radio play of the story of Harold Le Druillenec, who also narrated his experience.[4] Inevitably the analysis that follows in this chapter depends heavily on these sources. As all but one of the Islanders deported for their offences against the occupying authorities are now dead, we must rely heavily upon the memoirs of the few for an insight into the experiences of the many.

The compensation testimonies written between 1964 and 1966, the topic of a later chapter, also provide an additional excellent resource for similar insights but, although these are far more numerous, they are also often much briefer texts, sometimes only a page or paragraph in length. There are also a small number of newspaper articles. On their return to the Channel Islands in 1945, a small number of Islanders told their stories to the local press,[5] most often as a way of earning money to alleviate their desperate circumstances. This resource is scarce, but often longer than the compensation testimonies. It has the advantage of being immediate, and having been written when the memory was fresh and raw.

Now that the original authors have all passed away, we cannot ask them how accurate these accounts are. While we can compare them with other accounts of the same prisons and camps, these can be scarce for some of the lesser known places, and sometimes just don't exist. They are often rarely in English because, as we have seen, the Islanders were often the only Britons to have experienced these places. We also need to understand that the British experience was often not the same as that of other nationalities, and so the narratives offered by Islanders which may deviate from what we already know of these places should not necessarily be dismissed.

There are two further questions that we must consider when examining these sources. First, can we make the assumption that the earlier accounts are more accurate than the later ones because of the freshness of memory of the author? Second, who was the intended readership of the account? Were any of the published accounts exaggerated to increase sales – something that is perhaps more likely for newspaper articles where, after all, the stories were often told to a journalist first, and mistakes may have been made by the journalist in their write-up. Some former prisoners may have had something to hide. Hungarian woman Julia Barry née Brichta, for example, who had come to Guernsey in 1939 and married an Irishman in 1942, was a policewoman or kapo and interpreter in Ravensbrück concentration camp. In a recent volume on the camp based on eyewitness accounts and archival records, journalist Sarah Helm describes Barry as *'the only one of the group* [of British women in the camp] *who seems to have tried to keep an eye out for the rest. ... Amongst them only Julia Barry seems to have displayed any 'British solidarity' and tried to follow what happened to them all.'*[6] Yet we know from other accounts that camp police were greatly feared and very often cruel, sometimes to save themselves from punishment by the SS. As knowledge about the role of camp police grew, would Barry have admitted at a later date that this was her role in the camp?

Exaggerations are also more likely for the published memoirs (perhaps encouraged by the publishers to boost sales) than the unpublished accounts intended only for the family. And yet these unpublished accounts may also have been self-censored so as not to upset family members who might read them. All of the accounts may have omitted or sanitized the worst atrocities witnessed in their camps because of the inability of the author to bring themselves to write what they saw; indeed, there are a number of compensation testimonies which make statements such as '*I was in Buchenwald and what happened there will be well known to you*' – and then say nothing further.

Of all of the accounts available, the compensation testimonies would appear to be the most truthful. These, after all, had a closed and private readership with the Foreign Office and would never be seen by the general public – at least, not for fifty years. This suggestion of truthfulness may seem counter-intuitive; after all, surely the wilder the story, the more compensation could potentially be received. But this is to misunderstand the basis on which compensation was awarded. Former prisoners received compensation for the length of time they spent in a 'concentration camp or comparable institution', and for the degree of permanent disability they suffered. Both of these had to be independently verified.

We must also be aware that accounts – and their writers – were influenced by each other. The men who survived Naumburg (Saale) and Frankfurt-Preungesheim prisons had annual reunions for thirty years where they must often have talked about their experiences. When they came to write their compensation claims twenty years after the end of the war, their memories may have intermingled, especially as most of the testimonies of these prisons were written by one man, Frank Falla, who used his journalistic skills to help his colleagues frame their narratives.

Another more worrying example of possible deliberate exaggeration lies in the memoirs of Anthony Faramus, who presents us with two difficulties. First, he wrote two memoirs nearly forty years apart. They differ in some small details which has the result of placing both versions in doubt, although the first memoir was not written by Faramus but by Frank Owen, who interviewed Faramus extensively about his experiences. The second issue with which we have to contend is that Eddie Chapman, a criminal wanted by the police during the war, wrote his memoirs the year before Faramus. Faramus and Chapman knew each other, were alleged partners on the black market together, and were deported to Fort de Romainville prison in Paris together (Figure 2.1). Chapman left Romainville as a voluntary recruit to the German secret service, later becoming a double agent. Chapman paints himself as a James-Bond-type character, and a film was made of his memoirs. He also wrote the introduction to Faramus' 1954 memoir, and there is a feeling that Faramus tried to live up to Chapman's exploits. Both men, for example, describe the regular sexual encounters with female prisoners they had in Romainville after Chapman made a key to get into their wing. In his 1990 memoirs, Faramus makes no mention of his black marketeering or Chapman. In neither account does he repeat Chapman's claim, which was made in MI5 papers written in December 1942, that Chapman lived for a while with Faramus and together both men offered their services to the German secret service.[7]

While this may be the most startling of the discrepancies between the two men's statements, Faramus also says that he was in St Denis camp for three weeks rather than the single night that Chapman claimed, and paints Romainville as an even greater den of licentiousness than Chapman suggested in his account, with plentiful food, alcohol and sex in 1942. By the time of Faramus' first memoir, he had had some small-time success as a Hollywood actor. Perhaps Faramus' experience was truthfully portrayed but enlarged upon in his later memoirs. It is unfortunate that there are discrepancies in the two volumes as Faramus' 1990 memoir is especially compelling, well-written and gives an extremely detailed and almost visceral insight into the brutality of Buchenwald and Mauthausen. One feels that one would be doing a great disservice to those who suffered in these places to question Faramus' account. After all, there is clear archival evidence to show that he was in Buchenwald at least, and some of the events he testifies are independently verifiable.

Figure 2.1 The entrance of Fort de Romainville today. Copyright: Roderick Miller / Tracing the Past e.V

Many of the emotionally draining accounts encapsulated in memoirs and testimonies are often bleak to read. A number of them leave images in the imagination which are not quickly forgotten. Some of them testify to war crimes and horrific murders and tortures. All of them are diverse; each account is as unique as the author who experienced it. The reader cannot help but ask how each person survived to tell their account after the war. It is this central question of survival, and how it was accomplished, that drives this chapter.

Channel Islanders, prisons and camps

For all of our deported Islanders, the date at which they were deported often dictated their experience and chances of survival. For those deported at an early date with only a short sentence, their chances of returning to the Islands after serving their sentence in a single French prison were very good, if not guaranteed. Those who were deported at a later date, especially with a heavier sentence, were much more likely to die in a concentration camp in Germany or elsewhere. It is clear to see that the later the date of deportation, the more harsh the journey through Europe for the prisoner who was passed from prison to labour camp to concentration camp, especially after the Channel Islands were cut off from France in August 1944, preventing any return for released prisoners.

Patterning is visible in the available data for Channel Islanders' places of incarceration, although such observations do not encompass everyone. For the first two years of the Occupation, they were sent to prisons in Normandy after they were deported via the French ports of St Malo and Granville. Two prisons in Caen most commonly received Islanders during this period: the *maison d'arrêt* and Beaulieu

Prison (the *centrale*). While the records for Beaulieu do not survive, the prison records of fifty-two Islanders have been found for the *maison d'arrêt*. As an additional twenty-one Islanders were known to have been imprisoned in Caen, we assume at Beaulieu, this means that one-third of all deported Islanders passed through this city, many of whom served their sentence and returned to the Channel Islands.

In mid-July 1942, the prisons in Caen were emptied and most of the prisoners moved to Paris, to Fort de Villeneuve-Saint-Georges. Other prisons in Normandy, such as Saint-Lô, Lisieux and Coutances, began to be more commonly used. Those in prisons in Normandy with longer sentences by the middle of the war could expect to be transferred to prisons elsewhere in the occupied zone of France, such as Clairvaux, Fort d'Hauteville in Dijon, Haut-Clos Prison in Troyes and Châlons-sur Marne.

By 1943, Islanders were increasingly being transferred to Germany for forced labour after periods in France. Those still in France at the time of the expiration of their sentence after March 1943 stood little hope of returning to the Channel Islands,[8] although exceptions were sometimes made on grounds of age or the necessity of their job to food production in their island of origin. Instead, Islanders were transferred to an internment camp for the rest of the war; Saint-Denis on the outskirts of Paris was often the chosen destination for such people.

For those transferred to Germany in late 1943, the prison of Saarbrücken was sometimes used as the point of transit. Most who passed through this institution were sent to Frankfurt (Main) Prison and, from there, to Naumburg Prison. Islanders clustered at these three German prisons more than any other; however, as at least 125 prisons, labour camps and concentration camps have so far been found to contain Islanders, clearly some of these clusters were quite small.

For those who were to experience concentration camps, their journey by cattle truck often began in 1944 in the notorious Parisian prisons of Cherche-Midi, Fresnes and Fort de Romainville, or from Compiègne transit camp outside Paris. Internment in most if not all of these four led directly to camps such as Buchenwald, experienced by nine Islanders. However, Channel Islanders were also sent to camps such as Neuengamme, Bergen-Belsen, Hinzert, Mauthausen, Natzweiler-Struthof and Ravensbrück, and the routes there were often convoluted.

From late 1943 onwards, after their arrival in Germany, discernible patterns in the data begin to break down. Chaos begins to enter the system. Islanders were passed from overcrowded institution to overcrowded institution and from prison to labour camp, transferred to wherever they were needed for forced labour projects. The prisons in Bernau and Augsburg, for example, lent their prisoners out for labour projects; six Islanders worked at the brutal Neuoffingen labour camp, where all survived but suffered physically and mentally for the rest of their lives. It is no coincidence that nearly all of those from Jersey who did not survive were deported from the middle of 1943 onwards or later; they were sent away at a time when very few were allowed to return and when most prisoners were used for forced labour. They were in the system long enough to not survive it.

By 1944, those deported were mostly sent straight to Germany without any sojourn in French prisons. Islanders were also sent to Silesia, Poland, Austria and Bohemia. By this stage, those who were to survive managed it with permanent and serious lifelong consequences to their health. By the closing months of the war, a significant number of Islanders still in the prison and camp system joined death marches, from which few survived.

Whatever the length of sentence or date of deportation, one experience united nearly all Islanders: that of being targeted for special treatment by the guards because of their British nationality. The memoirs and testimonies speak of being singled out for violent verbal and physical abuse, and of being denied even the very rudimentary medical treatment extended to some other nationalities.

Occasionally there are accounts of other prisoners wanting to help the Channel Islanders because of their nationality, because these men and women were British and therefore represented the only unoccupied peoples of Europe whose army may yet have been able to save them from their nightmare. There is also a slight sense – a question that remains in the mind of the careful reader and unspoken by nearly all who wrote of their experience – that perhaps these solitary Britons in many camps were, in some sense, being kept an eye on. It would be too strong to say that they acted as hostages or special (and certainly not privileged) prisoners wherever they went, but one is left with the suspicion that there may have been a vested interest in knowing where these Britons were so that they could be plucked to safety or sent to a less harsh camp towards the end of the war if needs be. One does not always get the sense that these men and women were forgotten among the vast crowd. There is very little hard evidence to put forward to back up this claim, but testimonies like those of Kingston Bailey, who was plucked out of Dachau at the eleventh hour, and whose experience is described later in this chapter, is one such example. Stanley Green and Bill Symes were also removed from Buchenwald after outside intervention. We might also ask whether Sidney Ashcroft is another example of such protection of British citizens. Days from

Figure 2.2 Straubing Prison hospital today. Copyright: Gilly Carr

death and suffering from tuberculosis at Straubing Prison, he was taken out of the assembly of hundreds of prisoners before their forced march towards Dachau and put in the prison hospital (Figure 2.2). Whether or not these cases are exceptions, there is clear evidence that, towards the very end of the war, the Channel Islanders in certain locations, if still alive, found themselves being treated very much better by guards who wanted to save their own skins as Allied liberating armies drew near. It is important to emphasize that this was not the case for all; many Islanders also died in the closing months of the war in horrific circumstances.

'English swine': The impact of nationality on the prisoner experience

The title of this chapter is taken from a quote by Guernseyman Frank Tuck in the memoirs of his friend Kingston George Bailey. When he was sent to Neuoffingen labour camp, an offshoot of Augsburg Prison, he was overjoyed to find other Channel Islanders there. '*To be unable to converse freely with your fellow men because of a language barrier*', he later wrote, '*is to be alone amongst a crowd*'.[9] A feeling of isolation must have been experienced by many Islanders at prisons and camps across Europe, although when they found fellow Channel Islanders at their places of incarceration, immediate friendships resulted, although these also had their disadvantages. When Kingston Bailey was put on a working party from Bernau Prison, he was astonished to find Sidney Ashcroft, also from Guernsey. '*We managed to get side by side and, as we were marching, I received my first punch in the back for talking to my newly-found friend.*'[10]

Some Islanders were able to speak French; in fact, many could, at that time, also speak the indigenous patois, a form of Norman-French, or sometimes had a Norman, Breton or French parent or grandparent. French was also widely taught in schools from a young age. Those who were most disadvantaged in this respect were those who had been born and had grown up in the UK before moving to the Channel Islands in adulthood.

Many deported Islanders either stayed in French prisons for the duration of their sentence or were deported to French prisons before being moved to Germany, and they found themselves among mostly French political prisoners. Some Islanders were able to improve their foreign language skills during the long months of incarceration. Cecil Duquemin, for example, wrote in his unpublished memoirs that while at Bad Dürrenburg he was taken to '*a large hut close to a factory. In this hut there were between fifty and sixty prisoners of all nationalities. I palled up with a Frenchman who taught me the ropes. I could speak French and got to speak it almost like a native.*'[11] Learning French and, indeed, German, was vital for Islanders; most importantly, it decreased their sense of loneliness and broke down barriers between prisoners. While at Bernau Prison, where he was at that time the only Briton, Kingston Bailey remarked in his memoirs that '*we were of all ages from eighteen to sixty, mostly French. I was the only Englishman, and I was indeed glad that I had learned much French at Villeneuve.*'[12]

Foreign language abilities also allowed them to forge new friendships which could only be beneficial to their longer-term survival. Jerseyman Peter Hassall described the camaraderie that he and Maurice Gould built up with the French political prisoners at the brutal camp of SS-*Sonderlager* Hinzert, where the violence and humiliations were seemingly constant. The prisoners were able to offer each other solace and sympathy during their ordeal. Meanwhile, in some factory barracks in Swabmünchen, Bailey befriended a Greek who could speak English. He '*became one of my best friends*', wrote Bailey, illustrating how fellow-feeling could be induced in prisoners able to converse with one another. This Greek could '*also speak German, which helped us all considerably*'.[13] In this way, speaking a common language enabled the Islanders to strike up useful friendships.

Put simply, foreign language skills were of crucial importance for survival. Failure to understand and act upon orders from guards could lead to beatings. According to Kingston Bailey's memoirs, during hard forced labour in peat extraction works in Bernau labour camp, the German guard struck Kingston Bailey and Sidney Ashcroft across the shoulders with a stick, saying, 'English are you? Well, you will work here! Quicker, quicker; no work – no food. You are in Germany now, and in Germany you will work. Understand?' Sidney replied, '*I don't understand German*'. This made the guard worse and he struck him several times, yelling: '*You will understand before long. Quicker, quicker!*'[14]

An inability to learn a language or a lack of language skills in a camp could be as good as fatal to any of the Islanders. Sidney Ashcroft's resistance to disease was undoubtedly lowered by the beatings he received for being unable to understand German, probably contributing to his eventual death from tuberculosis at Straubing Prison. On arrival at SS-*Sonderlager* Hinzert, Peter Hassall (who spoke French and German) and Maurice Gould (who spoke neither) were told the rules of the camp by a senior Kapo or *Lagerälteste*, a man named Wipf. He finished his initiation speech by asking, in French, if the prisoners understood. Gould raised his hand to say that he did not. Hassall recorded in his memoirs what happened next. '*Hearing this, Wipf hurled himself through the first rank, then began pounding Maurice with his heavy club. After a dozen or so blows to his head, Maurice fell unconscious.*'[15]

Later on, the Room Senior of their barrack, a Frenchman named Callaux, overheard Gould and Hassall speaking English to each other. He screamed at them '*Who gave you two rosbifs permission to talk? I am in command here. You will not talk unless I say so, particularly in that foul English language. I don't understand it, so you, you big, filthy Englishman, had better learn French or German. I don't forget how the English abandoned France, and ran out on us like rats. I owe you for that.*'[16] Hassall and Gould learnt the hard way that they could not always count on people of Allied nations to like them because of their nationality.

After this initiation into the ways of the camp, Gould attracted attention for his lack of language skills and was nicknamed 'Churchill' by a sadistic member of the SS who was also their *Blockführer* (Block Leader). Callaux also waited for an opportunity to attack Gould. One day, when sent to collect coal for the camp, Gould's wooden clog fell off and Callaux used it as a pretext to attack him, shouting '*I'm going to kill you, you filthy English pig*'. Hassall, observing this, watched Callaux '*inflict a great deal of damage on Maurice, who collapsed in a ball in the middle of the road*'. As Hassall recorded in his memoirs, Callaux's brutality marked the beginning of the end for Gould.[17]

Figure 2.3 Fort de Villeneuve-Saint-Georges today. Copyright: Gilly Carr

Other Islanders found that, however good their language skills may have been, it was not always enough to get accepted by that nationality group, especially as food became scarcer. Kingston Bailey noted with regret that '*the French were not very generous, and kept their* [food] *parcels to themselves*' at Fort de Villeneuve-Saint-Georges Prison (Figure 2.3). In many of the French and German prisons to which Channel Islanders were deported, prisoners of that nationality were allowed to receive food parcels from their families. Islanders were too far away from their families and so relied upon the generosity – or its lack – of other prisoners to supplement their diets.

A fertile source for analysis of how Islanders worked together in friendship groups are the accounts of the German prisons of Frankfurt-Preungesheim and Naumburg (Saale) through which, respectively, fourteen and eleven Channel Islanders consecutively passed; three of the Frankfurt group moved on to other places of incarceration. Five of those who had been in Frankfurt survived to write compensation testimonies. Only three of the eleven who passed through Naumburg were able to do so. Frank Falla was one of them.

Falla was remarkably consistent in his description of these prisons over time, from his 1945 newspaper articles to his 1964 compensation testimony and his 1967 memoirs. His first description of these prisons was given in the two articles he wrote for the *Guernsey Evening Press* in July 1945,[18] just under three months after his release from Naumburg. Falla was still mentally suffering from the trauma of his lengthy incarceration, and wrote in his memoirs of this time that he was experiencing nightmares.[19]

In the first newspaper article, he described himself at his moment of liberation by the Americans as an '*emaciated and nervous wreck … physically and mentally*'. He reported that his friends who died in Naumburg were '*slowly starved to death in the course of six months and left to die like rats trapped in their cells'*. After relating to the reader his account of forced labour, starvation and beatings, Falla described how other prisoners could earn extra bread by informing the guards about their colleagues' misdemeanours. Islanders were forbidden English reading matter and communication with home, and had no food parcels to supplement their meagre prison bread-and-soup rations. They had to watch both the German prisoners and the guards' dogs being better fed than they were.

When Falla and his friends first arrived in Germany, they tried to cheer each other up. They *'cultivated our national spirit of trying to be cheerful despite skies black with clouds by quietly whistling, singing or humming songs while at our work. This was soon stopped by the workshop prisoner-bully, who reminded us that we were not in 'Merrie England' – how well we knew it, too! Persisting in attempting to be bright, we were threatened with 'arrest' – bread, water and solitary confinement'.*[20]

Beatings by the guards were a common feature of Nazi-run prisons. In Frankfurt this treatment was given especially when prisoners became noisy in their cells – in other words, when people in different cells attempted to communicate with each other by shouting through their windows. The British method of communication was to sing patriotic songs to see who replied; Falla described making contact with Allied airmen in Frankfurt this way, but the yells of the French prisoners prevented much communication as their noise attracted the guards. Knowing the way that the guards reacted to noisy prisoners, the final cause of death of Guernseyman Percy Miller, who Falla described as 'emaciated', must now be in question. Falla described how Miller had been punished for passing a note to another prisoner and subsequently put on a bread and water diet. He lost his mind, being driven mad with hunger, and died 'raving in his cell'[21] in July 1944. It is entirely possible that he was 'helped' on his way by the guards.[22]

Extracts from the more detailed compensation testimonies written by those in Frankfurt and Naumburg indicate clearly that the nationality of Islanders exacerbated their deprivations. Falla wrote that when he contracted pneumonia, he was refused even an aspirin because he was an *'Engländer'*, although they were freely given to Germans. Norman Dexter, also from Guernsey, wrote that most of the warders at Naumburg Prison were *'quite inhuman and kicked us about and called us 'English swine'*'. Such anti-English abuse seems to have happened at nearly all places of incarceration. The group of deported Guernsey policemen, who we will meet later, were also called 'English pigs' by the German secret field police in the Island,[23] an unhappy preparation for the reception that they would encounter throughout their places of incarceration.

Frankfurt and Naumburg were not the only prisons where telling tales on your fellow prisoner earned you privileges. While at a work camp of Bernau Prison, an exhausted Kingston Bailey asked his fellow Polish prisoners why they were *'working so quickly for Germany'*. One of them told the guard what he had asked. That guard *'became a madman and I thought that he would kill us on the spot. Cursing and swearing, calling us English pigs, he threatened to knock us down with his rifle; then he struck us many times with the stick that he always carried. ... The Polish prisoners were marched back to camp, but we were made to stay behind and work ...'*[24]

In Mauthausen, Anthony Faramus had learnt when to keep his mouth closed and when to speak. He was aware that being British and speaking English would bring him no favours. During registration on his entry to the camp, he remembered '*how the few British and American subjects in Buchenwald camp were held in contempt ... I decided to register myself as a Frenchman to escape attention and curiosity*'. This attempt backfired after he was unable to accurately say whether his proclaimed place of birth, St Malo, was in Normandy or Brittany.[25]

The list of Islanders who were ill-treated because of their nationality is a long one, and most remark upon it in their memoirs and testimonies. William Quin testified that, in his Austrian labour camp of Kematen, he was '*very badly treated*' once it was known that he was British.[26] Gerald Domaille wrote in his memoirs that he was denied extra food because he was British. He got on quite well with another warder but, when they discovered he was British, they treated him like '*scum*'.[27] The final days of Clifford Cohu's life in Zöschen work education camp in north-eastern Germany, in September 1944, gives a very clear picture of this (Figure 2.4). A letter from fellow prisoner and camp survivor Premysl Polacek from the Czech Republic was forwarded to the authorities in Jersey in October 1945 to bring them news of Cohu's death. Polacek knew that Cohu was from Jersey as they had managed to speak, but '*it was especially dangerous because he was the only Englishman in the camp and he was especially watched by SD[28] men. ... When we arrived in the camp I heard from the SD man, who*

Figure 2.4 The ruins of Zöschen labour camp today. Copyright: Gilly Carr

had accepted our transport, "Welcher is der Engländer?" [which is the Englishman?'] and when this man was shown, he roared: "Du wirst da bald krepieren" [you'll soon die there]. *Another prophesied him that in a week he would be dead … He was abused as "Du englische Sau, du wirst uns bombardieren, wir werden dir schon zeigen, du Krüppel"'* [You English swine, you will bomb us, we'll show you, you cripple].[29] Cohu was one of twenty-eight Islanders deported for offences against the occupiers who did not return; it is often the case that the final days or place of death is only known about today because of the friendship of fellow prisoners who were able to send the news back to the Channel Islands.

'The will and fortitude to endure': The power of the kindness of strangers

As much as Channel Islanders were targeted by prison and camp guards for their British nationality, they sometimes received the sympathy and friendship of their fellow prisoners. Many of these prisoners counted on the British, coming from an unoccupied country, to liberate them. Others wanted to learn English. Few prisoners, however, probably received as warm a welcome as Anthony Faramus claimed that he had experienced, somewhat improbably, at Fort de Romainville Prison in Paris. Once inside the building, '*women were in the stairwell and lining the banisters from the first floor. More animated laughter and ribbing. For the briefest of moments, all my cares became buried under an avalanche of hugs, squeezes and embraces.*' On the pillow of his bunk, a message had been left: '*Hôtel de Romainville. Ring for service. Pour la fille de chambre et la masseuse*'. A Belgian prisoner who worked in the cookhouse brought him and his American roommate a meal of food contributed by other prisoners, complete with half a bottle of wine, '*to honour the first British and American to the fort*'.[30]

While no other Islander claimed to have had such a hearty welcome in their prisons or camps, a number of others owed a more comfortable existence or even sometimes their very survival to the unlooked-for kindness of strangers inside or outside the prison or camp. In Cherche-Midi Prison in Paris, Ambrose Sherwill wrote in his diary for 26 November 1940 that he was '*visited by an American Quaker who is going to arrange to have my washing done and give me a clean towel. Thank God for a spot of human kindness.*'[31] While this kindness boosted Sherwill's morale, more crucial for most imprisoned Islanders was food. While in prison in Fort de Villeneuve-Saint-Georges, Kingston Bailey was visited by two Parisian women, Marie and Suzanne Hubert, who '*asked me what I needed in the way of food and clothes and said that they would do all they could to help myself and my English comrades*'. The women were able to smuggle in food parcels via a pro-British guard. '*It was very consoling to know that there was still some goodness in the world*,'[32] Bailey wrote later. He was very frank in his acknowledgement that '*we would have suffered much from hunger without those parcels to supplement our prison rations*'.[33] It was through periods of good fortune such as these that Bailey was able to survive his experience of Dachau despite his years in captivity.

During his period in Neuoffingen labour camp, Bailey's friend, Frank Tuck, was also fortunate in receiving the help of two local families related by marriage, the Stadler and Sailer families of Gundelfingen. Tuck was, at the time, helping to repair and build the German railways, where the work was extremely physically hard. The Stadler and Sailer families owned a nearby saw mill and farm, and two women from these families, Anna Stadler and Anni Sailer, asked the camp commandant for prisoners to work for them. When the prisoners arrived, they were well fed, given medical attention, and allowed to rest and listen to the radio. These women also left food in the nearby hedges and between the railway sleepers for the other forced labourers. Such kindness gave *much comfort and spiritual strength*[34] to the prisoners at a time when their lives were otherwise surrounded by violent beatings, ill-treatment and starvation. For Charles Friend, another Guernseyman in the same camp, this kindness '*softened our hearts and made us realise – perhaps for the first time during the war – that not all Germans were Nazis. Anna Stadler and her family bolstered us up and boosted our morale … the concern shown … gave us the will and fortitude to endure*'.[35]

Bailey was also fortunate, at a later period of his incarceration, to receive help again from three different strangers when he needed it most, this time in Dachau, when he was at his most vulnerable and weak. On his second day in Dachau, in December 1944, he was approached by a Serbian officer who spoke English and who told him that there were other Englishmen in Dachau, both from the armed forces. They offered to bring him food, and clothes to supplement his camp uniform to help him survive the sub-zero temperatures outside.

After a week in Dachau, he was introduced to the camp interpreter who became his '*greatest friend.*' The interpreter wanted to improve his English pronunciation. In exchange, he brought him war news and bread such that Bailey averaged double rations each day yet still lost two stone over three months. The interpreter also got Bailey moved into a better block, occupied by German political prisoners and – an almost unheard of thing for a concentration camp – a kind *Blockältester*, the senior prisoner in the barrack block whose camp life was more privileged than the other prisoners. This man '*was a perfect gentleman … he was kind and gentle to all and greatly assisted me by gifts of food and clothes … he was a great admirer of the British and believed sincerely in their victory*'.[36]

Bailey, Tuck, Sherwill and Friend were all extremely lucky in encountering such kind strangers willing to help them and provide physical and emotional support when they needed it most. While they were not alone, most other Channel Islanders had to rely only upon each other for succour.

'As good as a meal': The importance of friendship

Channel Islanders did not often encounter each other in the prisons and camps to which they had been deported. When they did, or when they were deported with each other, it provided them with much needed support and helped them survive. The importance of close-knit reciprocal relationships for survival has been previously identified and recognized in concentration camps,[37] and among Far East prisoners of war (POWs), where such groups were termed *kongsi*.[38] While there is no special term used by Channel Islanders to describe their own friendship groups, there is plenty of evidence that they existed and were of vital importance for survival in Nazi prisons and camps.

On a work commando from the prison in Bernau, for example, Kingston Bailey was overjoyed to bump into his old friend and fellow Guernsey policeman, Thomas Gaudion. In his memoirs he wrote that he was '*very pleased to be with him. I found that the company of someone you knew was as good as a meal*'. When Islanders lost their friends or were separated from them, the blow was a hard one to bear. When Frank Tuck and Kingston Bailey were separated at Villeneuve-Saint-Georges Prison, Bailey wrote that he felt a '*deep sense of personal loss, which was to take months to overcome*'.[39] To be apart even for a day was difficult for some. Peter Hassall later wrote that he and Maurice Gould '*had grown very close, and I became lonely when Maurice worked elsewhere. He had become my loving, big brother, and I hated not to be with him.*'[40] Although fifteen-year-old Hassall was three years younger than Gould, he had been the one to look after Gould because of his vital language skills. In Frankfurt-Preungesheim Prison, Gerald Domaille was the only Briton or person able to speak English in his group while working on grinding machines where he had to clean the surface of castellated nuts on emery wheels. To cheer himself up and give himself a '*feeling of confidence*', he sung English songs to himself at a volume that could not be heard above the machines.[41] Even when Islanders were alone, it provided them with comfort to hear a voice in their own language, even if that voice was their own.

In the radio play *The Man from Belsen* by Leonard Cottrell and narrated by Harold Le Druillenec about his own experiences, Harold describes his friendship group at Neuengamme concentration camp. This comprised Frank Le Villio, a Jerseyman fourteen years younger than himself, with whom he was deported. It also included other – mostly French – men. These men gave Le Druillenec advice on how to survive the camps by dodging work commandos, conserving energy or keeping on the right side of the *Blockälteste*. Another friend got a job as a night watchman in Neuengamme, which meant that he was able to steal from the camp kitchens and share food with his friends. Harold's entire story revolved around his friendship group in Neuengamme and, later, Belsen, and they supported and encouraged each other verbally as best they could. Words were all they had to offer, but the men formed an important support group for each other at a time when they needed each other most.

In Buchenwald, the Channel Islander group kept together. In a very lucid and detailed testimony, Emile Dubois described the group they formed, writing that '*James Quick, Freddy Baker, Stanley Green and myself teamed up with one hundred and eighty English and American soldiers or airmen, together we slept out in the little larger [sic] with only a blanket each for cover and the earth for our bed. They called me Pop because I was old enough to be their father ... we remained together until the Americans and British airmen went to another camp.*'[42] This short extract shows how family relations were recreated within the camp as an alternative to friendship groups, functioning the same way in helping Islanders to lean on each other for support.

At Frankfurt-Preungesheim and Naumburg prisons, where Channel Islander friendship groups were vital for survival, it was this survival that would, in the end, help keep memory alive as well. We are fortunate that Frank Falla documented these experiences in his memoir, as they offer our only in-depth source of information about their experience in these prisons.

The help they offered each other took many forms: emotional, psychological and practical. Each person was able to help according to their ability, skills and opportunities at specific moments in time. While some helped with food procurement or work tasks, others were able to keep spirits up or provide shoulders to cry on. Canon Clifford Cohu was '*optimistic*' and '*eager to cheer his colleagues*' in Naumburg. He also made continued requests to the prison authorities, as a Church of England clergyman, to '*bury his dead*' – the other Channel Islanders who died – but he was not allowed to do so.[43] Joseph Tierney, another Jerseyman who did not survive his experience, was, wrote Falla, a '*thoughtful and helpful man with some knowledge of German. In this way he was able to help those of us who didn't know the language*'.[44] Tierney was, at one time, given an apple by a German warder in Naumburg. Rather than eating it himself, he gave it to his fellow Jerseyman, Frederick Page, who was dying.[45]

Three Guernseymen, Gerald Domaille, Norman Dexter and Walter Lainé, who met in Frankfurt prison, became each other's lifelines. Gerald Domaille noted that '*they proved to be wonderful friends the whole of the time in Germany. ... It was wonderful to have a Guernseyman to talk to ... .*'[46]

While Frank Falla had neither physical strength, nor foreign language skills, nor access to extra food to help his friends, he had his journalistic skills, and these lay behind his desire to note down what he saw. During his time in prison, he recorded the many deaths of Islanders that took place, especially the deaths of Jerseymen:

> '*It was early in my life at Naumburg*', he wrote, '*that I did a swap which was to prove of value later. I exchanged with a German half a bread ration for a one-inch stub of pencil ... I was desperate to get this stub of pencil because I had a piece of thin tomato-packing paper at the bottom of my shaving-stick case and on this I recorded the days, dates and names of the eight Channel Islanders as they died.*'[47]

Later, Falla wrote that when he was ill with pneumonia, he was determined not to die:

> *I had to carry on as best I could for I was determined that someone would get back to Guernsey* [and Jersey] *with the news of what had happened to my colleagues, however gloomy that news might be. It was the least I could do for the relatives who waited in vain for those of my colleagues who had failed to pull through.*[48]

Falla, too, was able to benefit from the help given by his friends:

> *How good my friends were to me when they saw that I couldn't cope with the hard labour I was on! One day I joined them in an outside working party which was clearing the rubble from bombed-out Felnerstrasse ... soon my hands were so sore that I just couldn't handle any more as they seared into my blistered skin. Cecil Duquemin, who knew a little German, spoke to the guard who supervised us and, explaining my predicament, got me excused from the handling and put onto sweeping up rubble. Duquemin and Ernest Legg did my share of the brick handling between them.*[49]

Falla was able to repay Ernest Legg after they were liberated. In his testimony, Legg described how he suffered from hunger oedema due to starvation at Naumburg:

> When, along with Frank Falla, I was liberated by the American forces ... the American doctor with them said I might have lived 6 or 7 days but no more. I, too, could have died in the hospital to which we were taken, unless Frank Falla had complained to the American Red Cross that the hospital authorities were doing nothing to save my life. He was able to tell the doctors at the hospital when they were paraded near my bed that if I died, they, too, would die. ... As a result of this they immediately got to work on me and in a matter of 24 hours they drained 1½ buckets of water from my body.[50]

Not all Islanders were lucky enough to be liberated by the Americans. For those three Guernseymen who remained in Frankfurt, Norman Dexter, Gerald Domaille and Walter Lainé, the last weeks of the war ended with being forced into cattle trucks and later put on a forced march together from Straubing Prison towards Dachau concentration camp. Dexter wrote in his testimony that they were at this time '*able to help each other with moral and often physical support*'.[51] In his memoirs, Gerald Domaille expanded upon this. On the forced march, he was hit hard on his right ankle by the butt of a German rifle, probably fracturing it, and so had great difficulty in walking. However, his friends were there to help. 'Norman was great, he helped all the while ... it was at this stage we found Walter and another fellow named Sidney [Ashcroft]. Now there were four of us to help each other. Singly, I do not think any of us would have survived.'[52]

As this group started to fall behind and were unable to keep up with the others, Walter Lainé had to stop and lean against a hedge. Gerald wrote that

> Walter pleaded with us to leave him there; he said he could not manage another step. The warder then reminded us that if we left him there he would be shot. It was with a great effort that we got Walter to his feet, one each side of him, and plodded on. At this stage I can say that if we had not kept together, none of us would have survived. My ankle was swollen to such a degree that I could only just walk. During that period we were issued with a bowl of so-called soup; neither Norman nor Walter could get it for me. I had to get it myself so with one of them each side of me I managed.[53]

Gerald Domaille, Norman Dexter and Walter Lainé all survived. Sidney Ashcroft was separated from the group and died alone at Straubing Prison.

'It was because I was English': The impact of British nationality towards the end of the war

While Channel Islanders may have cursed their nationality for the trouble it brought them for most of the war, many of those still interned towards the end found that it earned them preferential treatment – although this depended on where they were in

Europe at the time. Some found that their guards treated them with new respect. In his memoirs, Falla noted that

> though not immune from occasional 'beatings up', the fact was that we British were treated by the majority of the Nazi guards with a certain amount of respect and this became more noticeable as the days and months moved into 1945, and defeat stared the Nazis in the face as the Allies and Russians advanced towards us.[54]

Anthony Faramus found definite advantages in his nationality which aided his survival. At the point of registration in Mauthausen, after trying to pass himself off as French so as to avoid attention, he was advised to be registered as British as it would grant him immunity from the quarantine camp. While at Buchenwald he had experienced the quarantine camp: it was a place where new arrivals congregated for a few weeks before being inoculated and declared 'healthy'. Faramus' own inoculation had been followed within hours by pneumonia. His job in the quarantine camp had been to empty the latrines, and '*convey human filth to the primitive and unhygienic cess pools*', a job which also involved climbing down into the latrines to retrieve bodies that had toppled over and drowned in the mire.[55] To be spared the quarantine camp was thus a definite advantage.

Later, when he developed diphtheria in Mauthausen, he was sent to the hospital in the camp reserved for '*prominent and highly favoured prisoners*'.[56] His friends, keeping an eye on him, remarked, '*Thank Christ for being British*'. Faramus himself acknowledged that his death '*had been averted only because of the privilege granted to my nationality*'.[57]

Faramus' accounts of what happened to him differ between his two memoirs (perhaps not unreasonably, given the time that elapsed between writing each one, and given that he was probably too ill during this period of his life to remember it with any clarity in any case). In his earlier memoir, it seems that the gangrene in his thigh was also treated at the same time in the camp hospital. In this version of events, a French friend in the hospital persuaded the '*unsympathetic*' Czech doctor who '*disliked me on account of nationality*' to treat him. The French friend is reputed to have said, '*Doctor, you ought to try to do something for him. I think he is the only Englishman in the camp, and who knows what may happen any time now?*'[58] In the later memoir, the treatment of his gangrene in hospital was an earlier and separate event, made possible by a sympathetic English-speaking Czech friend whose uncle was a prominent prisoner, a professor of medicine who worked in the camp hospital.[59] While the operation itself was crude and without proper anaesthetic, such treatment would not have been possible in either version had Faramus not been British. Either way, his nationality had saved him: '*I knew at last why I was still alive, why I had a bunk to myself [in hospital], why my leg had been treated, why I had received precious 'medicines', why I got my daily soup. It was because I was English*'.[60]

Faramus made a further friend while in the camp hospital: a prisoner-nurse named Lena, although once again his account of her differed in each memoir. In his earlier book, Lena was an Estonian prisoner who worked in a German hospital just outside the camp and who wanted to help him '*because he was English*'. In the later memoir,

Lena was a Czech prisoner who was forced to work under the SS doctor and was a friend of Faramus' English-speaking Czech friend. In both accounts, Lena was able to bring food to Faramus, although her own end differed in the two versions. In the first, she kissed him goodbye when he left the camp.[61] In the second, Faramus saw her charred remains after she went missing.[62] It is difficult to know which version, if either, to believe. The importance of this part of Faramus' story must surely be that his British status was responsible for enabling him to survive diphtheria and gangrene in a violently brutal and merciless concentration camp. These medical conditions were later verified by a medical report submitted with his compensation testimony in the mid-1960s.[63]

Many Islanders who survived until their liberation found that, if their liberators were British or American, they were given early (and perhaps better) treatment and preferential release before their comrades of other nationalities. At Naumburg Prison, Frank Falla was liberated on 13 April 1945 by the Americans. On discovering that he was British, his rescuer was reported to have said, *'That being so we'll have to get you out of this hell-hole, buddy'.*[64] Falla and his two surviving Channel Island friends were immediately taken away and put in the prison officers' quarters for the night and then to hospital for treatment by American doctors. Once released, Falla lived with the American unit in the best hotel in town during his recuperation. He also pressed the American doctors to apply pressure to the German doctors to make sure that his friend, Ernest Legg, had better treatment, and in that way saved Legg's life, as we have already seen.[65]

In Dachau, in February 1945, Kingston Bailey was losing weight rapidly and had contracted dysentery; he knew that this was as good as a death sentence. Typhus was also rampant in the camp. Late one night he was unexpectedly called, given his own clothes, and taken to Munich to be 'liberated'. Once there, he was *'treated with overwhelming kindness by the Germans'*[66] in contrast to his earlier experiences. He was then taken *'in comfort'* to Laufen civilian internment camp, where other Channel Islanders and Americans were interned. There he was looked after and nursed back to health by his friends.[67] To be unexpectedly singled out and plucked from Dachau while he was still just about alive could only have been because of his nationality. It also indicates that the guards were aware of and monitoring the presence of British prisoners in the camp.

In Belsen, Harold Le Druillenec was not plucked to safety before the end of the war. Instead, he endured violence and absolute starvation – he was given nothing at all to eat or drink for his last five days in Belsen. No authority, it seems, was keeping a special eye on him. However, when the British liberators finally arrived, Harold *'staggered to the compound gateway ... I saw ... by the roadside, a British radio truck with the officer sitting in it. I thought I rushed up to them but they told me afterwards that I groped my way to them ... 'Wait, wait please, I'm a British subject ... I'm from the Channel Islands'.* Harold was told to sit on the bonnet of the truck rather than invited inside as he was covered in lice. The soldier was unable to take his French friend. *'And so, on April 16, I left Belsen, sitting on the bonnet of a British radio truck because I was too lousy and dirty to be allowed inside. I weighed 90 pounds. And when I saw myself in the mirror for the first time, I looked behind it to see who was there. The army treated me with infinite kindness and in a few days I was in hospital in England. Some months later, when I returned to give evidence at the Belsen trial, I went to Luneburg to discover what had happened to my 150 comrades who had been left behind, only to find their graves.*[68] How narrowly he escaped their fate.

While we do not know the full circumstances of the eventual liberation of those deported from the Channel Islands, the detailed accounts of at least two more people survive. In his earlier memoir, Anthony Faramus wrote that, on 5 May 1945, his *'status as the only Britisher in the camp raised me to dizzy heights and consequently I had to submit to being carried on a stretcher to welcome officially the US officer* [who was the first to arrive at the camp]'. Although they offered to take him away with them, he claims to have refused, and limped back to the camp. There, he wrote that he was given a Sten gun by *'the other privileged prisoners'* and asked to *'take charge'* before helping to round up and execute the SS officers.[69] When the Americans returned, he was taken away on a stretcher. In his later memoirs, the broad series of events was much the same, except an American friend of his was taken away by the Americans during their initial visit. His role in executing SS officers was also played down.[70]

The early rescue and prompt medical treatment by Allied army personnel meant that liberated Islanders had a greater chance of survival. Unlike most other prisoners, they were not forced to wait in the camp while medical treatment and food was dispensed, and nor did they have to spend months moving between Displaced Persons camps, trying to get back home.

Even Julia Barry in Ravensbrück testified that, on 7 April 1945, *there came a new order: 'British prisoners are not allowed to work anymore'* … *At last on 25 April, early in the morning, came the unexpected order: 'British and Americans, with their bundles, are to be in 10 minutes at the office'* … *we called our people and went to the office. There the Commandant told us that the Swedish Red Cross people were outside the gates with their buses* … *we didn't cry, but a kind of hysterical trembling shook our bodies: we were saved from the most horrible death!*[71] The rescue of Scandinavians in concentration camps at the end of the war by the white buses of the Red Cross is well known.[72] What is less well known is the presence of other nationalities on board. Julia Barry, who only in 1942 had acquired a seemingly protective Irish citizenship, was fortunate indeed to have a place on board.

Those on forced marches were also sometimes rescued by the Allies. Gerald Domaille, along with his fellow Guernseymen, Norman Dexter and Walter Lainé, had ended their Nazi prison career at Straubing towards the very end of the war, as mentioned above. Leaving behind Sidney Ashcroft, they were put onto a forced march of seventy kilometres towards Dachau concentration camp in late April 1945. Their nationality offered no protection from this ordeal at a time when they were suffering from malnutrition, exhaustion and injuries. At some point in the journey they managed to escape from the column. As they approached Moosburg, which had been taken by the Americans, they were given a lift on the back of an American lorry to an Allied POW camp which had been recently liberated. By great good fortune, in the camp were two Guernsey officers, Lieutenants Mulholland and Porfins. The former was known to the men through their younger days in the Royal Guernsey Militia. Mulholland wrote them a letter that would ease their passage back home. This letter gave them access to an American officer who had taken over as mayor of the town. With the help of the American army, Domaille, Lainé and Dexter managed to get a train to France and were then flown to the UK.[73] While their nationality had not spared them during their time in Nazi hands, it had proved invaluable in getting them a fast ticket home.

'Tell our families what happened': The importance of testimony

For Channel Islanders who survived Nazi prisons and camps and returned safely to the UK or the Islands, they bore a heavy burden. They were responsible for testifying for their friends whose bodies they left behind in Germany and elsewhere. Only one made a promise to return to Germany and recover the body of a dead friend after the war.

When Maurice Gould was dying of tuberculosis in Wittlich prison, where the disease was rife, Peter Hassall visited his friend in the medical ward of the prison. During a lull in their conversation, *'Maurice suddenly blurted out, "Look, Peter, I'm finished! That means you have to stay alive! You must get back and tell our families what happened. ... After the war, come back and get me. Please don't leave me here."*[74] Hassall did not *'want to see my tall, gentle friend die, as we had been through so much together'*, but Maurice was too ill to make a recovery. He died in Peter's arms on 1 October 1943. *'I was alone'* wrote Hassall. *'I knew that I would have to fight harder to stay alive, as I had no one to turn to. Maurice had always been there to comfort me when I was demoralised. He had been my friend, my big brother, my shelter and my refuge.'*[75]

It took Hassall over fifty years to fulfil his promise to Gould. Although he made the attempt several times during that period, he was stationed all over the world and far from Wittlich or Jersey.[76] But after fifty years, and after the unveiling of the Lighthouse Memorial in 1996 to those who died in Nazi prisons and camps, and which raised public awareness about the stories of those who had died, the time was right to try again. The Jersey Branch of the Royal British Legion helped with the logistics of the operation, and the States of Jersey voted, in January 1997, to fund the return of Maurice Gould's body. He had at last been *'recognised as a hero worthy of repatriation'*, as Hassall later put it.[77] On 3 May 1997, Maurice Gould was reburied in the war cemetery of Howard Davis Park *'alongside other British fallen heroes ... it was not a sad event for me, as I had at my side my two dear Breton friends'* (who had been imprisoned alongside Hassall and Gould).[78] We will return to this reburial later in this book.

Each Islander who returned had their own crusade to fight. For some, it was a lifelong battle with their impaired health; for others, it was a struggle to cope with post-traumatic stress disorder (PTSD), as we shall see. But some were motivated to overcome personal travails to fight or act on behalf of dead friends to whom silent promises had been made. After his repatriation to the UK, Frank Falla was keen to honour the bonds of friendship forged in Nazi prison cells. Arriving back into the UK from Germany on 8 June 1945, within a month he sent articles to the *Guernsey Evening Press* and the *Jersey Evening Post* (JEP) about his experiences in Frankfurt and

Naumburg (Figure 2.5). He needed to contact the families of his friends who died in prison. In his compensation testimony, he wrote that

> when our kinsmen died, relatives were <u>not</u> informed. The first news of their deaths came from me in a letter to the Editor of the Jersey 'Evening Post' when I got back to England.[79]

Falla broke the news to the Jersey public, stating that '*the weakest of us, despite the cheerful and typical English spirit, went to the wall and I regret having to state that in a period of eight months, of the 11 Channel Islanders at Naumburg … only six of us are alive to tell the tale.*' Having secretly kept a note of which Islanders died when at Naumburg, Falla was able to then repeat this list in the JEP. The death of so many Islanders in Naumburg Prison was because they were kept apart in solitary cells in separate sections of the prison. '*Any contact was extremely hazardous to life and limb*',

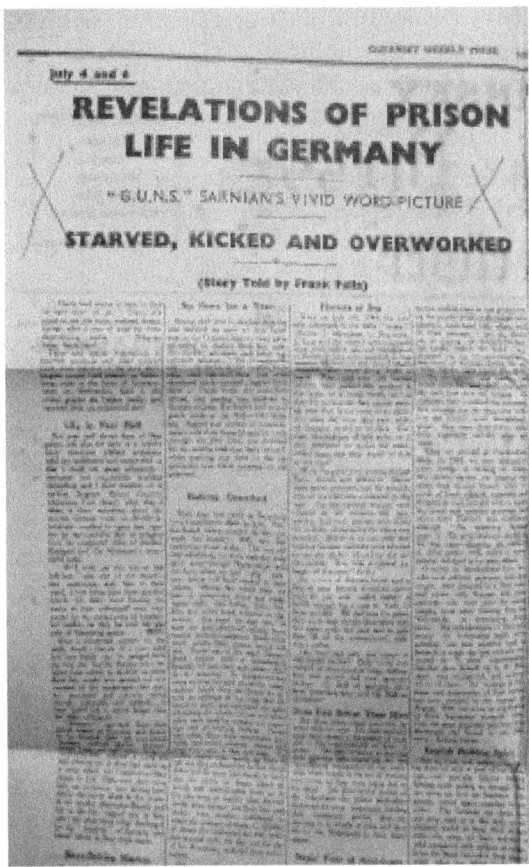

Figure 2.5 Newspaper article written by Frank Falla in July 1945. Copyright: Guernsey Press / Frank Falla Archive. Courtesy. Island Archives, Guernsey

as Falla put it. This separation prevented Channel Islanders from being able to help each other, unlike in Frankfurt.

When Falla wrote his article to the JEP in July 1945, he had been released less than three months earlier and the experience was still raw:

> *I very much regret that this article can bring little cheer or comfort to Jersey people and can only illustrate in a small way the hell-on-earth that we Channel Island political prisoners suffered at the hands of a vile enemy ... memories of which will never be erased from our minds and will haunt us to the end of our days. Even as a Christian people we can never forgive or forget all that we suffered at the hands of Hitler's Nazis.*

A year before his death, in an unpublished book manuscript, Falla confessed that this July 1945 article to the JEP was the most heart-breaking that he had ever had to write, and that it stood out above all those he had ever written. This article was the first communication that some Jersey families received about their family members. Falla followed it up by visiting these families personally to '*console them in their losses and answer questions about the circumstances*' of the death of their loved ones. Falla maintained a lifelong friendship with some of these Jersey people, including Eileen Tierney, the wife of Joseph Tierney who was never seen again after his supposed release from Naumburg.

Falla's formative early post-war experience was thus his role as the man responsible for bringing news of their loved one's decease to families. A number of families in Jersey still have those early letters from Falla, and have memories of his ongoing friendship with their families. As Falla knew well, the bonds of friendship and obligation survived death.

Falla was not the only Islander who brought back sad news and acted as a witness to the final days of their friends. In his Foreign Office case file for compensation in the 1960s, a 1945 letter to the War Office from Walter Lainé and Norman Dexter has survived. In it, they testify to the last days of Sidney Ashcroft's life before he was taken away from them, perhaps to be '*murdered in some brutal manner such as being gassed or shot*'. On the morning of 24 April 1945, they wrote, '*about 4,800 civil political and criminal prisoners were lined up in the prison yard and the director of the prison picked out the worst cases of illness, weak or most wretched-looking persons. Sydney Ashcroft was put with them.*'[80] They also took the opportunity to testify as to the presence of fifteen to twenty American and English parachutists in Frankfurt-Preungesheim Prison at the same time as they were there.

In July 1945, writing from Glasgow, Frank Tuck wrote to the Red Cross from his sick bed, anxious to inform the authorities about the death of his friend, Herbert Percival Smith, who was

> *tortured and left to die in Augsburg prison in April 1943 ... in common with all of us, Smith was badly shod and his feet were sore and bleeding. He was deprived of food and clothes when it was terribly cold, pronged with a fork, made to carry heavy sleepers, constantly tormented, beaten with a shovel and pick-axe in the stomach ... he was constantly tormented by the Camp Commander. Later he was taken to*

Augsburg and left to die in a cell and [was] refused treatment by the doctor there. I have as a witness a French aviation man who was a prisoner with him when he died and to whom Smith confided on his death bed.[81]

The importance of the survival of Islanders and their testimony for the families concerned should not be underestimated. This was the last act of true friendship that they could carry out for their deceased friends.

It was not only Islanders who could testify for each other; people of other nationalities who had formed friendships with Islanders wrote to Guernsey and Jersey after the war to let families know what had happened to their loved ones. We have already seen the letter written by Premysl Polacek about Clifford Cohu in Zöschen camp. The whereabouts of the bodies of other members of the Jersey 21 were provided by those who were with them at the end, including an unknown young man who testified to the death of James Houillebecq in Neuengamme in January 1945[82] and Frenchman Roger Hardy, who was able to tell the Painter family about the fate of Clarence and Peter Painter.[83]

Of those non-Islander friends who wrote to Island families to tell them of the last moments of their loved ones, perhaps the most moving and – much later – useful letters were those sent to Eileen Tierney in Jersey. Their contents were directly responsible for allowing the final resting place of Tierney to be determined and visited in 2016 for a BBC documentary discussed later in this volume. After he left Naumburg Prison in March 1945, where his fellow Islanders were aware of his departure, Tierney's movements were unknown. Although Tierney's mother, and wife Eileen, tried to search for him through the British and Belgian Red Cross, the Channel Islands Refugees Committee, the Soviet Embassy, UNRRA, the BBC, the Foreign Office, and as many different avenues as they could think of, they drew a blank. In May 1947, information arrived through the Red Cross from two Belgian men who had known Tierney, both of them survivors of the events that had claimed Tierney's life: Albert Sauvage and Albert Koch from Belgium. Sauvage wrote that he was with Tierney in '*Soechem camp*',[84] and they were then put on a railway wagon without food. He reported that Tierney died on 2 May 1945 either at 'Schels' or 'Theresine in Czechoslovakia, most probably in a common grave'. Koch, confirming Sauvage's information, said that Tierney had died 'between 30 April and 4 May 1945' between 'Schels and Kaschitz when the convoy was travelling towards Czechoslovakia'.[85] Koch had also written separately, saying that 'the person for whom you cry in fact escaped with me in Schelles and after we were recaptured on 28 April 1945 Joseph and myself were once again imprisoned in cattle trucks and it was only several days later that your dear departed husband died in my arms in Kaschitz'.[86]

Although his family tried to search for a grave for many years, and even into the 1950s, they were hampered by a lack of definite news and by the fact that 'Kaschitz' and 'Schels' or 'Schelles' no longer existed. As a village inhabited by ethnic Germans in German-occupied Bohemia, it was 'ethnically cleansed' of its inhabitants after the war as Czechs sought to rid their lands of much-hated Germans. The village became Kaštice, and those who might have witnessed anything were no longer there. In fact, before they were thrown out of Bohemia, in August 1945 the ethnic Germans had been forced to exhume the mass grave where Tierney's body had been thrown, and the decomposing corpses were placed in coffins and given a Catholic funeral and buried in the nearby village of Pšov. The details of this were found in the archives in Prague in December 2015.[87] The following March, Joseph's daughter Patricia, and her son Mark, were able to travel to his grave to pay their respects. They carried with them some of the ashes of Eileen Tierney to place with Joseph, to reunite them at last. This memorable pilgrimage is discussed in Chapter 8.

'Absent friends': The importance of friendship groups after the war

After the war, Frank Falla set up an annual reunion for the Guernseymen who survived Frankfurt and Naumburg prisons and Buchenwald concentration camp, sometimes inviting Harold Le Druillenec from Jersey too. On the last Saturday in April, the month in which the Frankfurt and Naumburg survivors were liberated, the 'Frankfurt / Naumburg crooks', as they collectively called themselves, got together. They ate what they liked, drank what they liked, and had as many cigarettes as they wanted in memory of their period of extreme deprivation and the things denied them by the Nazis. '*Our toast*', Falla explained in an interview in 1955, '*is 'Absent Friends', and we think about the chaps who died, like Canon Cohu – a fine and brave man. We rejoice that we lived – but we mourn those who died*'.[88]

In 1964, a compensation agreement with the West German government, the FDR, was signed and the British government received £1M in compensation for British victims of Nazi persecution. The States of Guernsey and Jersey declined to get involved in helping people claim compensation (beyond confirming to the Foreign Office that certain people had been tried by the German courts) and so it was Frank Falla who became a self-appointed 'unofficial official', as he called himself. He helped other Channel Islanders compose their testimonies and claim compensation, as we will see in Chapter 6. Falla derived a great deal of pleasure, satisfaction and happiness in being able to help other Islanders, especially those whose loved ones had died in Naumburg Prison. He did this on behalf of his dead friends as a last act of loyalty and friendship. Through his intervention, many families, brought low by poverty triggered by an inability of the head of the household to work or to pay expensive medical bills following ill-treatment in a Nazi prison or camp, were now able to pay off debts. With Falla's help, around 50 per cent of the 100 Channel Islanders who applied for compensation were able to receive it. This period of his life reawakened his desire to document the experiences of Channel Islanders deported during the Occupation. After the compensation claims he received a book contract from Leslie Frewin publishers and wrote his memoirs, *The Silent War*. It was an opportunity to put the side of the story of those who believed that their actions and motives were patriotic and legitimate. Falla was bitter that he and others like him were still perceived as 'naughty schoolboys' and 'troublemakers', and he wanted to change the way that people thought about those who had spent time in Nazi prisons and camps. Although it was still too soon after the Occupation for Falla's wishes to be granted, writing his memoirs proved therapeutic and enabled him to move forward with his life and '*get the experience out of his system*'.[89]

This group of friends continued to meet annually until their deaths in the 1970s and 1980s. During that post-war period, their bonds of friendship had been extended by bonds of family. Norman Dexter became the godson for one of Gerald Domaille's sons. The son of Kingston Bailey married the niece of Walter Lainé. Although such examples of intermarriage among former political prisoners were perhaps inevitable in a small island, it provides lingering evidence of the continued closeness of families of these men.

In Jersey, the great-granddaughter of former prisoner Emile Paisnel was on the committee of those who were behind the erection of the Lighthouse Memorial to the Jersey 21 in 1996. In Guernsey, the daughter and granddaughter of Joseph Gillingham campaigned for the Resistance Memorial, erected in May 2015 in memory of the Guernsey Eight. The families of others listed on the memorial came from across the UK and Channel Islands to witness the event. Each of those who attended came to remember their loved ones; those who had died in solitary confinement or alone, and those whose final resting place was discovered thanks only to their friends who fought to survive so they could bring home the news.

Conclusion

This chapter has put forward three key arguments. The first is that friendship groups among prisoners in Nazi prisons and concentration camps, comprising primarily those who could speak the same language, was vital to survival, although ultimately it could not guarantee it. Friends were able to help each other through illnesses and injuries, in food acquisition, in work parties, and in boosting morale. Those Islanders who died were often in a situation where they had become separated from their friends or were put in solitary confinement.

I have also argued that the British experience in prisons and camps was not an enviable one until the final stages of the war. Most Islanders reported being targeted for physical and verbal abuse because of their nationality. It was only as the outcome of the war became clear that Islanders were treated better by their guards who were scared of repercussions. British nationality also confirmed immediate medical treatment or liberation of Islanders if they made themselves known to their British or American liberators.

Finally, I have highlighted the sense of lifelong duty towards each other felt by former political prisoners – a duty that is often continued today by their children and grandchildren, as we shall see later on. It is possible that this phenomenon was heightened by the scarcity of Britons in the Nazi prison and camp system, which served only to tighten the bonds of friendship. The post-war friendship manifested itself as a fourfold duty: testifying for dead colleagues; informing the families of the dead of the loss of their loved ones; bringing home the bodies or the location of the bodies to the families; and a duty towards memory, most especially legitimating those memories. The importance of memory can be seen in memoirs, testimonies and, more informally, annual reunions. Those who survived the war owed each other their lives. Those who did not survive depended on the living to bear witness for them.

In the next chapter we examine what happened in the Channel Islands immediately after the war, when the local authorities had to justify their actions to their citizens and to the British government. This was done in the face of local dissent by the first groups of Islanders to speak up for the dead, who called for the prosecution of those whose actions led to the death of their fellow Islanders. Whose actions would be considered the more legitimate by history, what arguments were made, and who was the final arbiter?

3

1945–1946: Cementing De-legitimization

Introduction

The attitudes of the local authorities and the general public towards those who offended against the occupiers have their roots in the Occupation years. But the liberation of 1945 was, potentially, a chance for a different stance to be adopted. At the start of the Occupation, in July 1940, HM Procureur Ambrose Sherwill made a speech in Guernsey in which he described the relationship between the occupiers and the local authorities as '*not merely correct … [but] cordial and friendly. It is most important that they should remain so. Let no one jeopardise this by unseemly or unruly conduct.*'[1] But, as Frank Falla later wrote, '*even after the war when we ostensibly should have rid the island of its 'correct' behaviour, it was noticeable to the ordinary people of the Islands, like me, that no honour was bestowed on people of the calibre of the sole survivor of Belsen … Harold Le Druillenec*'.[2]

The continuation of the importance of the myth of 'correct behaviour' (and even cordial behaviour) between the occupiers and Islanders is something that lasted long after the end of the Occupation and formed a cornerstone to the narrative of Occupation memory. This narrative denies collaboration, resistance, and any wrongdoing on behalf of the occupiers. It insists that everybody behaved themselves and that the Occupation really was a '*model to the world*', as Sherwill put it in a speech the following month, in August 1940.[3]

The aim of this chapter is to examine how and why this narrative was perpetuated *after* the Occupation, but – more importantly – how former prisoners, the victims of Nazism, came to be either accidentally overlooked, perhaps as collateral damage, or deliberately excluded from playing a legitimate part in the story. The way that informers were treated will be singled out for particular scrutiny, as their actions caused the arrest, imprisonment and deportation of many Islanders.

This chapter focuses on the first year after the Occupation, when the narrative was still being constructed, and travels down four key avenues to understand the path eventually chosen. The first source examined, in the realm of officially sanctioned yet popular politics, is the film of the experience of the Channel Islands' Occupation, made by the Crown Film Unit (CFU) in 1945. The second source, so vital to understanding the stance taken by Guernsey, involves a dissection and analysis of a small number of important speeches made by senior members of the States,[4] the Island's parliament and government. In the examination of these texts we seek to understand why the politicians made the choices that they did. It will not escape the reader's notice that a narrative of 'correct relations' during the Occupation, coupled with the firm statement after the Occupation that this accurately described five years of civilian and military behaviour, not only steered the Channel Islands away from discussions of possible collaboration, but also avoided the possibility of post-war trials. The benefit or otherwise of such trials in the Channel Islands is something that has been discussed for the last seventy years, and we will also ask whether it would have been better to prosecute a small number of wrong-doers rather than avoid trials at all costs, with the resulting generations of finger-pointing and speculation that this engendered. However, the purpose of this chapter is not to decide whether trials were warranted or a good idea, or even to criticize the behaviour of the local authorities. Rather, it is to consider what role the discussion of trials played in legitimizing or negating the memory of victims of Nazism.

In the third part of this chapter, we shift to the voice of the people in the shape of the 'Jersey Loyalists', to explore how at least one group in Jersey felt about post-Occupation politics. While there was no similar group who pushed for justice in Guernsey, other archival sources can be drawn upon to see how those in that Island felt about the post-war choices that were being made by the local authorities.

The fourth and most decisive factor discussed here to have affected the final war narrative adopted was that which was negotiated privately, behind the scenes, between the local and British governments. This did not happen in a vacuum, without reference to the events of the Occupation. Rather, as we shall see, certain courses of action were decided upon for the 'good of the Islands' and in the 'best interest of the people'.

'They stole the truth and filled our papers with Goebbels and Haw-Haw': The Crown Film Unit's 1945 production

In 1945[5] the CFU, an organization within the British government's Ministry of Information, visited the Channel Islands to make a film, re-enacted by the Islanders themselves, about the Occupation[6] (Figure 3.1). At just over fifteen minutes in length, the film is narrated by a non-Islander,[7] although he refers to 'our', 'we' and 'us' when describing experiences in the Channel Islands. The narrator does not take the part of anyone in particular; rather, he is 'every man', and speaks for the average person. Although we do not know the full role of Islanders in influencing content of the film, it seems likely and, indeed, apparent that the script was made after much discussion with local people about real events. As the Ministry of Information was more used to making propaganda films, we might also question the extent to which the content or tone of the film was decided by London. If so, it is curious to observe the mismatch between this film and the resulting line negotiated between the Islands' and British authorities, where informers would not be punished and resisters were not rewarded.

The film opens with a group of men pushing a boat down to the water's edge, getting ready to escape from the island – one of three acts of resistance shown in the film (the others being radio resistance and the sheltering of Russian slave labourers). The

1945–1946: Cementing De-legitimization

Figure 3.1 Bailiff Alexander Coutanche in a cameo role in a still from the Crown Film Unit's production *The Channel Islands 1940–1945*, held at the Imperial War Museum, copyright expired[8]

voice-over begins with the words '*Good luck! When you get to England, tell them how we're getting on over here. Tell them we're having a tough time but the Germans can't get us down ... and tell them that we're managing to hear the BBC*'. In the opening frames, illicit listening to the BBC is emphasized; and in the speech in which (in a cameo role) Jersey's Bailiff, Alexander Coutanche, is listening to a radio hidden in the attic, Churchill intones '*any man or state who fights against Nazidom will have our aid*'[9] – an emphasis on the legitimacy both of resistance in general and of radio resistance and Coutanche specifically. Coutanche's role in this film is interesting: it is unthinkable that his Guernsey counterpart, Victor Carey, would have taken part, so strong a stance against resistance did the Guernsey authorities take. Coutanche is also positioning himself here as loyal to Churchill and anti-Nazi, an important signal to send to the audience watching the film in England given the accusations of collaboration that were circulating at the time.

The film names a small numbers of Islanders who played particular roles during the Occupation which were re-enacted in the film. Of those nine named people, seven were involved in resistance activities, all of which were connected with making crystal radios, illicit listening to the BBC, and making underground news sheets. This makes it clear which, of all the acts which defied German orders, was perceived as the most legitimate, common and uncontroversial to talk about. In fact, Sanders describes radio resistance as the 'iconic symbol of resistance during the occupation'.[10]

An analysis of the forty-six scenes depicted or enacted reveals an interesting balance of themes relating to different aspects of daily life under occupation (Figure 3.2). These we might broadly categorize under the headings of 'make do and mend / hardships' (such as food shortages, mending clothes or poorly shod children), 'resistance' (strongly weighted towards radio resistance), 'collaboration' (restricted to informing upon others who had hidden radios, and the black market), 'German wrongdoings'

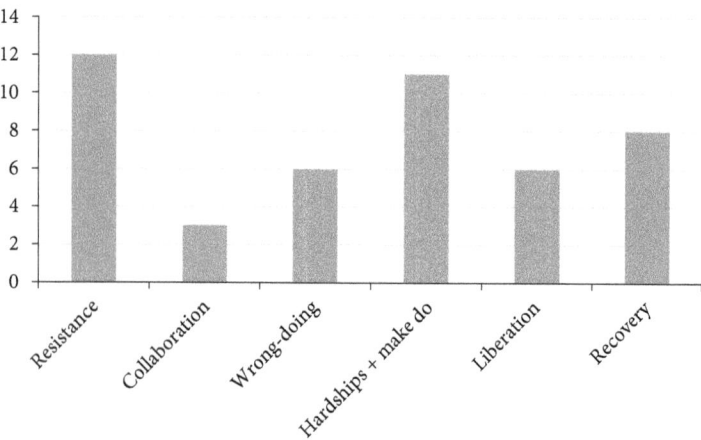

Figure 3.2 Graph showing number of incidences of themes in the CFU film, *The Channel Islands 1940–1945*

(depicted by graves of slave workers, and theft of civilian food and possessions), 'liberation' (inevitably revolving around the arrival of the Red Cross ship, the Vega, carrying Red Cross parcels), and 'recovery' (the shops filling with products once again, well-fed animals in fields, German soldiers removing barbed wire).

This balance of themes reveals that narratives of resistance are stronger than those relating to hardships / make do and mend, the latter of which is still a strong theme in Occupation memory today. Unsurprisingly, collaboration, or wrongdoing by Islanders, received the lowest number of references, and post-war recovery was a strong theme at the end of the film to let the British public know that the Channel Islands would be open for business again soon, with the words: *'Give us time to sort ourselves out and we won't let you down with our exports'.*

When we compare this graph, which we might say reflects the popular position in 1945, to the earliest of the phases of memory of the Occupation through which the Channel Islands have travelled since 1945, we find something slightly different. The years from 1945 until the early 1950s were marked by a celebration of victory and freedom, mourning for the war dead and cleansing the Islands from military hardware. The film touches only upon celebration and cleansing; it was perhaps made too soon to be counting the costs of the war. After this, the Islands entered a phase of deliberate and voluntary amnesia as people put the war behind them and focused on the future, a period which lasted until the late 1970s. At this point, the second generation started asking questions of their parents and exploring the Occupation for themselves through the medium of bunker excavation and restoration. This nostalgic approach, which also encompassed, from the mid-1980s, a focus on liberation, lasted until the mid-1990s, when victims of Nazism began to be 'remembered' for the first time.[11] And yet, when we refer back to this film, we can see that it touches upon victims of Nazism, such as slave workers and those imprisoned, although there is no mention of Jews. In fact, the imprisoned and/or deported were the single largest group referred to. Among them the film mentions real people such as '*André the hairdresser*',[12] who, '*after an informer gave his name to the Gestapo ... got six months in Jersey jail where, incidentally, he still carried on making crystal sets and listening to the news with the warders*'.

Other named prisoners included three of the five men who were deported for their work on GUNS, the Guernsey Underground News Service. The central character named in the film for this story, however, was a lesser known figure, Mick Robins, a junior reporter on the Star newspaper, who '*played a large part in the distribution of GUNS*'. The camera follows him as he delivers the news, and the narrator tells the listener how the Germans '*stole the truth and filled our papers with Goebbels and Haw-Haw. The remedy was simple but dangerous. We ran our own with the help of the BBC. One of our papers was called GUNS. ... The originator, Machon, of the Guernsey Star, was eventually caught and sent to Germany where he died, poor chap. Falla and Duquemin also went to prison.*' Although we perhaps shouldn't read too much into this, we might wonder why Gillingham and Legg, other deported members of the group, were not mentioned. Despite the abundant discussion of radio resistance, Machon is the only man described as having been deported or died for this offence, although twenty-eight Channel Islanders died in continental prisons or camps.[13] Radio resistance was the most frequent of all offences tried by the German courts.[14] These numbers were not yet known at the time the film was made; in fact, the full outcome of the Occupation as far as political prisoners were concerned was not fully known until many months – and sometimes years – later.

Radio resistance was clearly touted as a form of resistance par excellence: even the role of informers, listed twice, were informing on people who listened to the radio. '*We were very ashamed of our traitors; people who would split on you for a handful of dirty Marks. There weren't many of them but we shan't forget them. They used to write anonymous letters to the Gestapo, telling them where they could find hidden radios.*' The narrator makes it clear that the actions of these people wouldn't be forgotten; and yet that is exactly what Islanders would have to do after the Occupation, when nobody would be brought to trial or face prison for informing. And if informers would have to be forgotten, then those upon whom they informed were also destined to lose their place in the narrative of the Occupation for fifty years, despite the clearly prominent role they played in popular memory in the first year after the Occupation as exemplified by the CFU.

'Vital sacrifices': Leale's speech to the States, May 1945

There are two speeches to the States of Guernsey which might be thought of as effectively topping and tailing the Occupation, and both were delivered by Presidents of the Controlling Committee.[15] The first, by Ambrose Sherwill, was given on 7 August 1940, five weeks after the beginning of the Occupation. The German Commandant, Dr Lanz, his Chief of Staff, Dr Maass, and some German officers attended the sitting. The second was given by Jurat John Leale, two weeks after the surrender, on 23 May 1945. Leale later took over as President of the Controlling Committee after Sherwill was deported in October 1940.

During Sherwill's now-infamous speech, he declared:

May this occupation be a model to the world, on the one hand tolerance on the part of the military authority and courtesy and correctness on the part of the occupying forces and on the other dignity and courtesy and exemplary behaviour on the part of the civilian population. Perfect obedience to law and order, conformity, the strictest conformity ... When it is over, I hope that occupying force and occupied population may be able to say: '... we lived together with tolerance and mutual respect.' The German forces ... came to Guernsey and found the civilian population calm, dignified and well-behaved. Having us in their power, they behaved as good soldiers, sans peur et sans reproche. And we, the civilian population, were sober, law-abiding, giving no cause for offence, courteous and polite. We did our utmost, without exception, to avoid incidents and to assist in the maintenance of perfect order. ... We did not shed and were not asked to shed our loyalty to our King and Country.[16]

This 'model Occupation', to be characterized by correct behaviour on both sides, was sharply criticized by journalist Madeleine Bunting as being a 'deeply pragmatic policy [of] peace at any price', where protests were 'timid' and where the occupiers had to be 'conciliated and appeased at every turn', and resistance was rejected 'in any form'.[17] And yet Sherwill did not make his speech in a vacuum. On 19 June 1940, the Lieutenant-Governors of the Channel Islands received a letter from Alexander Maxwell, Permanent Under-Secretary of State, telling them that they should stay at their post and 'administer the government of the Island' to the 'best of their abilities, in the interests of the inhabitants.'[18] As the Lieutenant-Governors had already been recalled, the Bailiff and Attorney General in each Island received the letter. Quite how they interpreted the 'best interests of the inhabitants' can be exemplified in the address to the States that John Leale made in Guernsey two days later, and some six weeks before Sherwill's speech:

Should the Germans decide to occupy this Island, we must accept the position. There must be no thought of any kind of resistance; we can only expect that the more dire punishment will be meted. I say this: the man who even contemplates resistance should the Germans come is the most dangerous man in the Island and its most bitter enemy. The military have gone. We are civilians.[19]

While undoubtedly referring to military resistance – for he could not have foreseen the civilian resistance that was to later emerge[20] – Leale's speech set the blueprint for the way that the Occupation was to be conducted. When addressing the States five years later, in a speech which was subsequently published as a report,[21] Leale referenced Sherwill's speech rather than his own, perhaps indicating a subtle and delicate shifting of the blame for a policy which Captain Dening, an intelligence officer attached to liberating Force 135, was to consider to be a '*pusillanimous and material policy which made the States the willing puppet of an often contemptuous German administration. With such an example from the top, it is not surprising that the people of Guernsey found little incentive to indulge in anti-German activities which aroused the fierce and immediate condemnation of their own civic authorities.'*[22] As Dening later noted, such a policy effectively declared that an attack on the Germans was an attack on the States.[23]

Leale's post-Occupation speech in the States thus declared that

> *it has been our constant endeavour to make the occupation, to use the words of the first President of the Controlling Committee, a model. The generally excellent behaviour of the local population is, we think, proof that we have been not altogether unsuccessful in achieving our aim.*[24]

And yet, the Occupation had not been a model of good behaviour. There were many acts of protest, defiance and resistance, for which c. 1,300 people in the Channel Islands had been imprisoned locally, and over 200 deported for offences against the occupiers.[25] The Germans, for their part, had deported over 2,000 Islanders (including a handful of British Jews among this number) to civilian internment camps. They had forcibly brought thousands of foreign (many forced and slave) labourers to the Islands to build the Atlantic Wall under the auspices of the corrupt Organisation Todt, who had indulged in human rights abuses. The occupiers had also demanded the registering of the Orders against the Jews in the Royal Courts, which resulted in the deportation from Guernsey of one Polish and two Austrian Jewish women to France in April 1942, from where they were rounded up three months later and sent to Auschwitz.[26]

Leale's speech was billed as having the function of enlightening the audience on *'what the Controlling Committee has done or left undone'*. Leale made clear that it represented his own opinions which *'may or may not be held by my colleagues'*, and that he would *'try to state the truth as I know it ... I have the right to speak only of Germans as they behaved in Guernsey.'* He added that *'if we had to live over those years again, there are, of course, a number of things we should do differently, but we are entitled to ask you to remember that we are not trained diplomats ... our training was in the bitter school of practical experience.'* Indeed, this reminder by Leale was pertinent; the States of Guernsey and Jersey were not filled with international statesmen, trained and experienced in the black arts of dealing with the Third Reich, as intelligence officers attached to Force 135 bemoaned.[27] Instead, we learn from several later parts of Leale's speech that their primary modus operandi was to follow, to the fullest extent possible, the Hague Convention, a set of international rules governing the relationship between an occupier and the occupied. They clung to it with faith that it would lead them down the only possible path of survival and that it would guide them in the correct course of action in all circumstances. Three particular passages of the speech exemplify the degree to which it was adhered:

> *Under the Hague Convention the occupying force has both rights and responsibilities. The Occupied also have their rights, but they also have their responsibilities – good behaviour, for instance ... The Germans had been here for 12 months before we found a copy of the Hague Convention.*
>
> *In the long run I have no doubts whatsoever that our rights and interests as British people were best safeguarded by sticking to International law through thick and thin. ... We espoused the Hague Convention 'for better for worse, for richer for poorer, in*

sickness and in health.' To have flirted with the Convention would have been to have displayed bad morals and a patriotism based purely on opportunism.

Our position in this island was unique. We were a small community under the German Army, cut off from the rest of the world. The Hague Convention is real and solid. When you have it on your side, you feel less alone. It is something of civilisation which war with all its brutality cannot expel.

A fourth passage reveals the Leale's use of the Hague Convention as a blueprint for the perception of those who might 'rock the boat'; that is, only by behaving 'sensibly' could reprisals be avoided:

In our own Commentary on the Hague Convention we read: – 'If contrary to the duty of the inhabitants to remain peaceful, hostile acts are committed by individual inhabitants, a belligerent is justified in requiring the aid of the population to prevent their recurrence and in serious and urgent cases in resorting to reprisals.' … The behaviour of the people has except for a few isolated instances been seemingly sensible, realistic and in harmony with the rules of International Law.

These selected passages reveal the extent to which the Controlling Committee believed that the Hague Convention provided the correct path for them, as patriotic and civilized gentlemen. It validated that which they had already ordained would be the way forward. Their adherence to its tenets, and belief in its ability to guide them, explains their attitude, during and after the Occupation, to those who did not believe that their responsibilities towards the Germans merited 'good behaviour'.

Where the Convention was silent, Leale rationalized the choices he made, and explored options open to the Guernsey authorities when deciding how to act in response to the challenges and problems that the Germans demanded of them or threw in their path.

When we received an order, there were quite a lot of courses open to us. We could carry it out without demur or could risk doing nothing in the hope that this would be the last we would hear of it; or try by arguments to get it reversed; or accept, as a fait accompli, that something unpleasant was going to happen and to make the best of a bad job by suggesting alternative proposals, which, though unpleasant, would be less burdensome than the original order.

Leale drew upon the example of the mass deportations to civilian internment camps of September 1942 and February 1943 as a way of explaining how he and his colleagues rationalized their difficult decisions:

Among the cruellest problems we had to face, probably the cruellest of all were the deportations. We had to decide whether we should cut ourselves completely adrift on the grounds that the thing was unclean or take the point of view that if the deportations were due to take place there was nothing that we could do to prevent them. If we accepted the latter as our standpoint, we could work to ensure that everything was conducted in an orderly fashion; we could try to get the maximum number of exemptions; we could organise to that everything that was humanely possible was done to lighten the burden of those who had to go. We chose the latter alternative. I don't think we should have gained anything except a little notoriety by the former. We had to try to be realists.

However, although Leale was prepared to refer to any number of case studies when it came, for example, to the requisition of food or bicycles, he was silent on the subject of the ethical dilemmas surrounding the Orders against the Jews. The foreign labourers were referred to as '*unfortunate men*' who were in a '*pitiable condition*', mentioned only in passing to remark upon the '*inexplicable, tragic and puzzling*' fact that a '*proud race*' such as the Germans had allowed the '*British people, whom they undoubtedly respect*' to witness the men's plight. He did not discuss those who gave them humanitarian aid, as such people defied German orders. When it came to other victims of Nazism, such as people deported for acts of resistance, Leale was opaque and vague. In a section sub-headed 'The Iron Hand', Leale flagged up retributions for the arrival of the commandos, for sabotage and for V-signs:

However, the inhabitants of the island realised that such [resistant] *actions led nowhere ... Guernsey was, in fact, an impossible place in which to indulge in underground activities. Any attempt on these lines brought retribution on the population, and it was generally realised that getting other people into trouble is a doubtful way of displaying one's patriotism. Sometimes these awkward moments were of a different kind. Less stark they were none the less real and fraught with dire consequences involving members of the population in vital sacrifices.*

It is unclear precisely about whom Leale was talking, but in a paragraph on resistance activities (which occasioned the 'awkward moments' during which, we assume, these actions had to be discussed with the occupiers), the members of the population who were 'vital sacrifices' of the local authorities could only be those who were imprisoned or deported in order to somehow safeguard the majority of the population and protect them from retribution. This interpretation is further supported by a short passage towards the end of the report, where Leale thanked his colleagues on the Controlling Committee. '*I am not unaware that at times they had to make decisions which were resented by those affected. These decisions were taken only after weighing the private needs against the background of interests of the community.*'

An example of one of those who no doubt resented decisions made, whose case shows that an avowed adherence to the Hague convention was not just window dressing by Island authorities after the Occupation, nor something that was only used in Guernsey, is the Jersey case of Harry Ballantine. A retired army captain, Ballantine was caught with a radio set and wrote to the Attorney General on 12 February 1944 to ask what the rights were of '*political prisoners under international law*'. Duret Aubin replied two days later to say that he '*knew of no text book or other authority*' which dealt with the subject, and that the Hague Convention was '*silent regarding the position of civilians who may be prosecuted before, and convicted by, Military Courts in Occupied*

Territory' but that it was clear and '*well settled in practice*' that there must be a '*trial before punishment*' by such '*courts as the belligerent concerned may determine*'.²⁸ In other words, the Hague Convention was the authority to which they made primary recourse and, in the absence of any guidance, they did nothing to protect or help political prisoners. As long as the Germans held trials before punishing Islanders, they were behaving correctly as far as the local authorities were concerned. In the event, Ballantine was convicted on 26 February 1944 for '*failure to surrender a wireless set*' and given a sentence of three months.²⁹ It is not known whether he was deported.

Such a calculated sacrifice by the local authorities of individuals to protect the majority has been discussed by Paul Sanders as an example of a utilitarian doctrine. The 'greater good' argument, whereby it was better to sacrifice individuals for the greater good or safety of the community, was just too bad for the sacrificed people in question.³⁰ Such people were often from the 'out-group', among whom Sanders identifies as Jews, and 'deviants from the established path' – those who committed offences against the occupying authorities.

The policy of men in the States of Guernsey such as Leale and Sherwill, then, does not chime well with the popular narrative espoused in the CFU's short documentary. Having nailed his colours to the Hague Convention, and eschewed any chosen path other than one which called for 'sensible' or 'correct' behaviour, it would have gone against everything Leale encouraged in the population for five years to suddenly change his tune in May 1945. As a man of integrity and strong belief in his chosen actions, this is unlikely to have been something that he would have done. In fact, had he done so, he might have been accused of two-faced behaviour, or of trying to curry favour with the British liberating forces. To have suddenly espoused a strong pro-resistance stance would have made the population angry that such behaviour was not given more support behind the scenes during the Occupation, and that those given sentences by the German occupying authorities were not given more assistance and protection. To have publicly changed his mind about resistance would have been tantamount to declaring that his policy was wrong during the Occupation, and this he did not believe. Leale could have risked being removed from office by either an angry populace or the British authorities had he performed such a *volte-face*. As it was, Leale stuck to his guns, and continued to state a belief in the righteousness of the Hague Convention, which the British government could hardly have objected to. It was to prove to be his ticket to staying in office, to being publicly beyond reproach and, eventually, would lead to a knighthood. Under such circumstances, those who committed acts of resistance or defiance could not have hoped to share the stage with him.

Jersey Loyalists: The 'men of good standing'

One of the problems of acknowledging or giving honours to those who resisted, and especially those who were deported for offences against the occupiers, was that such people would have been raised in status and given a legitimate public platform. Once allowed a voice, that voice is likely to have condemned and drawn attention to informers and called for their arrest and trial. Once allowed out of the box, such people would have been hard to put back in again. Further, they were likely to have made complaints against the authorities for not doing more to protect them, and perhaps – rightly or wrongly – for having done too much to aid the enemy. Resisters had the potential to be dangerous for the local authorities because of their accusations of collaboration. It was perhaps fortunate for those in a position of authority that many of those who came home from the worst prisons and camps were in hospital or recuperating from injuries, illnesses and symptoms of PTSD (as we now recognize it) during the first few months after the end of the war.

One of the first things that Frank Falla did after his return to Guernsey was to go to the British military authorities to make a complaint against the man who informed on those involved in GUNS, and to ask that he be punished. He was told, more or less, to 'forget it'.[31] Falla was far from the only person who looked for justice. Local newspapers called for the Island officials to deal with collaborators[32] and journalists coming from the UK to the Channel Islands in search of sensational stories about collaborators and informers did not return empty handed, as numerous newspaper headlines of the period attest.[33]

Although we don't know how many people approached the British military authorities with complaints about the wartime conduct of other Islanders, they received a '*substantial number of letters, mostly anonymous, about the behaviour of certain members of the public*'.[34] Informers were being informed upon. What we do know, however, is that the people assigned to investigating possible war crimes were hopelessly overstretched,[35] and that they focused primarily on crimes committed by the occupiers. The Director of Public Prosecutions (DPP), Sir Theobald Mathew, was, from the start, not inclined to form a commission of inquiry into the conduct of the local authorities; he intended not to do anything in that direction if it could possibly be avoided.[36] Thus, although individual Islanders gave affidavits against individual Germans, such as men of the *Geheime Feldpolizei*[37] or German judges who presided over court-martials,[38] the main task of the investigators was to collect evidence relating to the 1942 and 1943 deportation of civilians, and the atrocities committed in the labour and concentration camps in Alderney. The Attorney Generals of the Channel Islands also wanted an investigation into the bombing of the Islands carried out as a prelude to occupation; the requisitioning of food in 1944; and the reduction of rationing as a reprisal for the sinking of German food vessels in 1943.[39] Nowhere on this list of priorities was the investigation of informers although, scarcely a fortnight after liberation, Major Haddock of the legal staff of Force 135 was advised that '*the question of persons having assisted the Germans whilst they were in occupation is a matter which should be tried by the civil courts; they are not war crimes*'.[40]

A number of men in Jersey, who represented several underground organizations, banded together soon after the Occupation by contacting each other through an advert in the local paper.[41] They called themselves the 'Jersey Loyalists' (JL). These underground organizations included the Air Raid Precaution (ARP) group (led by Major Crawford-Morrison, who was deported in 1943, and comprised other former officers among its members); the St Martin's Underground Movement; the Jersey Auxiliary Legion; and the Loyalists. Their self-assigned tasks during the Occupation were to gather military information, map German positions, and help escapees leave

Figure 3.3a and b Major John Manley and Major John L'Amy of the Jersey Loyalists. Courtesy: Jersey Heritage

the Island with copies of the maps or to try to get the information to England. They saw themselves as a '*self-appointed section of the British Secret Service*'.[42] They also compiled lists of collaborators.[43]

As the JL, they believed that the '*infamous collaborators and informers who had done so much to bring shame and disgrace upon the Island had to be brought to book*'. They pooled their resources and formed a '*strong Island organisation with a direct appeal to all loyal men and women who thought as we did and who were prepared to participate actively in our work*'.[44] Their aim was to petition the States of Jersey to ask for a special court to be set up to '*deal with persons accused of having collaborated with or assisted the German war effort*'.[45] The president and vice president of the JL were Major JCM Manley and Major J. H. L'Amy, both former members of the ARP, and both of whom had served as army officers during the First World War (Figure 3.3). L'Amy wrote a memoir within a year of the end of the Occupation, which is of great value in understanding the aims, actions and history of the JL.

On the JL's eleven-member executive committee was Harold Le Druillenec, the only British survivor of the liberation of Belsen, who joined as soon as he returned to the Island.[46] He and his sister Louisa Gould, who had died at Ravensbrück, had been informed upon.[47] On the hit list of the JL were informers ('*these individuals deserve one thing, and one thing only – the hangman's rope*'), fraternizers (i.e. women who slept with German soldiers), collaborators (among whom they included those who worked for the Germans) and black marketeers.[48] Paul Sanders described their petition as calling for a 'witch-hunt'. Under its terms, 'almost everyone could have been targeted for some offence' and the enquiry would have involved 'the invasion of the privacy of many hundreds of people'. The 'lack of measure' of the petition could have set the Island 'ablaze with anger and fury'.[49] It seems more likely that the JL themselves represented the anger and fury that was already present. It is also possible that a compromise position between them and the local authorities could have been reached, should both sides have been so minded, and had the British government not intervened.

On 21 June 1945 the JL presented a petition to the States of Jersey asking that '*a Tribunal, or Court of Inquiry, be set up before which members of the population against whom acts of disloyalty were alleged, could have their cases investigated*'. They also asked for the guilty to be prevented from leaving for the UK (where they might escape prosecution), and gave a detailed account of the '*different classes of persons against whom we sought an indictment and, so comprehensive was the list that every conceivable form of disloyalty was covered by it*'.[50] The JL saw themselves as '*strictly non-political*' and with a desire to '*proceed throughout in an absolutely constitutional manner*'. Their petition was drawn up '*under competent legal advice*'. They had also delivered their evidence to the British military authorities as well, who assured them that they were '*working on the right lines*'.[51]

After the petition was delivered, the States set up a special committee to examine and report on it. Unfortunately, it was not well received. By the end of August the JL had received no official response; however, one particular States Deputy had communicated with them, and this response was communicated by the JL to the local paper, presumably to publicly shame the States. They were told '*that the spirit of lawlessness was about was illustrated by the fact that the Petition was signed by people actually serving in the Civil Service of that island. ... It was the duty of the authorities to inform such officials that their action was contrary to the principles of justice and that unless they desisted, they themselves might be the first to suffer.*'[52]

The members of the JL were shocked and offended by such a response; they saw themselves as '*responsible men ... all men of good standing in the community. All are staunch Britishers.*' They deeply resented the way that they were being treated, for '*the Loyalists remember that many Jerseymen and Jerseywomen were sent to Germany and to death through the actions of informers. They remember Peter Painter and his twenty-year-old son, young Marsh, Davey, Tierney, Houillebecq, Canon Cohu and Mrs Gould. Over three months have passed and they fail to see any effort to trace the informers: they see no effort being made to trace those unfortunate citizens who have just "disappeared". That is why the Jersey Loyalists mean to expand and continue their work.*'[53]

The JL saw informers as indirect murderers, and they were foremost on their hit list. Among the victims of the informers were those today who we recognize as the 'Jersey 21' – those Islanders who did not return from German prisons and camps after the Occupation. The JL, like Frank Falla in Guernsey, wanted to see justice for those deported, and trials for those who were responsible.

Ten days after their article was published, the JL went to see the new Lieutenant-Governor of the Island, Lieutenant-General Arthur Grasett, to complain that insufficiently immediate and vigorous action was being taken against collaborators. Although the DPP was, at that time, investigating cases of treason and treachery, they were concerned about behaviour which fell short of these charges, namely the behaviour of informers and collaborationists. Grasett wrote to the Bailiff to express the hope that enquiry would determine whether any further legislation was necessary to deal with informers, and that the position and permission to reside in the Island of some of those who were too friendly with the Germans, many of them aliens, would be considered. The JL also repeated their concern that the States had not taken sufficiently vigorous action to discover the whereabouts of people deported to Germany still missing.[54]

In fact, this search was slow and piecemeal and, for the most part, conducted by others. While families were prime instigators in searching – often for years – for their loved ones, such as was the case with Joseph Tierney,[55] others were located through the letters of survivors to either the families concerned (such as in the case of Frenchman Roger Hardy's communications about Clarence and Peter Painter),[56] or to the Bailiff of Jersey (as we see with the letter of André Tournier, a second witness of the death of Clifford Cohu).[57] There is little evidence in the archives of prompt or active searches by the States of Jersey for missing civilians.

The JL were being kept waiting for a response from the States for their petition partly because the States themselves were waiting the termination of the investigations still being conducted by the DPP. Private communications between Coutanche and Grasett show that Coutanche feared that no criminal proceedings would be contemplated by the DPP because '*the facts do not support a charge of Treason or Treachery and because, in the present state of the Law, there is no criminal enactment which covers the case*'. He mused upon whether or not it would be desirable for the States to enact legislation '*designed to render retrospectively criminal acts which were not criminal at the time at which they were committed*'. However, having spoken on the subject to various authorities since the liberation, he had understood that '*any such Legislation was regarded as highly undesirable, and quite contrary to the principles of British Justice. I feel that the Public do not yet realize that this is so ... we must dismiss from our minds any possibility of retrospective criminal legislation.*' Meanwhile, Coutanche pressed for the deportation of former enemy aliens (the Italians and Austrians) in the Island, and noted that '*the Irish are being satisfactorily dealt with in the main*', but realized that they had no power to deport those who were British citizens. He asked whether the Home Office might suggest a way that Jersey could get rid of '*undesirable persons of British nationality*'.[58]

The States nonetheless asked the JL to supply a list of names, allegations and evidence which could then be forwarded to the DPP. They were told that the special committee set up by the States would recommend to the States '*if necessary, to seek an enlargement of the scope of their authority in order that there may be considered the possibility of dealing, by disciplinary or other action, with persons against whom the Director of Public Prosecutions decides that criminal proceedings do not lie*'.[59] The JL, however, did not see it as their duty to supply the special committee with lists of offenders and evidence; this list had already been submitted to the British intelligence corps. In any case, the JL did not have the authority or wherewithal to track down informers and collaborators; this needed to be done by a tribunal. They would, however, pass on all necessary information to an independent and public tribunal, as requested in their petition, if the States would set one up.[60] The JL were probably worried that if their information was submitted to the States alone, then it might not be acted upon and even covered up.

Were the States trying to wriggle out of holding a public tribunal? The JL could not have known that Coutanche was musing on the possibility of convening a tribunal, but why did he not push more vigorously for one? Was he concerned that some members of the States might have had allegations made against them? Or did Coutanche feel constrained by the limitations of the law and was anxious to be seen to comply with the DPP? Was it possible to please both the DPP and the JL, or was he not interested in pleasing the latter? It was important first of all for him to learn the conclusions of the DPP's investigations.

Meanwhile, Lieutenant-Governor Grasett had forwarded a list of thirteen people to the DPP '*against whom a prosecution in court might be brought, with good prospects of obtaining a conviction*', noting that the feeling in Jersey showed no sign of abating against those '*guilty of scandalous behaviour*' with the Germans who '*have been responsible for their fellow subjects being committed to prison*'. Grasett asked the DPP for advice as to what could be done because the situation was not improving with time and he was being pressed for action.[61]

In short, by November 1945, the population was still angry, although archive sources refer to this as being the situation only in Jersey. The DPP had not yet delivered his final judgement about what could be done with informers, and the States of Jersey were unwilling to act until he made his pronouncement. Would the English hold trials on their behalf, or would the States of Jersey have to do it? Was it even possible in law? David Fraser argues that the idea of the inapplicability of the law of treason and dislike of imposition of retrospective legislation '*could have been easily contested*'.[62] There was clearly no appetite for such contestation. But were there other laws which could have been invoked for such trials? A couple of options were still being considered at this date, such as Regulation 2A of the Defence (Jersey) Act,[63] or the English common law of 'misdemeanour of effecting a public mischief'.[64] However, the former was argued to have been revoked in August 1941, and the latter, while having the support of the DPP, did not enjoy such support in Jersey. Discussions indicated that this English law was inapplicable to Jersey, and it was doubtful whether '*a person could be tried in England for an offence committed in Jersey under the Common Law of England*'.[65] Journalist Madeleine Bunting presents this legal discussion as '*ignored advice*' and a decision by the British government not to have such trials because they would be a '*political minefield*'.[66] It seems more likely, however, that there were real legal issues at play, coupled with the desire of the local authorities to act correctly in the eyes of the British government. The hands of the States of Jersey were tied. They were effectively in limbo until the final report of the DPP was published, unable to act to satisfy the anger and frustration on their own doorstep.

The Channel Islands and the British government: Dealing with 'scandalous behaviour'

The JL were not yet out of the picture as 1945 drew to a close; they had not yet been satisfied. But the investigation to prosecute those who committed 'scandalous behaviour short of treachery or treason' was now out of their – and the States of Jersey's – hands. While this deliberation had been going on between the States of Jersey, the JL and the DPP, other forces had been writing reports on the same subject of collaborators and informers.

Intelligence officers, Captains Dening and Bake attached to Liberation Force 135, compiled a damning report as early as August 1945 on the conduct of the Islands (and its authorities) during the Occupation, writing that *'the loyal Islanders are in no mood to see matters glossed over, and indeed the Force Commander fears that when his Forces are withdrawn active armed disturbances may take place'*. The report also noted that there were approximately eleven cases (as opposed to the thirteen handed to the DPP by Grasett) where enough evidence had been accumulated to warrant consideration by the DPP. There were a further 180 cases of collaboration where it would be difficult to accumulate enough evidence for a prosecution, but where *'the people concerned undoubtedly deserve some form of punishment'*. These people included profiteers, informers (of which there was a *'considerable number'*), women who consorted with German troops and people who were too friendly with the occupiers.[67] Brigadier Snow of Force 135 dismissed the report as *'most partial and biased'* and based on *'tittle-tattle'* which *'made mountains out of molehills'*.[68] Paul Sanders also described the report as a *'manifest intelligence failure'*.[69] The gulf between the view of the Home Office and Brigadier Snow on the one hand, and that of the intelligence officers on the other, has been touted by amateur historian Barry Turner as something of a vendetta.[70]

This report was submitted at almost the same time as the Home Secretary, Mr Chuter-Ede, was making a statement in the Houses of Parliament which highly praised the Channel Islands' authorities. However, Chuter-Ede also stated in his speech that if evidence against any person emerged which warranted prosecution for treason or treachery, then they would be brought to trial in England as those offences were not triable in the Channel Islands.[71] A confidential letter from the prime minister to Chuter-Ede asked whether he had seen the 'adverse reports' from MI5 about the character of the authorities, who had by then been recommended for knighthoods.[72] Chuter-Ede replied to say that he had based his statement in Parliament on conversations with the DPP and the two Lieutenant-Governors of the Channel Islands (neither of whom had been in the Islands during the Occupation) after their first few weeks in office. If nothing else, Ede's speech had been premature given that the DPP had not yet finalized his report. Chuter-Ede also reveals that he received MI5's report the same day as his speech in Parliament, although he didn't reveal whether he read it before or after the speech.[73] Either way, Chuter-Ede's speech was the signal to the local authorities in the Channel Islands that they were officially off the hook.

Meanwhile, Captain Dening was not prepared to accept either the Brigadier's dismissal of his report or Mr Ede's speech in the House of Commons. The Brigadier, Dening said, in a letter to Major Stopford of the War Office, *'did not envisage the embarrassing possibility of ever having to reconcile his views with the existing evidence'*, and the Home Office *'preferred to accept opinions not related to existing evidence but based rather upon the apparently accepted policy of appeasements and the social impressions of high-ranking officers'*.[74]

Nonetheless, the die had already been cast. The Home Secretary had already made up his mind and the Bailiffs were still on course for knighthoods. While this said nothing about legal action against informers, the narrative of 'correct relations' had already been publicly stated in Parliament. This could only mean at least one nail in the coffin of public trials against informers, with the obvious knock-on effects on those who they effectively caused to be deported.

Before Christmas 1945, the DPP, Sir Theobald Mathew, and Duret Aubin, the Attorney General of Jersey, met in London to discuss possible prosecutions. The DPP wanted the cases to be dealt with by the Island courts because of the potential repercussions on the treatment of other British subjects who might have behaved badly in other occupied countries. It was also felt that there was little chance of success of prosecution in the English courts; the general feeling of a British jury, now so positively disposed towards the 'loyal Channel Islands', '*would be such as to lessen the chances of conviction*'. If those tried were acquitted, the resulting situation in the Islands was likely to be exacerbated. It was also noted that in England, it had '*never been necessary to legislate or to consider what conduct should be regarded as criminal during enemy occupation*'. There were also constitutional limits to the extent to which the Home Office could intervene in Island affairs. Aubin thought that it would be '*impossible to get a proper trial*' in Jersey as the '*public feeling in the Island was so high*'. Thus it was determined that the DPP would visit Jersey and make a statement that all allegations had been investigated and that he concluded that there were insufficient grounds for prosecution.[75] It seems likely that the Bailiffs were willing to accept whatever the DPP suggested because they, themselves, had also been in the frame (at least, as far as MI5 was concerned), and any protestations on their part might have looked like they had something to hide.

However, as the local authorities in Jersey and Guernsey were now in the clear, they might have pushed more vigorously for trials of informers at this point. The men of the States of both Islands were not, unlike the JL, activists for the prosecution of wrong-doers. The DPP was still, however, to make final his report, so still they had to wait and go along with recommendations being discussed at that point.

In December 1945, the Bailiffs of Guernsey and Jersey, Victor Carey and Alexander Coutanche, and John Leale, President of Guernsey's Controlling Committee, were given knighthoods. Honours were given liberally to other States officials. The British government presumably hoped that this would be an effective method of shutting down any criticism against the authorities while making a statement that the British government sided with the States and would not be sympathetic to any further allegations of collaboration or over-friendly dealings with the Germans. It was clearly seen as a method of quickly and firmly putting a lid on all further dissent and criticism.

In early January 1946, Grasett was able to inform Coutanche that the DPP had concluded its investigation into those alleged to have been guilty of '*scandalous and disloyal conduct*' in Jersey. The DPP was of the opinion that even though some cases showed evidence of '*conduct of a highly reprehensible and even possibly disloyal nature, none of them amount either to high treason or treachery, which are the only two offences for which an Islander can be tried in England in respect of acts done in the Island and which both carry only a death penalty*'. Instead, economic sanctions (i.e. taxes) or, in the case of aliens, deportation was advised.[76] The DPP also advised the Home Office that it was '*desirable in everybody's interests that this matter should be settled once and for all*'.[77] In short, Theobald Mathews' final report of January 1946 was not vastly different from his preliminary report of July 1945.[78]

Paul Sanders has argued that the British government decided very early on to do nothing about collaboration, and that their rhetoric of investigations was a screen whose purpose was to stem public discontent.[79] It seems more likely that if this was their decision and desire, then the DPP's report could have been concluded very much earlier. Stringing along the public – and the local authorities – was unlikely to have done anything to close down mounting anxiety and anger on the subject.

As retrospective legislation to deal with 'conduct not amounting to treachery or treason' could not be introduced, the people concerned could not be brought to trial either in Jersey or England. Grasett emphasized to Coutanche that it was '*not in the interests of the Island that considerations of this subject should be prolonged*' and that '*every possible effort has been made by the authorities in the United Kingdom and Jersey to deal with this very unprecedented situation in a manner in keeping with the British principles of equity, justice and law*'.[80] In short, the longer people like the JL agitated for action, the more adverse the publicity for Jersey (as reflected in national newspaper articles), and the worse the reputation of the Island.

Now that the DPP had reached a conclusion, the States could officially respond to the original petition of the JL, over seven months after it was delivered. The report by the special committee concluded that it was '*not possible to deal under the criminal law with any alleged acts of collaboration with the enemy done in the island*'. They had, they stated, considered setting up a tribunal to decide '*whether scandalous conduct has been established*', but had decided that it would be

> *impracticable and could serve no useful purpose. Any such tribunal would first of all have to define what conduct during the occupation could fairly be considered as 'scandalous'. To do this would involve the examination of the Hague Convention and the result would inevitably be that many types of conduct ... could not be condemned in law. What would, in effect, be a court of honour presupposes a code of honour and no such code exists dealing with this particular situation. Moreover it would be impossible to devise penalties that would operate equally and this, in the view of your Committee, would not be in the public interest ... any protracted investigation of this kind is not in the best interest of Islanders.*

The committee also reminded the JL that the States had passed legislation to empower the Lieutenant-Governor to deport aliens and '*certain other classes of persons*' and suggested that it be allowed to use those powers in cases where '*collaboration with the enemy is established*'. It concluded with the recommendation that no further action should be taken by the States.[81] All avenues, it appeared, were now closed.

In his memoirs, J. H. L'Amy of the JL ended with the bitter observation that '*as law-abiding citizens we have to accept this ruling. Rightly or wrongly, we regard the informer as something far lower than a common murderer ... the informer does his killing or his torture by proxy and by stealth and for no better motive than spite or filthy lucre. Belsen, Neuengamme, and Ravensbruch [sic] were his weapons. He had had his reward – "thirty pieces of silver"*.'[82]

The JL were disinclined to give up. Records show that even in July 1946 they were still pressing for a different conclusion and wrote to the Lieutenant-Governor threatening to write to the local newspaper. Grasett recommended that, although he couldn't prevent them doing so, it was suggested that '*the subject of your letter is now one which might with advantage be allowed to drop*'.[83] It appears that in January 1946, when the DPP wrote to Sir Frank Newsam at the Home Office, indicating that there was '*no longer any serious demand for criminal sanctions against alleged collaborationists by responsible public opinion*',[84] he did not consider the JL to be 'responsible'. They were now no more than a nuisance to the authorities.

The JL were not the only group in Jersey who wanted to act in the memory of those deported for offences against the occupiers. Although the JL were advocates for legal action against informers, the 'Ex-Convicts', as they called themselves, were former prisoners, and their goals are worth examining. They defined themselves as '*Islanders who had suffered imprisonment for various political offences against the Nazis during five years of occupation*', and in December 1945 held a meeting in a public hall, convened by a former political prisoner. They gathered together because they had '*heard with regret that many of their former comrades in Gloucester Street*[85] *were carried off to prisons in France and Germany, from which 20 would never return*'.[86]

It is worth pausing at this point to remark on this number and to note that somebody – an unknown Islander – must have made a list; a list that was unavailable or unknown to the Island's authorities at the time of the compensation claims in the mid-1960s. It would be pure speculation to suggest who was and was not on the list, given that the current number lies at twenty-one. However, at the time of the 1996 unveiling of the Lighthouse Memorial in St Helier, dedicated to the 'Jersey Twenty', the names probably matched those on the 1945 list. It was only through the painstaking research of Joe Mière from 1948 and Paul Sanders for his volume on the Jersey 21, *The Ultimate Sacrifice*, that the full details of those who did not return have been uncovered. In 1945, very few details of the deaths of Islanders were known.

The Ex-Convicts wanted to discuss two further issues: first, the question of raising funds to help the dependents of the twenty Islanders who did not return and to appeal to the States to provide immediate relief to those who needed it. Second, to discuss raising a memorial at a suitable spot in the Island to those who died. While funds were also collected at the meeting to help those in need, in December 1946 the States of Jersey passed an act to give an extra-statutory award in respect of the death or disablement of those who were deported during the Occupation.[87] Nineteen awards were eventually made,[88] but almost all of these went to civilian internees who had died of illness or diseases in their internment camps rather than victims of Nazism who had died or been disabled as a result of incarceration in a Nazi prison or concentration camp. Further, the scheme was only for those who were gainfully employed in Jersey at the time of their deportation ruling out anyone who was imprisoned by the German authorities and deported from the prison.[89] In fact, only one person in this latter category received an extra-statutory award: Anthony Faramus, who was in Buchenwald and Mauthausen concentration camps. Shockingly, documents survive to indicate that Faramus was deliberately not informed that he had received the award.[90]

A memorial would not be erected to the Jersey Twenty for fifty years, so we might assume that the Ex-Convicts' bid did not meet with success. It is possible, however, that when the States erected a memorial at Noirmont Point on the south coast of Jersey in 1947, in memory of 'those men and women of Jersey who perished in the Second World War, 1939-1945', that the Ex-Convicts were told that this included their people.

We can only assume that they were – or had to be – content with this, given the lack of any other memorial bearing names until 1996. As the Ex-Convicts do not recur as a fighting force after this period, we must assume that their political and charitable needs were met and so they disbanded, even if their bonds of friendship remained for a longer period.

Summary – Public and private memories

What emerges, in the first year after the strictures of the Occupation had been lifted after liberation, would appear to be two sets of memory which were diverging rapidly. On the one hand, exemplified by the JL and reflected in the short documentary made by the CFU, we see a population who were well aware of the actions of informers which led to the imprisonment and deportation of other Islanders. That population remembered with pride certain acts of resistance, pre-eminent of which was radio resistance and spreading the BBC news. Quite how the local population felt about other acts of protest, defiance and resistance is hard to gauge and varied according to the act and the member of the population observing it. The bottom line, especially in Jersey, was that informers were seen as the lowest of the low, regardless of who they informed upon or why. In Guernsey, as Paul Sanders observes, a culture of denunciation was almost cultivated by the authorities.[91] They had described resisters as enemies, and had passed an ordinance under which Islanders could be charged for 'uttering speech likely to bring about a deterioration in the relations between the German Forces and the civilian population'. Bailiff of Guernsey Victor Carey had even actively encouraged denunciation by offering a reward of £25 for people who came forward with information about those who put up V-signs.[92] With the fear of reprisals hanging over the population, and even an encouragement of denunciation from the Bailiff, informing was perhaps perceived by some to be less of an evil than resistance itself – unlike in Jersey. As Lord Justice du Parq observed, it would have been difficult to try informers in the Royal Court of Guernsey in the face of Carey's encouragement of denunciation.[93] It was probably no coincidence that no coherent group similar to the JL emerged in Guernsey.

Sanders has remarked that, in Guernsey, any fervour that existed in support of a purge died shortly after liberation. Although two petitions were submitted to the States of Guernsey, they did not muster enough support to be taken further. Sanders suggests that the lack of interest in collaboration trials was because of a lesser degree of political organization in Guernsey compared to Jersey, and because Islanders were encouraged to look to the future instead of the past.[94] It is also likely that the hard-line stance of the authorities, repeated again after liberation, made the population aware of the futility of protest.

When it comes to the narrative of the Occupation emerging from the local authorities, again the two Islands differ. On the one hand, in Guernsey the Hague Convention was being upheld as the only true course of action, and so any form of resistance – and any kind of resister – was a danger and a criminal. There could be no hope for any sympathy for those returning from imprisonment in continental prisons and camps under such a jurisdiction.

Among the authorities in Jersey there was more sympathy and even notional support for the prosecution of informers, with its associated (albeit unspoken) sympathy for those who died. And yet the situation was taken out of the hands of the local authorities by the precipitant actions of the Home Secretary, and by DPP. Although the States of Jersey could, perhaps, have used the intelligence reports by Captains Dening and Bake to push harder for prosecutions, the naming within the report of the shortcomings of people in positions of authority throughout the Channel Islands was a disincentive. Sanders' accusation of the report as an 'intelligence failure' was also, in his opinion, the 'most important impediment to collaboration trials'.[95]

In the end, the Lieutenant-Governor of Jersey was asked to advise the Bailiff that the Home Secretary could not recommend that the King approve retrospective legislation.[96] Citing His Majesty as the ultimate trump card, the Home Office knew that Alexander Coutanche could hardly have continued to push for trials after that. The case was closed, albeit only at an official level.

The discontent of former deported prisoners (and their supporters) would continue to rumble on. The work of other, later, agents or guardians of memory, such as Joe Mière, would make sure that the names of informers would not be forgotten either. Memory can be particularly long-lived in small, close-knit communities, and the default punishment of social ostracism or persuasion to leave the Island had to suffice.

We might take, for example, two publicly named informers from Guernsey to observe how that played out. Nellie Brewster and her daughter, Frances, were alleged to have informed upon and testified against John Ingrouille, one of the Guernsey Eight. Both women left Guernsey after the liberation. By 1947, when Frances tried to return to Guernsey with her new Polish husband, an Auschwitz survivor, she was told by the police to 'leave for her own safety'. Her mother was, at that point, living in Jersey. Frances was reported to have told reporters that *'when I came back, I thought everything of my foolish past would have been forgotten, but now I know it hasn't'.*[97] It is not known how many people with 'foolish pasts' were helped on their way by the local police.

The key casualty in the absence of trials against informers was, undoubtedly, the deported political prisoners. By failing to prosecute those whose actions directly led to the deportation and, sometimes, death of those who committed offences against the occupiers, the legitimacy of acts of resistance also failed to be stated. Such people were never going to be hailed as heroes in Guernsey, given the wartime stance of the likes of Ambrose Sherwill and John Leale, especially as they re-emphasized their position after liberation.

In Jersey there was more goodwill and effort made to enquire, behind the scenes, about prosecution, but the DPP invoked the highest power to prevent it. The names of informers do not appear in open files in the archives in Jersey, although they are available in The National Archives.[98] By ostracizing informers or encouraging them to leave the Island, and by denying them a place in public memory by not publicizing their names, the names of those they denounced were effectively similarly buried. Had retrospective (or other) legislation been allowed to be enacted, it is likely that the public prosecutions of informers that followed would have entailed the facts of the deeds and fate of deported prisoners to be established at an early date and recounted in court. This may have had the effect of elevating their memory and allowing this collated information to be recorded in the archives at a time when those affected and their families were still alive. Had prosecutions taken place, then a full roll of honour of those deported, so glaringly absent at the time that Alan and Mary Wood were writing *Islands in Danger* a decade after liberation,[99] may have been compiled in the first couple of years post war, especially as MI5 had found both what they described as 'German police records' and 'judicial records'.[100] As things stood, such research was only undertaken piecemeal much later. As Sanders notes, the absence of this archival information has meant that the historiography of the Occupation has relied upon oral testimony and memoirs written many years after the event, leaving the Channel Islands at a serious disadvantage.[101]

And yet we cannot exclusively twin the fates of informers and deported prisoners; after all, when the memory of the latter was rehabilitated in Jersey in the mid-1990s, this was done without undue reference to informers. Instead we must lay some of the blame at the feet of the Islands' authorities. We have already noted that for Leale to have legitimated the memory of resisters would have meant admitting that he was not only wrong, or had failed in his duty, but that he acted incorrectly during the Occupation. In Jersey, where resistance was not condemned so overtly, Coutanche, too, would have had to admit that aspects of the behaviour of the Island's authorities had fallen short of what was expected, at least by MI5. For the action of resisters to have been hailed as correct and legitimate, then the action of those who forbade it must, by definition, have been incorrect and illegitimate. Such an admission would have been too embarrassing for the authorities to contemplate. It could have led to loud calls for their dismissal from office. With people in both Islands calling, from 1945, for widespread reform of the States, then the Occupation-era authorities could very easily have found themselves persuaded from office during this period – in the 'best interest of the Islands'. Within a year of the liberation, resistance had been publicly and officially de-legitimized. Barry Turner suggests that the failure to acknowledge the efforts of resisters denigrated their hard work,[102] and this can hardly be denied. This did not stop grass-roots activists, often those who had been personally affected, from remembering others like themselves. It did, however, make resisters wonder if they had done the right thing.

In the next chapter we examine the former political prisoners who came home, and the range of their mental and physical health conditions and symptoms. While their friends in the Islands had had limited success in fighting for them and the legitimacy of their actions, to what extent was their ability to act constrained by their impairments to body and mind? And how did the attitudes of the Channel Islands' authorities compound their conditions, which in turn dwindled the number of people willing to speak out?

Part Two

1945–1965

4

The Impact of PTSD on the Agency of Victims of Nazi Persecution

Introduction

In the months following the liberation of Channel Islanders from their prisons and camps, these men and women slowly made their way back to the islands, often after months of recuperation in hospital. This chapter examines the impact of their wartime experiences on the former prisoners and knock-on effect on their families. Broadly speaking, this is the period between the end of the war and the mid-1960s, up to the time of the compensation claims which will be discussed in a later chapter. It is probably not too far from the truth to suggest that if these men were still suffering physically and mentally twenty years after the war, as described in their compensation testimonies written in the mid-1960s, then their conditions had probably become chronic and were unlikely to improve with time, especially given the lack of understanding in that period about how to treat what was later to be recognized as PTSD.

The deported women, who were in the minority at around 12 per cent of all those deported,[1] rarely applied for compensation and even more rarely wrote in their testimony about the impact of imprisonment on their post-war lives and mental health. It is thus the story of the men that inevitably and disproportionately colours our understanding. We also have greater evidence of the impact upon the wives and the mothers rather than the husbands and fathers of those deported. By gauging the impact of the men's sufferings on those with whom they had long-term primary relationships, we can better understand how their mental and physical ill-health effected them in their daily lives.

My central endeavour in this chapter is not just to catalogue the kinds of mental and physical ill-health suffered by victims of Nazism in the aftermath of war, even though such work is important in itself because it has never before been attempted for Channel Islanders. I also explore what impact this had on their abilities to represent and fight for those like themselves in later years. In short, I attempt to explore one of the several grass-roots causes for the lack of representation of victims of Nazism in later heritage of the Occupation. Cause and effect can, after all, be direct or convoluted and can play out over many decades.

The impact of the experiences of survivors led to, for many, poverty caused through ill-health; abandoning the Channel Islands in search of work in the UK; or debilitating psychological problems. Others simply did not want to return to the Channel Islands after the war because it was the place of the start of their problems and where they had been branded as troublemakers and criminals. Hinzert camp survivor Jerseyman Peter Hassall referred to this desire not to return to the place which brought back so many bad memories as 'Occupation syndrome', commenting that *'all concentration camp survivors'* have it.[2]

I believe that these factors contributed to the marginalization of victims from society, thereby robbing them of a voice, a platform, or agency to fight on behalf of their group for the right to be remembered in a positive light. We must also remember that many of these men and women died before the era of Occupation heritage in the Channel Islands, which really began only at the fortieth anniversary of liberation in 1985, when the first memorials began to be erected. Those who were proactive on behalf of their memory group were very small in number, and not widely encouraged by other Islanders.

The mental and physical ill-health of survivors therefore played a role in the small number of people who went on to become 'guardians of memory' for political prisoners. A desire not to talk publicly and continuously about their experience was another factor which inhibited growth in this particular narrative contributing to the memory of the Occupation. We must remember in all of this that in the kinds of small communities which characterize the Channel Islands, war narrative and memory has, to a greater or lesser extent, been driven by individuals who have been given a platform through occupying positions of power and influence. This is not a position often occupied by the victims of Nazism, although later in this volume I explore the role of 'guardians of memory' and the impact that they were able to have on the way that the Occupation narrative is remembered.

Those who were willing to speak out in the early days after the war in the form of public lectures or interviews in the paper were often drowned out by other narratives of Occupation. The Churchillian narrative of stoic endurance until victory[3] had quantitatively more people willing to promote it. It required strength, endurance, determination and a thick skin to champion actions perceived as criminal by others, and sometimes these qualities were eroded by the ill-health of victims of Nazism, as we shall see.

In this chapter I draw on three main sources in order to gauge mental and physical ill-health: published and unpublished memoirs and diaries; the compensation testimonies written in the mid-1960s which are the subject of Chapter 6; and interviews with the children and grandchildren of the people who spent time in Nazi prisons and camps. The number of diaries and memoirs are small, yet detailed, with unpublished accounts sourced from families and archives. Over 100 compensation testimonies from the Foreign Office and The National Archives have been examined, and around forty-five family members of victims of Nazism have been approached and interviewed, tracked down through articles in Channel Islands' newspapers and through social media.

Until now, no study has ever examined whether the Channel Islanders deported to various Nazi prisons and camps suffered from PTSD. We are now at the edge of living memory for this group, so it is too late to be able to interview them today to add their oral testimony to this study to contribute to any potential statistical levels of diagnosis.[4] While quantitative analysis of the available evidence would be unhelpful or misleading given the unevenness of the data and the patchiness of discussion of post-war mental and physical health in compensation testimonies, it is still possible to derive a qualitative insight into the lives of those who returned. By focusing on certain individuals whose case histories are known, we can observe the range of PTSD symptoms they suffered twenty years after the war. This study puts the symptoms described by the minority within the wider context of the kinds of problems potentially suffered by the majority of applicants for compensation, for it is in the compensation testimonies where these kinds of issues are discussed, especially where medical reports are included within the case files.

'The bullet still in my leg': Physical problems among returning Channel Islanders

While the core focus of this chapter revolves around discussions of PTSD and the problems it caused to the individuals concerned and their families, it is important not to divorce entirely the psychological and emotional after-effects of internment and imprisonment from the context of the physical. The primary endeavour of this chapter is to discover the extent to which physical and mental ill-health was a contributory factor in the lack of attention given to victims of Nazism in the Channel Islands. The two were, after all, caused by the same experiences. Injuries, diseases and chronic ill-health problems continued for many in the years after the war and sometimes lasted a lifetime, or even got worse in old age. Other conditions lay dormant after the war and came back with a vengeance as former prisoners retired and grew older. These conditions, and the scars on their bodies, served as daily reminders of experiences, keeping the times in camps and prisons ever-present in the minds of former prisoners and potentially hindering their emotional and psychological recovery.

Of all the testimonies of brutalities and post-war suffering, those of the Guernsey policemen stand out. In 1942, eighteen policemen (over half the entire force) were put on trial for stealing from German and local food depots. From the start the men claimed that their actions were patriotic and inspired by BBC broadcasts encouraging people in occupied countries to sabotage the German war effort. They also stated that they gave the stolen food to other Islanders in desperate need, and many recipients signed post-war affidavits to support this claim.[5] The police were tried by both the German military court and the Royal Court in the Guernsey and given long sentences of hard labour. The most recent re-analysis of the case can be read elsewhere.[6]

The policemen were not all sent to the same series of prisons and camps; each had a different trajectory although some of them clustered at different times in different prisons or camps. Because not all of the police applied for compensation, and because not all records survived to have been collected by the International Tracing Service, we cannot say with absolute precision who went where with whom and when.[7] Added to this, policeman Herbert Smith[8] was murdered in prison, and William Quin lost his memory, meaning that their journeys have been difficult to reconstruct in toto. However, we know that all of the men started their internment in Caen Prison followed by, for most of them, Fort de Villeneuve Saint-Georges Prison outside Paris, with clusters thereafter forming in Bernau Prison and forced labour camp (Kingston Bailey, Thomas Gaudion, Frederick Short and William Quin, although they didn't necessarily meet each other there), and in Augsburg Prison and its satellite labour camp of Neuoffingen (Jack Harper, Charles Friend, Frank Tuck and Herbert Smith). Kingston Bailey was the only one sent to Dachau, and William Quin was sent to Kematen forced labour camp in Austria. Frank Whare stayed in Villeneuve-Saint-Georges until its liberation, and Thomas Gaudion, Alfred Le Gallez and Eugene Le Lievre were eventually able to join their wives and children in Biberach civilian internment camp, where they had been deported because of the men's prison sentences and deportations. As we saw in Chapter 2, it was a great comfort to the men when they found each other in their prisons and camps.

Twelve of the men wrote compensation testimonies of various lengths and it is broadly true to say that the worse their experience, the more (and in greater detail) they wrote. The prolonged period of hard labour in prisons and camps experienced by many was marked by injury, disease, vicious cruelty, and 'brutal pre-meditated torture', as Frank Tuck put it afterwards.[9] By the mid-1960s, at the time of the compensation claims, many were still suffering the physical after-effects of their experiences. To compound matters, none of the policemen had been allowed to return to their old jobs because of their convictions. Appeals to the Privy Council in 1951 to overturn their convictions by the Royal Court ended in failure – a travesty of justice not yet rectified. Many of the policemen and their families moved to the UK to seek work, but very few of them were able to find employment of the same status or salary.

Frank Tuck's account is worth reproducing at length. His articulation of the problems caused by his disability speaks for the similar experiences of many. He wrote that

> *I spend my life in some degree of pain (almost unbearable at times) and have spent as long as six months at a time on my back in bed completely helpless due to a spinal injury caused by a blow from a German guard, which appears now to be affecting my head and neck. I also have internal trouble ... most likely caused by several attacks of dysentery ... my fingers are clubbed since Germany, and I suffer from rheumatism. As regards the attack of TB I suffered when I came home, resulting in the removal of part of my lung, I lost my job because I was considered unfit to pursue any occupation which involved manual work ... What disability and bad health has cost me since the war, it is impossible to estimate. Today I am unemployed and unwanted ... the money I have received as compensation for Nazi persecution to date has almost all been swallowed up in debts.*[10]

Tuck's statement gives us insight into his state of health and mind, allowing us only to imagine the impact of this on his family. With the main bread-winner unable to work and in need of care, and with debts accrued through medical and legal costs, it is easy to see how families such as Tuck's would have struggled financially. Compensation for men such as him would have been vital for keeping the family afloat.

Jack Harper, who like Tuck, had been in Neuoffingen labour camp, was also in a bad physical condition in the 1960s. At the time of the claims he also had suspected leukaemia. He had a disabled right shoulder and arm caused by tuberculosis and subsequent operations to treat it, and the beatings he received across his back and shoulders with pick-axes, shovels and forks were still troubling him. He had lasting signs of frostbite on his feet and right hand, a scar on his buttock from a bayonet stab by a guard, and still had the residual after-effects of malnutrition.[11] *'I was starved and beaten so many times that my mentality became impaired and my health was broken'*, he wrote.[12] Although Harper found employment at General Motors in America, after post-war emigration, the impact of the surgery on his shoulder led to his resignation. Charles Friend, who was also in Neuoffingen, also contracted tuberculosis. He still had problems breathing and struggled with pains in his legs.[13] Kingston Bailey was suffering with a duodenal ulcer, rheumatism, and muscular pains in his neck and head due to repeated blows on the head with a rifle butt by German guards. While the long-term implications to their lives of these injuries and diseases may not always have been stated in their compensation testimonies by these men, their families were able to provide this information, as we shall see.

Few in number were the deported men and women whose health was unaffected at the time of the compensation claims in the mid-1960s. Tuberculosis and other lung conditions were certainly the most common complaint.

A second group whose long-term health suffered were those sent to concentration camps such as Buchenwald and Mauthausen. Emile Du Bois and others in his cattle truck was machine-gunned on route to the camp and he endured Buchenwald with two bullets in his legs, which he had to conceal from the guards because *'they did not want cripples. They just disappeared'*. One of the bullets was *'removed by a Russian Doctor with the aid of a pen-knife which was sterilised in the flame of a cigarette lighter … the other bullet is still in my leg'*. He was also bitten by an Alsatian dog many times in the camp.[14] Anthony Faramus, who was in Buchenwald and Mauthausen, had gangrene in his thigh while in the latter camp, and also contracted scarlet fever, diphtheria and temporary blindness. His tuberculosis in both lungs led to the removal of seven ribs and the permanent collapse of a lung after the war.[15] Stanley Green was hit in the mouth with a rifle butt, knocking out five teeth while in Buchenwald. In his absence from Jersey, his wife had to sell household furniture and possessions and use up family savings in order to pay the rent and to live.[16] In 1966, when Alfred Baker asked for additional compensation for his time in Buchenwald, he had no fixed abode and was 'hunting for accommodation for his wife and children'.[17] He was beaten in the camp for holding his soup bowl in the wrong hand and had a scar under his chin for an unspecified operation carried out in Buchenwald.[18] Stanley Cordrey had, like many others, experienced a number of different prisons and labour camps. By the end of the war, he had two compressed fractures in his spine, a fractured skull, damaged feet and no teeth.[19]

While men made up the vast majority of deported Islanders, we have some information about the women who were sent to Nazi prisons and camps. June Sinclair and Louisa Gould from Jersey, for example, died in Ravensbrück.[20] Emma Constance Marshall was given a five-year sentence for buying food on the black market for her invalid husband and was deported from Jersey in late 1943. She went to around ten different prisons in France and Germany, and carried out forced labour in factories in many of them. Incredibly she received no compensation. Evelyn Garland, similarly uncompensated, went to many of the same prisons after being deported from Guernsey. She emerged from the experience weighing under five stone (seventy pounds) in weight. While in Bautzen prison camp, where she worked in a cotton mill under armed guard, she developed problems with her right arm. At the local hospital they *'opened it up from elbow to under the arm … I was in hospital for about eight weeks … but when I finally returned to the camp I could not use my arm at all, in fact the doctor said it was finished … sometimes I suffer quite a lot with it especially in bed at night. I cannot bear the weight of bed covers on it.'*[21]

These few examples give us just a little insight into the range of physical hardships suffered by Islanders after the war, many of which were endured for decades as long-term conditions. The impact of compensation is an important one to consider because, with it, token amount that it was, debts could be paid, physicians consulted and provisions for the family could be made.[22] It could also lift families out of poverty, thus potentially providing the men with time to do more than just focus on the search for work or housing.

We must also consider the added satisfaction that must have come with feeling that one had been listened to and one's sufferings acknowledged. It is likely that ongoing psychological distress was compounded by a failure to receive compensation. Writing about the experience may have re-traumatized some, and to have faced again the darkest period of one's life and submitted one's testimony to a faceless Foreign Office official only to be rebutted – or even risk being rebutted – must have been very hard for many. This is probably what lies behind some of the briefer testimonies. But in order to fully appreciate the later state of the mental health of many of those deported, we should turn to the subject of post-war ill-health, PTSD and its symptoms and an overview of those who were still suffering.

'My restless sleep': Mental health problems and PTSD

Many of those who had been deported to Nazi prisons, labour and concentration camps suffered from long-term mental health issues after their return, including nightmares, emotional numbness, anxiety and flashbacks. Some sought to block painful reminders in self-destructive behaviours including alcoholism. Others tried to self-medicate or manage their conditions in other ways. Many of the symptoms described by islanders in their compensation testimonies are among those recognized as PTSD today.

Although identified after the First World War as 'shell-shock' or 'war neurosis', PTSD first began to be recognized as a syndrome in concentration camp survivors in the psychiatric literature in the 1950s and 1960s, when it was known variously as 'KZ syndrome', 'concentration camp syndrome', '*Pathologie des Deportés*' or '*Maladie de la Résistance*', and was not fully understood.[23] The introduction of PTSD as a diagnosis was recognized as a consequence of war, especially as something experienced by Vietnam veterans.[24] The American Psychiatric Association first classified it as a 'gross stress reaction' in 1952, and as a 'temporary situational disorder' in 1968. Only in 1980, in the third edition of the authoritative *Diagnostic and Statistical Manual of Mental Disorders* (known as DSM-III), was it referred to as 'post-traumatic stress disorder'.

This recognition helped to lift the stigma associated with the condition, and facilitated compensation claims in various countries,[25] although this was many years too late to be of benefit to Channel Islanders.

Although such mental health issues were recognized in some European countries as having their origin in the camps, there is no evidence from their compensation claims that the various symptoms of Channel Islanders were diagnosed in this way. Not one of the testimonies uses terminology remotely approaching anything such as 'concentration camp syndrome' to describe their conditions, and only one uses the term 'psychoneurosis',[26] a medical diagnosis given by their doctor. Instead, other phrases were used such as 'mental agonies', 'nervous conditions', or a description of symptoms, indicating that whatever they were suffering, it had not been recognized by their doctor as a named condition. This is likely to be an indication of how much English or Channel Islands' general practitioners, very few of whom would have experienced prisons and camps themselves, knew about the condition or were up to date on the medical literature of this period.

A diagnosis such as 'concentration camp syndrome' or similar would at least have had the benefit of acknowledging the cause of the symptoms, which would have allowed victims of Nazism to maintain their self-respect, rather than being thought 'mad', insane or just odd. And yet, in an atmosphere in the Channel Islands of forgetting the darker aspects of the Occupation and especially the suffering of victims of Nazism, official or public recognition of a condition that called it to mind was, perhaps, unlikely.

In 1980, PTSD was defined by the American Psychiatric Association as something characterized by three groups of symptoms: those associated with reliving the trauma (such as nightmares or flashbacks); those related to avoiding any reminder of the trauma (such as memory loss, avoidance of certain situations, and feelings of detachment and the loss of the capacity to express affection); and heightened irritability (including sleep disturbances, a quick temper and outbursts of anger).[27]

The most recent, fifth, edition of the manual, dating to 2013, lists criteria for diagnosis. Briefly summarized, these are exposure to trauma; involuntary and intrusive memories of the trauma; persistent avoidance of reminders of the trauma; negative alterations of mood and cognition; alterations in arousal and reactivity; duration of symptoms for longer than a month; symptoms causing significant distress or social impairment; and being able to exclude other causes for the symptoms.[28] Many, if not all of these can be found in the testimonies of Channel Islanders, but because the disorder was not yet recognized and because the compensation claims form for disability did not encourage either physicians or applicants to ask or speak about mental health conditions, we have no means of judging whether those with some of these symptoms would be diagnosed with PTSD today.

Analyses have been carried out on victims of Nazism in other countries. While most of these studies have been carried out on Holocaust survivors,[29] some of which helped to identify the disorder,[30] many also exist on PTSD in resistance group members. Psychiatrists Kuch and Cox, for example, in a 1992 study of PTSD in Jewish Holocaust survivors, found that 48 per cent suffered from PTSD, and the more violence, brutality and trauma they had been exposed to, the worse their PTSD. They also found that survivors 'reported a disturbing lack of psychiatric care',[31] indicating, perhaps, that those who survived such terrible experiences did not seek out medical help, perhaps because of the stigma attached to mental health issues or because they did not even recognize their own behaviour for what it was.

In a comparative study of Norwegian resistance veterans which compared those who had been incarcerated in Natzweiler concentration camp with those who had been free to continue their resistance activities during the war, the former prisoners reported significantly more post-traumatic symptoms than the others.[32] Fifty-two per cent had sought help from health professionals for PTSD symptoms and 31 per cent had been hospitalized for war-related health problems. These findings were comparable to those obtained in a similar study with Holocaust survivors by the same author.[33] In a different study of Dutch resistance fighters fifty years after the end of the Second World War, of those currently in receipt of a disability pension, only 4 per cent had no symptoms at all of PTSD, showing the prevalence of this condition.[34]

Generally speaking, different countries have recognized the syndrome in different ways at different times, depending on the attitudes towards Jews and resisters within their national narratives, as well as the influence and former camp experiences of many of the doctors who studied them. This has also had an impact on compensation claims and war disability pensions.[35] While France, Denmark and Norway led the way in acknowledging the condition due to the strong position of the resistance in those countries,[36] it is unsurprising that Channel Islanders were unfortunate in this regard. The state of their mental health was not explicitly recognized as something worthy of mention or compensation during the compensation claims in the 1960s; indeed, such conditions were often still recognized as having a physiological cause at that time.[37]

While it might be thought that only those deported to Nazi prisons and camps on the continent (as opposed to being incarcerated in Channel Islands prisons) suffered from PTSD, one applicant for compensation, whose case file was anonymized, was held solely in Jersey prison. He was given an eighteen-month sentence for radio offences and was kept in solitary confinement for the first six months. '*I lived in constant fear of my life*', he wrote:

> *My cell was permanently lit by electric light. This resulted in never having any rest or sleep of any duration ... I was taken for three months daily to the Gestapo headquarters ... for interrogation. These interrogations sometimes took place during the day or at night. They lasted from 3-6 hours without food or drink. ... It was very painful for me to have to listen to the screams and beatings inflicted upon my fellow prisoners ... after about six months solitary confinement I could not stand the stress and strain any longer. I had a nervous breakdown. ... After about 12 months I was physically and mentally exhausted ... I had a further nervous breakdown accompanied by a mental black-out.*[38]

After the war, this applicant visited various doctors and saw a '*nerve specialist in Harley Street who could not cure me of my nervous disease*'. We might observe here that even a medical specialist in London, who we might expect to be better informed, had given this applicant to understand that he had a 'nervous disease'. The threat of deportation to Germany and the rigours of solitary confinement and sleep deprivation were enough to make the applicant have a total psychological collapse. Even up to the time of the compensation claims he was still suffering, writing that '*for the last 20 years I have suffered indescribable pain and mental agonies*'. His psychological condition meant that holding down a job was difficult. He asked for compensation so that he could buy '*additional items of food, [and] tonics coupled with a rest cure which I am badly in need of. These items are unobtainable under the National Health Service.*'[39] Thanks to this applicant we can understand another reason for lack of access to mental health care; the impact of the experience of internment upon a survivor's ability to work meant that such care was beyond their financial reach. Mental health conditions were apparently not yet well enough understood to be treated by the state.

Of those who were deported, one of the more common problems described in compensation testimonies were recurring nightmares. Frank Falla was particularly explicit about these in his memoir *The Silent War*, writing that after his return, he was worried about his health as he was '*experiencing severe sweats at night and the haunting hallucinations that I was back again in my prison cell at Naumburg … it was two hard years before I lost those night-sweats and hallucinations. I kept making noises and crying out in my restless sleep as though I was still in my cell*'.[40] Although Falla might have shaken off his night-time disturbances after two years, it was only in an interview following the publication of his 1967 memoirs that he revealed that '*I finally got the whole thing out of my system in this book*'.[41]

The trauma caused by the stress of deportation and imprisonment was too much for some. At least two Islanders lost their sanity following their incarcerations and spent the rest of their lives in and out of asylums. The first example of this is Walter Dauny, deported from Jersey. Described as a 'small-time juvenile delinquent' and a teenager with a troubled home life,[42] Dauny carried out a series of thefts of German property, and was deported to France in February 1944. He was sent first to St-Lô prison and then to Fort de Villeneuve Saint-Georges. As no record was found for him after the German withdrawal from France, it was assumed that he died in a concentration camp,[43] and was subsequently named on the Lighthouse Memorial in Jersey and listed as one of the Jersey 22.

However, in 2013 a nephew of Dauny's visited Jersey and saw his name on the memorial. He revealed that Walter was repatriated to the UK after France was liberated. In an interview he said that Walter did not die, but '*was terribly afflicted all his life as a result of his experiences in the camp*'.[44] He was in and out of hospital for tuberculosis, and asylums for his troubled mental health.[45] He died in 1989 aged sixty-three.

Flavian Emile Barbier, another Jerseyman, was assumed to have been the ring leader of the spontaneous mass demonstrations against the deportation of civilians in September 1942 to German civilian internment camps.[46] While most of those who took part were teenagers, Barbier was, at that time, thirty-three years old and married. On 12 October 1942 he was given a sentence of three years for 'organising a public meeting with anti-German demonstration',[47] and deported in January 1943.[48]

What happened next to Barbier can be gauged from his 1965 compensation testimony case file. He was deported to Fort d'Hauteville prison in Dijon and then, in June 1943, transferred to a prison in Germany. In October 1943 he arrived at Rodgau-Dieburg prison and was there until at least August 1944. Further records indicate that he was also in Rollwald penal camp.[49]

Flavian Barbier's application was submitted by his brother, Marcel, who by that time had been awarded power of attorney[50] over Flavian, who was in St Saviour's Mental Hospital in Jersey. Marcel was able to add that *As my brother is temporarily, we hope, in a mental hospital ... and his condition mainly due to his wartime experiences, it has been considered unwise to question him too much as to the correct name and address of the concentration camp from which he was released ... When found, he was unable to stand without aid, this being due to weakness induced by illness, malnutrition and ill-treatment. It is known that he was repeatedly beaten by the guards, knocked down an iron staircase and all-together badly ill-treated.* The medical report from the local hospital confirmed that Flavian had been initially cared for at home by a male nurse, but that Flavian had sacked him, five years previously, believing that '*he was in a concentration camp and that the nurse was a male guard*'. He had also turned to alcohol, presumably to block out the memories of the war. The report also revealed that Flavian had severe nightmares after the war from which he had to be wakened, and that he had only recently started talking about his time in the camps, at which point his wife learnt about it for the first time. It seemed that while in the camp, Flavian had experienced an operation on his spine, had surgery for a hernia, suffered from diphtheria and was now having memory lapses.[51]

While Walter Dauny did not submit a compensation claim in the 1960s, presumably because he was unable to, the situation would have been the same for Barbier had not his brother applied on his behalf. We know that other islanders were as badly affected, and this is very likely to be the reason behind the lack of application for compensation for some. Indeed, at least one was institutionalized while in an internment camp following his imprisonment, and soon afterwards committed suicide.[52]

We also know that those still affected badly, psychologically and emotionally, from their experiences put in claims, and this continued suffering is very evident from their case files. The example of Paul Gourdan is an interesting one, and the evidence for the impact on his mental state could be seen upon his return to Jersey. Gourdan, who worked as a labourer, had been given a sentence of three years and three months for committing 'serious larceny'. He claimed to have stolen German guns and thrown them in the sea.[53] Deported in June 1942, Gourdan spent time in the prisons of Caen, Fort de Villeneuve-Saint-Georges, and Saarbrücken before being sent to Neuoffingen labour camp, from which he escaped. He was then caught and sent on to prisons in Augsburg, Diez, then Amberg.[54] His series of prisons was confirmed by two of those interned with him at various points, namely, Guernseymen Frederick Short and Jack Harper, although neither was with him between his departure from Neuoffingen in the autumn of 1942 and the period of liberation, when Short saw him in Diez in 1945.

The next we hear of him is in July 1945, when he told his story to the *JEP*. In this article, he claimed to have been at Buchenwald for thirteen months and to have been given the job of skinning bodies to make lampshades. The article was remarkably detailed and included events known to have taken place at the camp. He testified to cannibalism, rape, murder, dismemberment and medical experimentation.[55] Yet, there is no official record of him having been at this camp. Was the story the product of a severely traumatized man who drew upon his real experiences but mistakenly or deliberately attributed it to Buchenwald in his stressed condition? Or was he simply making it all up, using information he read in the papers before returning to the Channel Islands? While the first explanation may seem more likely, he admitted to Major Francis Haddock, who was in Jersey in 1945 to make an investigation about war crimes, that the newspaper article was '*an exaggeration for the purposes of impressing the girls of Jersey (including his wife) who had consorted with Germans*'. Haddock found that his descriptions of Buchenwald differed from those of Jerseyman Emile Du Bois, who was also in the camp. Haddock could only conclude that '*in all probability he had never been to Buchenwald*'.[56] He then later discovered that Gourdan had also been convicted, before the Occupation, of crimes including forgery, false pretences, burglary and housebreaking.

Before we condemn Gourdan out of hand as a sick fantasist at worst or a time-wasting former criminal at best, it is worth fast-forwarding twenty years to get an insight into his state of health at the time of the compensation claims. In his file is a letter from Jack Harper, who said that he met up with Gourdan in October 1965. He was, he stated, '*highly emotional and suffering from loss of memory*'.[57] Frederick Short, too, made a statement about Gourdan, who he had last seen in May 1966, writing that '*he informed me that his mind has not been too good since his Nazi ordeal, and of later years seems to be getting worse, he cannot seem to remember anything, and his general demeanour, when he spoke to me, also gave me that impression*'.[58] Goudan's statement to the Foreign Office made no claims about Buchenwald. Instead, almost certainly a reflection of his confused state, he states that he was 'crucified and beaten' in Jersey as part of his torture,[59] then taken to Cherche-Midi Prison in Paris, then Mannheim and Diez-Lahn camps. This initially confused the Foreign Office, who thought at first that they had the wrong person. Gourdan then replied in a six-sided rambling letter, explaining that he had been '*knocked about in the camps*' by the Nazis and was unable to remember all of the camps he had been in. He then lapsed into retelling episodes, experiences and conditions in his camps and prisons, jumping confusingly from one to the other.

Although they were doing what they could to help Gourdan's case by seeking statements from other former prisoners who were interned with him, behind the scenes the Foreign Office were less sympathetic. In his case file notes, one official wrote 'I am not at all happy with this case. Either Mr Gourdan is lacking in something or he thinks we are'. Further, the same official thought that Gourdan's statement '*arouses suspicion*' and that his vagueness was '*convenient*'.[60] He was, none the less, awarded compensation which took account of his disabilities as a result of his internment.

Paul Gourdan was in a better position than William Quin; at least two men could vouch for being in prisons and camps with Gourdan for at least some of his experience. As we have already seen, Quin was alone in his labour camp and it was only due to the intervention of Frank Falla, who visited him on many occasions to try to piece together his story, that he finally got compensation. But, as Falla reported, '*the whole trouble with Quin is that the effect of his imprisonment has obviously caused serious loss of memory ... the man completely lacks the memory which could substantiate his case*'.[61]

If there were some former prisoners whose experiences caused them to lose both their sanity and their memory, there were others who emerged with a surfeit of memory that could not be readily expunged. The most well-known Channel Islander to have survived a concentration camp was Jerseyman Harold Le Druillenec, a school teacher, and the only British survivor of Bergen-Belsen at its liberation.

Le Druillenec, with his sister Louisa Gould, were caught and tried for sheltering a Russian slave worker for eighteen months. Le Druillenec was also charged for possessing a wireless set. While Gould died in Ravensbrück concentration camp, Le Druillenec was sent to a series of prisons and camps, including Neuengamme and Alter Banter Weg, the latter of which was '*a tough camp with torture and punishment the rule day and night. Means of putting inmates to death included beating, drowning, crucifixion, hanging in various stances … no-one escaped severe corporal punishment.*' Eventually he was sent to Belsen. He described the camp as a place of '*no food, no water, sleep was impossible … we had to rise at 3.30 am. All my time here was spent in heaving dead bodies into mass graves. … Jungle law reigned among the prisoners; at night you killed or were killed; by day cannibalism was rampant.*'[62]

Le Druillenec was in hospital for five months following his liberation, followed by six months convalescence. He was ill with septicaemia, dysentery, skin diseases and malnutrition sores; his weight had plummeted to six stones and he was left with a weak constitution which probably contributed to a series of heart attacks from 1961 onwards; he died of heart failure in 1985.[63]

Le Druillenec testified at the war crimes trials of Belsen, Neuengamme and Alter Banter Weg. He recorded an interview with the BBC in late 1945, which was broadcast at Christmas that year when he introduced the King's Speech.[64] Early in 1946, Leonard Cottrell produced a drama documentary on Neuengamme and Belsen, based on Le Druillenec's experiences, and which the latter narrated.[65] It was broadcast on 12 April 1946, on the anniversary of his liberation. These many experiences in testifying must have allowed him to rehearse and order his narrative in his mind in a way that would enable him to recall it clearly at the time of the compensation claims.

It is clear from his medical notes that Le Druillenec had become a man of iron discipline who would not allow his experiences to impact negatively on his life. In his application for compensation for disability resulting from Nazi persecution, he wrote that '*although my ability has been impaired, I had not meant to claim for disability till this form arrived inviting me to do so. I survived these concentration camps by a lot of luck and the ability to "live outside the carcase". I retain this trait. Rarely do I admit, even to myself, any physical weakness, ailments or discomfort and only see a doctor when it is imperative to do so. The filling in of this form has been somewhat of a trial.*'[66] Le Druillenec had learnt from experience that illness or the inability to work was a trait to be avoided in all circumstances in a concentration camp, as it usually meant imminent death.[67] He gives us an insight into other applicants who may have belittled or denied their condition.

Le Druillenec returned to teaching and, in 1949, was appointed headmaster of St John's school in Jersey. He had a very strong ethic of discipline for all in the school, teachers and pupils alike, and saw any illness as a weakness in himself or others. Much to their discomfort, he felt compelled to talk constantly to the other teachers about his experiences in Belsen. This culminated in a much-anticipated (among the staff) and clearly impending breakdown in the mid-1950s, and Le Druillenec took six weeks off before returning to teaching. When he returned, his character was 'much mellowed'.[68] However, in what seems like an extraordinary parallel to concentration camp roll-calls on the *Appelplatz*, one former pupil of his remembers that in the early 1960s he used to insist on outdoor assemblies for the whole school, who would have to stand outside together whatever the weather.[69]

In the 1950s, Le Druillenec was asked to write a book on his experiences. A friend of the family and former colleague, who started to type up his notes for him, reported later that Le Druillenec was unable to finish them as it was too difficult for him to write about Belsen.[70] The unfinished memoirs are still lost. This difficulty, coupled with his statement about finding the forms a trial to fill in, indicate that he had perhaps stopped speaking regularly about his experiences from the 1950s onwards, perhaps after his breakdown. The doctors may have recommended that he should stop speaking about the camps and focus on the future as part of a strategy for recovery.

It would be wrong to exclude discussion of the case of John Draper from this study of those with psychological difficulties following their incarceration. Seventy years old at the time of the compensation claims and living in Enfield, he visited the Foreign Office in person. The officials saw him as '*an old man with worries on his mind*', a '*simple soul*' who wouldn't '*stop talking about Dachau*', was '*rambling and incoherent*'.[71] While Draper had, it seems, only been in French prisons, his almost completely illegible testimony, which begins his story in 1933, is extraordinary to look at (Figure 4.1). The letters and words are so densely written as to be indecipherable and impenetrable, with the pen tracing each letter multiple times. The Foreign Office official who dealt with his case sent the testimony to be transcribed by a secretary. The contents were an accurate reflection of the man who had visited their offices. Within the incoherent content of his '*Journey through Dante's Inferno*' were details of Frenchmen shot in his prison, bombings, transportation from prison to prison, the deaths of various foreign nationals, and of Draper himself being hit on the head and in the eyes with a gun such that he now had only one working eye. He ended by saying, '*I've been waiting 20 years to write this*'.[72]

While it is impossible to tell whether the testimony was the product of a man with PTSD or whether Draper was an ill-educated man showing the effects of age-related

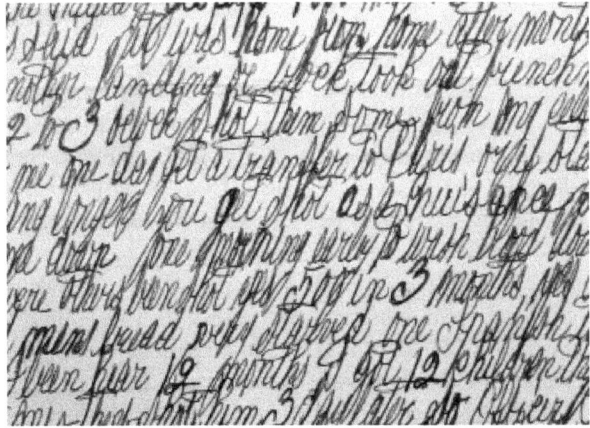

Figure 4.1 Segment of the compensation testimony of John Draper. Copyright: The National Archives. Contains public sector information licensed under the Open Government Licence 3.0

dementia, it is worth noting that the shorter letters to the Foreign Office in his file are more legible, with well-spaced words, although equally rambling; whereas the testimony itself switches immediately to an impenetrable scrawl which seems to relive non-chronological episodes from his life in real time as he writes. Such flashbacks are a known symptom of PTSD.

Because the Foreign Office struggled with the legibility and coherence of his letter, and because others who were in the same French prisons were not given compensation, Draper was also refused recompense. However, the details picked out from his testimony by the secretary who transcribed his case were such that, had they been composed by a man in full control of his faculties, could well have been sufficient to make a successful claim.

The experiences of Dauny, Barbier, Gourdan, Quin, Le Druillenec and Draper were just a few among many who noted in their compensation testimonies that they were still suffering mentally, twenty years after the end of the war. Ronald Beer, who had been in Rollwald penal camp with Flavian Barbier, wrote that he was suffering from '*nerves*' and '*severe nightmares*', and complained that the requirement to write his compensation testimony was '*all wrong*' and '*brought back everything*'.[73] Gerald Bird, who was in Buchenwald, reported that he was still struggling with '*psychoneurosis*'.[74] Charles Friend, who was in Neuoffingen labour camp, wrote that '*even after 20 years I still relive those terrible days*'.[75] His son confirmed later that his father became an alcoholic after the war.[76] Anthony Faramus was still suffering from nightmares after his time in Buchenwald and Mauthausen[77] and Frederick Short lapsed into the present tense in his six-page testimony of persecution and brutality, giving the impression to the reader that he was having flashbacks as he wrote. He described himself as '*suffering from a permanent mental disability*' which had changed his outlook towards his '*fellow beings*' and was now '*inclined to become very callous towards them*'.[78]

Given the number of Islanders who seemed to be suffering symptoms of PTSD, of which those described here are just a small sample, it is interesting to note the lack of sympathy of the medical board whose task was to assess applicants. Frank Tuck, who stated that he had experienced several nervous breakdowns and was constantly having treatment for bad nerves,[79] wrote in to make a complaint about the way that he was treated. '*I was appalled by the perfunctory nature of the interview … I was treated like an automaton, not allowed to speak except to answer the set questions put to me in a curt and cursory manner, and was completely unnerved. I do suffer from nervous disability and this was one of those days when I was particularly apprehensive. … Everything about the atmosphere was cold, detached, impersonal and hurried. The whole exercise left an awful lot to be desired. From what I was told there by others undergoing periodical examinations, this pattern is not an unfamiliar one*'. The medical board was, he complained, '*military-style*' in its method of dealing with applicants.[80]

If Tuck's experience of the official Ministry of Pensions and National Insurance medical board was typical of that of other applicants – and there is no reason to think that they changed their method of assessment just for him – then it is concerning that those struggling with PTSD were not treated with more sympathy and care. Tuck's complaint elicited a reply from the Foreign Office which was firmly in support of the medical board.[81] It appears unlikely that the medical board had been briefed adequately about dealing with those with mental health issues arising from their wartime experiences.

The suggestion that PTSD was not a recognized disability as far as the Foreign Office was concerned is reflected in their application form for compensation for disablement resulting from Nazi persecution. The questions on the form relate specifically to diseases and injuries and not to mental illness. After preliminary questions dealing with the patient's personal details, the form then asked claimants about the nature of the 'wound, injury or disease' for which they claimed. This was followed by questions asking where and how the wound or injury was inflicted, and when and where the disease began, and whether the applicant suffered from it before 'subjugation to Nazi persecution'. Just one and a half lines were provided for details; scarcely enough space to detail even the physical injuries. Tuck, like others, was forced to squeeze text into the margins and outside the space provided.

Frank Tuck's example is extremely valuable in shining a light on a compensation system which did not take into account mental illness or psychological trauma caused by Nazi persecution. Not only were applicants not asked about this directly, but the system of assessing disability by medical board disadvantaged those with mental ill-health. Whether or not the doctors on the board asked applicants about psychological trauma is unknown, but it seems that applicants were not offered an opportunity to volunteer information if not first asked about it directly. The procedure was also clearly frightening and off-putting to nervous applicants who perhaps did not even consider their nightmares, anxiety, and emotional distress to be a 'disability' in the terms specified by the Foreign Office. Only those who were now confined to institutions, such as Flavian Barbier, stood a chance of compensation for their psychological suffering.

Patients were compensated on a scheme of percentage of disability. As those who claimed for disability compensation were affected physically by diseases such as tuberculosis, it is difficult to know precisely how doctors arrived at a percentage. What percentage, if any, did they award to those with serious mental ill-health but who were otherwise physically able to work and earn a living? Such a calculation was probably not helped by applicants such as Harold Le Druillenec who saw any illness as a weakness and resolutely denied any help until it was absolutely necessary. Because mental illness was still stigmatized in the 1960s, it is probable that many (but not all) who suffered did not mention it, or marginalized its importance in their claim.

It seems likely that Le Druillenec was not the only one who saw physical disability as a weakness; we have already noted that he had not intended to apply for a disability award until he was invited to do so. Kingston Bailey, too, wrote at the bottom of his form, in capital letters and underlined, that his '*original claim was not for disablement*'.[82] Ronald Beer wrote on his claims form that he had '*not had a lot of treatment from the doctor*' and noted that he had not seen his named GP since 1938. While he listed his 'wound, injury or disease' as '*nerves and nightmares*', he noted that he had been self-medicating with '*goods bought from the chemists*'.[83]

Anthony Faramus, who was at that point living in America, did not fly to London to be examined by the medical board. Instead he was examined by a physician in California. This enlightened doctor filed a separate 'neuropsychiatric examination' report, which revealed that, '*in answer to leading questions*', Faramus didn't sleep well because of nightmares. Even for this more enlightened doctor, 'leading questions' rather than a direct and frank discussion, were deemed to be the way to elicit information of this sort.

Having focused on a sample of men and their physical and psychological difficulties, it is instructive to turn now to the women in their lives, and to examine the impact on them of their sons and husbands' problems. These accounts are extremely varied, depending on whether they married their men before or after the war.

'She was wonderfully brave': The mothers' and wives' tales

Of the women who married their deported men before the war, their experience would be one of long separation. This was the case for those who evacuated from the islands in 1940 and would not see their husbands again for five years, and for those whose husbands were deported to the continent for a prolonged period of time.

Some women became widows when their husband did not return. This was the case, for example, for Eileen, wife of Joseph Tierney, and Henrietta, wife of Joseph Gillingham. We shall meet both men again in this book; both had remarkably similar stories. Joseph Tierney was deported from Jersey for being caught as part of a ring of men who illicitly listened to the BBC and wrote down the news for dissemination. Joseph Gillingham was a member of the GUNS, an underground newspaper. The men met each other in Frankfurt and Naumburg prisons in Germany, according to the memoir of Frank Falla.[84] As each of the two men reached the end of their sentences, they were, or so they thought, going to be taken to Laufen civilian internment camp, where several hundred other Channel Island men were at that time being held. This, however, did not happen. Joseph Gillingham was never seen again and not a single trace of his whereabouts or body could be found. As for Joseph Tierney, final news of his death reached the Channel Islands via letters from his fellow prisoners which stated that he had died in 'Kaschitz', on the cattle truck which headed to Theresienstadt concentration camp.

For many years after the war, both wives, with the men's parents, searched for the bodies of their menfolk via as many different organizations as they could think of, but to no avail. It was not until the daughters of both men reached their own old age, when they bravely took a pilgrimage to Germany and the Czech Republic in 2016, that the final resting places of their fathers was discovered, as we shall see later. The pain of the loss of these men had stayed in their families for over seventy years.[85]

Some of the deported men were still teenagers or just out of their teenage years, leaving their parents waiting at home. The case of twenty-year-old John Ingrouille from Guernsey is a particularly sad one, is well known in the Island, and was relayed by his father in his compensation testimony. A young woman and her mother who had the reputation of consorting with German soldiers were said to have denounced Ingrouille for boasting that he could *'organise armed resistance of 800 men to oppose the Third Reich ... a pure figment of the(ir) evil imagination ...'* These women testified against Ingrouille both at his court-martials in Jersey and Berlin.[86] He was sentenced to five years imprisonment.[87] His sentence was spent in hard labour prisons in (among other places) Berlin and Brandenburg which, incredibly, he managed to survive, only to die in a displaced persons camp in Brussels after his liberation at the end of the war.[88] His body was exhumed in 1946 and relocated to the graveyard of the Vale Church in Guernsey. His parents received compensation in the mid-1960s, which they spent on a stained glass window of the crucified Christ at the church, in memory of their son.

Charlotte Ashcroft was another parent who could only sit and wait for her son to come home. Sidney Ashcroft was deported for the theft of food from a German kitchen and for exchanging blows with a soldier.[89] This was enough for him to spend his twenty-first birthday, which happened to be the first night of his incarceration, on the continent, in a French prison, the first of eight Nazi prisons in which he spent time.[90] He died of tuberculosis in Straubing prison[91] shortly before his twenty-fourth birthday, and was buried in a mass grave in a local graveyard in the town.[92] His mother was not notified, but the last person to see him alive, fellow Guernseyman Walter Lainé, saw him being led away with other weak and sick prisoners, before the rest of the inmates were put on a forced march to Dachau, which Lainé himself only just survived.[93] After Ashcroft failed to return to the island after the war, Lainé told Ashcroft's mother that he must have been killed. But because nobody had seen him die, and because there had been no notification of a grave for her to visit, she always believed that one day Sidney would come home to her. Although she and the rest of her extended family was from Kent originally, she resolutely stayed in Guernsey so that one day, should Ashcroft reappear, he could find her.[94] Charlotte did not apply for compensation; this is likely because of her strong belief that her son was still alive.

Dorothy Painter of Jersey lost both her husband and son, Clarence and Peter, in concentration camps. Nineteen-year-old Peter had been carrying out some amateur espionage and map-making of German fortifications; he also owned a souvenir First World War pistol and parts for making a radio. When the Germans searched their house, they found their evidence. While Peter admitted responsibility, Clarence was held to be responsible because of Peter's youth. Just before Christmas 1943, both men were deported under the NN decree, first to Cherche-Midi Prison in Paris, then Natzweiler-Struthof concentration camp, then a series of labour camps. Peter died at Gross-Rosen concentration camp and Clarence died on route to Dora-Mittelbau concentration camp.[95] In September 1964, Dorothy Painter put in an application for compensation for the deaths of Clarence and Peter, enclosing translations of the letters she received telling her of their deaths. '*If you wish to see the original letters*', she wrote, '*I will send them to you. They are very precious to us and I would be very distressed if they became lost or damaged.*'[96] These letters, her last links with her husband and son, were all Dorothy had left of these men.

Wives, mothers and children continued to be the ones who suffered after their menfolk failed to return home. After the Guernsey policemen were deported, for example, those wives and children that had not evacuated to England in 1940 and who still lived in the Island were themselves deported in February 1943. They were sent first to Compiègne transit and internment camp, where they could only look on helplessly at the ill-treatment of French Jews on the other side of the barbed wire, in a neighbouring compound. After three months, the Islanders were sent on to Biberach civilian internment camp.

For Irene, wife of policeman Herbert Percival Smith, the news of her husband's violent death in Augsburg Prison, where he had been the victim of great brutality, arrived while she was in Compiègne. It was too much for her to bear. Her daughter stated that the shock of the news was so much that Irene became very distressed and unstable. After the war, Irene was in and out of psychiatric hospitals for extended periods until 1952. Her children were sent to stay with other members of the family or with neighbours who had been with them in the camp.[97]

Another Guernseywoman, Rachel Symes, was deported to Cherche-Midi Prison in Paris with her husband, Louis, along with a party of other people from Guernsey, for their role in sheltering two British commandos who came to the island not long after the beginning of the Occupation. Just days before they were released, Louis was found dead in his cell. The German guards alleged that he had committed suicide by slashing his wrists with a razor blade,[98] although this was never proven. In support of this allegation, Henry Le Marquand, another of the party in the same prison, reported in his diary that he had been required to hand in his razor because of the suicide.[99] Ambrose Sherwill, also in the same party, noted that his own moods in prison were swinging violently from *'utter depression to elation'*,[100] showing the emotional volatility that that the prison environment could cause. However, Rachel Symes testified in 1964 that *'a man named Lotze or Losh who had been at Cherche-Midi at the time we were there claimed that my husband did NOT commit suicide'*.[101] Whatever the truth of the matter, a few days later Rachel Symes travelled home with the rest of the group to Guernsey. *'Poor Mrs Symes'*, wrote Ambrose Sherwill in his memoirs. *'In what a turmoil of mixed emotions she must have been ... she was wonderfully brave.'*[102]

The women who had evacuated to England before the occupation learnt very little about their husbands' fates. They were extremely lucky if they received a single letter from their imprisoned husbands. Iris, wife of Bill Symes who was imprisoned in Buchenwald, received an unexpected Red Cross postcard from her husband, smuggled out while he was still in the camp. Iris was living in Taunton, Devon, during the war years and was arrested by the police and interrogated at the local police station. She was accused of being a spy because the postcard had been written in German by Bill in order to avoid drawing attention to it. The experience of interrogation made Iris cry when talking about it for years afterwards.[103]

Often the first occasion on which many wives knew whether their husbands had survived (or were even deported) was when the men knocked on their doors in the summer of 1945. The daughter of Frederick Duquemin, for example, wrote a wartime memoir that recalled that when her mother received news that her father had returned to the UK, they travelled to meet him in London. *'Dad looked like a tramp; he had lost a lot of weight. He was wearing an old raincoat with box cord instead of a belt. He was carrying a duffle bag with a few things the Red Cross had given him and a prison blanket that he had brought with him from Germany; it was tied up with more box cord.'*[104]

Some men who had been deported in their early twenties found it hard to settle down after the war and find a partner. Anthony Faramus was particularly candid about his unsettled existence after his return from Mauthausen. After an extended period of treatment and recuperation in hospital and then with family in Lancashire, he went through a period of being unable to hold down a job, compounded by his 'criminal record' and lack of work experience, and eventually started to sleep rough and drink, and was in and out of prison. All the while, tuberculosis and PTSD extended its grip on him. '*Although I went to bed pleasantly exhausted*', he wrote, '*I had no resistance to recurring nightmares, hearing voices and screams; distorted images besieged me; the Devil himself paid me visits and hostile forces hunted me down. I felt the pain from bullets; I was hanged, decapitated, gassed, drowned and dispatched in a myriad ways.*'[105]

In the early 1950s he met his future wife, Mary, and it was only after their marriage that he was able to be honest with her about what he had been through. '*For many weeks* [after marriage] *I bore a sense of guilt. Before our marriage, I failed to own up to my shortcomings. The scars on my body I could fob off as souvenirs of war, but my bouts of insomnia and unconscious weeping and whimpering left Mary suspicious and led her to ask questions. Finally I unburdened myself, omitting nothing. My disclosures led to no ill-feeling; Mary put her arms around me and said: "You should have told me before, then I could have helped you sooner."*'[106] Even then, Faramus felt compelled to return alone to Paris periodically, where he was imprisoned in Romainville, to search for old friends. '*I was obsessed with war memorials, museums and reminders of the Occupation*'; but his trips '*left me with an easy peace of mind*'.[107]

For some men with PTSD, marriage was actually recommended to them as an aid to their recovery. The man imprisoned in Jersey jail whose period in solitary confinement led to a nervous breakdown was '*advised that it would be a great advantage to me if I would marry and settle down. My fiancée had followed me from Jersey and was agreeable to marry me knowing full well the position. I am glad to say that if it had not been for my wife's patience and loving care I would not have survived the most crucial time of my life.*'[108]

While the parents of some of the woman who married camp survivors were concerned about what their daughters were taking on,[109] the young women themselves seemed to have been less concerned, believing that '*that was war*'.[110] At least one wife was a nurse who met her future husband while he was recuperating in hospital, so presumably had a greater understanding of what she was committing herself to.[111] It is certainly true to observe that everyone in the Channel Islands had been occupied, evacuated, imprisoned or deported, and there was hardly a family who came through the experience unscarred. Even those who had spent the war years in the UK had experienced bombing, separation from family members and an uncertain future as refugees. The prospect of marrying a former prisoner was perhaps not quite as difficult as we might imagine now. The war had, quite simply, impacted everybody.

The women of these deported men – and indeed the husbands of deported women – must have carried a heavy burden at times. When the family struggled with poverty, they were the ones who went out to work while caring for their children and sick spouses. Some marriages suffered badly, with the husbands struggling with anger management issues, a symptom of PTSD following their incarceration.[112] Other survivors valued their wives and home life all the more for their experiences.[113] Bill Symes would often say that the thought of his wife and children was the only thing that enabled him to survive Buchenwald; his children described their parents' marriage as 'beautiful'.[114] Kingston Bailey, on the other hand, wrote in his memoirs that it gave him great pleasure during his incarceration to write to his wife and daughter, and that he longed for the day when he could be with them again.[115] After his experiences, however, he was unable to show his emotions again.[116]

Some wives were deliberately kept in the dark about their husbands' experiences; full disclosure of wartime experiences was by no means typical. Audrey, wife of Gerald Bird who, like Faramus and Symes, had been in Buchenwald, was led to believe that her husband had been in the Argyll and Sutherland Highlanders and had been taken a prisoner of war. It was only on the day of his funeral that she discovered otherwise.[117] There were also other men whose experience caused them to struggle to express any loving emotions, again a symptom of the PTSD, who chose wives who were similarly non-demonstrative and 'cold', allowing them to continue their post-war dysfunctional behaviour unchallenged.[118]

'I was able to recover completely': Concluding thoughts

This chapter has shown that, without a doubt, symptoms of PTSD were common among surviving deported Channel Islanders and that those symptoms often became chronic. Only a minority, it seemed, suffered no ill-effects at all – that we know of. The extent of physical problems can, to a certain extent, be difficult to judge given that many of the ailments of old age were blamed by Islanders on imprisonment. Psychological symptoms ranged from nightmares and amnesia through to anger and a lack of emotion; others suffered nervous breakdowns and periods of complete loss of sanity. This behaviour went largely untreated unless it was extreme or obvious enough to warrant institutionalization or urgent medical treatment. Otherwise, conditions were self-medicated with non-prescription 'tonics', alcohol or managed through marriage to sympathetic and caring women.

The lack of formal treatment was probably due to a range of factors including stigmatization of mental health issues, lack of affordability of this form of health care not then available on the National Health Service, and non-recognition of the necessity or availability of treatment, not to mention non-recognition of the condition itself. Brian O'Meara, for example, wrote in his testimony that he was 'able to recover completely' after Buchenwald.[119] His children were able to attest to the contrary, stating that he had an explosive temper and was not affectionate or tactile with them.[120] There was also no suggestion in any testimony or from any interviewed family member that the local authorities in the Channel Islands stepped in to pay for health care for deported Islanders. This would have been an acknowledgement of responsibility that they did not feel.

Some of the deported men tried to channel their energies and experiences into something positive after the war. Harold Le Druillenec testified at war crimes trials; Frank Tuck encouraged his fellow policemen to fight to clear their names through the Privy Council; and Frank Falla helped as many Islanders as he could claim compensation. These examples of strength of purpose and determination came from three men who exhibited symptoms of PTSD and were affected by continuing ill-health. Inevitably, physical and mental health problems intervened on occasions – sometimes for extended periods – to prevent many Islanders from working, from progressing in their careers, from supporting their families in the way that they might have liked, and from fighting for recognition. Indeed, Le Druillenec stopped speaking publicly after his breakdown, and Tuck did not continue his fight on the public stage for thirty years after the Privy Council rejection.[121]

Compensation was perceived by many applicants to be a lifeline. It could pay off long-standing debts and medical bills, bring some financial security, and even lift families out of poverty. A small number were disgusted by the paltry amount that they received, and it was not unknown for an angry wife to write a letter to the Foreign Office telling them off for their '*incompetence*'.[122] At least one wife, however, was very grateful for the money, which would enable her to visit the grave of her dead husband in Germany.[123]

These women had learnt to be protective of their husbands. Around half of the men and women who applied for compensation were successful in receiving it, meaning that the other half had their hopes raised and dashed, and their mental health conditions potentially exacerbated by the rejection.

This chapter has also suggested that the compensation forms were not designed for those suffering with mental health problems and neither was it worded in a way which encouraged the declaration of such conditions. Further, the modus operandi of the Ministry of Pensions and National Insurance medical board was clearly not prepared for applicants with mental health conditions. Its unsympathetic and military-style interrogations seemed to have exacerbated the anxiety of at least one Channel Islander. The system was, it seemed, discriminatory against applicants with non-physical disabilities. The methods of assessment were quite simply inadequate.

My closing thoughts for this chapter borrow from a study conducted by a Dutch team of researchers into resistance veterans. Their conclusions resonate with the situation in the Channel Islands and give us an insight into how deported Islanders may have felt. The Dutch team discovered that societal ambivalence towards Dutch veterans caused many of them to stifle their emotions, knowing that little sympathy would be forthcoming, which initiated feelings of isolation and rejection. The isolation was reinforced by feelings of '*doubt, guilt and shame … doubts about the risks taken, guilt about not having done enough, and shame emanating from intense feelings of anger, fear, and powerlessness. Small wonder that many civilian resistance veterans … became disillusioned.*' The same study found that '*social support in the form of understanding and attention from others, respect for suffering endured, and the provision of adequate opportunities for expression one's feelings*' can help psychological recovery. Yet Channel Islanders, just like Dutch resistance veterans, were deprived of such support outside their families and groups of fellow veterans. Like their Dutch colleagues, instead of '*being granted special status or attention, they were largely ignored*'.[124] Such treatment, coupled with a failure to legitimize their wartime actions, would have offered no relief from the symptoms of their condition. The low status of former political prisoners in the Channel Islands therefore may indirectly have compounded their symptoms and further hindered the ability of many to become proactive spokespersons for their memory group in the future. The numbers of people available to perform such acts were certainly curtailed by their mental and physical conditions. For a minority, their wartime experiences meant that that future campaigning or speaking out was simply impossible.

In the next chapter we examine the first twenty years after the war to assess the extent to which former political prisoners were silenced. Although this was not yet a period of the creation of heritage relating to victims of Nazism, were they afforded any legitimation about what they had experienced? We examine them in their own homes, and see the extent to which their families were aware of precisely what happened to them. We also observe them when in the company of each other, where champions began to emerge to fight battles with the local authorities over the legitimacy of their actions. But to what extent was the lack of legitimacy being compounded in a way that would affect them in the future?

5

The Decades of Silence? 1945–1965

Introduction

In the twenty years between the end of the Occupation and the compensation claims for victims of Nazism, what was the status of former political prisoners in the Channel Islands? While there was potential for them to be perceived as local heroes, taking centre stage in the first Occupation museums, this did not happen. What was happening to them instead? Were they trying to rebuild their lives and recover their health, or were they campaigning to be understood as people who did the right thing during the Occupation and acted legitimately? Did their early attempts to rehabilitate their memory bear any fruit?

As little progress was made in the rehabilitation of reputations of political prisoners in the first twenty years after the Occupation, in this chapter I want to explore this further. Did a lack of rehabilitation mean an absence and silence from those deported to prisons and camps? What was really going on behind the scenes in the first few decades after the Occupation? If the silences were real, what were the reasons for them? If these people were not considered a legitimate group for public memory, why was this? Does all the blame lie with local government, or has there been little interest in the population at large to hear stories of suffering in Nazi prisons and concentration camps? We must also consider why so few memoirs have emerged from this group to make their history mainstream. What forces have acted against them to restrain them from telling their stories and preventing them from becoming the main narrative of the Occupation and, in turn, acting to exclude that narrative from heritage for the first fifty years after liberation? Although former political prisoners were to become (in Jersey at least) the subject of pride and legitimacy after the mid-1990s, this was still a long way in the future.

This chapter, then, assesses the ways in which former prisoners of the Germans first asserted themselves to fight for greater recognition and credit for having stood up to Nazism and attempted to 'do the right thing'. I examine the first twenty years after the Occupation by exploring the actions of former prisoners in three settings. First, we encounter them in the home, as seen through the eyes of family members. We examine the legacies of the experiences wrought upon their minds and bodies, as narrated by their children, exploring the extent to which these survivors were silent in the home, or whether they were willing and able to speak out – setting the scene for whether they were later able to agitate for recognition. We then examine this group away from the family setting, exploring what happened when they were among themselves, both in private and entering a more public arena. We see them at reunions, in private correspondence, and as represented in heritage. In the third section of this chapter, we see former political prisoners negotiating face to face with the local authorities, becoming agitators, finding a voice, but then retreating to their own corners. In summary then, I want to explore the lack of public acknowledgement by examining whether it was caused by the victims of Nazism themselves, through their silence and passivity, or whether the public omission of the subject of political prisoners and their deportation to prisons and camps was a deliberate policy of those in positions of power and influence.

Our first question must be to ask this: if former victims of Nazism were going to fight, post war, for the loss of their reputations, who could speak for them? Whose offence against the occupiers was above reproach? Who might be seen as the most legitimate person for the job? While Frank Falla took on this job, the legitimacy of the spokesperson is an important consideration. Was the local population ready to hear this kind of 'special pleading' from people who their own governments had sought to label as troublemakers and criminals? In order to understand this group better, we must start to get to know their individual circumstances to better appreciate who was able to take this job on; who had the fortitude, the eloquence, and the physical and mental stamina to, effectively, fight the establishment.

'I didn't want to upset him': Silence in the home?

A good place to start to know these individuals better is in their own home, through the eyes of those who knew them best: their families.[1] After conducting written and spoken semi-structured interviews with around forty-five relatives – spouses, children and grandchildren of survivors of prisoners and camps – certain patterns were identifiable, especially when studied alongside compensation testimonies. What emerges clearly is that the majority of those who survived their wartime ordeal rarely spoke about their experiences with their families, and certainly not at length. When asked why this was, many of the second generation felt that their family member wanted to shield them or protect them, not wanting to burden them with traumatic images or knowledge. The children also quickly learnt not to ask questions, thus leading to the 'double wall' of silence identified by Dan Bar-On.[2] If the former victims of Nazism were not ready or willing to talk about their experiences, who, if anyone, could speak for them and champion them?

This broad observation of the suppression of traumatic memories within the home requires further analysis, for it feeds into the 'myth of silence' about the Holocaust recently challenged by David Cesarani and Eric Sundquist.[3] Broadly speaking, this myth suggests that, for a variety of reasons, there was silence by both survivors and scholars on the subject of the Holocaust, with the exception of publicity at the time of the liberation of the camps, until the 1970s. This has been shown by Cesarani and Sundquist not to be the case. They argue, instead, that the myth was nothing more than historical construction, based initially on evidence, but which subsequently turned into a set of beliefs almost immune to the contrary data which emerged later.[4]

Although the experience of Holocaust survivors and other survivors of Nazi persecution in concentration camps is not the same, there are clear parallels to be drawn. The shared experiences of internment, ill-treatment, starvation, disease and forced labour in certain – often the same – prisons and camps means that valid comparisons can be drawn. Further, clear parallels can be made between the after-effects on the survivors and their families from both groups. Holocaust survivors are thus a valid comparative group for the Channel Islander victims of Nazism.

To what extent was the 'silence' a myth in the Channel Islands? Did victims of Nazism readily speak out? When Channel Islands families were initially questioned, most of those interviewed agreed that they were told little or nothing about their fathers' experiences. But when probed more deeply, it appeared that many had, in fact, been told small anecdotes which emerged only on certain occasions. These were triggered by the most mundane of daily activities of home life. The most common irruptions happened at mealtimes, when the second generation soon learnt that their own fussy eating habits and food dislikes were given short shrift by men who had endured starvation. Nearly every person interviewed recalled having to sit at the dining room table for hours until their plate was cleared while being lectured about not appreciating food as they had not experienced real hunger, unlike the victims of Nazism.

The children of Brian O'Meara, who was in Buchenwald, remembered how much their father loved his food. *'He would eat anything. My mum would give him a larger portion than everyone else. He would pick up his plate and lick it afterwards. His table manners repulsed me ... You couldn't believe how quickly his food would go down. And he also used to take out his false teeth and lick them. Mum would say "anyone would think you were starving" – which he had been.'* Brian's son remembers the regular Sunday afternoon stand-offs, where he would have to sit at the table until he'd eaten his greens. *'I used to have to hide the food. I'd stuff it in my pockets, or throw sprouts down the side of the sofa, or spit them out in the loo. Hours would pass. Eventually mum would have to plead for dad to let me go.'*[5]

Frederick Duquemin, who had been in prisons in France and Germany, was supposed to have small and frequent meals after his return. *'That didn't work'*, recalled his daughter. *'If there was food around, he ate it. He hovered up everything. He once found a rasher of bacon that had been overlooked and it had maggots on it. He rinsed it off under the tap, patted it dry, and ate it. He said "you'll eat anything if you're hungry enough"'.*[6]

Gerald Domaille's sons testified that the food he ate in prison had an adverse reaction on their father later in life. *'There were certain things that dad couldn't abide: bread with caraway seeds and cabbage soup'.*[7] For Walter Lainé, whose family was very poor when he was a child, food was to be his tormentor later in life. He died of stomach cancer, possibly caused by his earlier period of starvation, and had to have almost all of his stomach removed the year before he died. He said to his daughter *'I've been starved three times in my life: when growing up; during the war; and now'.*[8]

In these ways, and through the medium of food, the children of those who had been deported began to learn small insights into their father's wartime experiences.

Food was not the only trigger for such recollections. Sometimes local events such as Liberation Day, or war films on television,⁹ also provided reminders. Even then, the men weren't always keen to elaborate on the trigger for their emotions. The frequent refrain of Gerald Bird (who had been in Buchenwald) to his wife was '*You wouldn't believe it if I told you what happened. You wouldn't believe it.*'¹⁰

Family finances, too, played an important role. Many among the second generation testified that there was little spare money around when they were growing up. When families were split up by war, deportation, or evacuation, homes and jobs were lost – sometimes in more ways than one. Frederick Duquemin's house in Guernsey was destroyed by the Germans while he was away in prison on the continent.¹¹ He, like many others, had to start from scratch on his return. Like all of the other Guernsey policemen deported for stealing from German food depots, he was not allowed to return to his job after the war and had to work in less financially rewarding positions. As many of the men had been treated so badly in labour camps and prisons across Germany, physical and mental ill-health prevented many of them from progressing in new careers. Compensation was thus a godsend for these families. Charles Friend's son recalled that it '*enabled us to get a leg up … it was used to make our lives easier. We were a poor family*'.¹² For the family of Frederick Duquemin, the later compensation '*made the difference between managing and not managing*'.¹³ Frank Tuck's compensation was likely to have been swallowed by medical and legal debts.¹⁴ To what extent the children of the family knew the reasons for the families' financial problems is debatable, but many were aware when compensation arrived because of the material improvement in their circumstances that it heralded.

Objects brought home from prisons and camps also became a way in for their children to learn about experiences. Gerald Domaille came home with an American army backpack. His eldest son learnt that after his father had escaped from a death march to Dachau, he'd managed to find American troops, who had given him army rations in the backpack.¹⁵ Frank Tuck had returned from Neuoffingen slave labour camp with a small Christmas card (Figure 5.1), hand drawn by Anni Sailer, the niece of Anna Stadler, who had saved the lives of many of the men in the camp by giving them shelter, food and medicine.¹⁶ Tuck's daughter and grandchildren were aware of the Christmas card and its story, but saw it rarely. It was kept locked up in a filing cabinet along with the rest of Tuck's war-related paperwork and memories.¹⁷

The children of Bill Symes, who was in Buchenwald, today treasure his wooden paperknife. Hand-carved by Symes in the camp, it depicts his camp number on one side and the name of the camp on the other (Figure 5.2). This paperknife was carved from the branch of an oak tree which was growing in the middle of the camp, and Symes' children associate the knife with his tales of their father eating acorns to try to satiate his hunger. Like Tuck's Christmas card, the knife was kept hidden in a drawer in Symes' room and nobody was allowed to touch it.¹⁸

Frederick Duquemin, too, brought back an item that only he was allowed to use: an old bone-handled knife that had been re-sharpened so many times that the blade was the shape of a crescent moon. His daughter was never told the specific story associated with the knife, but only knew that her father had – somewhat remarkably – kept it with him throughout his prison experiences. The knife was lost, probably thrown out, after her father's death, perhaps too powerful an object to keep in the house, given its association with bad memories.[19]

These items clearly functioned as memory objects so potent and redolent of a traumatic period that they had to be kept away from prying children who might be somehow burdened by the stories they contained just by viewing or touching them. Archaeologist Nicholas Saunders has discussed the power of such wartime 'memory objects' and the way they function. Although Saunders conceptualized the 'memory object' during his study of First World War trench art, it holds just as true for the items brought home from prisons and camps by Islanders. Inspired by the work of anthropologist Alfred Gell, Saunders sees these kinds of objects as representing human social relationships across time and space. As objects have 'biographies', just like people, so the objects can become receptacles and reminders of stories surrounding their making, their acquisition and their existence until the present day. Further, such objects are capable of forming a 'memory bridge' that could transport the viewer or owner emotionally back to their past.[20] It is no wonder that items brought back by Islanders were not often kept on display.

If objects were hidden to keep them from betraying their story, the men who returned also did their best to keep the full details of their stories hidden. Interestingly,

Figure 5.1 Frank Tuck's Christmas card. Courtesy and copyright: Angela McAllister

Figure 5.2 Two of the children of Bill Symes holding his paperknife made in Buchenwald, and a postcard smuggled out of the camp. Courtesy and copyright: Gilly Carr

interviews with the men's wives, daughters and granddaughters suggested that they knew less than the male members of their families. There is evidence that the women of the family were deliberately shielded (with varying degrees of success) from knowledge of what their menfolk had been through. For example, while Brian O'Meara's son knew that his father had been on a death march from Buchenwald, his two sisters did not.[21] They felt that their mother had also been protected by their father from knowledge about his time in Buchenwald. O'Meara's wife confirmed that she knew little. Her husband '*didn't seem to want to talk about it a lot. He brushed it off.*' She didn't even remember him successfully applying for compensation in the 1960s.[22]

The wife of Gerald Bird had been protected from knowing about what happened to her husband to such an extent that it was not until the day of his funeral that she learnt that he had not been a military prisoner of war, as she had been led to believe.[23] And while Bill Symes' son knew quite a few small anecdotes about his father's time in the camp, his daughter, who was older, knew less. '*He said some things*', she recalled, '*but he was very subdued if us girls were there. He'd tell funny stories instead to make us laugh. Sometimes he'd tell anecdotes but he'd stop them short. He never wanted to upset mum. He didn't want to put the emotions he felt on our shoulders. When I asked him about the camp, he said "I don't think you need to know about that."*'[24]

Kingston Bailey, who had been in Dachau, didn't talk about his experience at all with his daughter.[25] Frank Tuck's daughter felt that she was protected because she was female. '*I was a sensitive child. I think that he didn't want to upset me. But I was also sensitive enough to know not to ask about the camp. He would sometimes get upset talking about it … his eyes would fill up. Because he got emotional about it, we didn't push* it. I didn't want to upset him.'²⁶ Tuck protected his family to the extent that they weren't aware that he, too, was awarded compensation in the mid-1960s.

The daughter of Walter Nicolle felt that her father '*definitely spared me the details*' of his experience in French and German prisons. He '*definitely bottled things up. We'd let him speak if he wanted to speak, and he'd come out with little pieces, but we wouldn't force it out of him. It wasn't a taboo subject.*' His grandchildren clarified this further: '*It wasn't forbidden to talk about it but it would have been tactless of us to bring it up. We all knew he'd had the experience, but because he never spoke of it, it would have been inappropriate to mention it.*'²⁷

These comments were echoed in many interviews. While the subject of their fathers' prison and camp experience was not exactly taboo, it was more a question of sensitivity and tact among the children, of not wanting to be the one to bring the subject up in case it caused emotional upset. Gerald Domaille's sons also added further insight into this situation. More than wanting to be sensitive, one son recalled that '*I wouldn't have pushed him on it ... because I didn't want to be scared. I didn't want to upset him. I think people had more respect for their parents in those days ... you wouldn't probe.*'²⁸ Even though their father spoke about his time in captivity 'frequently' if something provided the trigger, the children had many reasons for not wanting to be the ones to ask. The children of Brian O'Meara confirmed that '*it was an unspoken thing not to ask dad about his experiences. It was a line not to be crossed. So much of his life was a closed book.*'²⁹

Other ways in which the second generation came to gain some insight and knowledge into their father's experiences was through obvious signs such as scars, which curious children naturally asked about. Charles Friend, for example, had an obvious scar on his cheek. His son knew that it had been caused by a French prison warder hitting him on the face with a bunch of keys with such force that it had ripped a hole through the cheek.³⁰ Gerald Domaille, on the other hand, had acquired tuberculosis in prison. After the war he'd had one lung deflated and many ribs removed. His sons remembered that he'd been unable to play football with them. '*He had a concave bit in his shoulder. He'd sink instead of swim if we went swimming. He had no natural buoyancy. These things would be explained by 'when I was in Germany', which was used as a euphemism to explain everything that had happened to him.*'³¹

The daughter of Frank Tuck, who was in Neuoffingen labour camp as well as a number of German prisons, remembered her father having a long and noticeable scar up his back, where they had to cut through ribs to get to his tubercular lungs. '*I remember long, long periods when he could hardly move because of pain. One of the exercises he had to do was to swing from the banisters to stretch his spine ... he was an invalid from my earliest childhood. I don't remember him running around and playing outside with me.*'³²

While not all of the children of parents who suffered ill-health knew the full story of how such injuries and diseases had been obtained, all knew that they had been acquired in prisons and camps, although only some of the parents were prepared to couple the marks on their bodies with anecdotes for their children. Frederick Duquemin returned from his prisons with a small blue-black tattoo, between his thumb and fore-finger, of a triangle – most probably a reference to the concentration camp classificatory symbol made by another prisoner who had experienced the camps. But beyond telling his daughter that he got it 'in prison', she had little further knowledge about how he had acquired the tattoo or who had made the mark upon her father's hand.[33]

The symptoms of PTSD, and other behavioural and psychological challenges which emerged in those who returned to the Channel Islands, had a large impact within families as we saw in Chapter 4; this alone challenges any suggestion of silence. For those with a sufferer within the family, PTSD was anything but silent. It was often the elephant in the room, the condition that had to be managed within the family. Walter Nicolle, for example, came back a changed man from his prisons. Although he was placid before the war, his daughter quietly admitted that his experiences had changed him. '*He wasn't violent with me but he used to get very angry. Sometimes he would be violent with mum. That had a bad impact on me.*'[34] Brian O'Meara also had problems with his temper for decades after the war, as his daughter explained. '*My father would fly off the handle at the most ridiculous things … my friends were scared of him … I wouldn't bring friends to the house. He would suddenly explode. He was a really difficult man at times. I loved him to bits but he wasn't easy to get on with.*'[35] When he lost his temper, he would also often shout at his children in German, a language he learnt in the camp. He also struggled with showing loving emotions. O'Meara's two eldest children found that their father wasn't tactile or demonstrative towards them, although he mellowed a little when his third child was born.[36] Kingston Bailey also shut down his emotions on his return from Dachau. His daughter felt that he '*wasn't a father … the bond wasn't there. I didn't have a happy childhood*'.[37] And yet, in his published memoirs, Bailey wrote about how much happiness it gave him to write to his wife and daughter while he was in a labour camp in Bernau, and how much he longed to be back with them.[38]

Charles Friend turned to alcohol after his return from Neuoffingen labour camp; it was, his son said, '*a classic sign of someone trying to self-manage a problem*'.[39] Even when methods of coping with or managing traumatic memories didn't impinge overly on other family members, they were still aware that their fathers were struggling with problems caused by their imprisonment. Alfred Hacquoil, for example, had bad dreams and flashbacks; he also developed a kind of obsessive-compulsive disorder in which he obsessively cleaned things over and over again because of effect of being in a mouldy and damp camp.[40]

After his early days of hallucinations and night sweats, Frank Falla overcame his experiences in prison to have an extremely happy marriage and two children, who look back with affection at their '*excellent father*' who simply didn't speak about the war within the home.[41] Given Falla's activism in later years, it is surprising that this part of his life was not discussed with his children.

Rather than characterizing the experience within the family in the decades following the war as being one of silence, with its associated implications of a total lack of knowledge or awareness being passed on to the second generation, it seems clear that in many ways the children of those who returned knew that their fathers had been exposed to horrors and traumas, to starvation, diseases and ill-treatment, and that the consequences of this were suffered in turn by the rest of the family unit. While the families were mostly shielded from the details of their fathers' experiences, it would not be correct to claim that the men were wholly silent. Rather, we can reposition life in the home as a place where the former prisoner's memories oscillated between being deeply buried or close to the surface, where they were acknowledged, partially shared, and often contained by the family, the primary buffers between these men and women and the outside world.

Today, the majority of families interviewed have scrap books, albums and family archives devoted to the men and women who were deported. These are filled with letters, archival records, and family photos. These, too, fight against silence and forgetting, helping to fill the gaps left by what was unsaid by the survivors. But who among these former victims of Nazism were willing to fight the establishment on behalf of themselves and their friends? What motivated them in that role? And what happened when they got together to discuss their experiences outside the home and make plans for promoting their cause?

'Absent friends': Political prisoners among themselves

Former political prisoners reached out to others like themselves and found solace in bonds of friendship forged in prison. This was the case in particular for Frank Falla from Guernsey and Joe Mière from Jersey, who operated later, and about whom we will hear more. It was these bonds and duties of friendship which lasted after the war, and sometimes after the death of their comrades, that spurred both men to become 'guardians of memory' in their own Islands for all political prisoners, as we shall see later. They were alone in the Channel Islands in the roles they took on; no others joined them in their quests during the period in which they were active, nor sought to rival their work from alternative bases in the Channel Islands. This is not to say that no other prisoner was active in supporting their friends. From his post-war home in Liverpool, Frank Tuck did his best to fight for his police colleagues and their reputations, but many of these men had left Guernsey after being unable to regain their old jobs or find something new which enabled them to support their families.

While in Naumburg Prison, journalist Falla found his journalistic impulse rise up within him and recorded events in writing as his friends died. Having found a piece of thin tomato-packing paper at the bottom of his shaving-stick case, he decided, as we saw earlier, to exchange '*half a bread ration for a one-inch stub of pencil*', and on the paper '*I recorded the days, dates and names of the eight Channel Islanders as they died.*'[42] As the prison commandant did not notify the Red Cross of the deaths, Falla was reliant on this aide-memoire when, after his liberation and return to England, he wrote articles for the *Guernsey Evening Press* and the *Jersey Evening Post* while he was waiting for his passage home. He named the dead men and described life in the Nazi prisons he had experienced so that their families would know what had happened to their relatives. When he returned to the Channel Islands, he '*called on them personally to console them in their losses and answer questions about the circumstances*'.[43]

Then, in 1946, Falla was invited to Vielsalm in Belgium to represent the Channel Islands at a gathering of Europe's Maquis leaders (Figure 5.3). The invitation was originally sent from Belgian war hero and BBC commentator Paul Levy to Bailiff Ambrose Sherwill. Levy had met Sherwill when he had entered Laufen internment camp upon its liberation, where Sherwill was the British Camp senior.[44] Sherwill had originally invited Harold Le Druillenec to represent the Channel Islands, given his fame as the only British survivor at the liberation of Belsen, but Le Druillenec was still recuperating, and so Falla was chosen instead. Falla described this later as '*the greatest honour ... I was proud to have been chosen to do this small task on behalf of those Channel Islanders who died and those, like myself, who were lucky enough to survive and return to our homes and loved ones, after our terms of German imprisonment*.'[45]

This reunion may have inspired Falla to hold his own in Guernsey. Annually, since his liberation, he organized a '*hotel get-together of the Guernsey ex-Hitler prisoners*':[46] the men with whom he was incarcerated in Frankfurt and Naumburg, plus Bill Symes who had survived Buchenwald. Photos exist of these annual reunions, and additional members around the dinner table sometimes included Harold Le Druillenec, and Hubert Lanyon from Sark who was one of the GUNS group imprisoned but not deported.

Undoubtedly these men spoke freely to each other about their experiences on these occasions. They were the only people who could truly understand what each other had been through. Whether the men looked forward to this annual rite of catharsis, or whether they dreaded it because of the painful memories it brought back, is unknown.

Figure 5.3 Frank Falla at a gathering of Europe's Maquis leaders, Belgium, 1946. Copyright: the Frank Falla Archive. Courtesy: Island Archives, Guernsey

But it was a time for memories and anecdotes, and for indulgences and solidification of friendships.

It is easy to see why and how Frank Falla became a spokesperson for Channel Islanders by the time of the compensation claims. Fate had spared him from death in prison when many around him were dying, and a scrap of paper and stub of pencil allowed him to testify after the war to the deaths of his fellow Islanders. He had represented his Island in Belgium, and organized annual reunions for the 'Frankfurt-Naumburg-Buchenwald crooks', as they sometimes called themselves. Falla had other virtues in his favour: his offence against the occupiers was an 'honourable' one that was beneficial to others. He was intensely proud of what he had done and not at all ashamed of his actions. He was still living in Guernsey at a time when around a third of former political prisoners had moved away; he was articulate, could write well, and was a respected journalist and member of the community. Importantly, Falla was no longer hindered by the PTSD he struggled with for the first two years after his liberation, and his health problems did not prevent him from doing whatever he could to help his friends. He was a legitimate – and ideal – choice of spokesperson, although he was self-appointed.

In the next chapter we examine in detail Falla's role in fighting for compensation for himself and his friends without the help of the local authorities. His large personal archive allows us to see the extent to which he operated alone, helping and encouraging his friends, fielding letters to Parliament and the Foreign Office, and to other victims of Nazism throughout the Channel Islands and further afield. When among his own friends, and without the 'interference' of the authorities, as he perceived it, Falla knew what he could achieve. And yet Falla was not the only former political prisoner to exhibit agency at this time. For every single man and woman who had been deported, and who wrote a testimony for compensation, this was an opportunity – perhaps the first that they had ever had – to tell their story. The period of the compensation claims was anything but a silent interlude for these people. While their testimonies may not have been repeated in newspaper articles at the time, and their opportunity to speak was not on a public stage, the possibility of having a willing listener in the Foreign Office had the potential to offer encouragement. While local government might have ignored their plight, the British government dangled what must have felt like the possibility of endorsing the legitimacy of their actions. For those who did not get compensation, such negation of their sufferings acted to undermine their self-belief in their own wartime choices. Many were probably too discouraged to tell their stories with anything approaching a sense of legitimacy again.

Former political prisoners versus the local authorities: The fight for legitimacy in the Channel Islands

By the time of the compensation claims in the mid-1960s, one-third of all of those Islanders who were awarded compensation – that is, those who suffered most – were no longer living in the Channel Islands, but had moved abroad to the UK or further afield. This is significant, because these people were no longer in the Channel Islands to fight on behalf of their memory group of those deported to prisons, concentration and labour camps. But there are further issues that must be unpicked here, because this statement is built on two assumptions. First, that it was necessary to 'fight' on behalf of a memory group; and second, that there was any such unified concept as a 'memory group' of former political prisoners in the first thirty years after the war. These are crucial issues to address, because they lie at the heart of understanding why the heritage and memory of political prisoners took so long to be acknowledged in the Channel Islands.

After the Occupation, we cannot talk about a 'memory group' in the singular for the simple reason that there was no unified resistance movement during the Occupation. Resistance in the Channel Islands was characterized by individual people or tiny groups operating alone.[47] This included providing humanitarian aid to escaped slave labourers, Jews and political prisoners; chalking V-signs in the street; clergymen giving loaded sermons from their pulpits; and intelligence gathering, to give a brief cross-section of the kinds of activities that took place.[48] People were not always even aware of who else was in their own group. Some of the five men deported for their involvement in GUNS, for example, met each other for the first time in prison.[49]

The reason for the small size of resistance groups or for solely individual action was because of the density of the German Occupation, which made secrecy and circumspection essential. As Paul Sanders has calculated, the Islands had one German soldier to every three Islanders, whereas mainland France had one German to every 100 Frenchmen after the occupation of the Southern Zone.[50] Many Islanders also had soldiers billeted on them. Further, there were no mountains or forests to hide any resistance groups. This meant that the conditions conducive to fostering large groups of people acting together did not exist.

After the Occupation, few knew the extent to which their neighbour had committed any act of protest, defiance or resistance unless they were imprisoned or deported for that act. Exceptions to this rule included the most common act of defiance: illegal listening to the wireless after radio sets were banned and confiscated in June 1942. Friends and neighbours would sometimes gather to listen together, or would pass the news to each other. Although such an offence could and did lead to death in a German prison, concentration or labour camp, such groups who listened together increased their chances of detection because of the numbers involved. This was the case for the five men deported for their role in GUNS; others who were involved either evaded detection or served their sentence in Guernsey prison.[51] This was also the case in the St Saviour's Wireless Case in Jersey, where a total of eighteen people were tried in 1943, and even more interrogated.[52] Groups of this size were definitely the exception rather than the rule, although another involving the same number of men in Guernsey resulted in a two trials in 1942: that of the Guernsey police who we encountered in the previous chapter. GUNS, the Guernsey police group and those who were in Jersey jail resulted in men prepared to fight for their own reputations just as much as for being judged in the right light by history.

Yet why did former political prisoners need to fight for this right? From the start of the Occupation, the States of both Guernsey and Jersey made it clear that acts against the occupiers would not be tolerated, as we have already seen. They reasoned that the only way that the Islands would get through the experience unharmed would be if everybody behaved themselves. Ambrose Sherwill was particularly vociferous in making an offence of any resistant behaviour likely to cause a *'deterioration in the relations between the occupying forces and the civilian population'*.[53] However, he was soon hoisted on his own petard.

Sherwill himself was in the first group to be deported from Guernsey in the first week of November 1940 for his part in what is referred to as the 'Nicolle and Symes affair'.[54] Guernsey Lieutenants Hubert Nicolle and Jimmy Symes, chosen for the mission because of their intimate knowledge of the Island's coasts, were commandos who came to Guernsey in the autumn of 1940 to gather intelligence. They were sheltered by their families and friends after a submarine failed to appear to take them back to England. Sherwill was included in the subsequent deportation as he didn't denounce them to the Germans as soon as he learnt of their presence on the Island, but tried instead to pass them off as POWs who had been in the Island since the start of the Occupation and had not yet handed themselves in.

Once the stance against acts of protest, defiance and resistance had been decided upon by the local authorities, diaries and private papers reveal that Channel Islanders were divided in their perception of acts against the occupiers, such as escape from the Island, or chalking up anonymous V-signs to indicate a hoped-for Allied victory. Those who were against such acts were simply scared for themselves and their families; it was in nobody's interests, they thought, if relations deteriorated or reprisals were taken. Those who rocked the boat were 'cowardly' and 'selfish'. Those in favour were of the opinion that the protagonists were 'brave' and 'patriotic'.[55]

It was against this backdrop that former victims of Nazism who wanted to be spokespeople for others had to fight for recognition that they had, in fact, behaved legitimately during the Occupation. As Frank Falla later put it, *'We were naughty lads who stepped out of line with the Germans. We were disowned by the civil authorities at the time .... And they never got round to owning us again.'*[56]

The first big litmus test of residual official antipathy towards people who committed offences against the occupiers came in 1951, when the Guernsey policemen sought post-war rehabilitation. The policemen had always seen themselves as latter-day Robin Hoods, pilfering – in order to give food to needy – from German stores and those of Islanders who dealt directly with Germans on the black market. Further, they argued that they were carrying out the orders of Colonel Britton of the BBC, who encouraged this sort of 'sabotage' of the occupier among occupied peoples.

In Paul Sanders' recent re-analysis of the 'miscarriage of justice' that applies to this case,[57] he argued that the Germans did not want to prosecute the men for sabotage. This was primarily because their cause were viewed with some sympathy by local people, and because convictions for sabotage could have led to death sentences, which went against Hitler's wishes about the way that Channel Islanders were to be treated.[58]

As the men were accused of stealing from local food depots as well as from German ones, they were tried by the Royal Court as well as the German military court. The Germans portrayed the policemen as common criminals in order to destroy their reputations, and this they achieved. This message was emphasized by parading the men, handcuffed, through the High Street on a busy Saturday afternoon on the way to the harbour for their deportation.[59] Their public humiliation was complete.

At the same time, the Royal Court was keen to preserve its own autonomy and needed to show the Germans that they were capable of tackling such 'offenders' properly. Headlines of the time show that Bailiff Victor Carey did not mince his words in condemning the men, declaring that their *'crimes have brought shame and humiliation on every soul in the island ... I am filled with shame. It is revolting to think how you have abused your position.'*[60]

The men received heavy sentences with hard labour and were deported in June 1942 to various French and German prisons, labour camps and concentration camps. All survived, except Herbert Smith, who died in Augsburg Prison as a direct result of the ill-treatment he suffered at Neuoffingen labour camp. The mental and physical health of most of the surviving men was impaired for the rest of their lives. Their wartime and post-war suffering was out of all proportion to the original offence for which they were prosecuted.

Led by Frank Tuck, the former policemen petitioned the Privy Council in 1951 to provide a ruling on the case brought before the Royal Court, whether it should be upheld, and whether they could expect rehabilitation. The Privy Court ruling came almost four years later: their plea was rejected. While they might instead have decided to ask for a Royal Pardon, this would have involved an admission of guilt, which the men were probably unwilling to make; and if this had been refused, then further doors would have been closed to them. Sanders argued that the case was rejected because of the limitations of the Privy Council purview. However, he also correctly and astutely draws attention to the way that, in 1945, the British government, led by the Home Office, had cleared the Islands' authorities of any wrongdoing during the Occupation, and had crowned this effort by awarding knighthoods to the Bailiffs. In the following decade they could not then be seen to revise the wartime ruling of an Island court presided over by the same man.[61] Indeed, this was the same man who also declared that acts of resistance were *'stupid and criminal'* and that it was the Islanders' *'duty and obligation to co-operate with them [the Germans] in carrying out their Orders and regulations'*, and also their *'duty'* to inform the police with information about saboteurs.[62]

We can see, therefore, that a decade after the Occupation, the British government was prepared to uphold decisions made by the Islands' authorities during the Occupation. This meant no sympathy for those who had been deported to continental prisons or camps, and a continuation of support for the wartime policy whereby, in the words of Frank Falla, *'if you offended the Germans and got punishment for it, that was your fault and the local authorities had no intention of helping you.'*[63]

Another insight into the common perception, among the general population, of former victims of Nazism is given in *Islands in Danger*, the first 'outsider' assessment of the German Occupation. The publishers, MacMillan, asked the Woods to make an *'independent enquiry into what happened during the five secret years'*. The authors were *'given the utmost help and co-operation in all the islands, with all the access we asked to official documents.'* They *'tried to set [the facts] out as plainly as possible, without passing any judgement.'*[64] This volume is useful because of the wealth of first-hand interviews that the authors carried out with Islanders and with former political prisoners in particular. In fact, this group received several dedicated chapters within the book, and a sprinkling of references throughout. Whether this is a reflection of the authors' interests or the narrative of the Occupation then being told ten years after the Occupation is an interesting question not easily answered, although it is worth setting out in full the authors' final assessment.

> *It seemed unfortunate that, for the most part, the [post-war] Honours were only given to those in high places and official positions, and included few who had risked their lives doing anything that might offend the enemy. ... It was understandable that the island authorities, fearing anything that might bring reprisals on their people, should have felt – rightly or wrongly – that they could not countenance anything like sabotage or resistance. But it seemed strange for this attitude to be carried over, by the Home Office, to the bestowal of awards after the war was over, and it struck the present authors as even more strange, when they began their work, that no attempt had been made to compile a Roll of Honour of those who ... had died for their courage. We found it hard even to get a complete list of Islanders who had ended their lives in gaols and concentration camps.*'[65]

Given that the authors had carried out interviews with many former political prisoners, as well as with the Islands' authorities, it is interesting to note that neither party had thought, at that date, of compiling a list of victims. There was, at that time, no pressing need to do so. The authorities had clearly not contemplated any kind of memorial on which the names of the dead might be listed, and there is no archival evidence to suggest that the families of the dead were pressing for such a memorial, even if some of them were asking for their loved ones to be included on military war memorials.[66] At most, we can suggest that *Islands in Danger* reveals a tension between the position held by the Islands' authorities with regard to victims of Nazism and the popular narrative told by Islanders, but that is all.

We might, however, add a further piece of evidence which supports this view. It came in the shape of Liberation Day in Jersey in the same year as the publication of *Islands in Danger*. Liberation Day every 9 May was and still is a time for commemoration and celebration in the Channel Islands. Jersey and Guernsey have historically remembered in different ways, but my recent analysis shows that they both followed the same 'master narratives' and phases of memory at broadly the same time, as we saw earlier.[67] While 1946 to 1949 was an era in which a patriotic memory of military victory predominated, the 1950s and 1960s ushered in a period of deliberate collective amnesia. During these years, people attempted to put the dark years of oppression behind them and focused, instead, on the future and rebuilding lives. Liberation Day was a quieter affair during this period. In 1955, Jersey decided to hold special tenth anniversary celebrations in the form of a 'Pageant of Jersey: from Viking to V-day'. The pageant was held in an arena and told the story of Jersey in ten vignettes; it is telling that the Occupation was relegated to a single vignette at this time.

The tenth vignette was 'The Liberation 1945' and one of the scenes enacted was a Gestapo arrest. For this to be included at all indicates that it was an important point of popular memory at the time, adding weight to the suggestion that such a popular memory may have been at odds with the way that the authorities wished the Occupation years to remembered, that is, where the heroes were the authorities themselves, who had acted as a buffer between the population and the occupiers, and for whom the post-war honours were well deserved.

By the 1960s, another chance arrived to test the waters of the position of Island authorities regarding victims of Nazism. Those who had suffered detention in a concentration camp or comparable institution were eligible to apply for compensation from 24 July 1964. The compensation claims offer us the perfect case study to see whether official attitudes had changed towards former political prisoners.

There had, since the Occupation, been a change of leadership in the Channel Islands: Sir Victor Carey had died in 1957 and had been succeeded as Bailiff by Ambrose Sherwill from 1946 until 1959. Sir Alexander Coutanche had retired as Bailiff in the early 1960s, but was still alive, as was Sherwill, who died in 1968. Two of the men who had helped lead their Islands during the Occupation were thus still living, and Coutanche was a peer in the House of Lords. They were not entirely out of the picture altogether, and obviously the institutional memory of the Occupation and, indeed, the Privy Council case had not disappeared.

While the subject and substance of the compensation claims will be dealt with in the following chapter, it is instructive to examine how they were received and handled by local government in the Channel Islands. Our two sources of information here are the writings of Frank Falla, who gives, admittedly, not an impartial view about the handling of the claims, given that he still felt himself to be perceived as a '*naughty lad*'. We also have the local government archival sources which testify the extent to which they cooperated with the Foreign Office's request for information about those who applied for compensation.

In his published memoir, Falla makes very clear that local government in Guernsey fell short of what he expected from them in terms of their obligations towards their citizens. '*I stood by anticipating a local awakening. Surely some official in the Channel Islands would realise that there were in Jersey and Guernsey people who merited compensation. I waited in vain ... I would have thought Statesmen in the Channel Islands would have stirred themselves and got things organised on an official basis. But not a bit of it. No one raised a finger to help, indeed no one seemed the slightest bit interested.*'[68] Falla himself 'took up cudgels' on behalf of his fellow Islanders, and enlisted help at the start of his crusade from MP Airey Neave, as we will see.

But was there a difference between what Falla was prepared to write in a published memoir and what he said in private? Indeed not. In his private correspondence, we can see that Falla was just as outspoken. In his archive is a wealth of letters sent to other Islanders who had come to him for help with their application forms, indicating a lack of help from other quarters.

In a letter of May 1964 to a Mr Wood, he wrote that he was '*leading an agitation for compensation for people who suffered under the Germans ... I must make it plain I consider the States of Guernsey have behaved shamefully for neither my colleagues or myself who were confined in German penal prisons have been compensated in any way at all, and no-one has taken up our case officially, and what is more they seem to want to know nothing about it.*'[69] Three months later, he wrote to a Dr Edward Aubert, saying that '*four months ago I showed the Bailiff, Sir William Arnold, my correspondence with Mr Airey Neave and the Foreign Office. His only comment for me, through his Secretary: "My goodness Falla's done a great deal of work there."*'[70]

Within a week of writing that letter, Falla seemed to concede that Arnold had shown only a little more than just surprise at the work he had done. In a letter to Stanley Green, a Jerseyman who had been sent to Buchenwald, and therefore a fellow former political prisoner unlike the former two correspondents, Falla wrote that '*in all the most surprising thing about it is that neither the States of Jersey or Guernsey seem to take the slightest interest in us or our claim. But I am perhaps happier about this than if they had put their ugly noses into my efforts as they might have fouled them up. The only person to take interest in Guernsey is our Bailiff, Sir William Arnold who has read the correspondence between Mr Airey Neave and myself.*'[71]

However, by the end of the period of the compensation claims, two years later, in a letter to a civilian internee, Falla accused the governments of Jersey and Guernsey of '*disinterest and apathy*'.[72] In a 1966 letter to Mr Littler at the Foreign Office, with whom Falla had communicated for the last couple of years, he thanked him, writing that '*the Foreign Office has remembered us where other people – many of them in authority – have forgotten us*'.[73]

But were Falla's accusations against the States of Jersey and Guernsey of a de facto policy of non-intervention and avoidance really justified? Had they washed their hands of the compensation claims, as Falla suggests? In reality, Falla could only speak for the response of local government in Guernsey. He had had no direct dealings with the authorities in Jersey, but he had been in contact with Jersey's former political prisoners known to him, and the widows of Jersey men who had died in prison alongside him. Their need for his help, and the lack of any indication of official help in Jersey, only convinced Falla that he was needed as an 'unofficial official', as he styled himself, for the whole of the Channel Islands. We might note that more people from Guernsey than Jersey received compensation, for which we can certainly credit Falla, even though more people from Jersey were deported.[74]

At the time of the compensation claims, the Bailiffs of Guernsey and Jersey were, respectively, William Arnold, who had succeeded Ambrose Sherwill, and Robert Le Masurier, who followed on almost directly from Alexander Coutanche, with only a brief year separating the two men during which Bailiff Cecil Harrison died in office. Both of the new Bailiffs had served in the armed forces during the Occupation and so had not been in the Island to have learnt of the court cases, deportations and deaths when they happened. While there is no evidence to suggest that either Sherwill or Countanche were looking over these men's shoulders and exerting their influence, their paintings were hanging in the Royal Courts and memories of the men and what they stood for and lived through were still fresh. With the Occupation having finished only twenty years previously, we cannot imagine that the new Bailiffs inherited no baggage at all from their predecessors.

The archival record for Jersey's dealings with the British government regarding the compensation claims is better than that for its sister Island, enabling us to get a better insight into that Island's attitudes towards former political prisoners. In fact, the first official discussions relating to monies for this group date to just seven years after the war, when the Ministry of Pensions in London contacted their opposite number in Jersey. They had been prompted by the French director of administration of war pensions to ask about the Island's underground resistance organizations and forced labourers and what pensions were made for those who died or were executed. While the UK had no people of this description, it thought that perhaps the Channel Islands might wish to respond about its own situation.[75] Cecil Harrison, who had been Solicitor General during the Occupation, and by 1952 was Attorney General, replied to say that there were no official records available. However, he also stated that there were no resistance movements in Jersey and that the number of casualties was 'not known definitely'. He wrote that he knew of four political prisoners who died in Jersey, but that it 'is quite possible that there were others'. However, he was able to state that, with regard to the 'payment of extra-statutory awards in respect of the death or disablement during internment of persons … removed during the German Occupation', nineteen awards were made.[76]

Correspondence between the Home Office and the Lieutenant-Governor of Jersey began seven years later, in 1959. Negotiations with the Federal German authorities were beginning and the Home Office wanted to know how many people were deported from the Island between 1940 and 1945 and the treatment they received.[77] Their letter was forwarded to Alexander Coutanche, who was still Bailiff at that time. He was able to reply with exact figures for those deported to civilian internment camps (which he described erroneously as 'concentration camps') in September 1942 and February 1943, but added that

> in addition to these deportations a number of people were sent from Jersey for imprisonment in France or Germany for offences against the Occupying Power. … These convictions were very numerous and many of them were for very trivial offences. If it were important to do so, voluminous records dealing with these offences could be searched, but I doubt whether an accurate figure of persons so sent from Jersey for imprisonment outside the Island could be ascertained. In this connection, however, my firm belief is that the number of persons concerned in this category were not numerous.[78]

He was, however, able to add that he had records of thirty-three people from Jersey who had been deported to Germany and were buried abroad. A sheet of torn scrap paper attached to the letter reveals some pencilled calculations which reveal how the thirty-three were constituted and who the authorities were aware of at that time. While few names were given, twenty-four were civilian internees; one was buried in Wittlich prison (presumably Maurice Gould, one of the Jersey 21); four in the British cemetery in Berlin (the four men who died in Naumburg Prison); and, in a column in the right-hand corner, obscured by a tear, is written '+ 2 Houillebecq, Mrs Berry + 1 Cohu + 1 Rossi'[79] This list shows awareness of eight[80] of the Jersey 21. Even though his colleague, Cecil Harrison, was still the serving Attorney General, and even though Harrison had established that pensions were being paid in respect of nineteen people who died, Coutanche neither drew upon nor referred to this information.

This shows the extent to which the local authorities were either not concerned enough to make a concerted check of the archives to answer the questions posed, or had not been concerned enough to keep good records relating to Islanders who died in continental prisons and camps. Neither reflects particularly well on them, and tells us something of the continued status of these people twenty years after the Occupation.

Given that these calculations were being made many decades before Jersey Archives was established, we can perhaps forgive the Island's authorities some ignorance on this subject. The papers relating to these cases were not professionally archived in the sense that we would understand it today. The search for those who died in prisons and concentration camps was something that was undertaken mostly by families, who spent years writing to agencies such as the International Red Cross or the International Tracing Service. For some, such as the wives of Clifford Cohu and Clarence Painter, and the mother of James Houillebecq, their knowledge of the place and circumstances of the death of their loved ones came only from eyewitnesses who made contact with the Island's authorities or newspapers.[81] Indeed, Frank Falla was able to be the man who relayed this news to a number of widows in Jersey. Overall, the fact remains that no centralized record or roll of honour had been compiled by the Island's authorities.

In 1963, Islanders began to petition the Bailiff of Jersey to ask about the forthcoming compensation claims and to ask for forms. At first the Bailiff seemed inclined to help, and wrote to the Home Office to ask for more information.[82] However, the Home Office recommended to the Bailiff that he leave distribution of compensation claims forms to the Foreign Office rather than letting the Bailiff's office become involved. '*If they were distributed locally, you might find that you became identified with them and were asked for interpretation of their contents, etc.*' The Bailiff was in full agreement with this suggestion.[83] This correspondence reveals that the Jersey authorities were prepared to be helpful up to a point; they were not inclined to become the kind of 'unofficial official' that Frank Falla was prepared to be.

In 1965 and 1966, the claims of a number of applicants for compensation were sent from the Foreign Office and Home Office to the Lieutenant-Governor and Bailiff's office for conformation and validation. These claims were duly consulted against available records of the military court of the Field Command 515 and the prison records, and help was given where possible. Indeed, the Jersey authorities seem to have been not entirely unsupportive in their perception of former political prisoners. In one letter to the Lieutenant-Governor, the Deputy Bailiff wrote to describe how the German courts worked in the Island during the Occupation, noting that

> *in so far as the local population were concerned, the German Courts dealt only with acts committed in contravention of German orders and regulations or to the prejudice of the Occupying Forces. It must be remembered that many of these activities were, in the circumstances of occupation, regarded as acts of patriotism and were, indeed, frequently encouraged by British broadcasts.*[84]

It is hard to imagine, in the light of the Privy Council appeal during which the Guernsey policemen cited Colonel Britton's broadcasts inciting sabotage as part of their defence, such a supportive statement about 'patriotic acts' emanating from Guernsey's authorities.

We are on slightly shakier ground when assessing Guernsey's reaction to the compensation claims. On the one hand we have Frank Falla's assessment that the authorities did not want to get involved at all. The unavailability of archival evidence on this subject in Guernsey means that we are left without any means to refute this other than to consult the other half of the correspondence in archives outside the Channel Islands. The very fact that the Foreign Office appeared to liaise wholly with Frank Falla,[85] asking him to track down people and provide information that the States of Guernsey might otherwise have provided, is indicative of the cooperation (or its lack) that they were receiving from the local authorities.

In fact, at the same time as the Home Office wrote to the Lieutenant-Governor in Jersey in 1959, they also wrote to Guernsey. Once again, the local authorities were able to give exact figures for the numbers deported to civilian internment camps as they had access to nominal rolls. With regard to those deported to continental prisons and camps, once again they did not have access to precise numbers. Ambrose Sherwill replied to the query, stating that, of those deported as a result of conviction of offences by German military courts, *'certain deportations'* numbered thirty-five and *'probable deportations'* numbered 6. *'It is not possible to be certain of accuracy'*, he wrote.

> *Some 450 persons were convicted of offences by German military courts and it was customary for the German military authorities to inform the Chief Office of the Guernsey Police Force merely of the convictions as they occurred. In the great majority of cases, the sentences were of relatively short duration and were served in the Guernsey prison. It is certain that thirty-five convicted persons were transferred to prisons either in France or in Germany and we have a list of the names of such persons. As regards the six persons shown as 'Probable deportations', this figure has been compiled from memory by police officers who were in the Force at the time although they are not certain that these people were deported to France or Germany. As regards one of the six, the only thing known is that he was transferred to Jersey from the Guernsey prison. It may be that other convicted persons were deported. Convicted persons who had completed their prison sentences in France or in Germany were not, I understand, usually released but were transferred to concentration camps and many suffered grievously ... Of those listed ... as certain deportations, five died. It would appear that death was caused or contributed to by the grave hardships they underwent.'*[86]

This degree of detail is interesting, as are the notes which Sherwill used when writing the letter.[87] The thirty-five were selected from a longer list of ninety-four men and women whose sentences were longer than six months. Presumably this selection was based on memory of definite 'known' cases, and included the deported Guernsey policemen and the five men involved in GUNS, but not those deported for sheltering commandos in November 1940, in whose number Ambrose Sherwill himself was included. It is interesting to note that of the five known to have died, Sherwill did not include in this count Louis Symes, who died in Cherche-Midi at the same time that he himself was incarcerated there. Had he forgotten his journey back to the Island with Symes' bereaved widow twenty-five years previously, or did suicide[88] not count? In any case, Sherwill's assessment of thirty-five deported people and five deaths was an underestimate. Such incorrect information about the numbers who died show that, like in Jersey, the local authorities had not, during the preceding twenty years following the end of the Occupation, attempted to establish precise figures.

In 1963 the Home Office wrote again to the Bailiffs of Guernsey and Jersey to update them about negotiations with the Germans for compensation. They had decided not to push for compensation for those deported to civilian internment camps, but only for those sent to concentration camps.

> *This may not be easy, since in many cases it cannot be shown that the victims were sent to concentration camps because of their 'political convictions, race, faith or ideology'* [as set out in the Bonn convention]. *But the Foreign Office will do their best, using the argument that the concentration camps were such typical instruments of Nazi persecution and stemmed from the odious tenets of the Nazi philosophy that all concentration camp inmates have a moral claim for compensation.*[89]

This might have been an opportunity for the Bailiffs to respond, providing more information about those deported, or to express their support or otherwise for the Foreign Office's position. However, a minute written in Foreign Office files ten months later reveals that neither Bailiff replied to the letter.[90] As we know, by the time of the compensation claims, the Foreign Office had resorted to liaising with Frank Falla instead.

Twenty years of silence? An assessment

This chapter began by assessing whether the first twenty years after the war, during which little or no progress was made in rehabilitating reputations, really was characterized by silence from the former political prisoners and, if so, to better understand its root causes. We saw that, on the contrary, and despite severe mental and physical health issues among many of them, there was no lack of communication between them and their families and colleagues about the fact of their suffering. Spokespeople among them emerged, such as Frank Tuck and Frank Falla, who were not afraid to challenge wartime rulings or seek compensation.

By examining the correspondence sent between Jersey, Guernsey, the Home Office and the Foreign Office in the period leading up to the compensation claims, we can clearly see that wartime feelings still held strong in Guernsey, refortified by the Privy Council ruling ten years after the end of the Occupation. In Jersey, where no such revivification of wartime memories had been triggered, attitudes may have softened slightly. Despite this, in neither Island had the authorities sought to make an accurate assessment of the number of people deported or who had died in French or German prisons and camps. While the archival evidence still extant for deportations is imperfect, especially in Guernsey, there is no way of knowing the state of the archives fifty years ago. We can perhaps be more forgiving of the local authorities for not knowing how many people were deported if they had to rely only on archives at the time of the compensation claims. But it is still valid to ask why, during or immediately after the Occupation, the authorities did not seek to undertake a head count, or to contact – even if only through the local newspapers – those who were deported to find out whether they had been ill-treated or had returned safely to the Islands. After all, then as now, the authorities had access to copies of the Occupation-period identity cards and so would have been able to work out who was present in the Islands at the start of the Occupation.

How might their position be defended? We might point out that in 1945 the Channel Islands received a massive influx of people as both evacuated and deported people returned to the Islands. An unknown number of evacuees decided not to return to the Islands. An equally unknown number left the Islands, determined to seek a new life after five years cooped up in a small island, wishing never to make the same mistake again of being trapped by war. With the population in such flux, tracking down 'lost' people would have been a difficult task. And yet there is no evidence that such an endeavour was ever attempted.

By the same token, we have seen that former victims of Nazism themselves, such as Tuck and Falla, did their best to fight for the legitimacy of their own actions and those of their comrades. Where their fight, such as that of the former Guernsey police, involved a face-to-face public legal battle with local authorities, they lost. Where they chose to fight privately and alone for recognition, as Falla did with the Foreign Office, they were free to act as they wished, with nobody to block their work. Falla showed that it was possible to move forward without any recourse to local government and to act outside their control.

Frank Tuck and Frank Falla were not representative of all former political prisoners. In the first twenty years after the war, they were the only ones who emerged who were willing to fight on behalf of others. Tuck did this despite having left Guernsey and despite his poor physical and mental health. The loss of the court case might have left him a broken man, but his extensive archive reveals that he continued to talk about his wartime experiences and the court case with his fellow policemen for the rest of his life, hoping to find a way to receive justice.[91] Falla, too, was driven by his work, although he achieved his objectives in the mid-1960s, when not only did he get compensation for himself and his friends – as we shall see in the next chapter – but he found a publisher for his memoirs.

Assessing the thoughts and memories of the children of other former political prisoners, we can see that memories of their wartime experiences were rarely deeply hidden. Among the men and women who were content to be represented by others, or who didn't want to speak or think about the Occupation years ever again, their children were aware in many different ways that their fathers or mothers had experienced something life-altering during the war years. Some were – or had been made to feel – deeply ashamed of their actions, but not a single child of a former victim of Nazism felt anything other than pride for what their parent had done and endured.

Neither in the home nor out of it were former political prisoners silent. But for the first twenty years after the Occupation there seems to be real evidence that the States of Guernsey and Jersey had little interest in letting these people's stories, experiences or losses become mainstream public – let alone championed – narratives of the

Occupation. In fact, it would take until the fiftieth anniversary of liberation for these stories to begin to be accorded legitimacy. It would also take this long for the first cracks to appear in the dominating Churchillian narrative, where tales of endurance until victory always held sway over experiences of victimhood.[92]

In the next chapter we pause in the mid-1960s for just a little longer to learn about work of Frank Falla, a guardian of memory for other victims of Nazism, as he fought for compensation for himself as his friends, both living and dead. It follows his correspondence with the Foreign Office and catalogues his successes in gaining compensation and victories in overturning rejected cases. Yet what were his strategies for success, and what did the local authorities do to help or hinder his work? And in the final analysis, what were the repercussions of the compensation claims for the legitimacy of victims of Nazism in the Channel Islands?

6

An 'Unofficial Official': The Role of Frank Falla

On 9 June 1964, the Secretary of State for Foreign Affairs, Mr Richard Butler, made a statement to the House of Commons.

> I am glad to announce that the Federal German Government have agreed to pay to Her Majesty's Government the sum of £1 million to compensate certain British victims of measures of Nazi persecution, that is to say, United Kingdom nationals, who, as a result of such measures, suffered loss of liberty or damage to their health, and the dependants of those who died as a result of such measures.[1]

In the Channel Islands, Frank Falla had been waiting for this announcement for many years. His excitement upon hearing Butler's statement was noted in his diary that day, as was his inability to sleep over the next few nights. This was the beginning of the end of a long journey for him, one that would be completed by the publication of his wartime memoirs a year after the compensation claims closed. The impetus for the memoirs had been triggered by the composition of his testimony of Nazi persecution. But in 1964, his testimony had not yet been written, although echoes of its early drafts can be read in the newspaper articles he wrote for the *Guernsey Evening Press* and the *JEP* soon after his release from prison.

In this chapter we delve into the details of Falla's role in the compensation claims as gleaned from his extensive personal files (Figure 6.1). More than anybody else in the Channel Islands, Frank Falla fought for the right of former political prisoners to receive compensation. His role is such that it merits its own chapter, and it stands as a tribute to all that he did for his fellow Islanders. Falla was determined to set out the case for legitimacy for himself and his friends, and this chapter explores the methods he used to achieve this.

Before the agreement: Making enquiries

After the war, and on his return to the Island, Falla became the chief reporter on the staff of the Guernsey Press, his former employers. He gradually rebuilt his life, marrying in 1949 aged thirty-eight, with the arrival of children in 1951 and 1954. Although he was

Figure 6.1 Frank Falla's briefcase containing his correspondence. Copyright: Gilly Carr

a family-oriented man, he did not and could not forget his wartime experiences; he still felt bitter at the lack of help or recognition that he and his colleagues received from local government in the Channel Islands.

On 2 December 1957, the Royal Court in Guernsey registered an Order which awoke in him a sense of purpose and drive that was to find its focus, seven years later, during the compensation claims. This Order, the original of which was signed in Balmoral on 23 August 1957, was entitled 'The Distribution of German Enemy Property (No.3) Order, 1957'. This money was to be put into a charitable trust to pay out sums not exceeding £250,000 for distribution among people who suffered persecution, for racial, political or religious reasons, in Germany, Czechoslovakia, Austria and any other country with which Great Britain was at war.

Falla was particularly interested in this because he sensed the beginning of the justice that he and his deported colleagues sought. Over a decade earlier, in February 1946, the Board of Administration in Guernsey had decided to recommend that permanent States (local government) employees who had been deported to Germany would be granted 50 per cent of their salaries, with increments, for the period of their deportation. The pay would act as recompense for the hardships that they were forced to undergo. Those who were not States employees would not receive unpaid salaries or wages. However, the payment was voted upon with those deported to civilian internment camps in mind. The same payment was made in Jersey. Falla's suspicions were being renewed that those deported for resistance crimes were being forgotten.

Although Falla later described the 1957 Order as '*the first straw that floated my way*',[2] in reality it was not. In May 1952, the United Kingdom, France and the United States had signed a treaty with the Federal Republic of Germany in Bonn which formally ended the Allied occupation of West Germany. Chapter Four, Article 1 of this treaty acknowledged an obligation to compensate victims of Nazi persecution, defined as '*persons persecuted for their political convictions, race, faith or ideology, who thereby have suffered damage to life, limb, health, property, their possessions or economic prospects*'.[3] Although the Allies were not completely satisfied by the provisions in the treaty, it was decided to sign it, but to then make strong representations to get the treaty amended. It was this treaty which sparked a series of bilateral agreements between formerly occupied territories and West Germany. Britain was late to come to an agreement because not only had the United Kingdom not been occupied, but all the other countries had numbers of victims to hand and Britain did not, which effectively scuppered earlier attempts to reach an agreement. The Germans would not write a blank cheque without having a reasonable idea of how many victims there were.[4]

While the later treaties and agreements no doubt emerged out of the 1952 Bonn agreement, Falla saw the 1957 Distribution of German Enemy Property Order as the first that might actually pay out compensation and offer recognition for those who were persecuted for acts of resistance. So in 1957, Falla wrote to MP Barnett Janner, a Trustee of the Nazi Victims Relief Trust which was charged with distributing the funds from the Order. He enquired whether the Order would be applicable to Channel Islanders, citing Schedule 2, which referred to those who '*may have suffered persecution on racial, religious or political grounds in any country in the Continent of Europe*'. Falla asked whether those deported to civilian internment camps on the grounds of having been born in the United Kingdom or political prisoners sent to penal prisons might apply for compensation. Crucially, he also wanted to know whether individual action should be taken or whether local government should pursue the matter on the people's behalf.[5]

Janner passed Falla over to the Secretary of the Trust, Joseph Cowen. Although promising to consult the Trustees, Cowen told Falla that

> the answer to the question whether the Order is applicable to Channel Islanders is fairly clearly in the negative. … The Fund is intended for 'victims of Nazi persecution'. … The persons you mention, however, were interned, imprisoned or otherwise ill-treated because they had resisted the enemy, or simply because they were enemies of Germany – as you yourself say, 'on the grounds that they were born in the United Kingdom … as a rough and ready guide, the persons whom it was intended should come within the scope of the Order are those who were deprived of their liberty pursuant to discriminatory legislation.'[6]

Cowen explained that Jews and Communists would be eligible, but not people who worked in resistance movements; Falla was left to surmise that this latter group had brought ill-fortune upon themselves.

Falla had to let the matter rest, realizing that further enquiries would yield no result. Three years later, however, he wrote again to Barnett Janner, having spotted a newspaper article which announced that Britain was shortly to reopen negotiations with Bonn on the subject of British victims of Nazi persecution.[7] Channel Islanders were specifically mentioned in the article, which gave Falla hope.

Falla noticed that again, no local government official '*had heard anything official … or stirred or raised a voice on behalf of we victims of the late occupiers of our islands*', so he asked Janner what his next move should be, because '*there exists a certain apathy in official circles here and through this I am afraid several worthy and possible recipients of merited compensation may be overlooked*'.[8]

Janner, now writing in his capacity as President of the Board of Deputies of British Jews, was prepared to share with Falla information which was *'founded on authoritative and reliable views obtained unofficially'*. He explained that although the British government in these talks had joined with other governments from countries which had been formerly occupied, it had *'not been the policy of the British Government to speed up its own talks with the German Government, because our Government presumably wish to see what the results were as far as the other European countries were concerned'*. As agreements had been made with most of the other countries, the current talks were mostly concerned with Nazi victims who became naturalized British subjects, and Channel Islanders.[9]

Falla wondered whether he dared to see *'a glimmer of light on the horizon'* for Channel Islanders, while at the same time expressing dissatisfaction that *'the needs of practically every other occupied nation has been given priority treatment and we British, as usual, place ourselves and our own people in the last place in the queue'*.[10] Although Janner had indicated that the agreement with the West German government might be concluded by the end of 1961, Falla waited another sixteen months before writing again to ask for news and to enquire whether they were *'fighting a lost cause'*.[11] He was told that there was *'no more than a slight possibility'* that Channel Islanders might get compensation.[12]

Keeping a watch on events in Parliament a year later, in July 1963, Falla followed a question raised by Airey Neave about the case of Miss G. Lindell, a friend and colleague of Neave's who had worked on the escape lines for captured Allied servicemen and POWs during the war. She had been caught and sent to Ravensbrück and other concentration camps, and had not received any compensation yet because the government was dragging its heels in negotiations with the Germans. Neave took issue with the Foreign Office for their *'dilatory'* and *'very slow manner'* with which the negotiations were being conducted. *'This'*, he argued, *'is not entirely a question of money. It is also a question of loss of prestige and dignity as a result of being placed in these concentration camps.'*[13]

Airey Neave had been a former prisoner and escapee of Colditz, where he was imprisoned as a POW during the war. He had subsequently worked for MI6 on his return to England in 1942.[14] His job was to help set up a network of escape lines and helpers across Europe for other escaped Allied servicemen. However, a number of these valued helpers had been caught by the Gestapo and sent to concentration camps, which upset Neave greatly as he felt partly responsible.[15] In August 1945, Neave was appointed to the British War Crimes executive. He took the job wishing to see posthumous justice for the agents he had lost in concentration camps.[16] Neave, like Falla, was thus concerned about compensation for his own group of friends and colleagues.

Peter Smithers, the Under-Secretary of State for Foreign Affairs, replied to Neave's criticism in Parliament in the summer of 1963 with recourse to the history of Conventions, and their associated legislation and amendments, with the Federal Republic of Germany. He blamed the long period of negotiations on the complexity of the situation with Britain, as an unoccupied country during the war, compared to that of other countries. He also argued that the details of the cases of the Britons concerned were *'difficult to ascertain'*. They were, he thought, complicated by the fact that these Britons were in other occupied territories when placed in camps, with the implication that they might have therefore been compensated by those other countries. One of the key stumbling blocks was that they could not reliably establish how many cases might be involved and therefore how much compensation to ask for. They also could not be sure which categories of people might be compensated.

> *We are at present engaged in reopening the negotiations on a new basis. We wish, first, to seek to agree in detail the different categories of case which might be covered by an ultimate agreement and also the types of suffering which are to be compensated. Having done this, and ascertained the area over which compensation could probably be obtained, we think it will then be possible – we hope expeditiously – to invite registration of applications for compensation within those categories. The applications for registration should then give us a reliable figure for the size of the problem. We should know approximately how many people would be compensated under an agreement arrived at and for what kind of suffering. This, therefore, should give a firm basis for the negotiation of a lump sum settlement.*[17]

Smithers' response to Neave was telling, for it revealed that not only did they have no clear idea of the numbers involved, but that the compensation figure would thus be based on guesswork. Only after the agreement was signed and registration invited would they really know how many were involved. At this point they would face the potential risk of under-compensating a large number of people, or over-compensating the few who applied. Both would have led to public embarrassment and criticism from the Germans. Smithers' reply to Neave was also misleading, for he implied that the method he outlined would provide a firm basis for the negotiation of a lump sum, whereas in fact the Foreign Office would only know the true numbers *after* the sum had been agreed upon. Negotiations, therefore, tried to emphasize that the German settlement would be a political one rather than one based on calculations of numbers of likely victims.[18]

In a letter written by a Foreign Office to a Home Office official a few months later, it was revealed that in the meetings with the Germans in October and November 1963 and in February 1964, two main difficulties manifested themselves. They were *'the German refusal to include resistance workers, or to make provision for refugee victims who took up British nationality after persecution but before October 1, 1953 (who therefore cannot claim under the Federal Compensation law)'*.[19] The problem was that these refugees were not British at the time of their persecution. The Foreign Office was thus still *'not really in sight of a solution to this problem'* three and a half months before the final agreement with the Germans was signed.

By mid-March 1964, the British government was *'quite resolved'* that resistance workers be included in any settlement, as it would not be acceptable to Parliament or the public if they were left out. This point had led to *'fierce argument'* with the Germans, who felt that resisters had no claim because *'belligerents have a right to curb sabotage and resistance activities in the countries they occupy'*. However, it was thought at this stage that the only chance of getting resistance workers accepted was the *'slight German hint'* that it would be up to the government to process the claims, and that *'if no attention is specifically drawn to resistance workers the Germans may not delve too deeply into the numbers of victims'* put forward.[20] Other countries had got around this problem with the Germans because their resistance workers were a smaller percentage of the overall total to be compensated and the Germans had left the distribution of monies to the governments concerned. The British could not hope to camouflage the high numbers of resisters within other viable claims (i.e. those by Jews). However, by focusing wording on those who were incarcerated in concentration camps, but without stating which categories of people they were (and by dissuading MPs from asking questions about this point in Parliament), the British hoped to come to an agreement with the Germans.[21]

By April, the chosen strategy was to urge the Germans to come to a 'political' settlement with the British government, in other words to give a lump sum and to leave it to the government to distribute it as it saw fit. The British wanted to uncouple the sum from the number of victims, but the Germans wanted the sum to bear some relation to the number.[22] If the Germans were to insist on relating the sum to the number of victims, a second line of approach was proposed whereby the British would ask for £2½ million to represent £500 per head for 5,000 victims as opening bid. As rough calculations had indicated that there might be around 1,500 claims (including around ninety Channel Islanders), it was suggested that £1¼ million might be the lowest acceptable figure.[23] In order to apply pressure on the Germans, it was suggested to the British Ambassador in Bonn that he should *'emphasise to the Germans the political and psychological importance of reaching a settlement'* to remove *'this long-standing irritant to Anglo-German relations'*. He should also emphasize to the Germans that the British were *'taking a risk in agreeing to a sum of money first and registering claims afterwards'*.[24]

By May, the British began comparing the bilateral agreements signed with other European countries and examining which categories of victims were compensated, by how much and in what kinds of places of detention they were held. Private discussions between the German and British officials before formal meetings indicated that the Germans might be willing to give £1 million in order to clinch an early settlement given that the British could not provide detailed numbers of categories of victims.[25] As this issue was causing problems to Anglo-German relations, the sum was accepted.

The final agreement was made on the condition that the pattern of the French–German bilateral agreement be followed, as this most clearly met both British and German requirements. The British government also agreed not to say anything prejudicial, in public or in Parliament, about the bilateral agreements made by the Germans with other countries with regard to the purposes for which the lump sum was paid. In other words, they were not allowed to state publicly that the Germans had agreed that money could be paid to resistance workers or refugees, but instead to fudge the issue by stating that *'Her Majesty's Government have decided, in the light of the discretion given to them … to include in the distribution of compensation all persons who suffered characteristic forms of Nazi persecution'*.[26]

Thus, the Agreement of 9 June 1964 was, in the event, to include both Jewish refugees who were not British at the time of their persecution, and resistance workers, without stating so explicitly. The Agreement stated that it would benefit '*United Kingdom nationals who were victims of Nationalist-Socialist measures of persecution and who, as a result of such measures, suffered loss of liberty or damage to their health or, in the case of those who died in consequence of such measures, for the benefit of their dependents*'. The distribution of the sum was also left to the discretion of the British government.[27]

Meanwhile, back in Guernsey, in the year leading up to the bilateral agreement, Frank Falla was doing his best to follow the progress made with the Germans and how this was being presented in Parliament and in the papers. Having read about the Parliamentary exchange in July 1963 in the *Daily Telegraph*, he wrote to Airey Neave to remind him about Channel Islanders who were sent to Nazi prisons and camps, most especially he himself and his friends who were involved in GUNS, and Harold Le Druillenec.[28] It is likely that in his correspondence to public figures, Falla made repeated reference only to his gang of five men and the well-known case of Le Druillenec, the only British survivor of Belsen at its liberation, because by associating himself and his group of friends with the surely water-tight case of Le Druillenec, he hoped to guarantee success. While he did not at that stage have the numbers and full list of names of others, Falla had contributed to *Islands in Danger*, published in 1955, which discussed the cases of many other Islanders, and he himself knew of Jerseymen who had died in his prisons. Therefore he had a ready source of information. However, while Falla was to be a spokesperson for all Channel Islanders, he felt a particular duty to those he knew and with whom he endured Frankfurt and Naumburg prisons.

Falla took the opportunity to voice his concerns to Neave about local government, complaining that '*no-one has bothered to do anything for us or our dependents in the way of compensation, nor are they likely to. For this reason I am wondering whether you can be of help to us in seeing that our claims for compensation are laid in the proper quarter at the right time*.'[29] Neave was able to reassure Falla that he would take up his case with the Foreign Office.[30] At last, Falla had an official champion in Parliament – somebody with the right history and motivations. Writing back with fervour, Falla took the opportunity to vent his frustrations again.

> *I started my agitation, Mr Neave, many, many years ago, and have rather wearied at the non-successful prosecution of it by members of the Island Parliament in Guernsey … the Home Office, under whose rule the island comes; or the Mother of Parliaments, the House of Commons. My state of mind has bordered on despair because I feel that worthy as all the Jews and foreigners may be of compensation from the Nazis, the state of the truly British subject (in the only part of the Empire or Commonwealth to suffer Nazi occupation), which is similar, has not only been overlooked but pushed aside and, obviously, chosen to be forgotten.*[31]

This was unusually candid of Falla; he rarely confided his feelings or state of mind even to his personal diaries. He apparently felt that Neave was a man he could trust. Neave duly passed Falla's letter on to Peter Smithers, Under-Secretary of State, who invited Falla to contact him directly. Falla again confessed to Neave that Smithers had '*given me heart and rekindled hope which, I must admit, was dimming with time*.'[32]

Keen to give Smithers some facts which might help with the drafting of the agreement with the Germans, Falla wrote to him in October 1963 to plead the case for '*not more* than 10 Channel Islanders who ... were imprisoned by the Nazis in concentration camps or penal prisons in Germany for what they chose to term "subversive activity"'.[33] At this stage, Falla was not yet in personal touch with other Channel Islanders who suffered in camps and prisons beyond his 'Frankfurt / Naumburg crooks', the name he gave to the attendees at his annual reunion. He felt that they had been categorized as 'crooks' not only by the Nazis, but by the Guernsey authorities because they had '*stepped out of line and not obeyed our temporary masters, the Germans*'.[34] Falla certainly did know of other Islanders who had been deported, such as the Guernsey policemen, but was probably aware that their case might not be seen as legitimate as that of political prisoners deported for offences similar to his own. Just as he felt that association with the name of Le Druillenec increased his chance of success, so he feared that association with those who had lost their honour and reputation so publicly might diminish it.

This point is worthy of further discussion. We know from Falla's archive that he was well-versed on the case of the Guernsey police, the eighteen men who, in 1942, were convicted by both the German and Royal Court for stealing from German and local food stores. Although the men pleaded after the war that they were carrying out acts of resistance encouraged by Colonel Britton of the BBC, and had stolen the food to give to those in need, their confessions at the time were made under torture and they had been made to sign statements in German that they could not read.[35] The men received severe sentences of hard labour and many of them subsequently suffered grievously in prisons, forced labour and concentration camps, where one was murdered. Falla had covered the case as a journalist in 1942, and had indeed shown his sympathies by publishing his article without running it past the German censor first.

As Paul Sanders has shown, when the former policemen tried, unsuccessfully, to get their wartime sentences overturned by the Privy Council in 1951, Falla supported the bid with evidence supporting their resistance credentials, describing them as an integral part of the Guernsey 'underground'.[36] Sanders argued that the subsequent puzzling absence of the police case in Falla's memoirs was because he found the '*grey zones*' in their actions a '*tad too ambiguous for his own more straight-laced understanding of resistance*'.[37] Indeed, in an unsent and undated letter from Falla to the Foreign Secretary, probably written in July 1964, Falla is categorical: in describing the categories of Channel Islanders likely to claim compensation, he outlined the police case, whose offences he described as '*not political*'.[38]

In 1963, when Falla contacted the Foreign Office to give them numbers from Guernsey, it seems that he 'played it safe' by excluding them from his calculation. At this relatively late – but still potentially fragile – stage in the game, Falla did not want to jeopardize his own chances of compensation – and that of his friends – by introducing complicated cases where the offences might not seem to be whiter than white. He did not know whether the type of offence might yet dictate who was to get compensation, so using a calculation comprising people with whom he was familiar, and whose cases were clear cut, he introduced the Foreign Office to those who occupied the upper echelons of his perception of a victim hierarchy, that is, those who suffered as a consequence of listening to the BBC and spreading the news via underground news sheets. The lower levels and more complicated cases would be introduced at a later date.

Writing on the same day to Airey Neave, Falla raised a concern that he had not aired with the Foreign Office, hoping not to disrupt the current flow of discussions which were moving, albeit slowly, in the desired direction. Were those imprisoned in penal prisons to be compensated in addition to those sent to concentration camps? Neave was unsure on this point; after all, the compensation was being demanded for those illegally detained '*insofar as concentration camps are illegal under international law. It might well be, however, that since detention in a civil prison led to ill-treatment in a concentration camp, this would be a relevant factor*.'[39]

Falla was left to sweat about this point for only a fortnight. The Foreign Office was soon able to reassure him that negotiations were resumed with Germany on 3 October 1963 and that the aim was to get compensation '*not only for inmates of concentration camps, but also for those who suffered comparable treatment*'.[40]

In late February 1964, the slow pace of the Foreign Office was highlighted again in Parliament following the death of Wing commander Yeo Thomas. Thomas had been a Special Operations Executive (SOE) agent, liaising with the Free French intelligence agency, but had been caught by the Gestapo and sent to Fresnes Prison outside Paris, followed by Compiègne transit camp and then Buchenwald concentration camp. In Parliament, Dame Irene Ward expressed her devastation that the Foreign Office had allowed people connected with the work of the resistance to go uncompensated.[41] Although she was assured that the negotiations were proceeding apace, Airey Neave and others continued to harass the Foreign Secretary in Parliament until, on 9 June 1964, Richard Butler made his historic speech, announcing that one million pounds of compensation would be given to British victims of Nazi persecution. Falla congratulated Neave the next day on the '*victory your persistence has gained you*'. However, like others in Parliament, he was not impressed as the sum extracted from the Germans.

> *After seeing what the Germans have had to pay other European countries, some of whom were not full-bloodedly in sympathy with the Allied cause when it was inconvenient so to be, I am startled that the sum is not again as much as the one million pounds agreed. Surely the victorious British should not only have not been the last to share the 'left-overs', but should have been paid at a higher rate than countries that were only occupied.*

Falla also expressed his unease about whether political prisoners would be included, realizing that he would have to wait and see how and if they would be categorized on the application form, but expressed his view that it would be necessary to include '*every detail of suffering and hardship inflicted by the Nazis*' on the claim form so that '*comparable treatment*' might be taken into account.[42]

At the very end of Butler's speech to Parliament on 9 June, both Airey Neave and MP Gordon Walker asked the Foreign Secretary whether victims of persecution in the Channel Islands would be included in the agreement, but Butler said that he would provide an answer at another time. To allay his fears, Neave later wrote to him to say that the Butler had written to assure him that they would be covered.[43]

While waiting for the claim forms for compensation to be ready, Falla took the opportunity of the hiatus to write again to the Foreign Office, where a special section of six staff had been set up to administer the claims.[44] This time, Falla provided a list of the differing categories those from the Channel Islands who might claim compensation – a full hierarchy of victim categories in order of those who he thought were most deserving.

> For example, the priority ones: those sent to concentration camps for political reasons and for resistance crimes; those sent to camps for having committed Black Market crimes both against the Germans and the civilian population; those sent to penal prisons in Germany for political and resistance crimes and their dependents who, while there is no proof that they were sent to concentration camps just disappeared on their release from these penal prisons and must presumably have been killed or to have died in these camps, or on forced marches (concentration camps were in the Nazi mind the natural next step from a penal prison for their promises of repatriation never materialised); and lastly the internees, some of whom may have suffered hardship of a different nature.[45]

Falla's ordering here is interesting. He placed himself and his colleagues who went to penal prisons only in third position, just above the internees sent to civilian internment camps. Those in second position are equally interesting: while Black Marketeers were looked down upon in the Channel Islands, Falla realized that anyone sent to a concentration camp would have a better claim than those sent to a penal prison, although he made clear his position, namely, that penal prisons were but an antechamber or waiting room before inevitable arrival at a concentration camp.

Once victims of Nazi persecution were allowed to start filing a claim, Falla asked the Foreign Office for twenty-four forms. His estimates of nine months earlier of '*not more than 10 islanders*' who were imprisoned for resistance acts had suddenly increased. Although he explained that he did not think that twenty-four would really be needed, he said that he knew of '*at least 16 ex-Nazi prisoners who would like forms*'.[46] The rapid increase was most likely due to the stipulated eligibility of dependents of deceased victims to claim compensation; fifteen Channel Islanders had been in Frankfurt-Preungesheim or Naumburg prisons. Guernseyman Bill Symes, who had survived Buchenwald, also periodically attended Falla's annual reunions. It seems likely that, now Frank knew who would be eligible, he realized that he could help the families of friends in Jersey as well as his own small gang.

'Fathering' the claims: The role of Frank Falla

Now that the Foreign Office was inviting claims, Falla turned his attentions to his fellow victims of Nazi persecution in the Channel Islands. By December, he had helped fourteen of them compile their claims, later describing his role as '*framing*' or '*fathering*' the claims through to fruition.[47] Most Channel Islanders wrote their own statements. However, for Frank Falla's group, he took an active role in helping them prepare their testimonies. These were the men who regularly attended the April reunion

Figure 6.2 Frank Falla and the 'Frankfurt / Naumburg Crooks' at their April reunion. Copyright: the Frank Falla Archive. Courtesy: the Island Archives, Guernsey

of 'Frankfurt / Naumburg crooks', as Falla referred to it in his diaries. The most regular attendees at these meals were Ernest Legg and Cecil Duquemin (Falla's co-members of GUNS), Norman Dexter, Walter Lainé and Gerald Domaille (Figure 6.2).

Falla's diaries and his papers give us an insight into the degree to which he composed the testimonies for his friends. October 1964 was a period when a number of the testimonies of the Frankfurt-Naumburg group were written. Falla's diary for this period records evening phone calls and visits to the homes of many of these men, their widows or the parents of those who lost sons. During these visits he distributed claims forms, discussed the composition of statements and collected filled in forms, which he posted to the Foreign Office in batches by registered post.[48] His method of collecting statements was sometimes done by interviewing the person concerned and typing up a statement which they later signed.[49] This method was particularly useful when a person had difficulty in remembering a coherent sequence of events or in composing a good case. On other occasions the person concerned would write their own statement or make some rough notes which Frank would discuss with the person concerned, adding extra notes of his own during the discussion, and then would later type up.[50] In the case of at least one applicant, Falla was given a treasured letter which was sent to the widow of deceased Jerseyman, Joseph Tierney, by a Belgian man, who had held the dying Islander in his arms, and made a vow to contact the man's wife after the war. Falla used this to help compose the testimony on behalf of Joseph's widow, Eileen Tierney.[51]

Norman Dexter's personal archive reveals a three-side handwritten testimony[52] which Falla typed up a few weeks later, correcting the grammar and changing words here and there to increase the perceived legitimacy of the claim without changing the factual content. The existence of the original testimony is immensely useful in demonstrating the ways in which Falla was able to change the text in small ways that he thought might increase the potential chances of compensation. For example, Falla added inverted commas around the references to Dexter's original 'trial' with the intention of drawing the attention of the Foreign Office to its illegality and illegitimacy in his eyes. Where Dexter had written that he '*remained*' in his cell during air raids at Frankfurt, Falla rephrased this as a place where he was '*forced to stay*' during air raids, adding that only prison officers and staff were allowed in the shelters. As he was also at this prison, Falla was able to add such extra details. Emotive additions were also made. Dexter had written that he '*witnessed several bodies of suicides being conveyed from their cells*' at Frankfurt. Falla rephrased this to say that Dexter '*witnessed the carrying from their cells of several prisoners who could endure it no more and had committed suicide*'. Dexter was on the forced march which left Frankfurt in March 1945. Where Dexter had discussed '*a journey ... on foot where we walked all day for several weeks*', Falla changed this to '*travelling on foot [we] were forced marched all day for several weeks*'. Where Dexter made reference to prisoners being '*allowed to bury*' the dead, Falla added '*though, God knows, they hardly had enough strength to dig the graves*'. Towards the end of the testimony, Dexter referred to being taken, after liberation, on a lorry with a '*crowd of Frenchmen*', which Falla changed to '*a number of French political prisoners*', emphasizing the similar status of the prisoners with whom they had been incarcerated.

Of course, these minor alterations were unlikely to have made much of a difference to the chances of getting compensation, but the subtle nature of the changes were a way for Falla and his fellow applicants to express their status as political prisoners and the illegitimacy of the way in which they were treated.

There were two forms for potential applicants. Form A was given to survivors of Nazi persecution, and Form B was for use in respect of a deceased victim. The form comprised three sections: applicants had to answer questions and provide proof about identity, nationality and persecution. While a narrative testimony about the experience of internment was not requested per se, the applicant had to provide the following details:

a. *Name of camp or other place of detention, its situation, its general conditions and regime;*
b. *Dates of imprisonment and of release; prison number; reasons for imprisonment and circumstances in which it arose;*
c. *If you are suffering permanent disability as a result of treatment received during your imprisonment please give full details of its nature and cause;*
d. *Any other information you consider useful and relevant. (Please attach all documentary evidence.)*[53]

While many applicants provided the bare minimum of information, others took the opportunity to write what amounted to short memoirs. As compensation was calculated – in theory at least – according to the length of time a person had spent in a concentration camp (or prison that was deemed comparable), it was in the interest of the applicant to show how severe their place of internment was. Therefore, when

Falla helped Dexter to rephrase his statement of persecution, he knew what he was doing, although the Foreign Office relied on official sources such as the International Red Cross and International Tracing Service when deciding how comparable to a concentration camp a place of detention was.

Falla sent off the first batch of seven files in late October 1964. Four of them were of members of the gang of 'Frankfurt / Naumburg crooks' (Falla, Legg, Lainé, Symes); a fifth was from Henrietta Gillingham, wife of the deceased Joseph Gillingham of GUNS. Mr Ingrouille, father of the deceased John Ingrouille, a Guernsey teenager deported for threatening the Germans with a non-existent 'resistance army', had supplied the sixth. Eileen Tierney made up the last person in this group. Joseph Tierney had been in prison with Falla and Falla had been the person to break the news to Eileen after the war. Since 1945, they had kept in touch and Falla had visited her whenever his work took him to his sister Island. He continued to look after her during the compensation claims. Falla was clear in his letter to the Foreign Office that he had typed additional facts when helping the group compile their claims, expressing a hope that it would help their cases.[54]

His second batch of half a dozen forms included three members of his 'gang' (Duquemin, Dexter and Domaille); Mrs Le Maitre, daughter of Percy Miller, who had died in Frankfurt prison; Rene Bessin, who was deported to Troyes prison in France for failing to surrender his wireless; and Rachel Symes. Rachel was applying on behalf of her deceased husband, Louis, who had died at Cherche-Midi Prison after the two of them were deported with a number of others from Guernsey in 1940 for their role in sheltering British commandos who had visited the Island. At the same time, Falla also distributed forms to Mary Bird and her brother Walter, who had also been among those deported to Cherche-Midi Prison. Roy Machon, deported for making V-for-victory badges, also received a form from Falla.[55] What Falla did not know, in the autumn of 1964, was that it was still far from certain whether he and his friends were eligible for compensation. A letter from the Foreign Office to the International Tracing Service asked whether Frankfurt and Naumburg were considered to be comparable to concentration camps.[56] Such queries made five months after the signing of the Anglo-German Agreement showed that the Foreign Office had no definitive pre-agreed list of prisons and camps before the compensation processing began. This was established on an ad hoc basis.

In December 1964, Falla discovered that he had become the Foreign Office's de facto point of contact for the Channel Islands in the absence of intervention by any member of local government. As he later wrote:

> *With local and national newspapers, television and radio featuring survivors' stories, and progress reported to the House of Commons by the Foreign Secretary, I would have thought Statesmen in the Channel Islands would have stirred themselves and got things organised on an official basis. But not a bit of it. No one raised a finger to help, indeed no one seemed the slightest bit interested. So I decided to do my best to find out what it was all about, and before long found that I had become a kind of unofficial 'official'.*[57]

Instead of writing to the Lieutenant-Governor or Bailiff's offices of Guernsey or Jersey, the Foreign Office now began to write to Falla, seeking information about Channel

Islanders from him. The Foreign Office had a list of seventeen more Islanders whose current addresses were unknown or who had not yet applied for compensation. These names derived from what they referring to as their '*1945 records*'.[58] In all probability these were either the records of Britons liberated from German camps and prisons, or else the records of interviews they conducted with returning prisoners, to which a number of claimants referred in their testimonies. Falla was delighted to help, and located his fellow Islanders in Guernsey, Jersey, France, the United Kingdom and United States through his own networks and the local newspapers. He was also able to confirm the identity of his fellow prisoners in cases where the Foreign Office was confused about names.[59]

Falla was also able to send the Foreign Office greater detail about the deaths of the Jersey men at Naumburg in order to facilitate the decision-making process on the claims of their next of kin. Falla had kept a scrap of paper hidden in the foot of his shaving-stick container while in prison and had kept a note of the details and dates of death of his fellow Islanders. As Falla had been the one to communicate the death of these men to their families, and these details were incorporated in their testimonies, Falla sent fuller details to the Foreign Office in April 1965, writing that '*in an effort to spare the feelings of the families of these men, I have never communicated the full facts to them as I do to you and you will readily appreciate why.*'[60]

There was little that Falla could do for Channel Islanders who had been deported to internment camps. Both the articles which Falla placed in local newspapers in both Guernsey and Jersey, and the Foreign Office adverts, emphasized the inapplicability of the compensation scheme to those who were held in such places. Despite this, many Islanders who were sent to the civilian internment camps of Biberach, Wurzach or Laufen in Germany wrote to Falla to ask for his help. A number of them had lost everything in the war and felt that they were still at a financial disadvantage twenty years later. Falla replied to (and kept) every letter that he received, explaining that the compensation agreement did not include POWs or those in internment camps. He could provide nothing but sympathy and regret that the local government could not do anything to help people in this position.

Falla was, however, able to fight hard on behalf of Islanders who were refused compensation, and exchanged many letters with the Foreign Office on their behalf. It is a clear indication of the status of Falla's role as an 'unofficial official' that the Foreign Office was prepared to discuss the personal details of individual cases at length with him. Although Falla appealed to Neave for help with their cases, Falla alone was able to overturn rejections, though he was not successful in all cases.[61] Neither was he able to fully dissipate the ill-feeling and dissatisfaction which followed the dissimilarity of compensation figures awarded to men who had had spent the same amount of time in the same prison as their colleagues.[62] Although compensation was paid in several instalments, one of these was specifically for physical disability resulting from Nazi persecution. However, when payments arrived, they were not labelled, which led to much misunderstanding and conflict between former political prisoners who confided their levels of compensation to each other. Neither was there any indication of further payments. In short, the entire process was a mystery to those who applied, and even Falla, who had probably studied the system better than any other Channel Islander, could not always understand the logic or methods of the Foreign Office.

The best example of this is the case of Roy Machon, whose greatest disadvantage was to be the only British man in his prison, and thus without anyone else to vouch either for his period of incarceration or the conditions of his confinement. Machon's case also exemplifies the difficulty faced by many in trying to understand what information the Foreign Office needed in order to give compensation. The case arguably shows that the Foreign Office acted beyond the boundaries of their own criteria when the information that they sought was not available.

According to the issued notes for guidance given to applicants,

> 'National Socialist persecution' means the infliction by members of the National Socialist Party or their agents for reasons of race, religion, political views or political opposition to National-Socialism of treatment involving detention in Germany or in any territory occupied by Germany in a concentration camp, or in an institution where conditions were comparable with those in a concentration camp. Hardships suffered in a normal civil prison, civilian internment camp or prisoner of war camp do not constitute Nazi persecution nor does treatment contrary to the Geneva Conventions and the rules of war, even though resulting in permanent injury or death. Applications for registration should not be made in respect of such hardships or treatment.[63]

Decision-making was not easy, and the Foreign Office team's notes, which can be found in most case files, make it clear that they debated every case among themselves, meaning that the criteria were not as clear cut as they may have looked at the outset. They acknowledged that '*the definition of Nazi persecution was drafted with sufficient flexibility to allow ... borderline cases where the line between Nazi persecution and German brutality is hard to draw*'.[64] After the period of the compensation claims was over, the Foreign Office admitted that the '*rules of the scheme were unrealistic*', and that the definition of Nazi persecution was '*a very difficult*' one.[65]

The Foreign Office team became more experienced as the period of registering claims progressed such that decisions were made based on earlier precedents that were accepted or rejected. This means that if early decisions taken about the regime in a particular prison were wrong, then that decision became compounded as time went on. Thus, although each case was judged on its own merits in so far as the elements of each case were assessed, it was not judged in isolation, and each judgement was heavily influenced by previous cases.

In trying to stay faithful to the guidance notes, however, the Foreign Office appeared to tie not only themselves in contradictory knots, but also the applicant as well. This is most clearly demonstrated in the case of Roy Machon.

'The true nature of what he suffered has not been properly grasped': The case of Roy Machon

Roy Machon was arrested in June 1943 for making V-sign badges (Figure 6.3). These badges were actually British coins with a safety pin soldered on the back. Machon, with

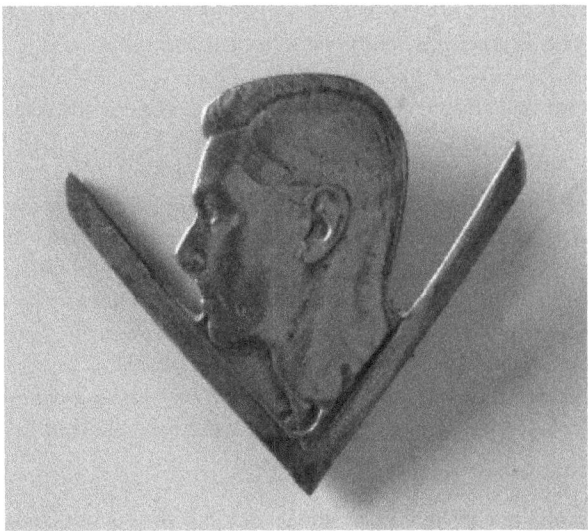

Figure 6.3 A V-sign badge made by Roy Machon. Copyright: Gilly Carr

his friend Alf Williams, filed around the profile of the King's head and scored the letter 'V' for victory underneath. These badges were very popular with the local population during and after the BBC's V-sign campaign of 1941, and were worn inside the lapel of jackets then flashed in the street to trusted patriotic friends.[66] While Williams was never caught, Machon unfortunately was. When Machon's workshop was searched, a BBC newsletter was also found.[67] Given the later involvement of Falla in this case, it is possible that this was a copy of a GUNS newsletter.

Machon was kept in prison in Guernsey for a month, where he was subjected to '*rough treatment*'. Six weeks after his release, he was informed that he would be deported on 1 October 1943. The night before he left, he organized a farewell party at which guests sang patriotic songs so loudly that German soldiers arrived and took him to prison. The next morning he and two other unnamed men from Guernsey were deported and sent to Laufen, a men's civilian internment camp to which hundreds of other male non-indigenous Channel Islanders had been sent in September 1942. Ex-servicemen from the Islands followed them in February 1943. In December 1943, Machon was informed that he had been tried in his absence and '*found guilty of holding a forbidden political meeting and singing forbidden songs*'. For this, he was to spend five months in prison with hard labour. Despite appealing, in February 1944 he was transferred to Stadelheim Prison in Munich where he was made to wear a jacket sporting a red diamond on the back. He was forced to splice steel cable for eleven hours a day for use in Messerschmitt planes; – work which was against the Geneva Convention for POWs. There is no question about the bad treatment of prisoners at Munich. Machon testified that

> *if any of we prisoners did not move quickly enough … we were punished by the guards who hit us about the head and neck with some heavy metal object or prison*

keys which they carried in a bunch. So many hittings about the head did I suffer that
I have sustained a permanent injury which resulted in deafness.

Beyond his own bad treatment, Machon also testified as to the fate of his fellow prisoners:

On Mondays and Thursdays in the prison guards would call out 10 to 20 names and these prisoners would be marched out to do work outside the prison. Many times, of that number, only 5 would return. The rest were either sent for further sentences ... or just killed where they stood. One such, a Pole, had his head cut off for stealing 10 Reichsmarks from a German ... Tuesdays and Fridays were the days of killings. On Wednesdays and Fridays we were given a small piece of blood sausage or a small piece of meat in our soup. It was commonly known and spoken about by prisoners, that we were eating the flesh and blood of fellow-prisoners who had been killed by the Nazis.[68]

After five months in jail, of which almost the entire time was spent in solitary confinement, with no Red Cross parcels, no medical attention, and no visits from any Protecting Power (such as the Red Cross), he was released back to Laufen where he was placed in hospital for several weeks. He and the others in Laufen were eventually liberated by the Americans in May 1945.

Machon's testimony was thus full, detailed and contained information on forced labour, ill-treatment and bad food. His period of incarceration at Munich, which resulted in permanent disability, should have earned him compensation. It did not. In fact, in a letter to Frank Falla concerning the case of Machon, the Foreign Office wrote:

Mr Machon was sentenced to hard labour and ... he first was put to work splicing steel cable then later, sorting dried peas and cutting webbing and leather and finally separating ferrous and non-ferrous metals. There would not appear to be anything wrong in the Germans employing him in these activities. In fact, they could have required him to undertake any kind of work as he was not a prisoner of war under the protection of the Geneva Convention which does prohibit the employment of captured servicemen on work directly concerned with the war effort, i.e., making munitions or guns, etc.[69]

The Foreign Office also contacted the ITS to discover what their files said about Machon and Stadelheim Prison. The ITS replied that they had no information about Roy Machon and their records revealed only the presence of an *Untersuchungshaftanstalt* (detention centre) and *Strafgefängnisse* (prison) in the Stadelheim district of Munich, but that they were not in possession of any documents from there.[70] Unfortunately for Machon, the Central Tracing Agency of the International Committee of the Red Cross in Geneva had a record only of his arrest and arrival in Laufen in October 1943. As Laufen was a civilian internment camp, inmates were not eligible for compensation.

The Foreign Office wrote to Machon explaining the problem and asked him for corroborative evidence of his imprisonment – a statement from a witness imprisoned with him – and more information on the conditions of his prison.[71] Machon wrote back a six-and-a-half page handwritten letter, stating his surprise at the response of the Foreign Office. He enclosed the names and addresses of men in Laufen with him who could vouch for his removal and return, a German prisoner, Walter T. and the names of two Dutch co-prisoners. He also gave more information on the conditions of his imprisonment, the lack of food, the exercise in the prison yard, and disappearance of any prisoner who collapsed during this.[72] Unfortunately, with no corroborative statements about disappearing prisoners, decapitations or the meat source of the blood sausages, it appears that Machon was simply disbelieved – or that this was not deemed sufficient to constitute Nazi persecution, whereas decapitation in Frankfurt prison was, which earned those interned in that prison the eligibility credentials for compensation.

A month later, Mr Wilson of the Claims Department at the Foreign Office wrote back to say that Machon had been turned down because

> *the regime at Stadelheim prison camp, as you describe it, was not comparable to a Concentration Camp. … The Concentration Camps, where suffering was an end in itself, were evolved as instruments to carry into practice the doctrines of Nazi ideology whereas the admitted brutalities and suffering often experienced during internment were incidental to and not the object of detention.*[73]

Such an explanation from the Foreign Office was unconvincing. The conditions in Stadelheim, while different in parts to Frankfurt and Naumburg as described by Falla, seemed no less harsh. The common elements of forced labour, ill-treatment, little food and lack of Red Cross parcels were all present. The difference for Machon is that no other Channel Islanders wrote to the Foreign Office with similar testimonies about Stadelheim. Being imprisoned alone, without his Island friends, was to have a negative impact on Machon's ability to get compensation.

He wrote again to the Foreign Office, this time with letters of support from Sir Ambrose Sherwill, the camp senior of Laufen, and with a testimony from fellow prisoner Walter T, arguing that Stadelheim was subject to '*Nazi tyranny*', '*was noted for brutal beatings*', and that prisoners '*worked fourteen hours a day on one bowl of soup. There were no Red Cross parcels in this prison. Surely this treatment amounts to cruelty & persecution?*'[74] Having made up their minds, the Foreign Office were unmoved, saying that they had '*little to add*' to their previous letter. They did, however, introduce a new element into the equation, saying that

> *it seems that you were imprisoned for an alleged civil offence, as indeed were many other Channel Islanders, and in spite of the hardships involved, this does not fall within the scope of the present distribution which is confined to compensation to victims of organised and deliberate persecution involving detention in Concentration Camps in furtherance of Nazi doctrines.*[75]

The Foreign Office were now placing weight on the offence which Machon had committed, which, in fact, was not a civil offence. Indeed, Machon had been tried by German military tribunal and convicted of '*Anti German manifestation*'.[76] Had they contacted the authorities in Guernsey, then this information could presumably have been provided. Within five days, Machon had written again to point out the political nature of his offence. To further his political prisoner credentials, he wrote:

> *I served imprisonment locally before being deported to Stadelheim for cutting telephone and electric main cables to German gun emplacements, and painting in tar the letters 'EV' [English Victory] either side of a laurel wreath which the Germans had painted on each building they occupied. I sabotaged German Military cars at the parking at the local cinema where I worked.*[77]

Offering to send proof if it was needed, Machon hoped that '*the above particulars will help to meet with the requirements necessary for the validity of my claim*'. By now it was looking suspiciously like the Foreign Office were trying to find any excuse not to compensate him. In their next letter, they again referred to the criteria for Nazi persecution, which stipulated that only those '*detained in Concentration Camps or institutions where conditions were comparable*' could be compensated. '*The evidence*', they insisted,

> *does not indicate that Stadelheim was such an institution. It is of course known that those who were detailed in <u>civil</u> prisons suffered considerable hardships, but ... [these] were different in kind from the suffering inflicted in pursuance of the evil Nazi ideology characteristic of the Concentration Camps, which alone the present scheme is designed to compensate.*[78]

Their reference to Stadelheim as a 'civil prison' here was deliberate. Machon had not noted who his jailers were and whether the prison was run by the SS or the Gestapo. Perhaps this might have made a difference. With six weeks left until the compensation scheme closed, the Foreign Office were clear that Machon's claim had fallen outside the scope of the scheme.

A fortnight later, Frank Falla joined the correspondence, writing to Mr Littler at the Foreign Office with whom he felt that he had struck up an acquaintance over the many letters they had exchanged over the matter of compensation for Channel Islanders. Falla asked Littler '*urgently to re-examine*' Machon's case because

> *so far as I can gather from talking to Mr Machon, the set of circumstances and conditions, generally, as applied to us in prison in Frankfurt-on-Main and Naumburg-on-Saale, also applied to him for his five month sentence ... conditions there seemed very similar to ours, plus the accompanying ill-treatment from the Nazis. I feel his case fully merits reconsideration and re-appraisal for ... he did suffer brutal treatment at the hands of the Germans.*[79]

Mr Littler responded, saying that the case had been examined very carefully and could not be accepted.

> *The Department has been in touch with the International Tracing Service of the Red Cross and it seems quite clear that Stadelheim prison can only be regarded as a*

normal type of institution and not one in which the conditions can be considered as comparable to a concentration camp. This is borne out by the statement Mr Machon made with the original application (which appears to have been prepared by you) and a more detailed statement given in his letter dated 20 September 1965.

Mr Machon, in his last letter dated 24 April, seems to think that it is the nature of the offence he committed which would influence his acceptance for compensation. This ... is not at all the case. The whole question hangs on treatment and on nothing else.[80]

This letter from Littler was disingenuous; the Foreign Office had specifically claimed that Machon's offence was a civil one and had seemingly encouraged Machon to pursue that line of argument to prove their statement to the contrary. Further, Littler's claim that, after contact with the ITS, it was '*quite clear*' that Stadelheim was a '*normal type of institution*', was not the truth. The ITS had not been able to furnish the Foreign Office with any such assurances. Given that '*the whole question hangs on treatment and nothing else*', it is surprising that Machon's ill-treatment and the comparability of Falla and Machon's experiences, established during their own private conversations in Guernsey, was disregarded.

Falla was clearly puzzled by the inconsistencies in Foreign Office policy and could not let the matter lie. Once again he got to work with his typewriter and wrote to Littler, explaining that

I cannot quite follow the reasoning which has put Mr Roy N. Machon outside the pale of compensation ... I rather feel that the true nature of what he suffered during his five months' imprisonment at Munich, has not been properly grasped.

Quoting from Walter T.'s testimony, and explaining the difference between the Stadelheim Prison during war and peacetime, Falla wrote:

And this I think is the bone of Roy Machon's plea: that it was a labour prison run by the Nazis who made them do work which no pact, treaty, agreement or law permitted them to do – and they were beaten up by the Nazis in their efforts.

Clearly at a loss to discover what the difference was between his prisons and Machon's, Falla added:

I would repeat that I think he should appear before yourself or one of your colleagues at the Foreign Office to be grilled and quizzed personally so that from his own lips you could get his story which I, in the writing, may have inadvertently minimised.[81]

At best, the Foreign Office acted opaquely. Its definitions of Nazi persecution seemed to be flexible only when deemed appropriate. Once again, Littler replied to Falla explaining that he was not denying that the inmates suffered brutality at Stadelheim, but that '*German brutality is not of necessity the same thing as Nazi persecution*'. Littler went on to state firmly that he had a set of criteria to apply and that Machon's circumstances '*do not match up to the requirements of eligibility*'. He also listed the work that Machon conducted during his forced labour, saying that there was nothing wrong in the Germans employing him in these activities as '*they could have required him to undertake any kind of work as he was not a prisoner of war under the protection of the Geneva Convention*'. In a second attempt to close the case, Littler again invoked Falla's own hand in Machon's case, clearly stating that he saw that Falla '*apparently prepared*' Machon's statement, implying in equal measure that a degree of responsibility and fault must lie with Falla. Littler ended the correspondence, or so he thought, with the firm and final statement that '*we must disappoint you and there the matter must rest*'.[82]

Anxious to keep good relations with Littler, and perhaps concerned lest his own testimony be downgraded and compensation withheld, Falla wrote yet again to express his gratitude and to say that no blame could be attached to either himself or Littler for their joint endeavours on Machon's behalf. Although the fundamental differences between the treatment received by Falla and Machon had still not been adequately explained, Falla clearly felt it better to preserve their good relations and indicated that he was quite content to accept his ruling '*as you have reasoned it out so well and lucidly that there should now be no doubt in his mind that he does not qualify*'. In fact, the key differences between Frankfurt and Naumburg on the one hand, and Stadelheim on the other, seemed to lie in the amount of information available to the Foreign Office and the number of people willing to add the weight of their testimony *in terms sought by the Foreign Office*, but which were not clearly specified by them. While Stadelheim indeed may not have been comparable to a concentration camp, and treatment may not have amounted to Nazi persecution, Machon's description of the prison did not differ greatly to other testimonies of Frankfurt and Naumburg. These prisons benefitted from the weight of multiple testimonies and ITS records.

'I am full of praise': The closing of the period of compensation claims

Whatever faults we may find with the officials at the Foreign Office, and notwithstanding the later Parliamentary enquiry about the administration of the claims,[83] Falla was not inclined to be critical. This was despite the dissatisfaction of some of his friends and the disappointment of unsuccessful Channel Islands applicants. In his final letter to Mr Littler, the man with whom he had liaised throughout his correspondence with the Foreign Office, he wrote:

> *I am full of praise for everything you have done for me personally and for those other Channel Islanders I have 'fathered' through this claims business during the past 2½ years. Perhaps you might be pleased to know that when speaking to me many of these people refer to you as 'Frank's friend at the Foreign Office'. I hope you like this, for that is the light in which I have looked upon you in all you have done for me and us. You have been a very good guide, counsellor and friend – when we needed one most and the happy outcome is that they are all grateful for what you have achieved for us. … Through all I do remember ex-Foreign Secretary R.A. Butler's assurance, reiterated by you, that the cases of the Channel Islanders who were in concentration camps or*

comparable institutions (prisons) would receive special consideration. And, I must stress that, in my own opinion that and nothing less than that has happened ... we are all extremely grateful and thankful for, believe me up till then I really did believe that we Channel Islander victims of the Nazis were forgotten people. That no longer applies for the Foreign Office has remembered us where other people – many of them in authority – have forgotten us.[84]

Having achieved compensation for himself and his friends who suffered in Frankfurt and Naumburg, including the widows of the Jerseymen who died in those prisons – women for whom he felt responsible after delivering the news of their husbands' deaths, Falla achieved everything he set out to do. It is perhaps unrealistic to expect him to have carried all former political prisoners from both Islands on his shoulders when he had no access to closed archival documents in the Channel Islands relating to the Occupation. Indeed, some of them are still closed to the public today. He did his best for all of those who came to him for help. Through his intervention, many families brought low by poverty, triggered by an inability to work or expensive medical bills following ill-treatment in a Nazi prison or camp, were now able to pay off debts. With Falla's help, around 50 per cent of all Channel Islanders who applied for compensation were able to receive it. Without his intervention, his ability to compose or structure a testimony, his valuable advice or his tenacity, the numbers would undoubtedly have been far lower.

Falla derived a great deal of pleasure, satisfaction and happiness in being able to help other Islanders claim compensation. Having kept a record of those who had died while in Naumburg Prison with him, the award of compensation to their families more than twenty years later reassured him that he had done his best to help his deceased colleagues. On receiving thank-you letters from a number of these families, he felt touched. It gave *'reassurance that all my efforts on behalf of my late fellow-prisoners was worthwhile'*.[85]

A week before the closing date for applications for claims, the Foreign Office announced that the deadline was being extended from 31 July 1965 to 31 March 1966. This was a positive move as it gave them more time to trace people, and gave potential victims a longer period to come forward with their claims. At the time, Frank Falla, however, was *'utterly astounded and appalled'* at the news; he had been waiting for twenty years for compensation and would now have to wait another eight months to discover how much he and his friends would receive.[86] The eight-month extension would, however, prove to be as beneficial for Channel Islanders as it would for others, and Falla was able to continue helping others.

In Parliament, after questioning by Airey Neave, Mr George Thomson, the Minister for State, revealed in July 1965 that 5,900 claims forms had been sent out and the claims of only 463 people had been registered by the end of July 1965[87] – a rate of less than eight per cent, although not all of those who received forms had returned them to the Foreign Office. Even so, these figures made Falla remark to Neave that the *'Foreign Office must have made it easier to get through the eye of the proverbial needle than to become registered for claims'*.[88]

As most of Falla's Channel Island colleagues had already had their claims registered, meaning that they had been successful, Neave was gearing up for another battle, and this time for ex-servicemen who had been denied compensation. Falla told Neave that there was *'considerable dissatisfaction'* in Guernsey with the non-registration of claims from people who were imprisoned in France alone, no doubt hoping that Neave would take the bait – and the cause – but Neave, who expressed his dissatisfaction with the way that the administration of claims were being pursued, was choosing his own battles to fight.[89]

Falla had received a number of letters from Islanders who had been sent to prisons in France but not Germany, who wanted to know whether they were eligible. Although Falla would once, undoubtedly, have encouraged them to apply, by 1966 it was clear that the Foreign Office was not compensating those who had only been incarcerated in France – at least, those from the Channel Islands and the particular French prisons to which they had been sent.[90] On these occasions, Falla had to inform such would-be applicants that the wording on the compensation notice, which invited applications from those who had suffered Nazi persecution in a concentration camp or comparable institution that *'the term "comparable institution" does not, unfortunately, cover prisons or camps in France'*.[91]

To celebrate their success in finally getting initial payments from the Foreign Office, which gave recognition for all that they had suffered, albeit not from local government in the Channel Islands, Falla organized a reunion dinner in Guernsey on 20 November 1965 (Figure 6.4). This was not just for the usual Frankfurt / Naumburg crooks, but for victims of Nazi persecution from Jersey and Sark as well. This event was billed as the *'Ex-Belsen, ex-Buchenwald, ex-Frankfurt, ex-Naumburg Channel Islands political prisoners of the Nazis'*. Falla had extended the invitation widely but it was difficult for many to make the journey; not all were well enough to do so. On the evening, twenty-two guests attended (compared to the usual group of half a dozen at the April reunions). Hubert Lanyon, the Sark member of GUNS who was imprisoned locally but never deported, wrote to Falla shortly before the event to say that he hoped to be in the Island to celebrate *'you heroes and to thank you all for the very noble, patriotic, inspiring and re-assuring work which was so grandly accomplished, albeit well knowing what risks were involved, yet never could you have thought of what an ordeal was before you'*.[92]

In his diary, Falla noted that he was joined that evening by Harold Le Druillenec and his wife from Jersey and the Lanyons from Sark, as well as an extended guest list from Guernsey, including, in addition to the usual attendees, Mr and Mrs Ingrouille (parents of the deceased John Ingrouille), Evelyn Le Maitre (daughter of the deceased Percy Miller), Bill Symes and his wife, and female member of GUNS, Henrietta Gillingham, whose husband, Joseph, had taken the blame for her and had died in Germany. Falla described the evening as *'wonderful'*, and was obviously delighted at the *'lovely surprise'* when *'the gang and others presented me with a lovely Ferguson TV set'*.[93]

Both Falla and Neave hoped that the 1966 General Election of 31 March would bring the Conservatives back into power, with a hope that perhaps they could *'right so many of the Labour Party's wrongs'* and could bring about a change of heart with regard to the borderline cases.[94] However, it was not to be. The Labour Party was re-elected and they showed themselves to be inflexible towards Channel Islanders and others with borderline cases.[95] The General Election date was also important to the two men for other reasons; it marked the closing date for applications for compensation. Falla hoped

Figure 6.4 The 1965 compensation celebration dinner for the 'ex-Belsen, ex-Buchenwald, ex-Frankfurt, ex-Naumburg Channel Islands political prisoners of the Nazis'. Copyright: unknown. Courtesy: Rosie Jeffreys

that perhaps the borderline cases might be '*brought into the fold*' should there be any money left over, but this is not the way that the Foreign Office chose to operate.

In January 1967, the final results of the compensation scheme were announced in Parliament. In all, 6,608 application forms had been sent out. While the number of forms returned or applications made was not reported, 3,046 were rejected. Most of the rejections were made on the following grounds: 913 (nearly 30 per cent) were on the grounds of nationality. 692 (23 per cent) had been in a civilian internment camp and 614 (20 per cent) were in a POW camp. A further 371 (12 per cent) were deemed to have been in an 'ordinary prison' and not in a concentration camp 'or comparable institution'. In other words, over half of those rejected, who felt that they had been subjected to 'Nazi persecution', had been in the 'wrong kind' of Nazi camp or prison, perhaps giving us an insight into the kinds of claims that the population felt *should* have been supported.

Only 639 people received compensation for imprisonment; 225 were compensated for death in a concentration camp or similar institution. One hundred and fifty-one received disability awards. In total, 1,015 awards were made.[96] Fifty of these, or around one in twenty, were from the Channel Islands. For a death, just over £2,220 was paid, and just over £22 and four shillings was awarded for each week in a camp.

However, these figures were premature; Neave's fight for compensation was still brewing for the British airmen murdered after the escape from Stalag Luft III, and for the survivors who were sent to Sachsenhausen. He went on to win this case,[97] although the money for these men was found from the interest earned on the one

Figure 6.5 Frank Falla typing *The Silent War*. Copyright: the Frank Falla Archive. Courtesy: the Island Archives, Guernsey

million pounds compensation because, as they were told by the Foreign Secretary, George Brown, '*Gentlemen, the cheese is all gone!*'[98] Tony Kushner has observed that the compensation claims should have been an occasion on which confront Britain's relationship to the Holocaust.[99] Instead it became, according to the British media, largely about 'compensation for British war heroes'.[100]

Concluding thoughts: Falla's fight for legitimacy

This chapter has focused on the details of Falla's long correspondence with the Foreign Office, and his dedicated fight for compensation for Channel Islanders. Throughout the long decade of keeping up pressure on civil servants and MPs, Falla followed every new development and did his utmost to persuade those with whom he dealt to see the legitimacy of his cause and that of his friends and colleagues.

Falla was galvanised from his success with the Foreign Office and the gratitude from his friends. In November 1965, the same month as his celebratory dinner with his former political prisoner friends, he agreed to write his memoirs of the Occupation and of his experience as a member of GUNS and a prisoner in Frankfurt and Naumburg prisons. He wrote *The Silent War* in just five months and the book was published in the autumn of 1966 (Figure 6.5).

The latter part of the book became his opportunity to tell the story at length which, up to that point, had been expressed only in newspaper articles, in letters to the Foreign Office, and in testimonies for compensation. The final chapter was devoted to the '*Forgotten People*', the Channel Islands victims of Nazi persecution and his struggle with local government and the Foreign Office to get compensation. Emboldened by his recent successes, he was uncensored in ripping into local politicians for abandoning those sentenced for offences against the occupiers and abandoning them again at the time of the compensation claims. Citing the 'top brass' cases of Harold Le Druillenec who was in Belsen; his sister Louisa Gould, who died in Ravensbrück; Bill Symes, who survived Buchenwald; and Guernseymen Canon Cohu and Charles Machon, both of whom died in captivity for their 'respectable' and highly legitimate acts of resistance, Falla was highly critical of the lack of recognition and honours given to such people.

Falla's book takes us up to around the same point as the last chapter: the mid-1960s, when, as shown, local government had shown neither willingness nor real interest in engaging with former political prisoners. In the next chapter we move into the final section of this book, and the period from 1965 to the present day. Here we discuss the role of guardians of memory and 'game-changers' in shifting the narrative in Jersey from the late 1980s onwards. Characterizing their actions and the events that they orchestrated as 'incremental memory events', and using these as inspiration, the chapter asks whether incremental memory events can be carried out by would-be game-changers in Guernsey with the same result?

Part Three

1965–Present

7

Game-Changers and Incremental Memory Events

More than fifty years have passed since the compensation claims of 1965. This period has seen a slow increase in the heritage of victims of Nazi persecution in the Channel Islands, picking up pace from 1995 in Jersey. In the mid-1960s, such a heritage existed only at private sites of memory, residing only in books, testimonies and memories. Today this heritage is fully embraced and championed with pride in Jersey alone. This chapter seeks to explore the steps made in Guernsey and Jersey in changing the way that victims of Nazism have been seen. Specifically, it assesses the acts of those who sought – and still seek – to change the game, playing particular attention to the impact made by these acts, both singly and cumulatively.

This chapter begins by examining the work of Jersey's guardian of memory of political prisoners, Joe Mière, his life's work, and his contact with Guernsey's guardian of memory, Frank Falla. I also examine his interactions with Jersey's game-changers, to whom he passed the baton towards the end of his life.

I then explore the how the tide turned against the old narrative of the Occupation in Jersey through the action of game-changers in the 1990s. I ask how it was that they succeeded in this endeavour where the guardians of memory had failed, and why these game-changers have emerged only in Jersey. Theoretically, this discussion is informed by the concept of the 'incremental memory event', which builds upon Alexander Etkind's original concept of the 'memory event'.[1]

The second part of this chapter is devoted to a study of a potential game-changer in Guernsey, and the work that he inaugurated on Holocaust Memorial Day (HMD) with the help of the author in 2015. I examine the difficulties and controversies that emerged during this activism. I also track the continuing efforts to encourage the tidal shifts to persist in following a new course through the deliberate instigation of incremental memory events during HMD in the years since. This attempt at game-changing has involved emulation of the example set by Jersey, whereby the memory and heritage of Jews and political prisoners are yoked together on HMD. While in Jersey there were specific reasons for the initiation and continuation of this association, neither of these events or preconditions are present in Guernsey. It is still too early to judge the success of the narrative of 'joint victims of Nazism' in Guernsey, but its adoption has been a recent and conscious decision. This chapter concludes by examining what remains to be done to change attitudes in Guernsey and when, if ever, this might take place.

'Naughty lads who stepped out of line':
The guardians of memory

While Jersey's first guardians of memory who spoke up for the missing and dead political prisoners might be said to have emerged in the form of the Jersey Loyalists and the Ex-Convicts we met in Chapter 3, Guernsey stood resolutely firm in rejecting the legitimacy of the memory of such people after the Occupation. The resolve of the authorities merely stiffened further following the Privy Council ruling against the Guernsey policemen in 1951. There was no evidence that the attitudes of the local authorities had softened by the time of the compensation claims in the mid-1960s. This period might have been a time when memories were stirred of interrogations, imprisonments and deportations, yet other than articles by Frank Falla in the local press, there was no flurry of stories in the papers of the Channel Islands during this period. The compensation claims might have been seismic in their ability to reawaken old memories, especially for former political prisoners; the event was certainly newsworthy. It might even have been a time for a reassessment of past attitudes, but there is no evidence that this happened in the Channel Islands, and no evidence that local government had any interest in seeing this emerge.

There is thus no evidence that the impact of the compensation claims was momentous enough to qualify in the Channel Islands as a 'memory event', as conceptualized by Alexander Etkind. Etkind's memory event is 'a rediscovery of the past that creates a rupture with its accepted cultural meaning. Memory events are secondary to the historical events that they interpret, usually taking place many years or decades later'. They are

> *defined temporally, as moments of the transformation of the public sphere, rather than spatially, as fixed locations on national territory ... memory events produce volatile effects that generate secondary waves and aftershocks ...* [they are] *simultaneously acts and products of memory ...* [and] *always have their authors and agents – initiators or even enthusiasts of memory – who lead the production of these collective events.*[2]

Frank Falla, as an agent of memory, had done his best, twenty years after the German Occupation, to reawaken public memory of the suffering of his former political prisoner colleagues – his 'fictive kin', as Jay Winter would term such a group whose bond was 'social and experiential' rather than biological.[3] Falla was more than a mere 'agent' of memory; he was a *guardian* of memory: someone who safeguarded the memory of his fictive kin group and became their spokesperson. While guardians of memory are usually typified by eloquence, good memory, good character during the war years, and a commitment to the legacy of the Occupation, the title is usually reserved for people who enjoy great longevity and garner more respect for their cause and their memory group the longer they live.[4] Falla died in 1983 aged seventy-two, and thus did not live long enough to see the benefits accruing to someone of his stature. His well-deserved status has only grown in the last few years.

As a journalist, Falla was able to get publicity for his cause in the local papers during the period of the compensation claims. When compensation was successfully obtained, he ensured that it made front page news on 23 August 1965 in the *Guernsey Star* and the *Guernsey Evening Press*. And yet this 'event' of compensation did not act as a memory event. While it may have acted as a 'rediscovery of the past' for the population, it did not create a 'rupture' with its 'accepted cultural meaning'. Resisters were still troublemakers and 'naughty lads [who] stepped out of line with the Germans'. As Falla put it, the local authorities had not yet got around to 'owning' the resisters.[5]

The Eichmann trial of 1961, just four years earlier, triggered a memory event in relation to understandings of the Holocaust because of its international TV broadcast of testimonies of Jews – the first time that the general public had heard Jewish survivors of the camps, in large numbers, speak these testimonies publicly. The newly recognized identity of the survivor emerged – someone whose new function was to be the 'bearer of history', as Annette Wieviorka put it.[6] Yet audiences in the Channel Islands seemingly drew no parallels between Jews and Islanders who suffered in concentration camps. There was, it seems, little sympathy – perhaps for either group. While the Eichmann trial 'freed the victims to speak' and 'created a social demand for testimonies' – indeed, marked the 'advent of the witness'[7] – this was not the case everywhere. Rather, it was the process of claiming for compensation itself, and the associated request for testimonies, that allowed camp and prison survivors in the Channel Islands to speak; but their words were read by Foreign Office officials alone. This was not an opportunity for the (re-)serialization of testimonies in the local newspapers. The public audience in the Channel Islands had little appetite to face a reminder of the darkest parts of the Occupation. They were not to show any willingness in this regard for another thirty years.

In Jersey, Joe Mière was keeping the flame alive of that Island's political prisoners. He had been a teenage resister who prided himself in being a thorn in the side of the occupiers after joining a small resistance group. He was fortunate in being arrested, for the third time, in 1945, after the occupiers had stopped deporting people to the continent because of the Allied liberation of Normandy in the summer of 1944. Mière was imprisoned and ill-treated during interrogation by the German Secret Field Police and the German Harbour Navy Police in St Helier.

After the war, Mière joined the army. In 1948 he was demobbed and started his collection of testimonies and photos of his fellow political prisoners:

> *Friends and people of the occupation were very kind to me, always ready to tell me their war history and give me their photographs … they were only too pleased that someone was recording the history. … As the years went by I added to the collection … the hours and days and years spent interviewing people seemed to never end. It was a labour of love and a great satisfaction to me which was my only reward. … By the time that I started work at the German Military Underground Hospital as a Deputy Curator in 1976, the collection was quite large.*[8]

While at the Underground Hospital, a concrete, labyrinthine, privately owned museum dedicated to the years of Occupation, he transferred his collection of photographs and stories, at his own expense, to glass cases (Figure 7.1). He retired in 1991 and died in 2006, aged eighty. Today, over a decade after Mière's death, his collection no longer

Figure 7.1 Joe Mière by Andrew Tift. Jersey Heritage Collections. Copyright: Andrew Tift

resides in the damp tunnels, but a part of it is in the café of Jersey War Tunnels, as the venue is now called. During his lifetime, Mière faced 'considerable indifference and even hostility' as he tried to build up his collection, but local tributes paid to him in his obituary show that he had become a respected figure in the community and a 'legend in his own lifetime'.[9]

Mière was the first person in Jersey, from 1976, to present the story of political prisoners in a traditional heritage format. He was passionate about speaking on this subject to visitors to the museum, and was committed to building up his list of former political prisoners. Frank Falla, on the other hand, was avid about journalism, and his public engagement was through the written word. It would not be true, however, to say that Falla had no dealings with heritage. The German Occupation Museum in Guernsey has a small section dedicated to GUNS, with additional information not found in Falla's memoirs, but most likely to have come from him given his commitment to his fellow political prisoners. It is also likely that the museum director would have sought out Falla for this information rather than the other way round, as Falla was a modest man, and preferred to tell his story through writing.

Such was Falla's modesty that, when in 1980 the Imperial War Museum wrote to him about their oral history programme to ask whether he could recommend people to interview who were deported from the Channel Islands, he did not suggest himself.[10] No interview with Frank Falla exists in the sound archive of the museum, although Joe Mière made a recording with them in 1989.[11]

Falla and Mière were in contact with each other only in the last few years of Falla's life. In 1980, Mière wrote to Falla to ask him how many people had been deported from the Island during the Occupation on the assumption that if anybody in Guernsey was keeping track of numbers, it had to be him. Falla replied with an answer that must have shocked Mière: 'I'm sorry, but there is no record of the number of Guernsey people imprisoned in the Island or elsewhere but I should think the number sent to prisons in Germany or France for offences against the Nazis would be around 30. I am very sorry but I've little that would enhance your Underground Hospital.'[12] Falla had also been assiduous in helping Islanders claim compensation. He had passed on addresses and names to the Foreign Office in the 1960s, and had helped advertise information about the compensation claims. But he had not, himself, compiled any kind of 'roll of honour', unlike Mière. His guess of around thirty deported Islanders was a considerable underestimate, and even fewer than that estimated by Ambrose Sherwill over twenty years before.

Mière was not content to be confined to the German Underground Hospital, his headquarters for so long. After his retirement in 1991 he gathered momentum in placing pressure on the local authorities in Jersey to recognize political prisoners and to publicly acknowledge that these people did the right thing. Mière wanted a memorial to political prisoners in St Helier outside the site of the former prison, but he had a fight on his hands. A memorial only became a reality in 1995, but Mière was denied an unveiling on Liberation Day, the most important Occupation-related date in the Channel Islands' calendar. He was also nearly denied his preferred location for the memorial. No publicity, as a deliberate decision by the authorities, was given to the unveiling until one day beforehand.[13] In the event, the new Bailiff, Philip Bailhache, unveiled the memorial (Figure 7.2). Bailhache had only taken office a few months earlier, but he showed himself to be a strong supporter of victims of Nazism and the man who would lead the Island through a re-evaluation of the years of occupation. Bailhache spoke the words that so many former political prisoners, gathered for the occasion, had longed to hear. He began by acknowledging the unusualness of erecting a plaque in honour of inmates of a prison, but acknowledged the ambiguities during military occupation of acts which 'breached the petty regulations and edicts of an occupying force' which 'were not criminal in any real sense of the word':

> *The site beyond these forgotten walls hold hundreds if not thousands of stories of courage and resilience most of which will never now be told. But enough stories have been told to make it right and timely that the island should now honour those who protested against the rule of the invader and who defied, often at enormous personal risks, the occupying force. Many of the men and women who defied the invaders have subsequently gone on to serve their island in a variety of ways. ... We gather today to salute the courage of all those who defied the invaders and showed the sturdy spirit of independence which beats in every true Jersey heart. We salute them and we thank them for giving inspiration to those of us who follow.*[14]

While Bailhache had not dwelt on whether the local authorities should have done more to protect political prisoners from incarceration or deportation, his words bestowed honour and respect on them, effectively acknowledging – albeit in so many words – that political prisoners had behaved correctly.

Figure 7.2 Philip Bailhache unveiling the political prisoners' memorial 1995. Copyright: *Jersey Evening Post*

Whether or not Bailhache's words pleased other members of the Island's elite was irrelevant; he set the tone, by his example and his words, for a new era of Occupation memory and a new approach to dealing with the past. Bailhache was not the only 'game-changer' in Jersey that decade, but as Bailiff he was probably the most important one. The actions of game-changers like him were able to puncture holes effectively in the previously impervious membrane of Jersey's Occupation narrative to usher in a new era of memory – and it is here that the role of the incremental memory event comes into play.

The game-changers and their incremental memory events

Game-changers – those who have been able to successfully change the way that the Occupation is perceived and understood – have had to fight against a number of counter-forces in the form of people who supported older narratives which shielded many old taboos and prevented them from being breached. The successful game-changer has had to find a way to challenge these narratives amidst opposition and unpopularity.

In coming to understand how the taboo surrounding fully honouring victims of Nazism was broken in Jersey, it is necessary to explain why this memory is taboo. It is important to preface this with an appreciation of the nature of the small communities that exist in the Channel Islands. The Islands are, in general, conservative and law-abiding places, where those who put their heads above the parapet to speak out against the status quo or seriously criticize local government can quickly find themselves ostracized. To take the example of Guernsey, it has never been politically expedient for any politician to criticize the actions of the local administration during the German Occupation. Although not a polite topic of conversation, it is generally agreed (sotto voce) that Alexander Coutanche of Jersey acquitted himself better than his opposite number in Guernsey because of his age (forty-eight versus Victor Carey's sixty-nine at the start of the Occupation), associated energy, and vigilant stance (behind the scenes) in standing up to the occupiers. Despite this, Carey has been beyond local criticism. Even though Jews and political prisoners were deported on his watch, no politician has been able to encourage self-reflection of this period of Guernsey's history for one reason: because Victor Carey's grandson, Sir de Vic Carey, became Bailiff himself in 1999. Sir de Vic became an advocate of the Royal Court in 1966, a Deputy in the States of Guernsey (an elected representative of local parliament) from 1976, and has held high office in the Island from 1977 onwards, becoming Deputy Bailiff in 1992 and Lieutenant Bailiff in 2005, upon his retirement. This means that for a significant number of decades, no politician has taken it upon themselves, out of respect, to criticize the wartime record of Victor Carey while his grandson, born in 1940, is still a prominent person in the Island. This taboo was also confirmed to me by a former Bailiff of Jersey, who also explained that post-war Guernsey Bailiffs before Sir de Vic had close family links to the Occupation administration of the Island and similarly had little inclination to encourage examination of Occupation consciences.[15]

I have termed the Guernsey taboo, the 'Carey effect'. In 1990, when Carey held the position of HM Procureur (second only to the Deputy Bailiff, who himself is second to the Bailiff), the playwright Julia Pascal was refused a licence to perform her play *Theresa* in Guernsey on the grounds that it was 'inappropriate'. Based on the life of Austrian Jew Therese Steiner, who came to Guernsey in 1939, was deported in 1942 and subsequently died in Auschwitz, the play highlighted the role of collaboration in the deportation of the Island's Jews. Luckhurst declared this ban as an act of 'politically motivated censorship' because of the emphasis the play placed on the role of Victor Carey in the deportations.[16] Whether or not Luckhurst was correct in her assessment, this play provides an interesting litmus test for Guernsey forty-five years after the Island was liberated.

Apart from this incident, and until 2015, Guernsey had no incremental memory events comparable to those which took place in Jersey over the previous twenty-five years. It had no Bailiff or other agent of memory prepared to usher in a period of self-reflection or self-criticism and acknowledgement of the potential sins of the grandfathers. This was not the case in Jersey.

By 1995, at the time of the fiftieth anniversary of liberation, the Bailiff of Jersey was Philip Bailhache, as we have seen. Joe Mière was the first of many guardians of memory to ask Bailhache to unveil memorial plaques and make speeches about victims of Nazism once it was known that he had an interest in the subject and the cause was close to his heart. As well as the political prisoner memorial, he also unveiled the 1996 Lighthouse Memorial, which recalled the death of the 'Jersey 21' in Nazi prisons and concentration camps, as will be discussed later. Thus, this slow increase in the number of memorials and heritage to victims of Nazi persecution in Jersey has helped to modify the everyday reminders of the Occupation years among the Island's population. Such was Bailhache's role in this acknowledged change in the Island's war narrative during his period of office, that this phenomenon became known as the 'Bailhache effect'.

Yet how did Bailhache manage to achieve so much – and apparently so easily – in contrast to the lack of progress made in Guernsey in promoting the memory of the victims of Nazism? In order to understand this, we must examine the role of the 'incremental memory event' and the game-changers who successfully created or enabled these events. Rather than having the power, in its own right, to 'change how people remember, imagine, and talk about the past',[17] I argue that the incremental memory event acts instead to create punctures – smaller explosions – which can act to perforate previously impervious membranes of memory or taboo, thus facilitating the power of the eventual full memory event to create ruptures with previously accepted cultural meanings. In short, incremental memory events act to 'soften up' their intended (or unintended) audience and to render them more receptive to memory events when they occur. I argue that memory events cannot or do not always achieve their effect or reach their true potential if people are not ready or willing to accept them as such. One might counter that a true memory event cannot be labelled as such if it lacks such power or potential, but I do not contend that this is always the case. While the impact of a memory event can be delayed, not always achieving its full potential at the time of its explosion, it can create a small tear (rather than a full rupture) in memory, which can be widened, made larger, and generally taken advantage of by the successful agent or game-changer.

Between 1988 and 2001 there were a series of incremental memory events in Jersey which had no equivalent in Guernsey at that time. By the time that Bailhache's interventions took place from the mid-1990s onward, they were largely uncontroversial, and not just because he was the Bailiff. One of the first incremental memory events was the Anne Frank exhibition, which visited the Island in 1988 at the behest of Jersey Heritage Trust (today Jersey Heritage) and included a section on Jersey's Jews and Channel Islanders who were sent to concentration camps (i.e. the political prisoners). This was judged to be the most popular exhibition ever to come to the Island and was visited by over 15,000 Islanders. As these two groups of victims of Nazism were presented together, it set the stage – and created a precedent – for the later combination of these two groups both in the minds of Jersey people (including those at Jersey Heritage) and on HMD. Yet still at that time, local people did not understand what the Holocaust had to do with Jersey, because the Channel Islands Occupation Society (CIOS) had portrayed the Germans in Jersey as 'good Germans' and not Nazis.[18]

The year before the Anne Frank exhibition, Jersey Heritage Trust appointed non-Jerseyman Michael Day as its new director. Day was struck straight away by how the Occupation narrative in the Island excluded narratives of suffering or victims of Nazism. Instead, the CIOS had taken ownership of the history of the Occupation and their interest was mostly confined to bunker restoration and the collection of militaria. Day wanted to change the narrative and push back against the establishment. He was perceived as subversive from the start because of this.[19]

Michael Day was able to work together with his staff and a group of people in Jersey in the 1990s who were in a position of power or influence, or who had passion, conviction, wealth or specialist knowledge, and these people were able to work together in a way that, through a series of incremental memory events, achieved change. For example, when Jersey Heritage Trust wanted to create the Tapestry Gallery within the

Maritime Museum to house a twelve-panel tapestry telling the story of the Occupation, and which was to be unveiled in 1995, Philip Bailhache was supportive and enabled the money to come from the States of Jersey to fund it. Freddie Cohen, the leading member of Jersey's Jewish community, had an energy and passion to make things happen, and was also wealthy enough to endow and support projects. These included the sculpture of a slave worker at La Hougue Bie, a site in the Island that comprised an underground German bunker dug into the side of a Neolithic tomb. The bunker had previously been an Occupation museum filled with memorabilia and militaria, but Jersey Heritage Trust turned it into a memorial for forced labourers.

Cohen helped to support historian Paul Sanders to come to Jersey to carry out work on his book *The Ultimate Sacrifice*, which was published in 1998,[20] and which drew and built upon the carefully curated stories protected by Joe Mière during his career. Sanders' book was commissioned in response to Madeleine Bunting's 1995 book, *The Model Occupation*, which made allegations of collaboration. Sanders' book detailed the stories of those whose names were inscribed on the Lighthouse Memorial in 1996: the 'Jersey 22', now known as the 'Jersey 21' after one man, Walter Dauny was found, in 2013, to have survived Villeneuve-Saint-Georges Prison in Paris.[21] Sanders later wrote that his book

> *reshaped the outlook and remains a landmark for anyone interested in understanding the different facets of the Channel Islands Occupation. This status of historiographical game-changer – a status it shares with Freddie Cohen's book on the* Jews of the Channel Islands *– gives* The Ultimate Sacrifice *a special place among the hundreds of Occupation books that exist today. The people of Jersey have never forgotten that it came at a critical time, when the wartime record of the Islands was subject to exacting scrutiny and adverse media coverage in the UK. By providing the antidote to another emerging narrative, namely the subsumption of the Occupation experience under a collaboration label, the book persuaded Islanders to hold firm.*[22]

Sanders was referring to the book Cohen wrote following his discovery, in the mid-1990s, of a very detailed lost wartime file relating to the Island's Jews. When Madeleine Bunting's book was published at the same time, it prompted the 'adverse media coverage' referred to by Sanders. It is impossible to overstate the impact and outrage Bunting's book caused in the Channel Islands for its allegations of collaboration and downplaying of resistance. Perhaps it can be said to have caused something of a memory event in itself, but Guernsey's membrane remained impervious and her findings were rejected, denied and heavily criticized in both Islands. The subject of collaboration was (and is) highly taboo, and the book caused huge offence. It spurred Cohen to write an extended article for the *Journal of Holocaust Education* in 1997, which was later extended into a book in 2000, based on what he discovered in the archives. While Cohen felt that he had to be 'reasonably careful' about how he presented his data so as not to be tarred with the same brush that was used on Bunting, his aims were to present the historical data so that the documents would 'speak for themselves'.[23] The role of the book, he wrote, was 'not to make judgements, assign responsibilities or to draw final conclusions'; rather, it was 'to present the evidence now available … as a source of information'.[24]

The data which Cohen collected was influential and compelling, even shocking, and the publication of his work was certainly an incremental memory event in itself. It laid bare the role of the Islands' authorities for all to see, although the information surviving in Guernsey's archives was far less detailed. As both president of the Jewish community at that time and as an agent of memory and game-changer, Cohen organized a memorial service held at Jersey synagogue in 1998 in memory of the Jews who suffered in the Channel Islands. He revised the text of his journal paper for a volume to complement the service. The speakers included Sir Philip Bailhache, Sir Graham Dorey (then Bailiff of Guernsey); Jon Kay-Mouat, President of Alderney; and Lord Jakobovits, Emeritus Chief Rabbi, among others. Bailhache's presence was important because it constituted another visible act of leadership, and showed to other Islanders that he had given the event his blessing. The event was also important for forging links and raising the profile and status of the Jewish community with the Island's establishment.

Bailhache's involvement was considered to have been pivotal for the Island as his address was the first occasion on which the suffering of the Islands' Jews had been officially commemorated. Graham Dorey's speech was considered to have been brief and avoided any acknowledgement of culpability on the part of the Island's authorities. Although the speeches were later uploaded onto the Island's Occupation Memorial website (now defunct), Dorey had meanwhile 'lost his notes' and so the speech that he sent over months later was changed.[25] It, too, was brief and entirely avoided pointing the finger of blame. Instead it briefly summarized the deportation of Guernsey's Jews. While there were only 150 people at the synagogue service, the event was heavily reported in the *JEP* and so the service became 'pivotal in changing minds', as Cohen later put it to me.[26] Michael Day described the event as one of a 'series of things that gradually moved consciousness'[27] – in other words, an incremental memory event.

Although Cohen's was not the only book on the Jews of the Channel Islands to be published in 2000,[28] his work had already made its impact over the previous few years and was on sale locally. Cohen was also a local man and his book was thus more likely to be read by Islanders. It is worth noting that in order to make any sort of real or lasting impact, new books on the subject of the Occupation often have to be accompanied by public lectures by the author and associated heritage initiatives such as exhibitions or memorial erections. This is hard for an outsider to achieve. Without this, new research which might make an impact among the academic community in the UK will receive only passing comment or interviews in the local papers, at best, in the Channel Islands. Bunting's book was an exception, and her allegations provoked local reactions in the heritage sphere, although not straight away. While it is hard to attribute direct cause and effect between her book and later heritage to victims of Nazism in Jersey, indirect links can be observed such as with Paul Sanders' book and the Lighthouse Memorial. However, Bunting was simply one of several actors who encouraged change in the 1990s. Michael Day's directorship and Philip Bailhache's period of office as Bailiff were unconnected to her work, and Jersey was already on a new and more inclusive trajectory.[29]

In January 2000, the Blair government in the UK announced the creation of an annual HMD.[30] The Channel Islands adopted the initiative in time for the commemoration of the first HMD on 27 January 2001. In Jersey it seemed a natural association to combine commemoration of the suffering of Jews with that of the Jersey 21, because both were co-victims of Nazism and both had already been joint subjects of other heritage ventures such as the Anne Frank exhibition. The decision to combine the two groups had the blessing of leading members of the Jewish community, who were happy for the day not to be exclusively Jewish.[31]

The Lighthouse Memorial to the Jersey 21 was an obvious focus for wreath laying during Jersey's ceremony given that the two small Jewish memorials were in the Island's synagogue and the Jewish cemetery. The Lighthouse Memorial was not in a space 'owned' by any particular group, and it stood outside the Tapestry Gallery.

Both Guernsey and Jersey commemorated that first HMD with large crowds, and in Guernsey a small brass plaque was erected at the harbour in memory of the three deported Jewish women. Guernsey's interfaith ceremony was held in St James assembly hall in St Peter Port, but thereafter the event rapidly dwindled to become a small handful of people – sometimes less than a dozen – clustered around the Jewish plaque for a five-minute outdoor ceremony held by a clergyman, with no member of the Island's elite in attendance (Figure 7.3). It was almost to be the same in Jersey, where the event was planned as a one-off, but many people were keen to continue the event. Bailhache was invited to speak in 2002, Jersey Heritage Trust supported the event, and an HMD committee was put together. Since then, the Lieutenant-Governor, the Bailiff, politicians and community leaders have attended, and the event has succeeded in attracting large crowds who fill the Tapestry Gallery of the Island's maritime museum in St Helier.

The Occupation Tapestry was inspired by the Overlord Tapestry in Portsmouth and the Bayeux Tapestry. It was created under the aegis of Michael Day, unveiled in 1995, and moved into the Tapestry Gallery in 1997. It tells the story of the German Occupation in twelve panels and includes depictions of victims of Nazism in the form of forced and slave workers, and Canon Clifford Cohu, an Islander who died in a concentration camp. The tapestry itself neglects the subject of the Jews, but the associated information panel recognizes this group. It is perceived today to have been a product of its time, that is, made at a time before victims of Nazism were part of the mainstream Occupation narrative.

In 2015 a thirteenth tapestry panel was commissioned, both as part of the seventieth anniversary of liberation celebrations, and as a way of recognizing the changes in Occupation memory and advances in research since the tapestry's unveiling in 1995. The content of the new panel was conceptualized by the author, and honours those men and women who have acted as agents or guardians of memory in the field of heritage in Jersey, especially those who have brought about incremental memory events in relation to the Island's victims of the Holocaust. The tapestry features Philip Bailhache, Joe Mière, Harold Le Druillenec, former political prisoners, deportees and slave and forced workers, watching over the memorials that they instigated.

The HMD ceremony in Jersey today includes a guest speaker, speeches from leading members of the community, the involvement with the local youth theatre, and ends with floral wreaths being laid on the Lighthouse Memorial by community leaders ranging from the Lieutenant-Governor, the Bailiff, the Constables[32] of the Island's parishes, the Island's Dean and other local elites.

Figure 7.3 Jewish Memorial in Guernsey after the brief HMD ceremony in 2012. The single small basket of flowers reflects the size of the crowd. Copyright: Gilly Carr

As we can see, Jersey positively reverberated with incremental memory events in the closing decade of the twentieth century, most of them safely ushered in by Philip Bailhache during this period as Bailiff, and only a few of which have been recounted here. Now in the twenty-first century, Jersey is in a position to look back at what it has achieved in overcoming its old taboos. There have been no parallels in Guernsey. It is likely that Bailhache would not have been quite so successful in his endeavours as an instigator or agent of memory had he not been Bailiff, thus revealing the clear relationship between memory and power in the Channel Islands. The office of Bailiff is held in high regard by Islanders and is rarely criticized. A lowlier person, such as a member of the public with no public office or recognized authority, would probably have been largely ignored. As it is, the game-changers of the 1990s – men such as Bailhache, aided by Day, Cohen, Sanders and others,[33] and even Joe Mière and his activism – punctured many holes in the membrane of memory and the taboo against invoking the Holocaust. They provoked, instigated or supported so many heritage initiatives related to victims of Nazism that, combined, they and their endeavours ushered in an acceptance and embrace of the Island's multiple victims of Nazism. The true memory event has taken place, but which of the incremental memory events achieved it would be hard to pinpoint. Cumulatively, they have done their work and the game has changed.

Guernsey had no parallel events at this time – or rather, it rejected any of the elements which might have had the power to disturb or puncture the status quo, such as Bunting's book. It has had no Bailiff or game-changers prepared to usher in a period of self-reflection and self-criticism, nor someone who has attempted to turn the tide.

In Jersey, the game-changers were able to take the baton – and the wealth of research – directly from the original guardians of memory and effectively continue their struggle. While the game-changers were in a position of authority or power and able to carry out this work, the guardians of memory usually were not. In Jersey, many such guardians were blessed with a longevity that carried them into the twenty-first century, endowing them with respectability as 'grand old men of the Occupation'. Joe Mière, for example, lived until 2006, witnessing many of the changes in Occupation memory in his Island. In Guernsey, Frank Falla died in 1983, and he was one of the last of his gang of 'Frankfurt-Naumburg Crooks'. He passed away almost twenty years before the beginning of HMD in Guernsey, and more than thirty years before the incremental memory event of HMD 70. The political climate of Guernsey has not yet been, since the end of the Occupation, one that has been conducive to the emergence of game-changers.

Social media and HMD 70 in the Channel Islands

By the year before the seventieth anniversary of liberation, and following the trail left behind in Frank Falla's personal archive, I had extracted from the Foreign Office archives around 100 Nazi persecution compensation claim testimonies written by Channel Islanders, and had given a number of public lectures in the Islands about them. I was thus asked to give the invited speech at Jersey's morning HMD 70 service. I also collaborated with the organizer of Guernsey's HMD service, local politician Deputy Elis Bebb, a Welshman who came to the Island in the mid-1990s, to make the evening event in the sister Island a success. I was interested to see whether I, as an outsider, could become a game-changer, using the reputation I had built up in the Islands over (at that point) eight years of heritage- and memory-related fieldwork. My strategy, inspired by Jersey's HMD, was to supplement the focus on the Jews (who had been given five minutes of attention a year since 2001 at the annual short ceremony in Guernsey) with the co-sufferers of Nazi persecution, the political prisoners (who were never spoken about). Specifically, the aim in 2015 was to see whether reading the personal testimonies of *other* Islanders in concentration camps could be used as a game-changing memory event. The experiences of Guernsey's Jews in concentration camps were not available because none of them survived.

A week before HMD, Elis Bebb had tweeted to advertise the HMD service and had contributed to an article on 21 January 2015 for the *Guernsey Press* where he spoke about how 'the [local] authorities were responsible [for the deportation of three Jewish women] and therefore it's important that, as a community, we commemorate and remember that'. Later, in the blog on his website, Bebb wrote that

> we in Guernsey deported the three Jewish women ... who were eventually murdered in Auschwitz ... we actively participated in the Holocaust ... the actions of the authorities in passing the anti-Semitic orders and those of the police in handing over people for deportation can only, in my opinion, be viewed as complicit.[34]

Bebb had felt compelled to speak out because, as he wrote in the same blog article, he perceived (as Michael Day had in Jersey) that the 'public narrative [of the Occupation] has become too narrow'. In short, Bebb had felt the power of the taboo in force in Guernsey and had tried to speak out against it by publicly pressing that most sensitive of buttons: a discussion of collaboration in the matter of the deportation of the Jews. His only saving grace was that he had not mentioned Carey; instead he used the word 'we' in discussing responsibility. The social media backlash was swift, violent in its intensity and led on Facebook by a local taxi driver, Neil Inder (who we shall meet again later), who posted on various Facebook groups to complain that Bebb was 'being offensive', that his comments were 'a sleight [sic] to all of those who endured the Occupation', and that he was calling the people of Guernsey 'Nazi sympathizers'. Hundreds of people commented on Facebook, encouraged by interspersions by Inder, who added comments such as:

> What Bebb is suggesting is that 'we' as in 'all' Guernsey people under Occupation actively participated and contributed to the Holocaust. Anyone with an Occupation history – we all have them – evacuated, starved, fought and died, should find wholly offensive.[35]

Inder and other Islanders called (without a trace of irony) for Bebb to be removed from his position and deported. Popular opinion was in full support of the local authorities who 'did their best' during the Occupation. They rejected the notion that 'Guernsey participated in the Holocaust', believed that the subject did 'not need to be investigated' and that unless Bebb was there at the time, he had no right to judge. There were a few dissenting voices, although they were silenced by the majority. Inder then filed a 'Code of Conduct' in the Royal Court against Bebb a couple of days later. The Code regulates the 'duties, standards, propriety and conduct, in public life', of the Deputies of the Royal Court[36] and Inder felt that Ebb had breached it. Inder's complaint was rejected on the grounds that it was not a function of the Code of Conduct Panel to be the arbiter between people who happen to hold strongly different opinions. The panel effectively sidestepped the risk of being sucked into historical discussions of taboo subjects.

This vitriolic exchange highlighted to me not only the strength of the 'Carey effect', which prevented Bailiffs and others in high office from speaking out, but the strength of the taboo which unwitting non-local Islanders could stumble into (even if they had joined the elite of local government), and which Islanders from all walks of life would take swift and strong measures to uphold. The impermeable membrane of memory in Guernsey was tougher than I imaged and, having collaborated with Bebb in the organization of the HMD service, we both wondered whether anyone would attend, or whether the church would be boycotted and picketed by Islanders holding placards. Not only had the incremental memory events in Jersey (including the publication of Freddie Cohen's authoritative book on the Jews of the Channel Islands) had no impact at all in Guernsey, where Facebook comments suggested that nobody had read it,[37] but I realized that forcing or creating an incremental memory event was going to be very difficult indeed.

On 27 January I delivered my speech about the experience of Channel Islanders in Nazi prisons and concentration camps at the HMD 70 ceremony in Jersey. Discussions with a number of people indicated that they were watching the social media row (which had spilled over into the local paper and radio) in their sister Island with a mixture of disbelief and amusement. Having passed through this phase twenty years earlier in discussing Occupation wrongdoings, they hoped that this incident would help Guernsey go through the same process.

On 27 January 2015, to my relief, the town church in Guernsey was filled to capacity. In the event, and for the first time, many more people attended the HMD service in Guernsey than in Jersey; even the Bailiff and Chief Minister were there. Last to arrive was Sir de Vic Carey, who made his way to the back of the church before the current Bailiff, Sir Richard Collas, invited him to sit at the front, next to him.

During the service, three children and one grandchild of local men who had experienced Nazi camps as political prisoners read out the testimonies written by their family member fifty years earlier (Figure 7.4). The effect was electrifying, and the gasps and shocked silence in the church made it clear that this was entirely new to Islanders. By the end, it appeared that Deputy Bebb had silenced his detractors.

The following day, the social media sites, which had been so full of bile just a day previously, fell silent. The *Guernsey Press* gave the event full coverage, and showed a picture of Paul Domaille giving the testimony of his father's death march towards

Figure 7.4 Peter Symes reading out his father's testimony about Buchenwald, HMD 2015, Guernsey. Copyright: Gilly Carr

Dachau. It seemed that those on social media had been outvoted by other Islanders, and the testimonies had brought home to people just one of the ways in which people in Guernsey, specifically political prisoners, had been co-victims of Nazi persecution and co-witnesses to the Holocaust.

Indeed, as the whole topic was still so sensitive, the process of changing narratives would inevitably be a long one, with the door being pushed open a little at a time. Had Bebb and I taken HMD 70 as an opportunity to talk only about the wrongdoing of the local authorities in not standing up for Jews and political prisoners, then this might not have received such a positive reception. We judged that it was important to make the evening ceremony a regular one before we tried to achieve all of our aims in a single evening only to have the event cancelled.

On 31 January, my full-page article entitled '*The night the Holocaust came home*' was published in the *Guernsey Press*. In it, I discussed how the Holocaust affected the Island; how Channel Islanders had experienced some of the darkest and most evil concentration camps; and how the toxic social media debate had revealed that the best legacy that HMD 70 could leave the Island would be 'education of the young and the provision of accurate and locally-meaningful teaching materials'.

But had a puncture mark been made in Guernsey's membrane of memory? One way to tell was to try to repeat the experiment at HMD in 2016 to see whether there could be a new status quo, or whether the situation would continue to be fraught for a few bumpy years. As HMD 2016 loomed on the horizon, I argued strongly to Elis Bebb that we should attempt to repeat the 2015 formula exactly so that the church service would begin to be seen as a 'tradition', replacing the five-minute widely ignored outdoor ceremony. This was especially important given the presence of the Holocaust memorial 'Requête' or bill which was currently coming up for debate in the local parliament, the States of Guernsey.

Elis Bebb had drawn up a Requête, signed by six other Members of the States, which made six statements, including that Guernsey should officially recognize Holocaust Remembrance Day (with the associated implications that States Members would not be requested in the Chamber at the time of the HMD lunchtime ceremony at the Jewish memorial). It also stated that Holocaust education should begin in schools; and that

> *for the avoidance of doubt, the Holocaust is recognised in Guernsey as the persecution and murder of all by the hands and policies of the Nazi forces of the Second World War, including the Guernsey Eight, the three Jewish women deported to Auschwitz-Birkenau and those who died building the Atlantic Wall.*[38]

The decision to include victim groups beyond the Jews in the local definition of the Holocaust was made by Bebb, and was threefold and political. First, Jersey remembers its political prisoners who died in prisons and camps as co-victims on HMD, which set an important and successful precedent. Second, to remember all local victims of Nazi persecution is arguably not an inappropriate endeavour for HMD because no other day in the local calendar presents itself as an obvious candidate for remembering this group. This argument is often made in the Channel Islands, and has led to more victims of Nazism receiving recognition when before there was none. Third, as the incorporation of this group had been such a successful part of HMD in 2015 – in fact, had been the highlight of the service – it seemed at that moment in time sensible and important to make it an official Resolution of the States of Guernsey[39] as a way of starting to wedge open (through public speeches) the tightly closed door of taboo on the wider subject of the Holocaust.

Thus, the inaccurate definition of the Holocaust remained in the Requête; it was signed on 17 November 2015 and became a States Resolution on 19 February 2016. Of course, to have an inaccurate definition of the Holocaust passed as a Resolution is not without serious problems, but there will likely be an opportunity to remedy this in time. However, for the time being it was arguably more important to press the local government to act on the other five statements in the new Resolution, such as beginning Holocaust education in schools, joining IHRA (with its associated injunction to open closed Holocaust-related archives), and to appropriately recognize HMD.

Thus, as HMD 2016 drew near, I volunteered my services to give a public speech from the pulpit – a feature not used the year before but, I felt, a good opportunity to press forward with the gains already made and to facilitate future public speeches on difficult topics by others – perhaps, one day, a future Bailiff.

What was my motivation for getting involved? Why should I, as an outsider, even take an interest, let alone try to influence memory culture in the Island? Self-reflection on this matter was important, and I was not the only one who asked myself these questions. As one of the very few academics in Europe who specialize in the German Occupation of the Channel Islands, with a particular interest in victims of Nazism, and as somebody with Guernsey heritage, I already had a legitimate interest in the subject. I was also very aware of the unbalanced and inaccurate popular perception of the Channel Islands in the UK as 'collaborators'. I had also read the various newspaper articles and popular accounts which criticized Guernsey for its insufficient inclusion of victims of Nazism within its narrative. My own previous research had also drawn the same conclusions.[40] I therefore wished to use my own expertise to help the Island develop a more plural memorial landscape and culture, with its knock-on effect upon the Occupation narrative.

The HMD 2016 service was perhaps more audacious than 2015 on several counts. Only as I climbed its steps did I realize that a woman speaking from the pulpit might be an unusual sight in this conservative Island. Neither was my speech meek; it fitted the HMD Trust's 2016 theme of 'Don't stand by'. Speaking about bystanders and those who did not intervene to prevent the deportation of the Jews and political prisoners, I praised the political prisoners as people who had done the right thing in standing up to the Nazis, but who had paid for their bravery with, in some cases, their lives. I also subsequently published the speech as an article in the Guernsey Press to drive the message home. I wanted people to acknowledge that this group were not the 'stupid criminals' that they had been labelled during the Occupation by the local authorities, but as brave and right-thinking men and women. The audacity of a woman – and an outsider at that – in delivering such a message from a pulpit can best be reflected not in words, but in the faces and body language of the clergymen of the Island sitting below the pulpit (Figure 7.5). I had clearly said what more cautious heads in Guernsey would not have – and had never – done, but I knew that I was playing to at least a small and

Figure 7.5 The author speaking at HMD in Guernsey in 2016. Copyright: Gilly Carr

appreciative section of the gallery, as some of the previous year's speakers – children of victims of Nazism – were there, and another row of them were due to speak during this year's service.

However, if I had been audacious in choosing to speak so plainly from the pulpit, I had not realized the problems that two of the other speakers were to cause: the children of Charles Friend and Frank Tuck, two of the sixteen Guernsey policemen deported in the summer of 1942 to a series of Nazi prisons, tortuous labour camps and concentration camps. As these men were tried by the Royal Court as well as by German tribunal, they represented yet another example of the failure of local government to protect its citizens.

Thus, to invite these men's children to speak about the horrors that their fathers faced was courting controversy, but I thought that it was right that the congregation should hear their testimony. That this would be an uphill struggle had already been brought home to me by the problems that emerged during the brief lunchtime outdoor ceremony by the Jewish memorial. Now that the Resistance Memorial had been unveiled the previous May, I was anxious (as were several people in the crowd) that the memorial, which stood next to the Jewish memorial, be incorporated into the ceremony so that wreaths could be laid at both locations.

While in January 2015 I had written to the Dean (who officiated at the short ceremony) to ask him to read out the names of the Guernsey Eight, in 2016 their memorial was there now as a visual reminder. After the ceremony, which acknowledged those listed on both the Jewish Memorial and (after interventions were made from the crowd) the Resistance Memorial, Angela McAllister, daughter of Frank Tuck, was interviewed by the Guernsey Press and was photographed holding flowers that she was laying by the memorial in memory of her father. This photo was chosen by the newspaper to accompany their coverage of HMD.

I later learnt that this did not go down well with certain factions of the community. The CIOS, who have local political and social leverage due to the dominant place of the German Occupation in local identity construction, were not happy that Angela McAllister had been chosen to represent the image of HMD in the Island that year. The CIOS see themselves as the guardians of Occupation memory, and are not of the opinion that the memory of the Guernsey policemen should be rehabilitated. Such was their unhappiness with the situation, about which they had been briefed in advance through sight of a draft of the order of service for the HMD evening programme, that they had decided to boycott the evening service altogether. Although Elis Bebb had invited their president to do a reading at the service about collaboration in the registration of antisemitic Orders, this was turned down. The official reason given was that they felt that the Jewish experience of the HMD service had been omitted. This, of course, was not so; other victims of Nazism had simply been added.

The following day the real issue was made clear to me. In what started as a conversation with a member of the CIOS about a Resistance Trail that I was designing for the Island (discussed in the next chapter), the topic quickly changed. I was told that the Occupation had already been written about and that they, the CIOS, were the experts and not me. I was told to stop trying to change things. I was also informed that that the CIOS had not attended the church service because the children of two of the Guernsey police were speaking, which was not deemed to be acceptable as the men were 'not heroes' and that they had 'shamed the Island'. The actions of the Royal Court in convicting rather than protecting these men were deemed to be wholly correct.

What I had up until that point perceived to be the 'Carey effect' in Guernsey was now revealed to be the 'CIOS effect' as well, whereby the current narrative of Occupation, which does not dwell on victims of Nazism, was safeguarded by this influential historical society. It wasn't necessarily that they were against victims of Nazism; it was just that this was not the narrative on which they had preferred to dwell over the last fifty years since the society was founded. Further, there were certain other clear problems with me being the one who was challenging this. I was an outsider (despite my mother coming from Guernsey) and, unlike many of the members of the CIOS, who are mostly older men, I was the wrong sex and age group. These were all clear violations of the status quo: the narrative was being challenged, and by the wrong sort of person.

Following this interaction, I fully intended to encourage Elis Bebb to press ahead in 2017 with the same formula for the evening church service. While Elis would organize the interfaith music, prayers, hymns, poetry and choir, I would source the speakers to give testimonies of their family member's experience in Nazi prisons and camps.

Meanwhile, at the end of November 2016, BBC Guernsey published a story about how I was working on Holocaust educational materials for the Channel Islands.[41] Within a couple of weeks, *The Times* newspaper picked up the story and published an inaccurate reported article, with quotes taken out of context, announcing how Guernsey was finally opening up '*about its Nazi past*'.[42] This caused another minor furore in the Island and, as Elis Bebb and I had been discussed in the article, we were embroiled. Another round of toxic social media debate commenced, with rhetoric not dissimilar to that which had taken place the year before, and this time more local politicians became involved. I wrote another article to the *Guernsey Press* to explain precisely what was planned for local Holocaust education to help calm fears.⁴³

The online discussions lasted until HMD 2017. However, after several months of preparation for the event by Elis Bebb, with speakers lined up to give testimonies, and with just a week or two before HMD, Elis was contacted by the Dean of Guernsey. He would now be organizing the service and apparently had not been aware of Elis's work behind the scenes, despite the fact that he had organized it for the last two years.

Nonetheless, Elis and I both attended the lunchtime and evening ceremonies to see for ourselves what was planned. Now that the Holocaust Requête had been passed, we also wanted to see who turned up at the ceremonies. We expected to see the full complement of States Members at the Jewish memorial lunchtime ceremony. Having decided not to stand for re-election, Elis was now a former Member of the States, but recognized just six of his former colleagues at the ceremony. However, for the first time the brief lunchtime ceremony saw the attendance of some local elites, including the Bailiff and the Constable of St Peter Port, who both laid wreaths. There were around forty people in attendance, which was more than normal, even though the weather was foul.

The brief ceremony took place with people clustered in front of the Jewish memorial as usual, but after the Dean invited wreaths to be laid, relatives of one of the Guernsey Eight pointedly laid a wreath at the neighbouring Resistance Memorial instead, to which the Dean had his back turned at that moment. After the Dean read out the names of the three deported Jewish women, the same relatives called out, 'And will you read out the names of the Guernsey people deported?' The Dean assured them that this was his intention, and after doing so he also surprisingly moved on to the nearby Deportees Memorial. The deportees were those English-born Islanders sent to civilian internment camps in September 1942 and February 1943 and are not connected with the Holocaust; nor had they been included in the victim groups mentioned in the Holocaust Requête. Yet, one of the States Members had been born in one of these internment camps and was quite possibly the instigator of the Dean including this group in his ceremony.

That evening, only a single States Member (besides the Bailiff) was seen at the service. The Dean's service lasted for only twenty minutes and he stayed at the lectern throughout. The only other speaker was the daughter of a deported British Jew who I had asked to speak. Rather than the choir and live music organized by Bebb, the Dean played recorded music, and the tape unfortunately got tangled up in the machine half way through, which adversely impacted the solemnity of the event.

Before the congregation (reduced to around fifty to sixty people) dispersed, a prominent member of the CIOS emphasized to the Dean and Bailiff how much better it would be in future years just to have an outdoor lunchtime ceremony in future, with no evening service. The service, after all, was the site of contestation, when un-vetted speeches might be given, and testimonies might be read out which challenged current narratives.

It seemed as if a coup had been staged to exclude me and Bebb. Bebb was later given to understand that 'some of what was emphasised' in the service in 2016 had caused 'displeasure' at a high level, and the service had been perceived to be too long. Whether the offending emphasis in 2016 was my speech which defended acts of anti-Nazi resistance, or the testimonies which challenged the status quo, or the focus given to children of two of the Guernsey policemen (which highlighted their conviction by the Royal Court), was unspecified.

Barely a year after the Holocaust Requête was passed, HMD in Guernsey in 2017 appeared to have taken several steps backwards. Bebb expressed doubt that his Requête would have been passed now, one year on, given the change in local politicians since the last election and the inclusion of more right-wing people. Much to my own surprise, the taxi driver who had expressed such bile on social media in 2015 towards Bebb, and shown such ignorance on the Holocaust, had been among those newly elected.

And yet, what would the future hold for HMD in Guernsey? If the evening service was to be disbanded altogether, then the Island might return to the five-minute outdoor gathering by the Jewish memorial, with all that this entailed in terms of silent wreath laying and prayers but no public speeches with the opportunities that they provided for soul-searching and introducing new elements into the narrative. If this were to happen, there was a real danger that the holes punched into the membrane of memory over the previous three years could close up and fade in memory, thus revealing incremental memory events to be potentially temporary rather than permanent. It seemed clear that any activism in this area must be patient and satisfied with small gains, with a view to providing fertile ground for later actions. If too much is demanded too soon, then events can be cancelled and opportunities for progress can be denied, regardless of new political resolutions.

In mid-2017, more than once the Holocaust Memorial Day Trust (HMDT) tried to contact the Dean and Bailiff's office to offer their help and guidance in forming an HMD committee and structuring a commemorative ceremony. This offer was not taken up. In the autumn, the Dean wrote to the Bailiff to suggest a meeting to discuss how HMD might be commemorated in future. Bebb was invited to the meeting, which finally took place in December, by which point it was decided that it was too late to organize a service for 2018, although plans for later years were discussed.[44]

In the event, the only ceremony that took place in 2018 was an outdoor lunchtime one by the memorials, and not in the church. A smattering of local politicians attended, with around fifty-five members of the public; the Dean led the ceremony. The Bailiff laid wreaths at the forced worker memorial, the Jewish Memorial and the Resistance Memorial, in accordance with the spirit of the States Holocaust Resolution. The CIOS laid a wreath only at the Jewish Memorial, but not at the Resistance Memorial; however, a number of resistance families came forward to furnish this memorial with more bouquets and wreaths than the others received. Although the Bailiff did not speak, the Dean spoke the following words at the Resistance Memorial:

During the Occupation, many Guernsey people demonstrated great courage and bravery and generosity, not least to the forced labourers and even to the German soldiers in the latter days of the Occupation, and perhaps none demonstrated greater courage than those known as the Guernsey Eight, who are commemorated here and whom we remember today because they were willing to stand up to the forces who were capable of the genocide that we know as the Holocaust. ... Some of these people came to the notice of the occupying forces through acts of betrayal ... Profound thanksgiving for their bravery and their courage, we keep silence to remember the Guernsey Eight.[45]

This slightly odd speech did not pay homage to *all* those who committed acts of protest, defiance and resistance (as per the memorial text), and named only the Guernsey Eight and those who were 'generous' to the forced labourers. The invocation of 'generosity to the German soldiers' seemed reminiscent of the 'good Germans' (as opposed to Nazis) who were supposed to have been the only kind of soldier of occupation in the Channel Islands.

But what would be the lasting impact of the events of HMD 2015 to 2018? Would any of them prove to be permanent incremental memory events? Certainly the presence of the 2015 Resistance Memorial and the passing of the Holocaust Requête made a difference. This new States Resolution requires HMD to be marked in collaboration with the HMDT, even if this still has yet to take place. If this is to mean anything at all, then it suggests a theme to the ceremony which should be addressed, and hopefully discussed in schools and local media as part of Holocaust education. The presence of resistance families at the ceremony, and their flowers at the memorial, suggests a new consciousness and pride in the heritage of their families – one that can find public expression without public opprobrium.

Guernsey is also now in a place where the Bailiff lays wreaths at the memorials to three victims groups of Nazi persecution. Even if the Bailiff does not give speeches at such events, his presence, and that of other members of the political elite and religious elite, signals a new respect being bestowed upon the victims. While the Dean's words did not address issues of culpability, or whether resisters or the local authorities did the right thing, the actions of the resisters were described as 'brave' and 'courageous'. This marks a departure from older parlance which used words such as 'stupid' and 'criminal'. Progress has indeed been made, but there is still further to go.

Sometimes public speeches by those in authority are not needed for the implied criticism of wartime activity to be voiced. Sir de Vic Carey was invited in April 2015 to give a public lecture about his late grandfather. He has long been notoriously reticent about speaking about his grandfather, but was persuaded to *'put the record straight'* as the *Guernsey Press* put it afterwards, in an article on 1 May 2015. In the lecture, he complained the Victor Carey had been *'badly treated by posterity'* and stated that he regretted *'the ongoing negativity and criticism of those who were doing their honest best for the island's people ...'* Sir de Vic was, it seems, commenting on the furore of three months earlier, even though nobody had criticized his grandfather by name.

There is thus reason to be hopeful that even if these years of HMD services are to prove but temporary, they took place at a time of other changes which are more permanent, both in the memorial landscape and in local legislation and education. These cannot help but have an impact, if only on the school-age children in the Island.

Conclusion

The number of incremental memory events in Jersey over the last twenty to twenty-five years has resulted in an island that is now comfortable in its own skin. The pre-existing taboos were broken during Bailhache's period of office as Bailiff and in the years immediately before. In 2010, this Island was even involved in putting forward successfully the names of four Islanders for the British 'Hero of the Holocaust' award.[46] A further candidate from Jersey was given the award in 2018 after the submission of her case by the author.[47]

Guernsey, on the other hand, has lacked similar incremental memory events until much more recently, and has shown itself to have acquired a largely impervious – even self-healing – membrane of memory when it comes to historical taboos. We may still have witnessed several incremental memory events over this period; small explosions which may have succeeded in making some small yet significant punctures in that tough membrane. Now that the event has begun to be endorsed by public elites, the desired longer-term impact may have begun to be achieved, although it is perhaps too soon to tell. The question remains of whether a place has truly come to terms with its past if it does not verbally address its earlier deeds or misdeeds, but instead lays wreaths to the victims. It surely signals a beginning of that process.

Thus, we may not always identify an incremental memory event when we see it; it may be that only a sustained and ongoing attack on tightly held taboos will reveal itself to have been successful in the long run. Perhaps we might better understand some of these events as 'delayed memory events'; sometimes the reverberations take time to fully play out.

I once thought that the final incremental memory event which causes the large tear along the perforations of the memory membrane in Guernsey would be the moment when Victory Carey's grandson departs the stage. However, I now recognize the additional strength of both the 'CIOS effect' and public feeling. It seems clear that there are now three ways open for the future in terms of Guernsey's memory of the Holocaust. Either the would-be game-changers admit that it is still too soon after the Occupation to hope for public discussion on the subject, or they continue to fight in the current fashion (or in a more low-key manner) on HMD, facing annual battles which attempt to pave the way for public speeches and the facilitation of activism – even future elite activism in the vein of Sir Philip Bailhache. It is beginning to appear, however, that neither of these waiting games will give rise to desired result in the near future. The third way forward is now enshrined in the Holocaust Requête: Holocaust education in schools. If the second and third generation are resistant to change and still protective of their grandparents' experience, there is potential for the fourth generation and beyond, who have yet to build their own membrane of memory or to decide for themselves the legitimacy of the actions of victims of Nazi persecution.

In the final chapter I examine the potential for the scattered legacies of victims of Nazi persecution to be turned into a fragmented heritage which can be brought together in formats such as digital heritage. When brought together for the first time, can such interventions in the heritage arena provide effective incremental memory events? Through proposing the concepts of 'reparative heritage' and 'acts of rescue', this chapter asks whether such heritage can raise awareness, especially through social media, to establish a new baseline of legitimacy for victims of Nazi persecution.

8

Acts of Repair, Acts of Rescue

Scattered legacies and fragmented heritages

After an event such as a war or military occupation, a legacy can be left behind in many forms. These include traumatic memories, a swathe of military debris, abandoned forts, bunkers or military strongholds, commandeered prisons, labour camps, the material culture of occupation, and destroyed buildings, to name just a few. All of these kinds of legacies can be found in the Channel Islands today. Some are visible and able to be visited as tourist sites. Others have been metaphorically or literally buried beneath the soil for over seventy years. But how can legacies such as these be mobilized to form heritage?

The diagram below (Figure 8.1) helps us to conceptualize how post-conflict heritage is formed from the multiple legacies of military occupation.[1] These legacies need some form of intervention to turn them into heritage; it is not a process that happens automatically by dint of each legacy lasting in various forms into the present. Examples of intervention include collecting traumatic memories and creating memorials or museum exhibitions that honour those who suffered; the excavation of the remains of labour camps by archaeologists; and the restoration of former political prisons, which can be opened to the public. The legacies chosen for such heritage intervention strategies are directly linked to a place's war narrative. The resulting heritage both proclaims and reinforces the story that a community tells about itself and its past, and facilitates the transmission of that narrative to the next generation.

But how easy is it to turn a legacy into heritage? Heritage is rarely created for those deemed unworthy to receive it. If a person or group is deemed to have acted wrongly or illegitimately, or to have brought a place into disrepute, then a memorial or museum exhibition in their honour will be a long time in coming. Indeed, they will often need to wait until perceptions have changed. That waiting period can last a very long time, and sometimes a helping hand is necessary. But how long is long enough, and how can we test the water to see if a community is ready to reassess past perceptions?

This chapter examines my own attempts to contribute to commemoration of victims of Nazism by creating fragmented heritages from their scattered legacies. It is driven by the central questions of whether and how such interventions in the heritage arena can be effective. While the previous chapter examined the headway made in legitimizing the narrative of victims of Nazism on consecutive HMDs in Guernsey

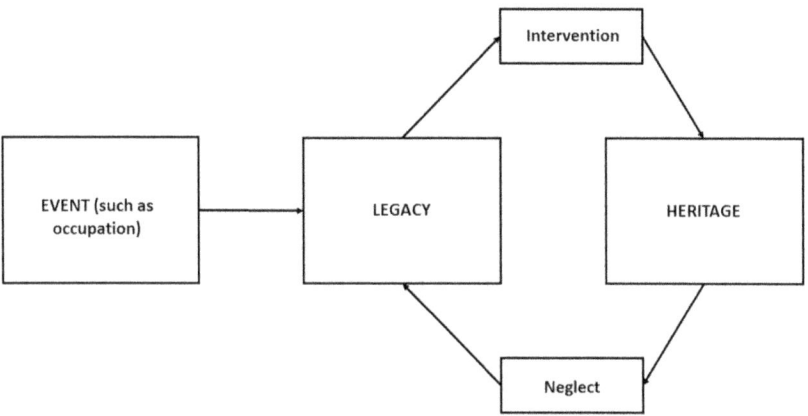

Figure 8.1 Diagram to show the relationship between an event, its legacy and its heritage. Copyright: Gilly Carr

using the concept of the incremental memory event, this chapter brings together other interventions made in the heritage arena. Three examples will be discussed of scattered legacies brought together to attempt to augment the heritage landscape. The first case study concerns the Resistance Memorial in St Peter Port. Proposing the concept of 'reparative heritage' for this memorial, I examine its role in legitimating the reputation of those it promotes. The second example explores the impact of digital heritage and the 'acts of rescue' that it performs. I examine how this format provides a platform not only for collating scattered legacies (with the implications of facilitating easier interventions into the heritage landscape), but also for the restoration of the public memory of a generation now gone, and the dissemination of information for educating the next generation. The third example concerns the creation of heritage products especially suited to fragmented heritages: the heritage trail. Resistance trails were created for the capital towns of both Guernsey and Jersey, and I discuss the difficulties encountered in each case. To a certain extent each of the case studies presented here overlaps, as we will see: each of them – and the publicity surrounding them – deals with rehabilitation of memory through the legitimation of victims of Nazism.

Reparative heritage

In 2012, two colleagues and I were in the Channel Islands to carry out research for our book on resistance during the German Occupation.[2] At that time there were no memorials in Guernsey to those who carried out any such acts, unlike in Jersey. It did not escape our notice that Guernsey also lacked any guardians of memory who might have made it their business to campaign for memorials. Although the children of resisters were individually interested in seeing such public recognition for their family members, there had been no collective action on their part towards this aim.

Having received Frank Falla's extensive resistance archive in 2010 from his daughter, and having successfully brought to fruition our book on resistance in 2014, I wondered whether I, personally, could pick up Falla's baton (given that neither of his children were interested in that role) and become a memory activist or game-changer. Although my family is from Guernsey, I have never lived there, and neither was my family involved in resistance activities during the Occupation. However, just as there are those who aspire to be memory activists, rescuing stories from oblivion and promoting them as part of a respect for the dead and the causes for which they died, so there are also counter-forces. Such persons or groups can counteract the work of the memory activist either through obstruction (deliberate or otherwise) or through promoting or amplifying different narratives. Such different narratives are, in Guernsey, still mainstream and of long duration.

After more than a decade of research into the German Occupation and its victims of Nazism, I wanted to offer my expertise and time to gauge whether the resistance families wanted recognition and, if so, in what form, and to liaise with heritage authorities to see whether they were receptive to heritage initiatives. If so, what initiatives were possible?

Resistance legacies that have not been chosen for heritage incorporation, in places where nobody has disturbed them for many generations, tend not to sit patiently waiting to be noticed in dark corners of archives and museum storerooms. Indeed, after many decades of neglect, we must augment our language. From simply 'intervening' in pre-existing legacies, we must begin to speak of 'saving' them, because these legacies often become lost, scattered and forgotten. Often, because that legacy has not been seen as important for speaking about the experiences of the community or their identity, it survives only in the memories of those who experienced it. After this generation dies, the legacy is often lost. It does not survive as a neatly arranged and collated 'thing', ready for researchers to pick up and turn into a museum exhibition. Thus, our conceptualization of the link between an event and its legacy indicated above begins to look both idealistic and unrealistic after several generations of being ignored or silenced. Any heritage intervention thus becomes harder to achieve and results in fragmented heritages which require more work in the process of putting them together to form any kind of challenge to the heritage status quo. Yet how might we go about making that challenge?

Scrutinizing motivation and a right to involvement is an important exercise when undertaking activism, especially in a place where one does not live. My close family roots and deep ancestry in Guernsey, as well as more than a decade of regular fieldwork in the Channel Islands, has ensured a thorough understanding of the culture, history and legacies of the German Occupation. I have been motivated, as a direct consequence of my research, and as a person to whom important records have been entrusted, to act on behalf of neglected victims of Nazism. I have observed a historical reluctance to engage with this legacy and heritage in both Guernsey and Jersey, a reluctance that Jersey began to overcome from the mid-1990s onwards, and one with which Guernsey still struggles. I wanted to use the results of my research to give some recognition to those who had suffered or died in Nazi camps and prisons. I wanted to enable their voices and their heritage to become as mainstream, uncontroversial and legitimate as the restoration of German bunkers and the museum displays relating to the hardships of ordinary families struggling to survive the rigours of occupation. In the swiftly changing political climate in Britain, Europe and the United States, I wanted to focus the spotlight of attention on those who stood up to fascism and Nazism in their own way, to emphasize that these people ultimately did the right thing – a narrative that has in the past proved to be a step too far in Guernsey.

Each of the colleagues with whom I worked in writing the book on resistance has taken it upon themselves to change the memory landscape (both figurative and literal) in the Channel Islands in their own way. Each of us has been motivated by our own perceptions of historical injustices towards the memory of those we have studied. We have also each worked with the families of those for whose memories – and right to be remembered – we fight. For us, it has been important to rescue and legitimate the memory of those we have studied as a personal tribute to and support for the cause of the dead.

None of the three case studies explored in this chapter were planned in private; all were carried out in collaboration and discussion with local heritage authorities and with the families concerned. In the case of the digital heritage most especially, I made sure that the concept and plans were disseminated through many articles in the Channel Islands' press and radio, and on social media, where local families were invited on many occasions to contact me and share their stories. This, therefore, was not an ivory tower project, but was carried out for and with the local community, albeit a segment of the community that comprised the resistance families.

Conceptually, this chapter is inspired by Hirsh and Spitzer's 'small acts of repair'[3] and considers its heritage equivalent. While this term can be applied to heritage creation, as I discuss, I develop it further to propose 'acts of rescue', which are sometimes necessary when dealing with scattered legacies and fragmented heritages.

For Hirsch and Spitzer, 'small acts of repair' involve illuminating forgotten and denied chapters of Holocaust history, asking whether it is possible to repair and find redress in the aftermath of the Holocaust for events for which nobody has accepted responsibility, or for which judicial recognition has not taken place, or which have not even been nationally acknowledged. Working within the field of literary studies, they explore this concept through the lens of poetry. Taking poems written by young Holocaust victims from Transnistria (once part of Romania), they carry out 'small acts of repair' by reading them aloud at conferences, or publishing them within their own writings. Their aim is to ensure that these people, their voices and the stories that the poems represent become connected within the larger group and national histories. Such poems can form links with other small stories and forgotten histories across space and time and add context within a wider historical setting. They see these 'acts' as reparative rather than redemptive or as heroizing the young victims. To carry out such 'small acts of repair' are, for them, of importance where the history of a place the poems speak of has been contested, erased or forgotten. In Romania today, the sites of the camps, cemeteries and mass graves are unmarked. There is also a lack of education and much local ignorance about the story of the Jews of Transnistria.

But how are such 'acts of repair' or rescue to take place within the field of heritage? Adding the largely neglected experiences of victims of Nazism to the history of the Second World War is an easier task. To include their voices – their memoirs, diaries and testimonies – in historical texts is straightforward and uncomplicated, but what we might term 'reparative heritage' is less easy to achieve.

Acts of 'reparative heritage' might include erecting memorials, holding museum exhibitions, or adding elements to commemorative ceremonies to make the wider heritage arena more inclusive of forgotten or neglected victims of Nazism. It gives voice to those whose experiences have been erased, marginalized and forgotten, but also to those whose acts have been denied legitimacy, or are even still seen as illegal. In the spirit of Hirsh and Spitzer, I see reparative heritage as requiring effort and even activism to come to fruition, for this heritage seeks legitimacy and acknowledgement for those whom it represents.

Such reparative heritage is allied to – although not the same as – the concept of 'healing heritage': the notion that heritage is able to heal communities by righting past wrongs through giving voice to victims. There are various ways in which heritage might be thought to have a healing function. Lynn Meskell and Colette Scheermeyer argue that heritage should be seen as a form of therapy, of benefit for the 'disempowered, dislocated and disadvantaged', and that cultural productions such as museums, memorials, heritage sites and public spaces of commemoration can provide therapeutic arenas for empowerment. They believe that heritage can 'play a recuperative role in allowing otherwise marginalized histories to be brought to the fore'.[4] Such therapeutic heritage can be seen as an antidote to dissonant heritage which, John Tunbridge and Gregory Ashworth argue, dispossesses and disinherits certain groups or communities as a statement about what 'contemporary society chooses to inherit and pass on'.[5]

Such therapeutic solutions in the heritage arena for marginalized and excluded groups would seem to fit the concept of reparative heritage very well, although Tunbridge and Ashworth caution us against simply adding the dispossessed and marginalized to heritage and imagining that we have done our job. They express concern that adding 'new heritages' to the old simply leads to each having decreased historical significance now that they have to share audience attention with each other. They ask how we know what balance to aim for and when the correct balance has been attained. If all heritage (i.e. heritage meaningful to all groups) is given equal weighting, then it will increase dissonance among the large or majority groups.[6] Furthermore, adding historical plaques to those previously marginalized is an exercise limited by the 'willingness of the consumer … to stop and read them'.[7]

Some people, such as Dacia Viejo-Rose, argue that memorials (in particular) do not heal; this is not their function and we should not look at them with this expectation.[8] Such cautions are depressing for the heritage activist to read, a depression both compounded and relieved in turn by the two schools of thought in the literature identified by John Giblin. The first argues that heritage (as a whole) does not heal;[9] the second, that it might heal if conducted correctly.[10] However, research by Giblin suggests that heritage is neither an 'essentially positive nor negative … strategy to select or avoid respectively' but can better be understood as a 'common element of post-conflict[11] renewal, as part of a healing complex'.[12] He suggests that we should move beyond asking *whether* heritage ultimately heals or hurts, as this is 'a distraction'. Instead we should examine *how* heritage functions during the memory negotiations and contestations that typify the post-conflict situation. This is because 'an idealised "healed" is unlikely to ever be achievable and may even be undesirable'. In the Channel Islands, the German Occupation is one of the prime aspects of identity today. A 'healed' status may involve letting go of this traumatic memory, which is unlikely to be a suggestion which would find much support. Instead of aiming for the healed state, then, we should, according to Giblin, be concerned with identifying and exploring the healing-heritage processes in culturally specific and subjective terms, which might encompass a process that includes many reverses, spirals and trajectories, and 'thousands of individual multi-directional paths'.[13]

Giblin is right to stress that the 'healed' state is unachievable through heritage or even an undesirable position to aim for. Hirsch and Spitzer make clear that their 'acts of repair' cannot make up for the original injury or loss; they are specifically modest acts of historical redress where 'political and legal acknowledgement and reckoning are largely absent'. Small acts 'respond to the vulnerabilities of personal and familial archives that come to light'. They are carried out in a spirit of solidarity with the victims.[14]

Reparative heritage, then, aims neither to heal nor to make up for the loss suffered; it knows it can do neither of these things. Because it takes place in a location where political acknowledgement is (in Guernsey) currently absent – or only slowly and belatedly beginning to show its face – such heritage aims to acknowledge loss in a way that makes legitimate the stories and experiences of those who are no longer alive. In this it moves beyond, and is less modest, than Hirsch and Spitzer's aims, which were not explicitly political, nor sought acknowledgement from those in authority.

The Resistance Memorial as reparative heritage

The importance of political acknowledgement of the legitimacy of victims was an aim from the beginning of planning for a memorial in Guernsey to those who committed acts of resistance against the occupiers. An earlier letter proposing a memorial had been sent by a local family to a local politician in the States of Guernsey, but this had not been met with much interest. Jean had lost her father, Joseph Gillingham, when she was a few months old. He died in an unknown Nazi prison after being deported for his role in the news sheet GUNS. Gillingham had last been seen leaving Naumburg (Saale) Prison in February 1945. Jean and her mother, Henrietta, who died in 1998, had keenly felt the lack of a grave to visit to remember him. In December 1949, Henrietta Gillingham asked the Bailiff if Gillingham's name could be added to the war memorial in St Peter Port, which was being updated with names of the military dead of the Second World War. The Bailiff turned down the request on the grounds that the memorial was only for 'those who died while serving in the Armed Forces of the Crown and not to civilians who died as a result of the war'.[15]

After Henrietta passed away, Jean placed a memorial plaque to her father on her mother's grave, commemorating his role in GUNS. As Gillingham had no known grave at that point, was not allowed to be added to the Island's war memorial, and had no other place where his family could go to remember him, this became a substitute grave. On Armistice Day each year, Jean placed a small wooden 'poppy cross', with her father's name written on it, in front of the same war memorial where he had been denied a place in the Island's public memory in 1949.

In mid-2014 I worked with Jean's family on the Resistance Memorial, inviting into the conversation the chair of the Guernsey Deportee Association (GDA). In Guernsey, the deportees were those Islanders deported to civilian internment camps in September 1942 and February 1943. Those sent away in February 1943 included many of those who had previously spent time in prison for offences against the occupiers. They were deported with their families, and so a number in the GDA today had a shared interest in seeing the erection of a memorial remembering their own family members who had been imprisoned pre-deportation, even though the deportees as a group had a memorial erected to them in 2010.

The Deportees' Memorial was (to my eyes) problematic in its text. At the bottom of the polished granite plaque were the words: 'Also remembering other Islanders who were *for other reasons* deported and died in labour camps and prisons in Europe' (my emphasis added). The reluctance to name the reason for the deportations to other places of incarceration was a spur for having another memorial.

With the aim of having a resistance memorial unveiled in May 2015, the seventieth anniversary of liberation of the Channel Islands, letters were written to the Bailiff and Lieutenant-Governor of Guernsey, as well as the director of Guernsey Museums and Art Gallery (GMAG) and the Guernsey Press in order to gauge their support. Various concerns were raised at this point. While the director of GMAG was concerned about who might fund the project and was already overstretched with different initiatives,[16] the Lieutenant-Governor suggested that the Deportees' Memorial was already sufficient and, in any case, it was not within his remit to decide; rather, it was for the 'people of Guernsey to determine whether or not such a memorial is required'.[17]

The Bailiff, who was asked for his support for a memorial unveiling followed by a *Vin d'Honneur*[18] for resistance families, replied that while he was happy in principle to lend his support, he couldn't commit to attending given how busy his calendar was for the period around Liberation Day.[19] I replied proposing an earlier date and suggesting that he might like to host the *Vin d'Honneur* at the Royal Court, as his predecessor had done for the Deportees' Memorial.[20] The Bailiff replied to decline, saying that it would be neither 'practical nor appropriate' to 'select a limited number from such an enormous group'.[21] I replied once again suggesting that perhaps the families of the Guernsey Eight (a term I had recently coined, following the use of the 'Jersey 21' in the sister Island, to describe those from Guernsey who had died in Nazi prisons and camps) might be invited. This was eventually agreed.

In September 2014, when agreements had been reached with the director of GMAG about commissioning the memorial, the names of the Guernsey Eight were put forward and a suitable formula of wording was decided on to encompass all those deported for offences against the occupying forces. I suggested the formula used on the title of a book which I had just co-written,[22] and so the memorial was dedicated to 'the memory of all Islanders who committed acts of protest, defiance and resistance during the German Occupation 1940-1945, those who were imprisoned or deported, and those who died in captivity'.

Before the names of the Guernsey Eight were added, the families were contacted where possible to see if they were content to have their family member's name listed publicly and to see if they could attend the memorial's unveiling. However, it became apparent that the memorial would only display seven names. The daughter of Herbert Smith did not want her father's name to be honoured in this way. Smith was one of the Guernsey policemen deported for stealing food from German and local depots, and he had been publicly disgraced. He and the other convicted policemen had argued that they acted patriotically, following advice and directions from the BBC's Colonel Britton. However, the German version of events, constructed from confessions signed after physical and mental ill-treatment of the policemen, has long been preferentially believed.[23] Herbert Smith was brutally treated at Neuoffingen labour camp in Germany and died of his injuries while alone in a cell at nearby Augsburg Prison.

Although Smith's daughter had recently located and visited for the first time her father's last resting place in a mass grave in a cemetery in Germany, she struggled to fully forgive him for his actions. They had resulted in the deportation of the rest of her family (including herself) to an internment camp in February 1943. She had also had an unstable childhood caused by her mother's mental ill-health, which was triggered by learning of Smith's death while she was in a camp. Because the Guernsey policemen had never received a pardon or had their convictions overturned, despite their best efforts, their names are still dishonoured. The daughter of Smith did want to risk facing any public backlash by having her father's name carved on a public memorial. In fact, the chair of the GDA (an association of which Smith's daughter was a member) was also opposed to having Herbert Smith's name on the memorial because of this controversy.[24]

The Guernsey Resistance Memorial was thus to list only seven names. While the presence of a public memorial bearing her father's name was to be a proud and healing experience for the daughter of Joseph Gillingham, it was also a site of potential hurt and shame for Herbert Smith's daughter. The agreed compromise position was to leave a space on the plaque for Smith's name to perhaps be added at some unspecified time in the future.

And yet, despite being a potential example of both a 'healing' and a 'hurtful' memorial (without having the aim of being either), it is also an example of 'reparative heritage' in that it counters ignorance and denial about resistance in the Channel Islands, but cannot (and does not aim to) compensate for the original injury or loss in Nazi prisons and camps. It acknowledges the loss, makes it a legitimate one to grieve for, and seeks acknowledgement and legitimation from those in authority. And yet it inevitably breaches the boundaries of 'small acts of repair' and what they try to achieve. While the memorial was erected in the spirit of solidarity with the victims, publicly naming those who died inevitably risks raising them to the level of 'heroes', of redeeming those once considered villains. Redemption and heroization are not the aims of acts of repair, but are perhaps no bad things in themselves given that reparative heritage acknowledges its activist aims as part of its goal of achieving acknowledgement and changing narratives. While creating heroes can risk turning imperfect people into 'cardboard saints', the second of the case studies presented here helps to mitigate that risk by presenting online the details of the lives of each of those deported so that the details of their story can be understood.

Yet perhaps the memorial strayed too far from the spirit of Hirsch and Spitzer. Their reading of poems of the Jews of Transnistria was done in a way that was 'neither critical, nor analytic, nor apologetic, nor redemptive' but, indeed, reparative.[25] Does this mean that the acts of the Guernsey Eight and Jersey 21 should not be criticized, analysed or apologized for, nor their memory redeemed? Should we consider it enough of a 'repair' to simply place their names upon a memorial? This is difficult when dealing with people who were once branded as criminals by those in authority, and is not something with which Hirsch and Spitzer had to deal when reading their poems of Jews who did not survive the Holocaust. The Jews of Transnistria did nothing to trigger their fate other than be Jewish. This was not the case with those who committed acts of protest, defiance and resistance. The very nature of this group meant that a political dimension arguably has to be part of what constitutes reparative heritage.

The political activism connected to the memorial meant that suggestions of placing it away from other memorials related to the German Occupation was headed off at an early stage. This already-marginalized group did not need further marginalization. That it was to be placed in the same memorial space as other plaques to victims of the Occupation (such as the Deportees Memorial and the Jewish Memorial), as well as monuments to the act of liberation, meant that resisters were allowed into the accepted narrative (albeit into its memorial arena) of the Occupation for the first time in seventy years. This in itself was an important step forward.

Therefore, by the autumn of 2014 the obstacles to the erection of the memorial were overcome. Jean's family and other resistance families funded the memorial costs, and the Bailiff agreed to unveil the memorial and to hold a *Vin d'Honneur* for the families of the Guernsey Eight, although the Bailiff's office was not in favour of unveiling the memorial as part of the liberation celebrations, given the number of his commitments at that time of year. The fact that the memorial unveiling was not seen as either high enough in priority or profile to be part of liberation celebrations was telling, but the date of 4 May, five days before Liberation Day, was a very good compromise.

The process of tracking down resistance families began, especially those of the Guernsey Eight, so that they might attend the memorial unveiling. While Herbert Smith's daughter did not want to attend, I wanted to give the same opportunity to all relatives. In trying to trace them, it soon became apparent that the location of the bodies of four of the Guernsey Eight were lost and had no known grave. While Major Marie Ozanne of the Salvation Army (imprisoned for writing to the German *Feldkommandant* to criticize his actions against Jews, forced labourers and deportees) and John Ingrouille (who was falsely accused of threatening to raise an army of 800 men against the Germans, for which he was given a five-year sentence[26]) were buried in a local parish churchyard in Guernsey, the other six were scattered throughout Europe. Herbert Smith was buried in Augsburg *Westfriedhof*, and Percy Miller (deported for listening to the radio) lay in the *Hauptfriedhof* in Frankfurt, where he was placed after his death in Frankfurt prison. A search for the other four was needed.

My hunt for the families of the Guernsey Eight was unproblematic as most lived locally. The last to be tracked down was that of Sidney Ashcroft, deported for theft of food from the occupiers. I quickly established that his family was no longer in Guernsey. Occupation registration cards showed that Ashcroft was born in St Helen's,

Lancashire, and that his mother, Charlotte, was from Tunbridge Wells, in Kent. My public appeal in those counties for people who knew his family caught the attention of a regional BBC station, who agreed to televise my appeal for those who knew him. This was successful and I was subsequently contacted by relatives of Charlotte Ashcroft.[27]

The story of Ashcroft's life, deportation on his twenty-first birthday, and subsequent journey through Nazi prisons and camps was compelling.[28] Ashcroft was last seen by another Guernseyman, Walter Lainé, in Straubing Prison. While Lainé was assembling in the prison yard with hundreds of other prisoners as a precursor to their forced march in the direction of Dachau in April 1945, Ashcroft was led away with other sick and weak prisoners. The assumption for seventy years was that he was shot or taken away to a concentration camp.

After consulting the records of the International Tracing Service, I learnt that – unexpectedly – Ashcroft had in fact been placed in the hospital building in Straubing prison, where he had soon afterwards died of tuberculosis. He was subsequently buried in the nearby cemetery of St Michael. After the final resting place of Ashcroft had been discovered, the BBC flew to Germany with me and a second cousin of Ashcroft's to make a short documentary[29] about the search for his grave. Ashcroft's body had been placed in a seemingly empty grassed area in the cemetery (which was in fact a large area of unmarked graves for prisoners), with a single memorial stone euphemistically commemorating 'victims of the Second World War and of tyranny'. After consulting old records, the cemetery manager was able to show us the location of Ashcroft's body, where his relative laid a memorial stone in his memory (Figure 8.2).

Finding Sidney Ashcroft was a defining moment. Researching his family history, and learning how his mother had waited even until her death in the 1980s for her son to return home, convinced me that collecting scattered legacies across Europe to create fragmented reparative heritage was an important task. Laying a small memorial plaque to Sidney Ashcroft had, too, been an act of reparative heritage. While the official memorial stone in the cemetery had hinted at 'victims of tyranny', it had shied away from naming who these people were and how and why they had died, denying them acknowledgement and legitimacy. Finding Ashcroft's body and placing a memorial plaque was also a gesture of comforting the dead, of giving our company for a short while, and of friendship. I had come to know Ashcroft through my research and had developed what felt like bonds of friendship with him. The trip to Straubing felt like a pilgrimage, a tribute to a brave young man and an act of solidarity. His name on memorials in Guernsey and in Straubing seemed more than a small act of repair. Although it could never bring him back, it was, in a way, an act of rescue. And it was not the last of such acts that I could make.

In early May 2015, the Bailiff of Guernsey, Sir Richard Collas, unveiled the Resistance Memorial in front of representatives of the families of the Guernsey Eight, and a crowd of other resistance families (Figure 8.3). The chair and members of the GDA attended, and the Salvation Army band played in honour of Major Marie Ozanne, one of the people named on the memorial. It was not, in the event, a political occasion, nor an occasion on which the Bailiff would address the marginalization of former political prisoners, their absence from the narrative of Occupation, nor the lack of assistance given to those arrested by the local authorities. In his speech before the unveiling, and

Figure 8.2 Sidney Ashcroft's memorial plaque, Straubing, Germany. Copyright: Gilly Carr

in recognition that this acknowledgement would not be forthcoming, he remarked that 'many will say that we should have officially recognised their (the resisters') courage a long time ago, but now is not the time to dwell on those thoughts'.[30] Instead, the Bailiff reflected on the location of the memorial – the harbour of St Peter Port – as a place of deportations, evacuation, bombing and arrival of forced labourers. He reflected on the abandonment of the Channel Islands by the British, the endurance of the general population, and he paid tribute to the acts of bravery committed by many civilians, many of which, he acknowledged, were not recorded anywhere except in the memory of those who committed them.

Despite the opportunity for challenging or signalling a change to the status quo of the narrative of Occupation provided by the unveiling of the Resistance Memorial, the Bailiff's speech reinforced it. Other aspects of the ceremony, such as the playing of the Last Post and the minute's silence, evoked elements of Armistice Day commemorations, absorbing the Guernsey Eight into the pantheon of a different group of war heroes. This was clearly not a time for questioning the narrative, opening it up or introducing new elements. Time will tell whether the memorial unveiling and the resulting publicity created an incremental memory event. Perhaps the very

Figure 8.3 The Resistance Memorial, 4 May 2015. Copyright: Gilly Carr

presence of the memorial will, through the very dint of existing and being used on Holocaust Memorial Day, as we saw in the last chapter, form another perforation in Guernsey's fabric of memory.

Acts of rescue and the Frank Falla Archive

'Acts of rescue' – something that goes significantly beyond the small acts of repair described by Hirsch and Spitzer – is an important part of collecting scattered legacies and fragmented heritages of victims of Nazism. The first step in this process was taken in 2010, when Frank Falla's daughter gave me her father's extensive archives as well as the unpublished manuscript of a second memoir and a collection of his published articles and wartime photos. This archive contained Falla's full correspondence with the Foreign Office during the period of the compensation claims, and copies of many of his colleagues' testimonies of Nazi persecution in prisons, labour and concentration camps, glimpses of which we have seen earlier in this volume.

This archive, with its testimonies which indicated the presence of many more in Foreign Office archives, also contained important clues about the journey taken by many Islanders whose stories were neither published nor had been passed on to family members. I realized that these scattered clues needed to be assembled to facilitate piecing together the stories of many victims of Nazism. While Sidney Ashcroft was now the first of four missing members of the Guernsey Eight whose story had recently been pieced together and whose last resting place had been found, I knew that there were others in Jersey and Guernsey who were missing and whose families still mourned their loss.

By the time of the Resistance Memorial unveiling, I had known Jean and her family for several years. After researching the work of Frank Falla and his GUNS colleagues, I had known that Jean had grown up without her father after he was deported when she was a few months old. No trace had ever been found of Gillingham after 1945, and even the International Tracing Service archives had no further records on him after Frankfurt and Naumburg prisons, destinations known to the family because Frank Falla and Gillingham's brother-in-law and fellow prisoner, Ernest Legg, were able to inform them after their release. Gillingham's family had long suspected and accepted that he had been swallowed up in the concentration camp system.

The story of Joseph Tierney of the Jersey 21 was similar to that of Joseph Gillingham. Tierney had also helped to spread the BBC news and had been deported around six months before Gillingham. He, too, experienced Frankfurt and Naumburg prisons. According to Frank Falla, who was with both men during their incarceration, they were in the two prisons at the same time and knew each other, although Tierney arrived in Frankfurt several months before Gillingham. Tierney had been deported in September 1943, just after the baptism of his baby daughter, Pat, and had then experienced two other prisons before Frankfurt. Like Gillingham, he was never seen again after he left Naumburg Prison. After the war, his wife, Elaine, received messages through the Red Cross from two men who were eyewitnesses to Tierney's last days in a cattle truck, as it headed towards Theresienstadt concentration camp.

Having found Sidney Ashcroft, I wanted to find Gillingham and Tierney. I had also got to know Pat, Tierney's daughter, in Jersey, and wanted her to meet Jean, given the similarity in the two women's experiences, growing up with the grief of their mothers and grandparents, and with the traumatic loss of their fathers. The BBC commissioned a second documentary that would follow Jean and Pat on a journey into Germany and the Czech Republic in the footsteps of their fathers.

At the very end of 2015, and with the help of a Czech colleague at the University of West Bohemia,[31] I was able to piece together the prison and camp trajectory of Tierney. We discovered that he had been sent to a prison in Halle, followed by Zöschen labour camp, and then put on a forced march from which he had escaped but been recaptured and put in a cattle truck. In April 1945, he died in the arms of a friend, as we learnt in an earlier chapter, and his body was thrown by the SS into a mass grave of 234 people near the village of Kaštice. He was exhumed and reburied in a Catholic cemetery in the village of Pšov later that year, in the presence of Allied representatives. Remarkably, the archives in Prague had a film of the exhumation and reburial.

Three weeks later, I was able to visit Pat and let her and her assembled family know that we had found her father's grave, and that she would be travelling in her father's footsteps, along with Jean, with the BBC accompanying us. I was concerned that the film would reunite only one of the women with their father's graves, but given the harrowing nature of Tierney's end, I wondered if Jean was better off not knowing what had happened to her father.

Although others, including the post-war aid agencies, and a colleague of mine had tried to find Gillingham without success over the years, I tried a new line of research provided by Frank Falla's archives, which I was still working through. Encouraged by the success of finding Sidney Ashcroft, who had not died in a distant concentration camp as his friends had feared, I created a distribution map of the first destinations of all Islanders after they had left Frankfurt or Naumburg prisons. I was surprised to find that they all clustered roughly within a fifty kilometre radius of the prisons. I subsequently contacted all of the archives in Saxony-Anhalt, the province in which Naumburg lies, to see if they had any relevant records.

In March 2016, four days before filming began, I received an email from the archives in Halle[32] to say that they had Joseph Gillingham's death certificate and that his body had lain in the city's *Gertraudenfriedhof* cemetery for over seventy years. Gillingham had died in Halle police prison on 11 March 1945, one month and nine days after he had said goodbye to his brother-in-law and left Naumburg Prison. This news was both incredible and deeply moving as I knew how much it would mean to Jean and her family. The BBC was keen to keep the surprise for when we arrived in Halle.

Four days later, Pat, Jean, a BBC crew and I flew to Germany, stopping first to film in the now-empty and bitterly cold Naumburg Prison. The week of filming was emotionally draining for everybody. On the day we arrived at Halle Archives, the cameras captured Jean's reaction when her fingers stopped at her father's name in the death register, precisely seventy-one years to the day since he had died. Her seven-decade search for him was at an end.

We laid flowers on his grave the next morning (Figure 8.4), an act that Jean has been able to repeat on two occasions since with her family. Joseph Gillingham had been fortunate to receive a headstone for his cremated remains, unlike other prisoners whose ashes were placed in an anonymous mass grave nearby, most likely because his name had been Germanicized to Josef Gillinghamm. Prisoners assumed to be German had been given headstones.

The next stage of our journey, into the Czech Republic, was more traumatic. Passing through the grim ruins of Zöschen labour camp, we met my Czech colleague, Pavel Vařecka. We visited the semi-derelict train station of Kaštice, where the dead men were taken from their cattle trucks. Vařecka then took us to the original site of Tierney's mass grave, where he had begun an archaeological project to search for any personal effects or clothes of victims left behind when their bodies were exhumed in August 1945. Finally, in the hamlet of Pšov, where the last snow of winter had recently melted, we were able to lay flowers at a memorial within the demarcated area where Tierney and his fellow prisoners were placed in the summer of 1945 (Figure 8.5).

In that week in March 2016, we were able to restore Pat and Jean's fathers to their families. While the bodies of both men were left behind in Halle and Pšov, Pat and Jean had made an extraordinary journey, travelling in their fathers' footsteps in a way that enabled them to come to know their fathers for the first time in their lives. The two men, who both women had previously referred to as 'Joe' rather than 'Dad', had properly become their fathers at last. While their fathers had both lain in their graves for over seventy years, these resting places had been utterly unknown to their families. Joseph Gillingham and Joseph Tierney had been rescued in a very real sense. For me, the discovery of their bodies was far more than a 'small act of repair'; it was an act of rescue. And through the BBC documentary,[33] with its associated news headlines

Figure 8.4 Jean at her father's grave in Halle. Copyright: Gilly Carr

in the Channel Islands and further afield,[34] the resistant acts of both Gillingham and Tierney became known to a wider audience. The discovery of their graves had helped to counter the ignorance about Channel Islander victims of Nazism, as well as the perception that resisters were criminals who 'rocked the boat' for everyone else. While the documentary could not trigger political acknowledgement of the legitimacy of the actions of resisters, it helped to challenge popular perceptions.

Ashcroft, Tierney and Gillingham were not the last Islanders for whom acts of rescue have been carried out. In June 2018 I travelled to Hamelin in Germany with Philip, the grandson of Charles Machon, originator of GUNS. While at the time of the Resistance Memorial unveiling in 2015 we did not know where Machon's body lay, he had been confirmed as still lying in *Am Wehl* cemetery in Hamelin after dying in Hamelin Prison. Earlier records at the International Tracing Service had stated that his body had been exhumed in 1949 and moved to somewhere in France, but this was shown not to have been the case.

We were helped in Hamelin by local activist Bernhard Gelderblom, who had fought on our behalf to get a memorial erected in the cemetery for Machon. His local memory association,[35] which works to preserve the memory of victims of Nazism, had paid for most of the memorial costs. It could not be erected over Machon's last resting place,

Figure 8.5 Pat in Pšov, Czech Republic, at the place where her father was reburied in 1945. Copyright: Gilly Carr

as his grave had been reused twice and two bodies lay on top of his. The relatives of the most recent occupant of the grave were therefore not to be contacted or disturbed over this issue, and Machon's memorial stone was erected a short distance away, in the company of other victims of Nazism (Figure 8.6).

Like the daughters of Tierney and Gillingham, Philip Machon felt that he had begun to know his grandfather for the first time through visiting his prison, travelling in his footsteps, and paying homage to him at the place of his death. He was also touched at how people in Hamelin were prepared to treat his grandfather with such respect. Charles Machon's memory had been, in effect, rescued.

The discovery of the graves of all these men became part of a new project. Inspired by the work of Frank Falla, who had collected testimonies of his friends and colleagues who he knew had been victims of Nazism, I started work on creating a website which would record the wartime story of all Islanders deported to Nazi prisons, labour and concentration camps.[36] While most of the deported survived the war, more than 10 per cent did not. The trajectories of the vast majority were unknown, and the website would provide the platform for all known archival documents scattered across Guernsey, Jersey, the UK, France and Germany, that related to the deported, to be gathered

Figure 8.6 Philip Machon by his grandfather's memorial in Hamelin. Copyright: Gilly Carr

together in one place (Figure 8.7). It would feature court records, prison, police and camp records, as well as the now-digitized records of the International Tracing Service, which predominantly contains the surviving German prison and camp records. Most importantly, the website would provide a sustainable educational resource that could be used by members of the public, by researchers and by students and their teachers.

I named the website after Frank Falla, and each person's page showcases their testimony (where it exists), their records in the Channel Islands, and their prison and camp records. The families of those deported have, in a number of cases, supplemented what is known about those on the website with anecdotes, photos, and family documents. These are the scattered legacies of the many victims of Nazism in the Channel Islands, and bringing them together within the Frank Falla Archive represents the most extensive act of rescue ever performed on this group to date. But it is certainly not the first vehicle to attempt to present this task, as we have seen.

Collating the records and writing personal histories of the deported has been started from scratch because there was no pre-existing accurate list of names of the deported. Because of the unreliability of a list created by Joe Mière, which contains no information about sources, it has not been used as a basis of research. However, thumbnails of stories

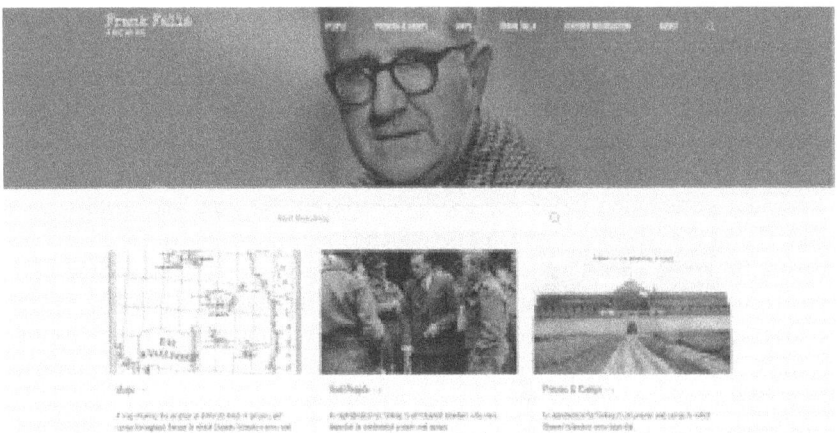

Figure 8.7 The homepage of the Frank Falla Archive, www.frankfallaarchive.org Copyright: Gilly Carr

of fifty-seven people from Mière's list are displayed in the café of Jersey War Tunnels, each presented with their photograph. Once a person has been proved to have been deported, only then does the Frank Falla Archive provide Mière's data as supplementary information alongside other versions of stories. In some places, Mière's collected oral testimony is simply incorrect. For example, Wilfred Le Mercier claimed to have been sent to Flossenbürg concentration camp in November 1942, although documents in Jersey Archives show that he was actually deported to Kreuzburg internment camp in February 1943. In other places, Mière's oral testimony is all that exists.

The names on the Frank Falla Archive have therefore been compiled from archives such as logs of those deported from Jersey (no similar log exists from Guernsey), coupled with names taken from compensation testimonies, from Occupation memoirs and from court cases. It was not unusual for the occupiers to deport people without trial, or without notifying the authorities, and so some people vanished without trace. The difficulty of tracing the names of the deported has been compounded by the not entirely complete nature of the collection of Occupation registration forms held in Jersey. Different kinds of records have survived in Guernsey and Jersey, enabling us largely to work out what has not survived in the sister Island. After observing that those with a sentence of three months or more were likely to have been deported, in 2014 I estimated that the minimum number of Islanders deported was likely to lie between 226 and 253 people.[37] To date, I have accounted for 215 of these people, but the total continues to grow.[38] The Frank Falla Archive also presents interactive maps of the Channel Islands and continental Europe, showing where those deported once lived, and the locations of their prisons and camps. It also has a social media presence so that acts of rescue and new discoveries can be disseminated online.

Every profile written is a small act of rescue from oblivion. Every person on the website has left a scattered legacy existing now only in the archives of Europe and in the anecdotes recited by their children and grandchildren. The website is a bringing together of fragmented heritage in digital form. The aim is to use it in education in

Channel Islands schools, thereby facilitating the legitimation of this heritage for the next generation.

Writing profiles for each deported person has led to archival revelations and the chance to uncover long-held mysteries. For example, the member of the Jersey 21 about whom we know the least is a man called Peter Bruce Johnson. Our only knowledge about his life comes from the memory of Joe Mière; we have neither photograph, Occupation registration forms nor court case records for him, and neither has a single record of anybody of that name been found in the International Tracing Service archives. Mière recalled that Johnson was Australian, was hearing-impaired, non-vocal (apparently unable to speak) and worked as a timber cutter. He also witnessed an accident at work in which Johnson accidentally cut his thumb off in the wood-cutting machine. Mière also noted that Johnson was deported in 1944 and died in Mittelbau-Dora concentration camp, but the source of this information is unknown.

When writing the Frank Falla Archive profile for an Australian man residing in Jersey named Thomas Patrick Nelson, I discovered that he cut wood for a living. He was deported in 1944 to French prisons only and survived the war but did not return to Jersey. Nelson's granddaughter contacted me to say that her late grandfather's name was really Thomas John Nanson, and that he moved to Jersey under an alias, possibly to escape the law, and that his hearing had been lost since his service in the Royal Artillery in the 1920s. I wondered whether Nelson / Nanson was really Peter Johnson, and Mière had misremembered the name. Although Nelson / Nanson's granddaughter said that her grandfather was not missing any digits and did not have scars on his hands, I was interested to note that his French prison records noted that he had distinguishing marks on his hands and forearms, perhaps consistent with a recent accident that was less severe than Mière remembered. I wrote up the theory as a news item for the website, which was picked up by BBC Jersey.[39] Meanwhile, the HMD committee in Jersey, who organize the annual commemorations around the Lighthouse Memorial, gave a statement to say that they did not think that Nelson / Nanson was Johnson because he was in possession of all his fingers and thumbs.[40] I was also contacted by the director of Jersey Heritage, who was concerned that such public speculation over the identity of people on the memorial could undermine public confidence in it. Such is the risk with some acts of rescue; digital heritage has the potential to overrule or undermine more traditional forms of heritage. However, presenting the stories of people online in a freely accessible format can also contribute to future heritage creation for victims of Nazism, and can present a wealth of stories about which a new generation can learn.

The challenges of creating legitimate heritage: The resistance trails

As the seventieth anniversary of the act of liberation grew close in 2015, and following the publication of *Protest, Defiance and Resistance in the Channel Islands*, I was inspired to create resistance trails for Guernsey and Jersey, featuring sites that had been identified as key places where such acts took place. I wanted to use the opportunity to both draw upon uncontroversial sites that were already part of the Occupation narrative and introduce new sites. I also wanted to bring together sites scattered around both Islands – fragmented heritages – that already had memorial plaques or information boards attached and to combine them with sites not yet marked. The idea was to combine taboo heritage[41] (i.e. sites that resist heritage creation because of their extreme sensitivity) with already accepted heritage as a way of using the latter to encourage the legitimacy and acceptance of the former.

I created the first trail for Jersey Heritage, identifying fifteen sites that would make an interesting tour for both tourists and Islanders. This trail included houses which marked people already honoured and/or respected in the Island such as that of Albert Bedane, who sheltered Jewish woman Mary Richardson during the Occupation and had been honoured by Yad Vashem as Righteous Among the Nations; Louisa Gould, who had died in Ravensbrück concentration camp for sheltering a Russian slave worker; and the 'Surrealist Sisters', artists Lucy Schwab and Suzanne Malherbe (better known as Claude Cahun and Marcel Moore), who were imprisoned and sentenced to death after being caught for their two-woman resistance group activities. The trail also included an escapee, Maurice Gould, who died in Wittlich Prison after brutal treatment in Hinzert concentration camp and whose body had been returned to Jersey in 1997; and St Saviour's Church, inside which a memorial plaque remembered Canon Clifford Cohu, former priest of the parish, who had died in Zöschen labour camp for his leading role in spreading the BBC news in Jersey. The trail would also draw upon the rather neglected and increasingly illegible Political Prisoner Memorial, erected outside the site of the former prison in 1995 after years of petitioning by Joe Mière; and the Lighthouse Memorial to the Jersey 21 unveiled in 1996. I was keen that sites where there was nothing to 'see' would be included, sites which existed only in 'resistance legend' and in the memory of those who were there, such as the place where hundreds and possibly thousands of Islanders protested against the September 1942 deportations. The proposed sites of taboo heritage included 'Silvertide', the former headquarters of the *Geheime Feldpolizei*, the closest thing that Jersey had to the Gestapo; and the Folie Inn, headquarters of the German naval police and also a place of interrogation for many. Silvertide kept its name and returned to domestic housing stock after the Occupation, while the Folie Inn also kept its name and turned back into a pub. Neither site has yet been claimed for heritage incorporation in telling the story of the Occupation. Jersey Heritage was happy with the concept, including the sites of taboo heritage (see Table 8.1), although three of my proposed sites were replaced with others, including recognition of Victoria College House, a location of one of the several German courts where Islanders were convicted.

The resistance trail for Jersey was to be available both as a printed walking guide and map for tourists to take with them, and as an online trail, illustrated by a series of videos narrated by either the original resisters, where they were still alive, or their relatives or friends telling the story of each site.[42] The logo for the trail featured the two most popular forms of resistance: a V-for-victory sign and a pair of headphones, indicating somebody illicitly listening to the BBC on a homemade crystal radio set. The associated sound was a 'V' in Morse code followed by people singing 'There'll always be an England' (a popular wartime patriotic song) sung over the noise of marching German soldiers (Figure 8.8).

Table 8.1 The sites on Jersey's resistance trail

Site	Narrator
Victoria College House (HQ of occupiers and location of one of the military courts)	Expert (the author)
19 Peirson Road, St Helier (location of Jersey Communist Party meetings)	Occupation generation narrator; friend of original resistance activist
Silvertide, HQ of *Geheime Feldpolizei*	Brother of political prisoner interrogated in house
V-sign, Royal Square, St Helier	Grandchildren of original resistance activist
Occupation Tapestry Gallery, St Helier	Local actor on 1980s TV series set in the Island
St Saviour's Church, focus of event which led to deportation of a group of Islanders	Daughter of resistance activist
Mount Bingham, St Helier, focus on demonstrations against deportations	Original resistance activist
House of Albert Bedane (Righteous Among the Nations)	Member of Jewish community
Political Prisoner Memorial, St Helier	Daughter of political prisoner
Grave of Maurice Gould, an escapee who died in a concentration camp and whose body was repatriated	Original resistance activist who also tried to escape from the Island.
Lighthouse memorial to Islanders who died in concentration camps	Jersey Heritage staff member
Fauvic embarkation point where many Islanders attempted to escape with help from a local family in the area	Original resistance activist
La Fontaine, Millais, St Ouen, home of Louisa Gould who was sent to Ravensbrück for sheltering an escaped Russian slave worker	Niece of original resistance activist deported as part of same group
La Rocquaise, St Brelade's Bay, home of two-woman resistance group imprisoned in Jersey	Jersey Heritage staff member

The role and potential of digital heritage as an alternative to traditional heritage has been discussed elsewhere by Caroline Sturdy Colls.[43] She has argued that it can be a suitable way of presenting controversial or difficult heritage when more traditional forms of memorialization are neither wanted nor suitable. The Frank Falla Archive sets a precedent for the heritage of resisters and promotes the marginalized stories of victims of Nazism to let them become better known to locals and tourists alike in order to challenge existing dominant narratives which often exclude such stories.

With this in mind, the second trail was designed for GMAG, which has one-third of the budget of Jersey Heritage and is funded by the Island's Department of Culture

Figure 8.8 The Jersey resistance trail. Copyright: Jersey Heritage

and Leisure. It is therefore under government control, unlike Jersey Heritage. Being accountable to politicians, they are perhaps less inclined to take risks with controversial heritage, and in any case have less money and fewer staff with which to do it.

In the last chapter, I identified two factors which help explain why Guernsey has not made the same progress as Jersey since 1995 in coming to terms with the darker aspects of the Occupation. The first is that the Island's Occupation narrative is held very firmly in place by the CIOS, the founder of which is also the owner of the private German Occupation Museum, which has helped construct and shore up the mainstream narrative. Although this museum has an extension which tells the story of the some of the victims of Nazism, it is not the primary or dominant part of the museum. The second factor is the 'Carey effect'. Because victims of Nazism have not received the same attention and acknowledgement in Guernsey as they have in Jersey, it was especially important to create a resistance trail in this Island. While I was commissioned to create the trail in Jersey, I was not in Guernsey, although I offered to create it without charge. This offer was accepted and I was asked to select ten sites for inclusion (Table 8.2).

Resistance heritage is far less visible in Guernsey, with fewer memorials in existence; in fact, I played a hand in the erection of all three memorials related to resistance in the Island (two Blue Plaques and the Resistance Memorial). Even so, there was less in the way of fragmented heritages that I could draw upon, although there are just as many resistance stories, even if they were less well known because of the greater marginalization of victims of Nazism.

After the three existing memorials, I selected the remaining seven sites according to certain criteria: I wanted to choose some of the most well-known sites, which had already entered folk memory, rather than those which no longer meant anything to anyone. These would help legitimate the trail. My second criterion was to choose controversial sites to create balance and to push back against the more conservative culture in Guernsey, knowing that their equivalent sites in Jersey had now been accepted for inclusion in that Island's resistance trail.

Table 8.2 The sites of Guernsey's resistance trail

Site and event / memory
Resistance Memorial, unveiled 2015
Blue Plaque at house of Marie Ozanne (local resister), unveiled 2013
Vale churchyard (burial place of two resisters)
GUNS plaque (Guernsey Underground News Service), unveiled 2017.
Site of former prison (where political prisoners were held)
Grange Lodge (*Geheime Feldpolizei* HQ)
German Occupation Museum (prisoners' room)
St Sampson's Harbour (where Captain Noyon escaped from the Island in 1944, carrying information for England)
Commandos' memorial, erected 2010 (where two commandos came ashore; they were sheltered by family and friends who were sent to prison in France)
Charybdis graves at Foulon cemetery (bodies of British naval personnel were washed ashore after their ship, the HMS Charybdis, was sunk. Their funeral was attended by thousands of defiant Islanders)

In order to help certain difficult legacies become digital heritage, even if traditional forms of memorialization were not viable, among the sites selected were the former location of the Island's prison, where political prisoners were held, which is today the site of the new buildings of the Royal Court. Unlike in Jersey, no memorial to political prisoners has ever been placed there. Another potentially provocative location was Grange Lodge, today a hotel. During the Occupation it was the headquarters of the *Geheime Feldpolizei*. It was also the location where half the Island's police force were held in 1942 and repeatedly physically and psychologically assaulted during interrogation after they were alleged to have entered German food stores. Because the judgements against them have never been overturned, to include Grange Lodge in the resistance trail was thus to make a political statement about my own stance towards a wartime injustice.

Having chosen two potentially provocative sites for the resistance trail, I decided to strike a more conciliatory note by adding the prisoners' room in the German Occupation Museum, owned by the aforementioned founder of the CIOS. I had previously written to him to consult and ask his thoughts on the trail and its sites. On receiving no reply, I decided to discuss it with him in person when I was next in the Island. On this occasion I was told explicitly that the CIOS did not want a resistance trail at all. The real problem may have been that the CIOS was not the organization designing the trail and choosing the locations and, thus, the promoted narratives. Despite this potential setback, the director of GMAG confirmed that they were still happy for me to continue designing the trail.

It is worth stating that, at the time of writing,[44] Guernsey's resistance trail still has yet to come into being as a heritage product. In late 2015, when I proposed the trail, I was told that it could be placed on the GMAG website as a PDF for people to download, but this has not yet taken place. There are plans afoot for it to be turned into a smartphone App in due course. Until it goes live, the impact or reception of the trail in political or popular circles cannot be gauged. In the meantime, the list of sites has been added to the Frank Falla Archive website.[45]

Digital heritage has great potential for putting online that which is too controversial to place on the ground, in the landscape or townscape. While the former can be a substitute for the latter, inevitably more traditional forms of heritage can sometimes feel more important in challenging existing narratives because of their greater visibility. In places where this is indeed the case, digital heritage can form a primary step for raising awareness and familiarizing people with alternative stories relating to the places where they live or visit. That which is controversial or provocative can be tried out online, to get audiences used to these narratives, such that more traditional heritage inclusion can be an easier step when it is attempted.

Conclusions

Like the examples in the previous chapter, the creation of the Resistance Memorial, the Frank Falla Archive and the resistance trails are all potential examples of incremental memory events. Time will tell how much of a puncture in the fabric of memory they achieve in Guernsey but, by their presence, they act to familiarize the general public with the victims of Nazism in their heritage landscape and to engender their acceptance.

Rather like Michael Billig's 'banal nationalism',[46] whereby flags and other symbols of the nation are constant banal reminders of nationhood, so memorials of resistance in the landscape (physical and digital) have the potential to become so normalized and internalized that they could become a form of unthinkingly accepted 'banal heritage' in the form of 'banal memorialisation', even though this form of heritage is anything but banal.

The case studies discussed in this chapter are also attempts at what I have termed reparative heritage, a concept which takes inspiration from the work of Hirsch and Spitzer, but with a stronger activist stance. For many decades, victims of Nazism were not just ignored, but cast as troublemakers who rocked the boat and made things more dangerous for everyone else. Because of this, they have not, since the Occupation, been allocated more than small sections of museums. Even then, only the most 'worthy' among resisters are often featured. The Frank Falla Archive addresses this lacuna and makes sure that the story of every deported person will now be available online. It also brings together in one place the scattered archival legacies of those who were deported, which has allowed acts of rescue to be performed and the bodies of the lost to be recovered. These acts of rescue, as I have termed them, coupled with BBC coverage in documentaries and online news items, have also acted to make a new generation of audience members familiar with victims of Nazism, and to see them as brave forebears of whose actions they can be proud. Whether the case studies discussed here can be classed as successful examples of reparative heritage is yet to be fully gauged, but their very existence establishes a base line of legitimacy. This is why the Resistance Memorial, the heritage trails and the Frank Falla Archive can all be classed as effective: they raise awareness of victims of Nazism, especially when stories can be shared through social media and pique curiosity. To get such heritage products erected, established or presented online in the first place means that the metaphorical and literal landscape becomes pluralized and victims of Nazism can become part of the visual narrative of Occupation.[47]

As in the previous chapter, there has been resistance to these initiatives, and even self-censorship by the daughter of one of the men whose name has been withheld from the Resistance Memorial in Guernsey. Those who have not supported the creation of new heritage are those who fear that they have something to lose, whether that is their reputation or a monopoly on Occupation narratives. There are also those who fear what the silenced will say if given a platform. Will they point the finger of blame at those who did not defend them against the occupiers? Or has that moment long passed: will resistance families now look to the future and be proud that their relatives are being remembered with honour and respect at last?

When scattered legacies and fragmented heritages are reunited, collated in one place, there is potential for them to become something that they never were during the Occupation: an organized force, working together for a common cause. Those who committed acts of protest, defiance and resistance acted alone or in very small groups, and were never part of a 'resistance movement' in the Channel Islands. Yet there is potential for them to be brought together for the first time, and not necessarily to challenge those who once denigrated their memory or their actions. Studying the larger group has allowed many new patterns and facts to emerge about the experience and trajectory of deportation and imprisonments. It has also allowed the fates of some to be uncovered and those of others to contest what was once established fact, even if that does involve changes to current heritage provision.

The future for this new body of work is not just in the field of heritage, but in education as well. Conversations which have long been left unspoken can be discussed safely in the classroom. What is politically too sensitive to voice out loud to those in power can be more safely harnessed to discuss in a safe space in schools so that the next generation in the Channel Islands, and especially Guernsey, can grow up with a better understanding of the past and with victims of Nazism being a legitimate subject of study and constituting a legitimate heritage at last.

9

Conclusion: A Legitimate Heritage?

It has been my aim in this book to build a historical picture that seeks to explain the long-term processes which have marginalized Channel Islander victims of Nazi persecution in history, memory and heritage. Just as much as external factors have excluded them, they have been silenced through other internal processes. Early in the book I wanted to give an insight into precisely what their experiences were within prisons, labour camps and concentration camps on the Continent. It is important to show that, even though they were, according to the *Geheime Feldpolizei,* supposed to have been treated leniently in the Channel Islands because of their British nationality,[1] this was not the case once they were deported. Their places of incarceration were every bit as unpleasant, violent, cold, squalid and deprived as that faced by victims of Nazi persecution from other countries. Despite this, I wanted to explore whether there was a uniquely British experience in Nazi prisons and camps and, if so, what it was. Through analysing post-war memoirs and testimonies written in the 1960s I showed how Islanders benefitted from friendship groups where they could be united by their language and lack of skill in the common languages of the camps. They also sought comfort from each other due to the ill-treatment that their nationality provoked among the guards, who seemed to derive pleasure from targeting the 'English swine'. By contrast, their fellow prisoners from Allied countries on occasion shared their food or made friends with British prisoners. While this was no doubt triggered by genuine friendship and anti-German feeling, there were probably also aspirations for preferential treatment when the Allies finally liberated them. Such friendship groups are crucial to our understanding of long-term processes at play in this book because they transcended death. After the war they motivated survivors to keep alive the memory of their dead friends and to speak for them. The survivors also encouraged others to remember and recognize them and their deeds as legitimate, patriotic and honourable, even though the task took decades. The mission and duties of the guardians of memory, who we met later in the book, were shaped by and in the prisons and camps of Europe.

Returning to the Channel Islands, we observed in Chapter 3 the actions of the local authorities both during and immediately after the Occupation in terms of how they perceived – and encouraged others to perceive – resisters and those who committed acts of protest, defiance and resistance. This chapter focused on the way that the local authorities stuck, limpet-like, to the Hague Convention as the only correct and legitimate course of action, and one to which their loyal adherence could not be criticized by the British government after the war. When confronted by a situation that was not covered by it, they were paralyzed by inaction, which included failing to act to protect those prosecuted by German courts.

Such fidelity to the Convention was to prove their ticket to staying in office. However, the local authorities were not preaching to the converted when it came to the local populations. Grass-roots opinions immediately after the Occupation showed, in film, who the ordinary Islanders thought were the troublemakers to be punished: the informers. Resisters were not given honours after the war as this would have raised their status and given them an aura of legitimacy that the authorities did not believe they possessed or should possess. This would then have given them a platform and a voice, which they might have used for condemning the authorities for not supporting them or protecting them, even behind the backs of the Germans. Survivors might not have been willing to let the calls be dropped for the prosecution of informers, as the Jersey Loyalists were pressurized to do. The States of Guernsey and Jersey were more interested in pleasing the British government post-war rather than their own people. It was to lead to knighthoods for them, and not for any brave victim of Nazi persecution. Awarding knighthoods was also the British government's way of shutting down dissent and further criticism, and it allowed the Channel Islands' governments to remain in office. Had the action of resisters been declared correct and legitimate, then by definition that of the authorities would have been illegitimate. Self-interest and self-preservation on behalf of the Islands' governments made sure that victims of Nazism were denied a voice.

In Guernsey there could be no action taken against informers given that Bailiff Victor Carey had encouraged denunciation, and given the hard-line stand that the authorities took against resisters during and after the Occupation. There could be no hope of sympathy for men and women returning from prisons and camps. In Jersey there was some support in local government for prosecuting informers and sympathy for those who died but, in the end, the fact that the local authorities' shortcomings had been noted by intelligence officers made them anxious to toe the line taken by the British government. By burying the names of informers, the names of those they denounced were effectively buried at this time too. By not trying informers in a court of law and making public the repercussions of their acts, the facts and fates of those who died was not established and the appropriate documents were not collated at an earlier date. This left a legacy of oral testimony, rumour and myth.

In the fourth chapter we returned to the perspectives of the returning victims of Nazism, observing how rife mental and physical ill-health was among survivors. For many, these developed into chronic conditions that lasted throughout their lives. For some, these conditions improved with treatment after the war. For others, the long-term impact of incarceration on their health would only emerge in later years, after retirement and a lifetime of trying to blot out painful memories of the war years by burying themselves in work. A now-unquantifiable number of Islanders who returned exhibited symptoms of PTSD, but because mental ill-health was stigmatized in the 1960s, and because the range of symptoms of the condition was not fully recognized, nor named as a condition until 1980, the right treatment was neither available, affordable, nor sought in most cases. Indeed, the ill-health of many returnees meant that they were unable to hold down work that would enable them to support their families, let alone seek expensive medical treatment. Instead, Islanders tried to self-medicate their symptoms and focus on the future.

Those who managed to transcend their conditions to take on the authorities, testify against war criminals, or help their friends from their prison days, were few in number, decimated to a now-unknown degree by their conditions. By making comparisons with Dutch resistance veterans fifty years after the war, we can suggest that the political atmosphere in the Channel Islands was such that former victims of Nazism received little official sympathy or public support and understanding beyond their own families and friendship groups. Their suffering served only to remind others of their lack of courage during the Occupation. The failure to legitimize their wartime actions would have compounded symptoms of PTSD and further hindered the ability of many to become guardians of memory in the future.

The fifth chapter illustrated how the first twenty years after the war was not a period of silence for victims of Nazism, despite the apparent lack of public attention they received during this period. Despite the political climate in the Channel Islands where the local authorities were still not sympathetic towards them, and still denied their legitimacy, former victims spoke out. While there are very few examples of men or women who recited everything of what they had experienced to their families, there is ample evidence to suggest that the children and spouses of victims of Nazism gained, in other ways, insight into the sufferings of those who returned. When gathered or communicating among themselves, however, those who survived were more willing to speak about what they had experienced. They drew strength from each other which enabled a few people, such as Guernseymen Frank Falla and Frank Tuck, to emerge to begin their fight with the local authorities to argue for the legitimacy of their actions and that of their friends. Unfortunately this proved to be simply another opportunity for the Islands' leaders to restate their wartime position, and yet another opportunity to publicly de-legitimate the narrative of the victims of Nazism.

Denying these men and women legitimacy since the end of the war has meant that the archival records in the Channel Islands relating to victims of Nazism have remained inadequate, scattered and messy. When the British government began to gather the necessary data, from the late 1950s onwards, for the early stages Anglo-German compensation agreement, they needed to know how many victims of Nazism there were. Their communication with the Channel Islands' leaders reveals the latter's ignorance and a massive underestimate of the numbers of victims and survivors. This points either to poorly kept archives on the subject, or else a lack of willingness to spend the time to gather together the appropriate records or to ask an employee to carry out this job. This, in turn, implied a lack of care for the fate of victims. By the mid-1960s, the dominant Churchillian narrative, upheld by the authorities, still held sway without the slightest of cracks.

In Chapter 6 we arrived at the mid-1960s and the period of the Anglo-German compensation agreement which saw the Federal Republic of Germany give a million pounds of compensation to the UK government. Just over 100 applicants were from Channel Islanders. Although small in number, this total was high in terms of success rate. While almost half of all applications from the Channel Islands were successful, the UK success rate overall was 22 per cent. This was almost entirely thanks to the work of

Frank Falla, who became the 'unofficial official' in his dealings with the Foreign Office because the Islands authorities exhibited a *'certain apathy'*, as he put it, towards the compensation claims and did not want to get involved.

Falla used his own concepts of legitimacy to fight the case for Channel Islanders to be involved in the compensation claims, which was far from certain at the outset given that that Islands are not part of the United Kingdom. Nevertheless, Falla held tight to the description of his actions and those of his colleagues as 'political', knowing that political opposition to Nazism was likely to be compensated. He played down the status of the Guernsey policemen, whose cases had already been dismissed by the Privy Council in 1951, as 'non-political'. Instead he associated himself and his colleagues with those whom he thought would increase his chances of success: people such as Harold Le Druillenec, whose legitimacy was beyond reproach and who had testified at war crimes trials. Falla's fight with the Foreign Office revealed a system that was not always fair, leaving one questioning whose concept and knowledge of Nazi persecution was the more legitimate: that of the applicants or Foreign Office.

Falla felt so bolstered and emboldened after the successes of the compensation claims that he went on to write his memoirs in 1967. This book marked the first public platform of a victim of Nazism, and it held nothing back. His outspoken condemnation of the Channel Islands' authorities was now in print, and drew a line in the sand in its statement of where legitimate behaviour lay during and after the Occupation.

The third part of the book, beginning with Chapter 7, explored the period from 1965 to the present, looking at the role of guardians of memory and their successors, the game-changers. The guardians of memory for political prisoners were those of the first generation, their fellow victims of Nazism, who made it their duty, and sometimes their life's work, to fight for those who survived or died during incarceration. The game-changers, on the other hand, were the people who emerged in various positions of power and authority and were willing and able to continue their work, albeit in different ways. The game-changers were successful in Jersey in breaking the stranglehold of the Churchillian narrative. They changed the historical conversation permanently to include victims of Nazism through using incremental memory events, most notably in the field of heritage activism.

In Jersey, the new heritage involved yoking together Jews and political prisoners, most especially during HMD commemorations. Inspired by this success, this chapter also explored the extent to which such a strategy might be successful in Guernsey. By charting the attempts at creating such incremental memory events through changing the format of successive commemorations of HMD from 2015 onwards, the blocking agents still in force in Guernsey today were identified. However, real changes have taken place. There is now a Resistance Memorial, a States Resolution on the Holocaust which has led to public endorsement of HMD by some political and religious elites, and the beginnings of Holocaust education. In the end, this will make the difference because, as Andy Pearce has argued, 'when a period of history is marginal in both the education system and the wider cultural realm, it follows that degrees of ignorance, indifference and disinterest will ensue'.[2]

The eighth chapter offered two new concepts to think through the kinds of fragmented heritages that now exist for victims of Nazi persecution, especially in

Guernsey. The first concept considered 'reparative heritage', which built upon Hirsch and Spitzer's concept of 'small acts of repair'. Acts of reparative heritage include erecting memorials or holding exhibitions to those whose experiences have been marginalized, forgotten and denied legitimacy. This form of heritage requires activism to come to fruition and seeks public and political legitimacy and acknowledgement for those it represents. It is not modest in its demands.

Reparative heritage often starts with acts of rescue, examples of which include finding graves of the dead, laying memorial plaques or reconstructing the lost stories and trajectories of victims of Nazi persecution through archival records. Digital heritage, too, can be used to marry reparative and fragmented heritages to create projects ideally suited to the medium, such as heritage trails and education projects. Digital heritage can be used to raise awareness and to allow audiences to become more familiar with and accepting of alternative narratives relating to the places where they live. The Frank Falla Archive, highlighted here, is an example of a reliable source for the next generation for whom victims of Nazism can become a legitimate subject for study.

The role of incremental memory events

The concept of the incremental memory event is presented here as a useful conceptual tool for thinking about change and how it happens. It potentially presents a strategy for adoption in other places where change is sought through the use of heritage activism. It is clear that incremental memory events do not offer a quick fix. Rather, by their nature, they take advantage of existing opportunities (such as HMD), and create new ones by seeking to help facilitate new projects in the form of memorials and exhibitions. While the events recorded here have been instigated with the help and support of local people, there are still ethical issues to consider.

If the researcher or activist wishes to help facilitate change, then that person must be sure that their agenda has support among the group for whom they speak or act. The activist must also be sensitive enough to understand the motives of any blocking forces. Are they blocking activism because of self-interest, or wanting to preserve the status quo because it shores up their own work and narratives, or because the aims of the activist are wrong-headed, unsuitable for that community, or due to a lack of historical knowledge or understanding of the local situation? There is a danger of paternalistic attitudes, of assuming that the activist know best. The activist should be prepared to question their motives as they work and to ask in whose interest and name they work. Does working on behalf of a group who one believes to be morally or ethically legitimate guarantee that the project is a just one? Will the community in question always be better off as a result of the activism, or is there a potential for harm? While there are no correct answers to these questions, the activist must be prepared to question themselves and their actions continuously, and to discuss plans with the local community first to ensure that any heritage project will be valued and supported rather than vandalized as soon as is completed. Digital heritage projects are always viable alternatives to more traditional forms.

While a number of incremental memory events have been discussed in this volume, it is interesting to observe that events similar to – but not as effective as – these have taken place in earlier decades, and have not had the same impact or ability to punch holes in the fabric of memory. They have not qualified as incremental memory events. This has been because the political and historical milieux in which they have taken place has not been conducive to change. A good example of this can be seen in an episode which took place in Jersey in 1966, during the Cold War.

In March of that year, a delegation from the Soviet Embassy in London, headed by the *chargé d'affaires*, Mr Vassev, came to the Island to award gold watches to those who sheltered Russian forced labourers during the Occupation. Such high-ranking guests to the Island were welcomed by local officials and members of the States. They stayed at Government House with the Lieutenant-Governor, and were also presented to the Bailiff, Robert Le Masurier. At the evening reception, gold watches were presented to twenty Islanders (or rather to thirteen, as five were not present and two were deceased). Harold Le Druillenec acted as a spokesperson, giving a speech during which he thanked Mr Vassev for the awards and for 'showing the appreciation of his Government for what the Islanders had done during the war'. He also thanked the 'many distinguished guests from Jersey who have graced the reception with their presence'.[3] This speech of thanks was more than politeness; Le Druillenec must have been touched to have been recognized at last, and in the presence of the Bailiff, Lieutenant-Governor, and Alexander Coutanche, the Occupation-period Bailiff. Indeed, he may have been surprised to learn that the names were provided to the Russians by the Bailiff after they wrote to request them two months earlier.[4] Quite how the Bailiff's office sourced the names is unknown. Perhaps Le Druillenec himself had helped in this regard.

This was the first time that recognition of the actions of Le Druillenec and his sisters[5] had been given. That the tribute had not come from the government of Jersey, nor Westminster, but from the Russians, was telling and perhaps not surprising. Over the preceding years, the family sometimes felt that they had 'done something wrong',[6] such was the lack of appreciation that they received. Needless to say, the event of the award of gold watches was not one which sparked a reassessment in the Channel Islands of those who had helped forced labourers, or been sent to prison or deported for their humanity. The politics of the Cold War arguably prevented this ceremony from becoming an incremental memory event, even though it occurred at around the same time as the compensation claims. Had the political climate been different, these two events might have been able to pack quite a punch; and yet it wasn't to be.

Thirty years later, the projects of the game-changers in Jersey came thick and fast, and it is arguably this density of events, activism and projects that helped to cement change. While I have discussed some of the major exhibitions and memorial projects that they oversaw, there were smaller supporting acts. Some of these were instrumental in helping to change attitudes. Others ensured that the change in attitudes would be permanent. These smaller acts were unlikely to have been possible at earlier dates, nor to have created an impact.

In 1997, as we saw in an earlier chapter, former *Nacht und Nebel* prisoner from Jersey, Peter Hassall, fulfilled a promise made many decades earlier, and managed, with the help of others in Jersey, to repatriate the body of his friend, Maurice Gould, who lay in a military cemetery in Wittlich, having died in the nearby prison. Fifty-five years to the day after they tried to escape, Maurice Gould's remains were reburied in the Allied war cemetery in Howard Davis Park in St Helier. That his remains could be buried with 'war heroes', rather than in a family plot in one of the parish church graveyards, was an indication of the changed climate in the Island and the elevated memory that victims of Nazism could now command. In fact, Hassall's repatriation of Gould's remains is an early example of an 'act of rescue' of the kind discussed in the last chapter (Figure 9.1)

Such acts still continue in Jersey. In September 2018, the remains of Frank Le Villio, one of the Jersey 21, were reburied in Jersey having been exhumed from a paupers' grave in Nottingham. Le Villio had died of TB in 1946 after experiencing and surviving a number of concentration camps, including Neuengamme. A local historian had discovered his final resting place and had campaigned to return Le Villio's body to the Island. The repatriation drew much local support and media attention, and a local funeral director donated his services free of charge. Despite the fact that Le Villio was originally convicted of larceny, the return of his body to the Island was not greeted with any complaint or opposition – quite the opposite.

If we view the respect with which we treat the dead and their graves as indicative of the extent to which a society honours their memory and – in the case of victims of Nazism – their cause, then we might pause to contrast Gould and Le Villio's grave with that of John Ingrouille, one of the Guernsey Eight. Twenty-year-old Ingrouille was deported in March 1941 after being falsely accused of threatening the Germans with an army of 800 men. He passed through one French and three German prisons, where he was ill-treated, and was liberated only to succumb to the effects of tuberculosis on his journey home. He died in a hospital in Brussels and his parents repatriated his

Figure 9.1 Allied war cemetery with Maurice Gould's grave on the right, Howard Davis Park, St Helier. Copyright: Gilly Carr

body to Guernsey in 1946. They received compensation for his death in the mid-1960s and spent the money on a stained glassed window in the local church in their son's memory. Inevitably, after they died, there was nobody to take care of his grave. Its state of repair in 2010, 2015 and 2018 showed that it was still in a process of active decay and neglect, despite being tidied in 2015 (Figures 9.2a, b and c). The wooden cross raised above Ingrouille's grave by his parents had fallen apart and the grave was covered in weeds. After I wrote an article for the local paper about the state of the grave, a distant relative living in England came forward in August 2018 with an offer to pay for marble chips to be placed on the grave to discourage weeds.

At the same time as past victims of Nazism were being honoured in Jersey and neglected in Guernsey, the children of some of the Guernsey police deported in 1942 to concentration and labour camps were seeking legal redress, in 2018, for their fathers. At the time of writing, the Attorney General's team in Guernsey has yet to cooperate with the police families' law firm in London. Several extensions have been sought and given with no progress yet made. This court case – if it gets that far – will be

Figure 9.2a John Ingrouille's grave in 2010. Copyright: Gilly Carr

Conclusion 203

Figure 9.2b John Ingrouille's grave in 2015. Copyright: Dave and Rosie Bradshaw

an extremely interesting litmus test to see the extent to which the Island is ready, after seventy-eight years, to take the side of victims of Nazism.

The *grands absents*

We might think that once the climate has permanently changed (if this position is, indeed, ever reached) and we reach a position where victims of Nazi persecution become part of the mainstream narrative of Occupation, with their stories told in schools, then we have achieved our aims. But we are still left with the dark underbelly of two unresolved issues. The first is the problem of where this leaves the informers– those whose actions led to the arrest and deportation of many victims. The second is the Islands' local authorities, who did not stand up for, nor support, those given custodial sentences and deported. To what extent do we need to find resolution for these issues, or can they be left in the past? If we do so, are they likely to remain yet another aspect of the Occupation that continues to be spoken about in hushed tones, standing in the way of the Islands finally coming to terms with all aspects of their past?

In Jersey, now that the victims of Nazism have taken their place in the Occupation narrative, the informers are the *grands absents*, with seemingly no further role to play. Despite that, in 2008 Channel Television reporter, Eric Blakeley, made the documentary *Betrayed to the Nazis*. In this he showed recently unclassified documents which named

Figure 9.2c John Ingrouille's grave in 2018. Copyright: Molly Paul

the two sisters who were thought to have denounced Louisa Gould. This documentary earned him an award nomination. Despite this, the key difficulty in incorporating informers into any narrative is that most are nameless. Many of the victims of Nazism had a very good idea of who had denounced them, and names of informers are often passed down through the generations in the Channel Islands. Without proof, it is hard (if not ethically problematic) to create a 'perpetrator wall of shame' in any museum exhibition.

Despite that, such a 'rogues' gallery' exists today at a tourist attraction, Jersey War Tunnels, comprising photographs and stories collected by the late Joe Mière (Figure 9.3). This exhibit, on display in the café, is grouped into various colour-coded categories. One is labelled 'Persecuted and Persecutors', the latter displaying photos, coded in black, of the men of the German Secret Field Police. Another, coded red, is headed 'Fraternised with the Enemy', and tells the story of notorious 'Jerrybags',[7] people who traded preferentially with Germans, and two collaborators. The latter were deported English men who came to Jersey just before the war with the Peace Pledge Union, who ended up being recruited into the Nazi British Free Corps from their internment camp of Marlag and Milag Nord. While Jerrybags were suspected of acting

Figure 9.3 The café of Jersey War Tunnels. Copyright: Gilly Carr

as informers, this particular aspect of the display is more concerned with fraternization than with denunciation per se.

Although the names of some informers are known to the extent that their identities are recorded in archival documents, we return once again to the problem created by the lack of post-war trials. The guilt or innocence of certain individuals was not established at a time when it may have been possible to do so. While that of many alleged Jerrybags was not established in law, it has not prevented their names being reproduced in books and exhibitions, unlike that of the informers.

The lack of trials has also meant, as we have seen, that it was not established who ultimately did the right thing: the Islands' authorities, who condemned those who offended against the Germans, or those who were prepared to disobey both them and the Germans. But given the consequences for those who were deported, should we expect a belated apology today from those in positions of authority? Is an acknowledgement of not doing more, of failing to protect all of its citizens, necessary in order to move forwards? Or is it too late given that the original actors have long since passed away? Speeches expressing this kind of regret have been given in Jersey and are regularly repeated in that Island on HMD. It is unclear whether this has this been a necessary part of allowing victims of Nazism to take their place within the master narrative of Occupation in that Island, but it has certainly facilitated the process.

In Guernsey the situation is complicated by the associated deportation to France of three Jewish women without British citizenship, who later died in Auschwitz. An admission of guilt in the failure to protect one victim group would be difficult without an apology for the deportation of another. In this regard, yoking together the memory of the Jews and the political prisoners for commemorative purposes in Guernsey may prove problematic (or serendipitous, as the case may be); it would be difficult to apologize for wrongdoing against one and not the other. The case of the Jews is more clear-cut than the political prisoners, given the varied nature of the latter's offences. The advantages and disadvantages of combining the two groups together on HMD have yet to make themselves clearly apparent.

HMD in Guernsey is still in a state of flux and has yet to settle down into a fixed formula. At present, a ceremony with floral tributes rather than verbal expressions of regret seems to lack some essence of the day's purpose. Without adequate recourse to the past, the day seems to lack conviction or sincerely held intentions. There is a danger that Guernsey's new Resistance Memorial, coupled with the Jewish Memorial, will function as sites that facilitate a process that allows elites to pay lip service to honouring the dead, but without reflecting on what they represent. As James Young has pointed out, such sites can take over from us the responsibility to remember.[8] They become instead what Geyer has called a 'wreath drop zone'[9] – an insincere expression of regret when it is politically necessary. Memorials on their own are not enough.

The Channel Islands and the Holocaust

At the start of this book I asked *how* and *why* the particular victims of Nazism under discussion here should fit into the British narrative of the Holocaust. The Channel Islands are perennially marginalized in this historical discussion (except to allege collaboration) because of their small size and the small number of Jewish victims. There is the additional problem of a lack of knowledge of the precise number and names of Islanders who were in camps, apart from the oft-cited Harold Le Druillenec, but the Frank Falla Archive website is now in a position to resolve this.

Like the British POWs discussed recently by Russell Wallis,[10] Channel Islanders in concentration camps and labour camps were highly likely to have been witnesses to the way that Jews were treated, and a number of compensation testimonies refer to Jews. We know that at least three of those deported from the Channel Islands testified to war crimes investigators,[11] and many more were co-victims of starvation, disease, brutality and ill-treatment in the same places of incarceration as Jews. And yet those deported for offences against the occupiers were, bar one person,[12] not Jewish and so, by definition, not part of the Holocaust, even if they were witnesses to aspects of it. What, therefore, is their place in history? Are they of no interest outside the Channel Islands, or can their experiences of incarceration in around 125 different prisons and camps[13] help inform us about the British experience of the Second World War and its co-witnesses to the Holocaust? The Channel Islanders' testimony deserves to be better known and to sit alongside that of POWs sent to concentration camps or sub-camps, and members of the SOE who were caught by the Gestapo. In fact, some deported Channel Islanders were also witnesses to both of these groups, especially in Buchenwald and Ravensbrück. The weight of Islanders' testimonies, alongside that of others who had 'endured the co-presence of the "Final Solution"' as 'intimate witnesses', as Tony Kushner put it,[14] is yet another argument for all of these groups to be incorporated more fully within Britain's memory of the Holocaust. And yet Kushner has also argued that an 'analysis of Britain's relationship with the Holocaust has to have, as its starting point, a humility that accepts' a 'gulf in experience' between that of Jews and British citizens.[15] While he was referring to British POWs held in camp E715, who worked in the Buna factory of Auschwitz, the gulf is not quite so large when we consider the experience of SOE agents and some of the Channel Islanders who were victims in camps just as much as they were witnesses. There were British witnesses in varying degrees of 'intimacy' and victimhood when it came to Nazi persecution and the Holocaust.

At the time of writing, preparations are underway for a new learning centre and memorial for the UK Holocaust Memorial Foundation. The Imperial War Museum's Holocaust gallery is also being redesigned. There is scope for additional British voices in both of these projects, for witnesses / co-victims as well as for Jewish victims. The compensation testimonies newly released to The National Archives provide us with a wealth of new material. There is also a case to be made for a greater role in UK Holocaust education for the testimony of these kinds of witnesses and co-sufferers. School students may find it easier to relate to stories of people from their own shores who were sent to Nazi prisons and camps, as well as those who came to the UK as refugees and gained British nationality after the war. It would certainly help to address the misconceptions that the Second World War was something only 'fought on the continent by continentals'[16] or, by extension, that only continentals were occupied, deported or incarcerated by the Nazis.

There is yet another potential role for this element of the Channel Islands' story – one that is illustrated equally by the narrative of the Islands' Jews and other victims of Nazism, and that is the subject of failure. The failure of the Islands' governments to adequately protect their citizens or monitor who was deported; the failure of both the British and Islands' governments to hold trials after the war; the failure of the British government to admit more Jewish refugees before and after the war; and the failure of the Foreign Office to better understand Nazi persecution and to compensate more people than they did.

As Kushner has recently shown, Britain has long had a triumphalist wartime narrative with regard to the Holocaust – and the Second World War in general: what Mark Donnelly calls the 'good war' paradigm.[17] Kushner argues that Britain has had a 'tendency towards self-congratulation that has never really disappeared, and is unlikely to in the foreseeable future (given Britain's unique and untarnished – in its own mind – relationship to the Second World War)'.[18] This attitude is despite evidence of behaviour which should provoke a more humble response. Where the UK has boasted about the number of Jewish refugees it took in, it is rather more silent about the many more that it turned away or prevented from reaching Palestine. When there were calls to bomb the railway lines leading to Auschwitz and the camp itself, it did not do so. The UK has remained, according to Kushner, 'several decades behind' other countries in terms of a critical and self-reflective perspective towards its own wartime actions and inactions.[19] Guernsey has not been so different in this respect, even if Jersey seems to have (perhaps unknowingly) led the British Isles in self-reflection and self-criticism.

At a time of 'increasing ethnic and racial tensions at a global level, and the worst refugee crisis since the Second World War', argues Kushner, 'critical perspectives are more than ever required in the dialogue between "then" and "now"'.[20] The problems of the current era have also provoked a need for more people to stand up to fascism and far-right ideology. School children need more British role-models of those who were 'upstanders' and rescuers, or who exhibited high standards of ethical or moral behaviour in the face of Nazism and far-right ideology. Channel Islander victims of Nazism can fulfil those roles, providing balance to others who have brought criticism upon the Channel Islands for their facilitation of antisemitic legislation and its implementation.

Among those honoured as British Heroes of the Holocaust in 2010, when the award was instigated by the Holocaust Educational Trust, were Harold Le Druillenec and two of his sisters. Albert Bedane, who sheltered Jewish woman Mary Richardson, was also honoured that year. Since then, the name of Dorothea Weber née Le Brocq was added to the list in 2018 after her case was put forward by the author. These are stories which can be recited with pride alongside those which represent a failing. As Paul Sanders put it, after he proposed four Islanders for the award in 2010, 'Islanders could no longer be portrayed as having behaved like a bunch of pathetic or venal accommodators – a storyline still touted by parts of the UK media only a decade earlier – but had tried to do their bit as well'.[21]

The role of the Channel Islands' victims of Nazism and their governments give us yet another response as to *why* the Holocaust should become part of Britain's memory culture. While there was scepticism when Holocaust Memorial Day was first introduced in the UK because mainland Britain had not been occupied and the Holocaust was perceived as a geographically distant event,[22] such disinterest can be shown as misconceived when the wider British Isles are taken into account. On the same theme, Caroline Sharples and Olaf Jensen have drawn attention to the myth that 'Britain's physical remoteness from the Holocaust can be seen as facilitating a limited dialogue with the crimes: they happened in a different land, in a very different political climate; they could not possibly happen here'.[23] The case of the Channel Islands clearly destroys that myth, increasing the potential of Channel Islands' case studies to increase engagement with the Holocaust.

Although this book ends here, there is clearly more work to be done. Guernsey has not yet come to terms with its past and is currently at least twenty years behind its sister Island. It is difficult to say how long this process will take and whether the two Islands are destined to follow the same trajectory. Guernsey still lacks game-changers – or at least, enough game-changers – who are willing to work together to broaden Occupation narratives to encompass victims of Nazism. One of the most important game-changers in Jersey was the Island's Bailiff, who made speeches and unveiled memorials to create change. Guernsey has yet to witness such a Bailiff, and there is no predicting whether the next Bailiff, or the one after that, will be the same sort of figure as Sir Philip Bailhache. Perhaps the person to create change will come from a different field altogether. However, it seems to this author that while some vital foundation stones in the form of incremental memory events have been laid – the Resistance Memorial, the States Resolution on the Holocaust, and Holocaust education, not to mention the Frank Falla Archive – the momentum needs to be kept up. If it is not, progress could be very slow indeed and we will need to look to the next generation, who will now be given Holocaust education, to see the Occupation through new eyes. Perhaps it is only they who can decide, in the end, whether victims of Nazism are a legitimate heritage.

Notes

Chapter 1

1. Carr, G. 2014. *Legacies of Occupation: Heritage, Memory and Archaeology in the Channel Islands*. Switzerland: Springer International Publishing, pp. 286–9.
2. Rousso, H. 2007. 'History of memory, policies of the past: What for?' pp. 23–77 in K. Jarausch and T. Lindenberger (eds), *Conflicted Memories: Europeanizing Contemporary Histories*. New York: Berghahn Books, p. 207.
3. Sanders, P. 2012. 'Narratives of Britishness: UK war memory and Channel Islands occupation memory', pp. 24–39 in J. Matthews and D. Travers (eds), *Islands and Britishness: A Global Perspective*. Newcastle upon Tyne: Cambridge Scholars Publishing, p. 25.
4. Sanders, P. 2005. *The British Channel Islands under German Occupation, 1940–1945*. Jersey: Jersey Heritage Trust, p. 256.
5. Ramsden, J. 2010. 'Myths and Realities of the "People's War" in Britain', pp. 40–52 in J. Echternkamp and S. Martens (eds), *Experience and Memory: The Second World War in Europe*. New York and Oxford: Berghahn Books, p. 40.
6. Connelly, M. 2010. 'We can take it! Britain and the memory of the home front in the Second World War', pp. 53–69 in J. Echternkamp and S. Martens (eds), *Experience and Memory: The Second World War in Europe*. New York and Oxford: Berghahn Books, p. 54.
7. Sanders, *The British Channel Islands under German Occupation*, p. 256.
8. Jorgensen-Earp, C. 2013. *Discourse and Defiance under Nazi Occupation: Guernsey, Channel Islands, 1940–1945*. East Lansing: Michigan State University Press, p. 58.
9. Jorgensen-Earp, *Discourse and Defiance under Nazi Occupation*, p. 59.
10. Cottrell, L. 1950. 'The Man from Belsen', pp. 97–110 in L. Gilliam (ed.), *BBC Features*. London: Evans Brothers Ltd.
11. Stories such as these are told in *Islands in Danger* by Alan and Mary Wood, published in 1955. The reader is referred here or to www.frankfallaarchive.org to read the stories of Lillian Kinnard, Kathleen Norman, Winifred Green, Nan and Edward Ross, William Symes and William Green, for example.
12. Advertising poster. TNA ref. FO 950/765.
13. Agreement between the UK of Great Britain and Northern Ireland and the Federal Republic of Germany concerning compensation for UK nationals who were Victims of National-Socialist Measures of Persecution. TNA ref. FO 950/741.
14. TNA ref. FO 371/183129.
15. Cohen, F. 2000. *The Jews in the Channel Islands during the German Occupation 1940–1945*. Jersey: Jersey Heritage Trust; Fraser, D. 2000. *The Jews of the Channel Islands and the Rule of Law*. Brighton: Sussex Academic Press; www.frankfallaarchive.org [accessed 15 July 2018].
16. Political prisoner logbook, Jersey Archives ref. D/AG/B7/1.

17. Carr, G. 2014. 'Heritage, memory and resistance in the Channel Islands', pp. 307–37 in G. Carr, P. Sanders and L. Willmot (eds), *Protest, Defiance and Resistance in the Channel Islands: German Occupation 1940–1945*. London: Bloomsbury Academic, p. 311.
18. Those from Jersey who died in prisons and camps. The number has varied slightly over the last twenty years. What started as the Jersey 20 became the Jersey 22 after new names were added to the Lighthouse Memorial which remembers this group. After one person was found to have survived the Occupation, the number is currently 21.
19. Sanders, P. 2004. *The Ultimate Sacrifice* (2nd edition). Jersey: Jersey Heritage Trust, p. 13.
20. Sanders, P. 2018. *The Ultimate Sacrifice* (3rd edition). Jersey: Jersey Heritage Trust, pp. xix–xx.
21. Sanders, *The Ultimate Sacrifice*.
22. Ibid., p. xix.
23. See Carr, G., Sanders, P. and Willmot, L. 2014. *Protest, Defiance and Resistance in the Channel Islands: German Occupation 1940–1945*. London: Bloomsbury Academic.
24. Sanders, *The Ultimate Sacrifice* (3rd edition), pp. xix–xx.
25. TNA ref. FO 950/999.
26. Sanders, *The Ultimate Sacrifice* (3rd edition), p. 112.
27. Willmot, L. 2014. 'Sabotage, intelligence-gathering and escape', pp. 213–42 in G. Carr, P. Sanders and L. Willmot (eds), *Protest, Defiance and Resistance in the Channel Islands: German Occupation 1940–1945*. London: Bloomsbury Academic, p. 225.
28. Willmot, 'Sabotage, intelligence-gathering and escape', p. 226.
29. Hassall, P. 1997. *Night and Fog Prisoners*, unpublished memoir, https://www.frankfallaarchive.org/wp-content/uploads/2016/08/Peter-Hassalls-memoirs.pdf [accessed 1 August 2018], pp. 154, 158 (references to insomnia and nightmares); email conversation with Andrew Hassall (the son of Peter Hassall), 3 August 2018.
30. Carr, 'Heritage, memory and resistance', pp. 308–9.
31. Ibid.
32. Eighteen policemen in Guernsey were tried for stealing food from German stores to give to the hungry; eighteen people in Jersey were tried in connection with the 'St Saviour's wireless case', as it was known. Both cases are discussed in more detail later in this volume.
33. Those from the Island who died in Nazi prisons and camps.
34. Butler, J. 2010. *Frames of War: When is Life Grievable?* London and New York: Verso, p. 31.
35. Extract from speech made by John Leale, 21 June 1940, Guernsey, reproduced in Captain Dening's intelligence report, IWM ref. 13409.
36. In the police case of 1942, the policemen were tried by both the German court and the Royal Court. The conviction of the latter has never been overturned. See also Cruickshank, C. 2010 [1975]. *The German Occupation of the Channel Islands*. Oxford: Oxford University Press & Guernsey: The Guernsey Press. [Reprint, Stroud: Sutton Publishing], p. 117.
37. For example, in the case of the GUNS case, Frank Falla states in his memoirs that they were 'not allowed a defending counsel'; Falla, F. 1967. *The Silent War*. London: Leslie Frewin, p. 106.
38. See the case of the four men from Guernsey, accused of black market offences, sent to Jersey for their trial. Their Guernsey lawyer, Advocate Martel, asked for them to be defended but the Jersey advocate was successful only in being able to plead in mitigation of sentence; this plea was rejected. JA ref. D/Z/H6/3/23.
39. Letter from Victor Carey to Feldkommandantur 515, 26 February 1942. IA, ref. CC 14-05, 95A.

40 Falla, *The Silent War*, p. 106.
41 Weisberg, R.H. 2014. *In Praise of Intransigence: The Perils of Flexibility*. Oxford: Oxford University Press, p. 107.
42 For example, when the local authorities in Guernsey and Jersey made a stand to complain against the deportations of civilians in September 1942 and February 1943; see Carr, G. 2014. 'Defiance and deportations' pp. 127–52 in G. Carr, P. Sanders and L. Willmot (eds), *Protest, Defiance and Resistance in the Channel Islands: German Occupation 1940–1945*', London: Bloomsbury Academic.
43 Sanders, *The British Channel Islands under German Occupation*, pp. 77, 142–3.
44 *The German Occupation of* Jersey by John Hamptonne L'Amy, Société Jersiaise Library ref. MIL/GO/D/12.
45 Wood, A. and Wood, M. 1955. *Islands in Danger*. New York: Macmillan, p. 237.
46 *The Bitter Years* by ITV Channel Television, 1970. https://www.youtube.com/watch?v=rN-XA8Ms1Ns [accessed 22 June 2018].
47 The Guernsey Underground News Service.
48 Mayne, R. 1974. 'Forgotten Islanders', *Channel Islands Occupation Review*, 15–18.
49 Cruickshank, *The German Occupation of the Channel Islands*, pp. 158, 162.
50 An organization whose members collect stamps and postmarks from envelopes of letters written to and from the Channel Islands during the Occupation.
51 Harris, R.E. 1979. *Islanders Deported*. Ilford, Essex: CISS Publishing, p. 163.
52 King, P. 1991. *The Channel Islands War 1940–1945*. London: Robert Hale, p. 188.
53 King, *The Channel Islands War 1940–1945*, p. 158.
54 Ibid., p. 161.
55 Bunting, M. 1995. *The Model Occupation*. London and New York: HarperCollins Publishing / BCA, p. 193.
56 Bunting, *The Model Occupation*, p. 336.
57 Ibid.
58 Mière, J. 2004. *Never to be Forgotten*. Jersey: Channel Island Publishing, p. 197.
59 Falla, *The Silent War*, p. 167.
60 Letter from Joe Mière to President of the Prison Board, 26 February 1996, Joe Mière Collection, c/o Mick Mière.
61 Letter to Philip Bailhache from Joe Mière, 8 March 2001, Joe Mière Collection c/o Mick Mière.
62 Letter to Joe Mière from Stephanie Nicolle, Solicitor General, Law Officers' Department, 1 March 2001. Joe Mière Collection c/o Mick Mière.
63 Letter from Joe Mière to Freddie Cohen, 15 March 2004, Joe Mière Collection c/o Mick Mière.
64 Channel Islanders who were transported to concentration camps or prisons, www.thisisjersey.co.uk/hmd/html/570.html [accessed 31 October 2014]. The website www.occupationmemorial.com, which also contains this data, is currently in abeyance.
65 Arguably, this number should not be included when calculating how many Channel Islanders were deported during the German Occupation.
66 Mière, *Never to be Forgotten*, p. 14.
67 See Carr, G. Sanders, P. and Willmot, L. 2014. 'Conclusion', pp. 329–54 in G. Carr, P. Sanders, and L. Willmot (eds), *Protest, Defiance and Resistance in the Channel Islands: German Occupation 1940–1945*. London: Bloomsbury Academic, p. 351.
68 Number correct as of 1 August 2018.
69 Although the Germans sometimes deported people without notifying the authorities.
70 British subjects tried by the German military courts in Guernsey. Captain JR Dening files, IWM ref. 13409.

Chapter 2

1. The reader is invited to peruse www.frankfallaarchive.org, written by the author [accessed 15 July 2018].
2. Bailey, K.G. 1979 [1958]. *Dachau*. Guernsey: CI Marine Ltd; Falla, *The Silent War*; Faramus, A. 1990. *Journey into Darkness*. London: Grafton Books; Hassall, *Night and Fog Prisoners* (published online); Sherwill, A. 2006. *A Fair and Honest Book*. Lulu. com.
3. For example, Domaille unpublished and Duquemin unpublished, both in private ownership but available on the Frank Falla Archive website (www.frankfallaarchive.org).
4. Cottrell, 'The Man from Belsen'.
5. For example, Falla, 'Revelations of prison life in Germany', *Guernsey Evening Press*, 2 July 1945, 1; 'Revelations of German prison life', *Guernsey Evening Press*, 4 July 1945, 1; Barry, 'From Ravensbruch [sic] to Guernsey', *Guernsey Evening Press*, 17 August 1945; 'I was condemned to death', *Guernsey Evening Press*, 18 July 1945; 'War disclosures of Mrs Julia Barry', *Guernsey Evening Press*, 20 July 1945.
6. Helm, S. 2015. *If This Is a Woman*. London: Little, Brown Book Group, p. 431.
7. Statement by Eddie Chapman, 16 December 1942, TNA ref: KV 2/455 to KV2/463 ('Edward Arnold CHAPMAN, codenamed ZIGZAG').
8. *Sujets britanniques sous contrôle de l'Administration Pénitentaire Français*, document dated 11 March 1943, Archives de Paris, reference 1807W 46. My thanks to Paul Sanders for this document.
9. Bailey, *Dachau*, p. 48.
10. Ibid., p. 69.
11. Duquemin, C. n.d. Unpublished memoirs. https://www.frankfallaarchive.org/wp-content/uploads/2016/10/Cecil-Duquemin-Memoir-edited-RM-GC.pdf [accessed 23 August 2018].
12. Bailey, *Dachau*, p. 69.
13. Ibid., p. 85.
14. Ibid., p. 70.
15. Hassall, *Night and Fog Prisoners*, p. 79.
16. Ibid., p. 83.
17. Ibid., p. 101.
18. Falla, 'Revelations of prison life in Germany'; 'Revelations of German prison life'.
19. Falla, *The Silent War*, p. 45.
20. Falla, 'Revelations of German prison life'.
21. Testimony of Walter Lainé, Foreign Office compensation testimony, HNP 1195.
22. The reader is encouraged to read the following story of Percy Miller written by the author, in which his death is suggested to have been hastened by the beatings of guards: https://www.frankfallaarchive.org/people/percy-william-miller/ [accessed 7 June 2018].
23. Bailey, *Dachau*, p. 37.
24. Ibid., p. 71.
25. Faramus, *Journey into Darkness*, p. 248.
26. Testimony of William Quin, TNA Foreign Office HNP case file 3608.
27. Gerald Domaille, unpublished memoirs, https://www.frankfallaarchive.org/wp-content/uploads/2016/10/Gerald-Domaille-memoirs.pdf [accessed 23 August 2018], p. 23.
28. The SD or *Sicherheitsdienst* were the security service of the SS.

29 Letter from Premysl Polacek to British Embassy in Prague, dated 25 October 1945, forwarded to Jersey authorities. JA D/Z Law Officer's Department.
30 Faramus, *Journey into Darkness*, pp. 75–7.
31 Sherwill, *A Fair and Honest Book*, p. 312.
32 Bailey, *Dachau*, p. 44.
33 Ibid., p. 45.
34 Words of Frank Tuck in Dutot, L. 1974. *Bread between the Rails*. Liverpool: F.H. Tuck, p. 26.
35 Words of Charles Friend in Dutot, *Bread between the Rails*, p. 27.
36 Bailey, *Dachau*, pp. 107–10.
37 Davidson, S. 1984. 'Human Reciprocity among the Jewish Prisoners in the Nazi Concentration Camps', pp. 555–72 in *The Nazi Concentration Camps*. Yad Vashem. http://www.yadvashem.org/odot_pdf/Microsoft%20Word%20-%203554.pdf [accessed 8 June 2018].
38 Hovinga, H. 2010. *The Sumatra Railroad: Final Destination Pakan Baroe, 1943–1945*. Trans. Bernard J. Wolters (5th edition). Leiden: KITLV Press; Oliver, E. 2014. *Interpreting Memories of a Forgotten Army: Prisoner of War Narratives from the Sumatra Railway, May 1944–August 1945*. Unpublished PhD thesis, University of Leeds.
39 Bailey, *Dachau*, p. 46.
40 Hassall, *Night and Fog Prisoners*, p. 103.
41 Gerald Domaille, unpublished memoirs, p. 31.
42 Foreign Office case file TNA ref. HNP 949, Emile Dubois.
43 Falla, *The Silent War*, p. 124.
44 Ibid.
45 Ibid., p. 125.
46 Domaille, unpublished memoirs, p. 21.
47 Falla, *The Silent War*, p. 123.
48 Ibid., p. 126.
49 Ibid., p. 116.
50 Foreign Office, TNA ref. HNP case file 1197.
51 Foreign Office, TNA HNP case file 1235.
52 Gerald Domaille, unpublished memoirs, p. 42.
53 Ibid., p. 53.
54 Falla, *The Silent War*, p. 119.
55 Faramus, *Journey into Darkness*, pp. 188–90.
56 Faramus, A. 1954. *The Faramus Story*. London: Brown Watson Ltd, p. 133.
57 Faramus, *Journey into Darkness*, p. 275.
58 Faramus, *The Faramus Story*, pp. 134–5.
59 Faramus, *Journey into Darkness*, pp. 254–6.
60 Faramus, *The Faramus Story*, p. 139.
61 Ibid., p. 152.
62 Faramus, *Journey into Darkness*, p. 291.
63 Foreign Office, TNA ref. HNP case files 1901 & 1831.
64 Falla, *The Silent War*, p. 131.
65 Ibid., pp. 131–6.
66 Bailey, *Dachau*, p. 117.
67 Ibid., pp. 115–20.
68 Cottrell, 'The Man from Belsen'.
69 Faramus, *The Faramus Story*, pp. 147–9.

70 Faramus, *Journey into Darkness*, pp. 290–2.
71 Barry, 'From Ravensbruch [sic] to Guernsey'.
72 Persson, S. 2009. *Escape from the Third Reich: Folke Bernadotte and the White Buses*. London: Frontline Books.
73 Gerald Domaille, unpublished memoirs.
74 Hassall, *Night and Fog Prisoners*, p. 117.
75 Ibid., p. 123.
76 Ibid., p. 158.
77 Ibid.
78 Ibid.
79 TNA Foreign Office, HNP case file 149. Original emphasis.
80 TNA Foreign Office, HNP case file 1195.
81 Letter from Frank Tuck to British Red Cross Society, 12 July 1945.
82 Sanders, *The Ultimate Sacrifice* (2nd edition), pp. 63–4.
83 Ibid., p. 59.
84 This is actually a reference to Zöschen camp, the same place where Clifford Cohu had been several months before. Tierney was in this camp from 31 March until 7 July 1945.
85 Undated and typed official communication to Eileen Tierney.
86 Letter from Albert Koch to Eileen Tierney, 2 May 1946.
87 My eternal thanks to Dr Pavel Vařeka of the University of Western Bohemia for this discovery.
88 Quote in Wood and Wood, *Islands in Danger*, p. 233.
89 Quote from Falla in a review of *The Silent War* in *Guernsey Life* magazine, dated March 1967, scrapbook cutting, Frank Falla Archive, IA, Guernsey.

Chapter 3

1 Quoted in Falla, *The Silent War*, p. 156.
2 Falla, *The Silent War*, p. 157.
3 'Today's States Meeting', *Guernsey Evening Press*, 7 August 1940.
4 The parliament and government in both Guernsey and Jersey is referred to as the States. This is short for the States of Deliberation (Guernsey) and the Assembly of the States (Jersey).
5 The film was probably shot in late summer / early autumn, judging by the clothes worn in the film.
6 IWM ref. UKY 727, *The Channel Islands 1940–1945*, directed by Gerry Bryant. Crown Film Unit 1945.
7 This assumption is made on the basis of the accent of the narrator, and the mispronunciation of two Channel Islands' surnames. St Helier is also referred to as St Helier's – a rather antiquated terminology not used today, despite the common local reference to other Island parishes in the possessive (e.g. St Martin's, St Saviour's, St Clement's, etc.). The author has not been able to gauge the extent to which this was still used in 1945, when the normal nomenclature even then was 'St Helier'.
8 IWM ref. UKY 727.
9 Quote from Churchill's speech of 22 June 1941, on alliance with Russia. http://www.winstonchurchill.org/resources/speeches/1941-1945-war-leader/809-the-fourth-climacteric [accessed 26 July 2016].

10. Sanders, P. 2014. 'Radio days', pp. 65–96 in G. Carr, P. Sanders and L. Willmot (eds), *Protest, Defiance and Resistance in the Channel Islands: German Occupation 1940-1945*. London: Bloomsbury Academic, p. 65.
11. Carr, *Legacies of Occupation*, pp. 286–9.
12. This is André Aune, a French hairdresser.
13. The twenty-eight Islanders deported for offences against the authorities are the 'Jersey 21' and seven of the 'Guernsey Eight', noting that Marie Ozanne was imprisoned and died locally, and was not deported. Three Jewish women were deported from Guernsey in April 1942 and died in Auschwitz; their names are not counted among the political prisoners here as they belong to a different category of Nazi victim outside the confines of this book.
14. Sanders, 'Radio Days', p. 68.
15. The Controlling Committee was an emergency committee convened to steer the Island through dealings with the occupiers, the president of which liaised between the committee and the German Commandant's staff.
16. 'Today's States Meeting', *Guernsey Evening Press*, 7 August 1940.
17. Bunting, *The Model Occupation*, p. 78.
18. Pocock, H.R.S. 1975. *The Memoirs of Lord Coutanche*. Chichester: Phillimore, p. 12; Sherwill, *A Fair and Honest Book*, pp. 82–3.
19. Speech made by John Leale, 21 June 1940, Guernsey, reproduced in Captain Dening's intelligence report, IWM ref. 13409.
20. See Carr, Sanders and Willmot, *Protest, Defiance and Resistance*.
21. Leale, J. 1945. *Report of Five Years of German Occupation*. Guernsey: Guernsey Press.
22. IWM ref. 13409, Report of Captain Dening IO(b), file 9, August 1945.
23. Ibid.
24. Ibid.
25. Current estimated figures lie at c. 1,300 imprisoned locally and at least 215 deported as a minimum number; Carr, Sanders and Willmot, *Protest, Defiance and Resistance*, 351; www.frankfallaarchive.org [accessed 8 June 2018].
26. Cohen, *The Jews in the Channel Islands*, pp. 49–55.
27. TNA ref. KV 4/78, the I(b) Reports on the Channel Islands.
28. JA ref. D/Z/H5/348.
29. JA ref. D/Z/H6/7/46.
30. Sanders, *The British Channel Islands under German Occupation*, pp. 64, 77.
31. Falla, *Silent War*, p. 143.
32. 'Deal with traitors', *Jersey Evening Post* 19 May 1945; 'The case against the farmers', *Jersey Evening Post*, p. 31, May 1945; 'Those who worked for the Germans', *Jersey Evening Post*, 2 June 1945.
33. For example, 'Sorting out Channel Island traitors', *Daily Herald*, 19 July 1945; 'Germans and Channel Islands: Collaboration was unavoidable', *Liverpool Post*, 19 July 1945; 'Channel Isles Collaboration', *Daily Telegraph*, 19 July 1945; 'Collaborators get off Scot Free', *Daily Herald*, 28 July 1945; 'Punish Our Quislings, Jersey Demands', *Daily Worker*, 25 May 1945; 'Purge needed', *Daily Worker*, 11 July 1945; 'Don't annoy the Nazis Rules Jersey', *Daily Worker*, 9 July 1945.
34. TNA ref. HO 45/22399, complaints about administration in Jersey and Guernsey, statement dated 4 June 1945.
35. Captain Dening, who worked in the intelligence section of Force 135, notes that he and another colleague working alongside him were struggling with their work load and that they had fewer numbers and a lower status than the Public Safety Section,

36 which had six officers. These men had NCOs at their disposal, but very few of them. Thus we might conclude that any investigation had to have a narrow focus if it was to carry out the job in hand with any hope of success. IWM ref 13409, JR Dening file 9.
36 TNA ref. HO 45/22399, statement about meeting between Frank Newsam (DPP) and Lord Justice du Parcq, 6 June 1945, dated 9 June 1945.
37 TNA ref. WO 311/11, affidavit by Alfred Howlett about treatment at hands of GFP.
38 TNA ref. WO 311/105, statement of Mrs Harriet Cohu, 10 December 1945.
39 TNA ref. WO 311/11, letter of 14 June 1945 on war crimes in the Channel Islands.
40 TNA ref. WO 311/11, letter from the Judge Advocate General to Major Haddock, 26 May 1945.
41 SJ ref. MIL/GO/D/12, The diary of J. H. L'Amy, p. 23.
42 Ibid., Chapter VI, p. 2.
43 Ibid., p. 23.
44 Ibid., p. 23.
45 'Deal with the Quislings!' *Jersey Evening Post*, 18 June 1945, front page.
46 SJ ref. MIL/GO/D/12, The diary of J.H. L'Amy, p. 24.
47 'Betrayed to the Nazis', presented and directed by Eric Blakeley, Channel TV documentary, Jersey, 2008.
48 SJ ref. MIL/GO/D/12, The diary of J. H. L'Amy, p. 27.
49 Sanders, *The British Channel Islands under German Occupation*, 239.
50 SJ ref. MIL/GO/D/12, *The Diary of J.H. L'Amy*, p. 28; Jersey Archives ref. A/F/5, copy of the petition submitted by the Jersey Loyalists.
51 'Who are the Jersey Loyalists?' *Jersey Evening Post*, 30 August 1945.
52 'Who are the Jersey Loyalists?'
53 Ibid.
54 JA ref. A/F/5, letter from Lieutenant-Governor to Bailiff, 11 September 1945.
55 My thanks to the family of Joseph Tierney for letting me examine their family archives.
56 'Tragic news for Jersey family', *Jersey Evening Post*, 2 June 1945.
57 JA ref. B/A/L15/6.
58 JA ref. A/F/5, letter from Bailiff to Lieutenant-Governor, 15 September 1945.
59 JA ref. A/F.5, letter from States Greffier, H. Le Riche Edwards, to Jersey Loyalists, 22 September 1945.
60 JA ref. A/F/5, letter from Mr Poole, Honorary Secretary of the Jersey Loyalists, to Mr Le Riche, Greffier of the States, 17 October 1945.
61 TNA ref. HO 45/22399, letter from Lieutenant-Governor Grasett to Director of Public Prosecutions, 2 November 1945.
62 Fraser, *The Jews of the Channel Islands and the Rule of Law*, p. 148.
63 TNA ref. HO 45/22399, letter from Duret Aubin, Attorney General, Jersey, to JB Howard, Home Office, 7 August 1945.
64 TNA ref. HO 45/22399, letter of 26 November 1945 from Alexander Coutanche to Lieutenant-Governor Grasett.
65 Ibid.
66 Bunting, *The Model Occupation*, p. 311.
67 TNA ref. HO 45/22399, 'The Channel Islands under German Occupation', report by intelligence officers attached to Force 135, submitted to MI5, and forwarded to Brigadier Snow, 20 August 1945.
68 TNA ref. HO 45/22399, letter from Brigadier Snow to Frank Newsam, 24 August 1945.
69 Sanders, *The British Channel Islands under German Occupation*, p. 244.

70 Turner, B. 2010. *Outpost of Occupation*. London: Aurum Press Ltd, p. 254.
71 TNA ref. HO 45/22399, statement in House of Commons by Mr Ede, 17 August 1945.
72 TNA ref. HO 45/22399, letter from Prime Minister to Home Secretary Ede, 31 October 1945.
73 TNA ref. HO 45/22399, letter from Home Secretary Chuter-Ede to Prime Minister, 2 November 1945.
74 IWM ref. 13409, JRD 9, letter from Captain Dening to Major Stopford, 26 August 1945.
75 TNA ref. HO 45/22399, letter to Lieutenant-Governor Grasett 26 November 1945; statement of Mr Howard, Home Office, 31 December 1945.
76 TNA ref. HO 45/22399, letter from Theobald Mathews, Director of Public Prosecutions, to Lieutenant-Governor of Jersey, 7 January 1946.
77 Ibid.
78 TNA ref. HO 45/22399, 'The conduct of the population and administration of the Channel Islands under German Occupation', Theobald Mathew, Director of Public Prosecutions, 9 July 1945.
79 Sanders, *The British Channel Islands under German Occupation*, p. 234.
80 TNA ref. HO 45/22399, letter from Lieutenant-Governor Grasett to Alexander Coutanche, 12 January 1945.
81 TNA ref. HO 45/22399, Rapport du Comité Spécial nommé avec mission d'étudier une Pétition du Comité Central d'Organisation des 'Jersey Loyalists', 2 February 1946.
82 Société Jersiaise ref. MIL/GO/D/12, *The Diary of J.H. L'Amy*, p. 29.
83 Jersey Archives ref. A/F/5, letter from RMH Lewis to Major JCM Manley, 27 July 1946.
84 TNA ref. HO 45/22399, letter from Theobald Mathew to Frank Newsam, 7 January 1946.
85 Jersey Prison was also referred to as 'Gloucester Street Prison' and 'Newgate Street Prison' after its particular location between these streets in St Helier.
86 'Ex-convicts meet in Lyric Hall', *Jersey Evening Post*, 12 December 1945.
87 Jersey Archives ref. B/A/W21/1.
88 Jersey Archives ref. D/Z/H9/8.
89 Act of 2 December 1946 of the Social Assurance Committee with report in respect of Extra-Statutory Awards in respect of death or disablement during internment of persons who were originally resident and gainfully occupied in Jersey and who were removed during the German Occupation; see also correspondence of February 1948 surrounding the case of James Dale; Jersey Archives ref. D/Z/H5/473.
90 Letter from G. Le Cocq to C. Harrison on the subject of Anthony Faramus, 12 July 1949, Jersey Archives ref. D/Z/H5/473.
91 Sanders, *The British Channel Islands under German Occupation*, p. 82.
92 8 July 1941, notice in the *Guernsey Evening Press*.
93 TNA ref. HO 45/22399, Statement by Lord Justice du Parq, 14 June 1945.
94 Sanders, *The British Channel Islands under German Occupation*, p. 247.
95 Ibid., p. 249.
96 TNA ref. HO 45/22399, letter of 9 January from A. Maxwell, Home Office, to Lieutenant-Governor of Jersey.
97 'Couple without a home or country', *Guernsey Evening Press,* 29 May 1947.
98 TNA ref. KV4/78.
99 Wood and Wood, *Islands in Danger*, p. 237.

100 IWM 13409, JRD 9, 'Report on German judicial records' and 'German documents held in I(b) office'.
101 Sanders, *The British Channel Islands under German Occupation*, p. 254.
102 Turner, *Outpost of Occupation*, p. 273.

Chapter 4

1 At the time of writing, the current number of Islanders securely known to have been deported, stands at 222; twenty-seven of them were female. This list is still a work in progress.
2 Hassall, *Night and Fog Prisoners*, p. 154; Mière, *Never to be Forgotten*, p. 185.
3 Sanders, 'Narratives of Britishness'.
4 To the best of the author's knowledge, there is only one living former victim of Nazi persecution.
5 Today some of these affidavits are in Guernsey Archives, AQ 1214/30. A larger number are in the papers of Frank Tuck, privately owned.
6 Sanders, P. 2014. 'Economic resistance and sabotage', pp. 277–306 in G. Carr, P. Sanders and L. Willmot (eds), *Protest, Defiance and Resistance in the Channel Islands: German Occupation 1940–1945*. London: Bloomsbury Academic.
7 Although see entries on the Frank Falla Archive, which represents the best reconstruction of their journeys to date: www.frankfallaarchive.org [accessed 15 July 2018].
8 The full names are given of the various victims of Nazism referred to in this chapter. The decision to do this is threefold: their names are already in the public domain; their children have given permission for their names to be cited; and the people in this group have historically been marginalized and silenced.
9 Letter written by Frank Tuck to the British Red Cross Society, 12 July 1945, copy placed within Foreign Office case file HNP 133, Frank Tuck. TNA ref. FO 950/962.
10 Letter from Frank Tuck to Claims Department, 10 March 1966, Foreign Office case file 133, Frank Tuck. TNA ref. FO 950/962.
11 Medical report by Benjamin Kaufman MD in Foreign Office case file, HNP 1358, Jack Harper. TNA ref. FO 950/2187.
12 Testimony of Jack Harper, Foreign Office case file 1358. TNA ref. FO 950/2187.
13 Testimony of Charles Friend, Foreign Office case files 853 and 920. TNA ref. FO 950/1748.
14 Testimony of Emile Du Bois, Foreign Office case file 949. TNA ref. FO 950/1777.
15 Testimony of Charles (Anthony) Faramus, Foreign Office case file HNP 1381. TNA ref. FO 950/2730.
16 Testimony of Stanley Green, Foreign Office case file HNP 2085. TNA ref. FO 950/2914.
17 Letter from Alfred Baker to Claims Department, 30 March 1966, Foreign Office, claims file HNP 114. TNA ref. FO 950/943.
18 Testimony of Alfred Baker, Foreign Office claims file HNP 114. TNA ref. FO 950/943.
19 Testimony of Stanley Cordrey, Foreign Office claims file HNP 1463. TNA ref. FO 950/2292.
20 June Sinclair is a mysterious character in that no archival details of her exist anywhere; her fate is known only through oral testimony. More details on her case

can be found here: https://www.frankfallaarchive.org/people/june-mary-sinclair [accessed 15 July 2018].
21. Testimony of Evelina Garland, Foreign Office claims file HNP 334. TNA ref. FO 950/1162.
22. There is no NHS in the Channel Islands; those without medical insurance have to pay for every doctor's visit and every prescription.
23. Eitinger, L. 1961. 'Pathology of the concentration camp syndrome', *Archives of General Psychiatry* 5(4): 371–9; Withuis, J. 2010. 'The management of victimhood-long term health damage from asthenia to PTSD', in J. Withuis and A. Mooij (eds), *The Politics of War Trauma*. Studies of the Netherlands Institute for War Documentation. Amsterdam: Aksant.
24. Gersons, B.P.R. and Carlier, I.V.E. 1992. 'Post-traumatic stress disorder: The history of a recent concept', *British Journal of Psychiatry* 161: 742; Crocq, M. and Crocq, L. 2000. 'From shell shock and war neurosis to posttraumatic stress disorder: A history of psychotraumatology', *Dialogues in Clinical Neuroscience* 2(1): 47–55.
25. Gersons and Carlier, 'Post-traumatic stress disorder', p. 742.
26. Foreign Office case file HNP 1696, Gerald Bird, letter from Bird to Foreign Office dated 4 March 1965. TNA ref. FO 950/2525.
27. Ibid; American Psychiatric Association 1987. *The Diagnostic and Statistical Manual of Mental Disorders* (3rd edition) (DSM-III). Washington DC: APA, pp. 236–9.
28. https://www.nimh.nih.gov/health/topics/post-traumatic-stress-disorder-ptsd/index.shtml [accessed 15 July 2018]; DSM-V.
29. For example, Kuch, K. and Cox, B. 1992. 'Symptoms of PTSD in 124 survivors of the Holocaust', *American Journal of Psychiatry* 149(3): 337–40; Yehuda, R., Kahana, B., Southwick, S.M. and Giller, E.L. 1994. 'Depressive features in Holocaust survivors with post-traumatic stress disorder', *Journal of Traumatic Stress* 7(4): 699–704.
30. For example, Eitinger, 'Pathology of the concentration camp syndrome'.
31. Kuch and Cox, 'Symptoms of PTSD in 124 survivors of the Holocaust'.
32. Major, E. 2003. 'Health effects of war stress on Norwegian World War II resistance groups', *Journal of Traumatic Stress* 16(6): 595–9.
33. Major, E. 1996. 'The impact of the Holocaust on the second generation: Norwegian Jewish Holocaust survivors and their children', *Journal of Traumatic Stress* 9: 441–54.
34. Op den Velde, W., Frey-Wouters, E. and Pelser, H.E. 1994. 'The price of heroism: Veterans of the Dutch resistance to the Nazi occupation and the Holocaust in World War II', *Holocaust and Genocide Studies* 8(3): 335–48.
35. Withuis, 'The management of victimhood'.
36. Ibid., p. 320.
37. Ibid., p. 293.
38. Compensation testimony in Foreign Office case file HNP 352, name redacted; TNA ref. FO 950/1180.
39. Ibid.
40. Falla, *The Silent War*, p. 145.
41. Review of *The Silent War* in March 1967 edition of *Guernsey Life* magazine, article in Frank Falla's scrapbook, Frank Falla archive.
42. Sanders, *The Ultimate Sacrifice* (2nd edition), p. 94.
43. Ibid., p. 96.
44. Interview with Paul Dauny, BBC news website 15 October 2013, http://www.bbc.co.uk/news/world-europe-jersey-24523007 [accessed 11 June 2016].
45. Interview between Trevor Dauny and author, 17 May 2013.

46 See Carr, 'Defiance and deportations', p. 138.
47 JA ref. D/Z/H6/4/36.
48 JA registration card for Flavian Emile Barbier.
49 https://www.frankfallaarchive.org/people/flavien-emile-barbier/ [accessed 15 July 2018].
50 In Jersey law, the role of 'Curator', the term used for Marcel Barbier, was used to describe someone who has a legal and financial duty to the person and property of the person incapable of managing their own affairs by reason of mental infirmity, profligacy or alcoholism. This is decided by a 'Curatelle' of seven reputable citizens, one of whom must be a doctor. By this point, Flavian Emile Barbier had been 'certified as insane' by two doctors and had been appointed Curator over his brother's affairs in February 1964; letter dated 13 January 1966 to Mr Wilson of the Claims Department of the Foreign Office from the Home Office. Letter contained in Foreign Office case file HNP 916 for Flavian Emile Barbier. TNA ref. FO 950/1744.
51 Foreign Office case file HNP 916 for Flavian Emile Barbier. TNA ref. FO 950/1744.
52 https://www.frankfallaarchive.org/people/arthur-wilfred-queree/ [accessed 15 July 2018].
53 'Jerseyman's Amazing Story of "Horror Camp"', *Jersey Evening Post*, 9 July 1945.
54 Foreign Office case file HNP 435 for Paul Gourdan. TNA ref. FO 950/1263.
55 'Jerseyman's Amazing Story of "Horror Camp"', *Jersey Evening Post*, 9 July 1945.
56 IWM, Channel Islands War Crimes Papers, IWM MISC 172/2640.
57 Statement from Jack Harper's lawyers to Foreign Office dated 20 July 1966 in Foreign Office case file HNP 435 for Paul Gourdan; TNA ref. FO 950/1263.
58 Letter from Frederick Short to Foreign Office dated 29 June 1966 in Foreign Office case file HNP 435 for Paul Gourdan. TNA ref. FO 950/1263.
59 His allegations of crucifixion at Jersey Prison are, without doubt, false.
60 Case file notes dated 1, 6 and 29 June 1966, Foreign Office case file HNP 435 for Paul Gourdan. TNA ref. FO 950/1263.
61 Letter from Frank Falla to GC Littler, Foreign Office, dated 21 February 1966. Foreign Office case file 3608 for William Quin. TNA ref. FO 950/4437.
62 Testimony by Harold Le Druillenec, Foreign Office case file HNP 272. TNA ref. FO 950/1100.
63 Le Druillenec, Harold Osmond (1911–85) by Francis Corbet, *Oxford Dictionary of National Biography*. Oxford University Press.
64 http://www.bbc.co.uk/archive/people/55/41.shtml [accessed 10 June 2016].
65 Cottrell, 'The Man from Belsen'.
66 Notes in application form for compensation for disablement resulting from Nazi persecution, Foreign Office case file HNP 272, Harold Le Druillenec. TNA ref. FO 950/1100.
67 Op den Velde, Frey-Wouters and Pelser, 'The price of heroism', p. 339.
68 Interview between author and anonymous former teaching colleague of Harold Le Druillenec, 24 September 2014.
69 Email of 13 July 2015 to author from Alice Allen about her aunt, Marion Laurens (born 1951).
70 Interview between author and a friend of the family and former colleague at St John's school of Harold Le Druillenec, 25 September 2014.
71 Notes made by officials in Foreign Office case file 544, John Draper. TNA ref. FO 950/1732.
72 Foreign Office case file 544, testimony of John Draper. TNA ref. FO 950/1732.
73 Foreign Office case file HNP 939, Ronald Beer. TNA ref. FO 950/1767.

74 Foreign Office case file HNP 1696, Gerald Bird, letter from Bird to Foreign Office dated 4 March 1965. TNA ref. FO 950/2525.
75 Foreign Office case file HNP 920, testimony of Charles Friend. TNA ref. FO 950/1748.
76 Interview between author and Keith Friend, 5 May 2015.
77 Foreign Office case file HNP 1381, medical notes of Anthony Faramus. TNA ref. FO 950/2730.
78 Foreign Office case file HMP 396, testimony of Frederick Short. TNA ref. FO 950/962.
79 Foreign Office case file HNP 133, letter of 11 May 1964 from Frank Tuck to Airy Neave MP. TNA FO 950/962.
80 Foreign Office case file HNP 133, letter 10 March 1966 from Frank Tuck to Miss A Windham, Claims Office. TNA ref. FO 950/962.
81 Letter from Foreign Office Claims Department to Frank Tuck, 1 September 1966. Foreign Office case file 133, Frank Tuck. TNA ref. FO 950/962.
82 Application for compensation for disablement resulting from Nazi persecution; Foreign Office case file HNP 525, Kingston Bailey. TNA ref. FO 950/1353. Original emphasis preserved.
83 Application for compensation for disablement resulting from Nazi persecution; Foreign Office case file HNP 939, Ronald Beer. TNA ref. FO 950/1767. Original emphasis preserved.
84 Falla, *The Silent War*, pp. 116–25.
85 The author was privileged to travel to Germany and the Czech Republic with the daughters of Gillingham and Tierney in search of their fathers for a BBC documentary, *Finding Our Fathers: Lost Heroes of WWII*, screened in May 2016.
86 Testimony of Mr John Alfred Ingrouille, 25 September 1964, Foreign Office case file HNP 1194. TNA ref. FO 950/2023.
87 Political prisoners' log book, entry 15, JA ref. D/AG/B7/1.
88 Testimony of Mr John Alfred Ingrouille, 25 September 1964, Foreign Office case file HNP 1194. TNA ref. FO 950/2023.
89 Police log book, Guernsey police station, entry 103, conviction dated 14 May 1942.
90 Political prisoners' log book, entry 125, shows that Sidney Ashcroft left for France on 1 June 1942, JA ref D/AG/B7/1.
91 TNA ref. RG 32/31.
92 Cemetery log book (alphabetical) for the graveyard of St Michael, Straubing, entry 45.
93 Letter from Walter Lainé to War Office, 23 October 1945, inside Foreign Office case file HNP 1195.
94 Interview with Maureen Cowley, neighbour of Charlotte Ashcroft, 30 September 2015.
95 Sanders, *The Ultimate Sacrifice* (2nd edition), pp. 53–63.
96 Application for compensation submitted by Dorothy Painter, Foreign Office case file HNP 245. TNA ref. FO 950/2362.
97 Written statement from daughter of Herbert Smith to author, 24 October 2015.
98 Testimony of Rachel Symes, Foreign Office case file HNP 1239. TNA ref. FO 950/2068.
99 Diary entry of 23 December 1940, unpublished diary of Henry Le Marquand. My thanks to Peter Creasy for giving me a copy of this diary.
100 Sherwill, *A Fair and Honest Book*, p. 308.
101 Testimony of Rachel Symes, Foreign Office case file HNP 1239. TNA ref. FO 950/2068. Original emphasis preserved.

102 Sherwill, *A Fair and Honest Book*, p. 163.
103 Interview between author, Joan Hall and Pete Symes, 10 December 2014.
104 Wartime memoirs of Rose Short, daughter of Frederick Duquemin.
105 Faramus, *Journey into Darkness*, p. 236.
106 Ibid., p. 239.
107 Ibid., p. 240.
108 Compensation testimony in Foreign Office case file HNP 352, name redacted; TNA ref. FO 950/1180.
109 Interview between author and Audry Bird, wife of Gerald Bird, 3 May 2014.
110 Interview between author and Kathleen O'Meara, wife of Brian O'Meara, 14 December 2014.
111 Interview between author and Phil, Ian and Paul Domaille, sons of Gerald Domaille, 27 July 2014.
112 Interview with Jean Duquemin, daughter of Walter Nicolle, 14 December 2014; interview with Bryan O'Meara, Sally Nicolle and Karen McGee, the children of Brian O'Meara, interviewed 14 December 2014.
113 For example, Gerald Domaille, as testified by his three sons, Phil, Paul and Ian Domaille, interviewed 27 July 2014.
114 Interview between author and Pete Symes and Joan Hall, 10 December 2014.
115 Bailey, *Dachau*, p. 79.
116 Interview between author and Dawn Crowson, daughter of Kingston Bailey, 9 June 2016.
117 Interview between author and Audrey Bird, wife of Gerald Bird, 3 May 2014.
118 Interview with Bryan O'Meara, Sally Nicolle and Karen McGee, children of Brian O'Meara, 14 December 2014.
119 Foreign Office case file HNP 3637, Brian O'Meara. TNA ref. FO 950/4466.
120 Interview with Bryan O'Meara, Karen McGee and Sally Nicolle, children of Brian O'Meara, 14 December 2014.
121 Sanders, 'Economic resistance and sabotage', p. 293.
122 Letter from Beatrice Dexter to Foreign Office, case file HNP 1235, Norman Dexter. TNA ref. FO 950/2064.
123 Undated letter from Rubina Thorne, wife of John Nicolle, Foreign Office case file HNP 392. TNA ref. FO 950/1220.
124 Op den Velde, Frey-Wouters and Pelser, 'The price of heroism', pp. 344–5.

Chapter 5

1 As many more men than women were deported, the children of male former political prisoners were more numerous and dominate the database of those interviewed.
2 Bar-On, D. 1995. *Fear and Hope: Three Generations of the Holocaust*. Cambridge, MA: Harvard University Press.
3 Cesarani, D. and Sundquist, E.J. 2012. *After the Holocaust: Challenging the Myth of Silence*. London and New York: Routledge.
4 Cesarani and Sundquist, *After the Holocaust*, p. 2.
5 Interview with Bryan O'Meara and Sally Nicolle, 14 December 2014.
6 Interview with Rose Short, 13 December 2014.
7 Interview with Paul, Ian and Philip Domaille, 27 July 2014.
8 Interview with Jill Robilliard, 27 July 2014.

9   Letter from Howard Hacquoil, 19 May 2014.
10 Interview with Audrey Bird, 3 May 2014.
11 Interview with Rose Short, 13 December 2014.
12 Interview with Keith Friend, 5 May 2016.
13 Interview with Rose Short, 13 December 2014.
14 Interview with Angela McAllister, 4 August 2014.
15 Interview with Paul Domaille, 27 July 2014.
16 Dutot, *Bread between the Rails*, pp. 14–16.
17 Interview with Angela and Clare McAllister, 4 August 2014.
18 Interview with Peter Symes and Joan Hall, 10 December 2014.
19 Interview with Rose Short, 13 December 2014.
20 Saunders, N.J. 2001. 'Apprehending memory: Material culture and war', pp. 476–88 in P. Liddle, J. Bourne and I. Whitehead (eds), *The Great World War, 1914–45*. London: HarperCollins.
21 Interview with Bryan O'Meara, Sally Nicolle and Karen McGee, 14 December 2014 and 16 December 2014.
22 Interview with Kathleen O'Meara, 14 December 2014.
23 Interview with Audrey Bird, 3 May 2014.
24 Interview with Joan Hall, 10 December 2014.
25 Interview with Dawn Crowson, 10 June 2016.
26 Interview with Angela McAllister, 4 August 2014.
27 Interview with Jean, Jo and Andrew Duquemin, 12 December 2014.
28 Interview with Paul, Ian and Philip Domaille, 27 July 2014.
29 Interview with Bryan O'Meara and Sally Nicolle, 14 December 2014.
30 Interview with Keith Friend, 5 May 2015.
31 Interview with Paul, Ian and Philip Domaille, 27 July 2014.
32 Interview with Angela McAllister, 4 August 2014.
33 Interview with Rose Short, 13 December 2014.
34 Interview with Jean Duquemin, 12 December 2014.
35 Interview with Sally Nicolle, 14 December 2014.
36 Interview with Bryan O'Meara, Sally Nicolle and Karen McGee, 14 December 2014 and 16 December 2014.
37 Interview with Dawn Crowson, 10 June 2016.
38 Bailey, *Dachau*, p. 79.
39 Interview with Keith Friend, 5 May 2015.
40 Letter from Howard Hacquoil, 19 May 2014.
41 Letter from Tim Falla to author, 3 May 2014.
42 Falla, *The Silent War*, p. 123.
43 Falla, 'Brevities', *Guernsey Ink in my Veins*, p. 14.
44 Falla, 'Personal Postscript', *Guernsey Ink in my Veins*, p. 6.
45 Ibid.
46 Falla, *The Silent War*, p. 155.
47 Carr, Sanders and Willmot, *Protest, Defiance and Resistance*.
48 For a full insight into the kinds of resistance that took place in the Channel Islands during the German Occupation, see Carr, Sanders and Willmot, *Protest, Defiance and Resistance*.
49 Falla, *The Silent War*, p. 104.
50 Sanders, *The Ultimate Sacrifice* (2nd edition), p. 128.
51 Falla, *The Silent War*, p. 110.

52 Sanders, *The Ultimate Sacrifice* (2nd edition), p. 23.
53 Sherwill, *A Fair and Honest Book*, p. 140; this legislation was, according to Sherwill, passed in order to save a shopkeeper, Mr Collins, imprisoned for 'propaganda against the German army'. It was hoped that by trying him in the Royal Court rather than making him face a German military tribunal, he could be acquitted, which indeed he was.
54 See, for example, Sherwill, *A Fair and Honest Book*, pp. 143–53.
55 Carr, 'Heritage, memory and resistance', pp. 308–9.
56 Falla, *The Silent War*, p. 167.
57 Sanders, 'Economic resistance and sabotage', pp. 277–306.
58 'History of the GFP in the Channel Islands', the papers of Captain JR Dening. IWM ref. 13409.
59 Durand, R. 1946. *Guernsey under German Rule*. London: The Guernsey Society, p. 83.
60 *Guernsey Star*, 'Bailiff denounces ex-policemen', 2 June 1942.
61 Sanders, 'Economic resistance and sabotage', pp. 291–3.
62 *Guernsey Star*, 22 March 1941; see Carr, 'Heritage, memory and resistance', p. 311.
63 Falla, *The Silent War*, p. 156.
64 Wood and Wood, *Islands in Danger*, p. 8.
65 Ibid., pp. 236–7.
66 Guernsey Archives ref BF 26-09, letter dated 11 December 1949 from Henrietta Gillingham to the Bailiff of Guernsey, asking for her dead husband, Joseph Gillingham, to be included on the war memorial in St Peter Port, Guernsey.
67 Carr, *Legacies of Occupation*, Chapter 5.
68 Falla, *The Silent War*, p. 162.
69 Letter from Frank Falla to Mr GEP Wood, 19 May 1964, Frank Falla archive.
70 Letter from Frank Falla to Dr Edward Aubert, 23 August 1964, Frank Falla archive.
71 Letter from Frank Falla to Stanley Green, 29 August 1964, Frank Falla archive.
72 Letter to Mrs Margaret Beaumont from Frank Falla, 6 March 1966, Frank Falla archive.
73 Letter from Frank Falla to GC Littler, Claims Department, Foreign Office, 30 November 1966, Frank Falla Archive.
74 At the time of writing, the list of those deported compiled by the author, and based only archival records and not any prior list compiled by others (and therefore on unknown sources), stands at 215. One hundred and twenty-six of those were from Jersey.
75 Letter from TW Casey to Cecil Harrison, 30 December 1952. JA ref. D/Z/H9/8.
76 Letter from Cecil Harrison to TW Casey, 21 January 1953. JA ref. D/Z/H9/8.
77 JA ref A/F/5, letter from Home Office to Lieutenant-Governor of Jersey, 17 November 1959.
78 JA ref A/F/5, letter from Alexander Coutanche to Home Office, 1 December 1959.
79 JA ref B/A/L10/92, scrap paper accompanying letter from Bailiff Alexander Coutanche to Lieutenant-Governor, 1 December 1959.
80 Mrs Berry is not one of the Jersey 21, and neither did she die in an internment camp; she is reputed to have died in Sweden during her early repatriation. JA ref. B/A/W85/5.
81 Sanders, *The Ultimate Sacrifice*.
82 JA ref B/A/L10/92, letter from Bailiff of Jersey to Mr Burley, Home Office, 17 June 1964.
83 JA ref B/A/L10/92, letter from A. J. Langdon of the Home Office to Francis de Lisle Bois (Deputy Bailiff), 18 August 1964; letter from R. de Masurier (Bailiff) to Home Office, 20 August 1964.

84 JA ref B/A/L10/92, letter to the Lieutenant-Governor of Jersey from Francis de Lisle Bois (Deputy Bailiff), 28 July 1965.
85 TNA ref. FO 950/765.
86 TNA ref. FO 371/146013, letter from Ambrose Sherwill, 30 November 1959.
87 Copies of these notes (original source unstated) are available in the Island Archives, Guernsey, Review File 6, compiled by Tom Remfrey, Guernsey Deportee Association, case notes on the deportations from the Channel Islands to Compiègne internment and transit camp and its legality.
88 It has never been established whether Louis Symes committed suicide or was murdered in Cherche-Midi. His wife, Rachel Symes, believed that it was murder; compensation claim testimony, TNA ref. FO 950 2068.
89 TNA ref. FO 371/177981, letter from Mr Langdon, Home Office, to William Arnold, Bailiff of Guernsey, 31 July 1963.
90 TNA ref. FO 371/177981, minute written by L. Heaton, 8 May 1964.
91 My thanks to the daughter of Frank Tuck for allowing me access to her father's archives.
92 Sanders, 'Narratives of Britishness'.

Chapter 6

1 Hansard, 9 June 1964, vol. 696, cc.242–6.
2 Falla, *The Silent War*, p. 162.
3 Convention on the Settlement of Matters Arising out of the War and the Occupation between the United Kingdom of Great Britain and Northern Ireland, France, the United States of America and the Federal Republic of Germany. Bonn, May 26 1952. Chapter Four – Compensation for victims of Nazi persecution. [copy editor: please note: this is the official original title: do not change it]
4 'The visit of Mrs GM Lindell and Mr Airey Neave MP to the Foreign Office on March 17 [1964] to discuss compensation for British victims of Nazi persecution'. TNA ref. FO 371/177980.
5 Letter from Frank Falla to Barnet Janner, 12 December 1957, Frank Falla Archive.
6 Letter from Joseph Cowen to Frank Falla, 2 January 1958, Frank Falla Archive.
7 *The Daily Telegraph,* 16 November 1960, 'Nazi's British Victims: Restitution issue to be reopened', p. 20.
8 Letter from Frank Falla to Barnett Janner, 5 January 1961, Frank Falla Archive.
9 Letter from Barnett Janner to Frank Falla, 26 January 1961, Frank Falla Archive.
10 Letter from Frank Falla to Barnett Janner, 2 February 1961, Frank Falla Archive.
11 Letter from Frank Falla to Barnett Janner, 24 June 1962, Frank Falla Archive.
12 Letter from CD Rappaport to Frank Falla, 9 July 1962, Frank Falla Archive.
13 Hansard 15 July 1963, vol. 681, c.299.
14 Routledge, P. 2002. *Public Servant, Secret Agent: The Elusive Life and Violent Death of Airey Neave*. London: Fourth Estate, p. 127.
15 Routledge, *Public Servant, Secret Agent*, pp. 132, 136.
16 Ibid., p. 162.
17 Hansard 15 July 1963, vol. 681, cc.302–3.
18 Scheme to compensate UK victims of Nazi persecution. TNA ref. FO 950/766

19 Letter from Lorna Heaton to Mr Langdon, 25 February 1964, HNP file 149, Frank Falla.
20 'The visit of Mrs GM Lindell and Mr Airey Neave MP to the Foreign Office on 17 March [1964] to discuss compensation for British victims of Nazi persecution'. TNA ref. FO 371/177980.
21 Ibid.
22 Confidential memorandum to British Ambassador in Bonn, 9 April 1964. TNA ref. FO 371/177980.
23 Ibid.
24 Ibid.
25 Cypher from Bonn to Foreign Office, 14 May 1964. TNA ref. FO 371/177980.
26 Confidential draft of Anglo-German agreement to compensate British victims of Nazi persecution, 22 May 1964, signed by WBJ Ledwidge. TNA ref. FO 371/177980.
27 Agreement between the United Kingdom of Great Britain and Northern Ireland and the Federal Republic of Germany concerning compensation for UK nationals who were victims of National-Socialist measures of persecution, Bonn, 9 June 1964. Copy in TNA ref. FO 950/741.
28 Letter from Frank Falla to Airey Neave, 21 July 1963, Frank Falla Archive.
29 Ibid.
30 Letter from Airey Neave to Frank Falla, 29 July 1963, Frank Falla Archive.
31 Letter from Frank Falla to Airey Neave, 7 August 1973, Frank Falla Archive.
32 Letter from Frank Falla to Airey Neave, 19 August 1963, Frank Falla Archive.
33 Letter from Frank Falla to Peter Smithers, the Under-Secretary of State, 12 October 1963, Frank Falla archive.
34 Falla, *Guernsey Ink in My Veins*, Chapter 13, p. 15.
35 Sanders, 'Economic resistance and sabotage'.
36 Guernsey Archives AQ 1214/17. William M Bell Collection. Affidavit Falla, 17 February 1951. Sanders, 'Economic resistance and sabotage', p. 293.
37 Sanders, 'Economic resistance and sabotage', p. 293.
38 Undated and unsent draft of letter from Frank Falla to Richard Butler, Foreign Secretary, Frank Falla Archive.
39 Letter from Airey Neave to Frank Falla, 23 October 1963, Frank Falla Archive.
40 Letter from WBJ Ledridge, Foreign Office, to Frank Falla, 5 November 1963, Frank Falla Archive.
41 Hansard, 23 March 1964, vol. 692, c.10.
42 Letter from Frank Falla to Airey Neave, 10 June 1964, Frank Falla Archive.
43 Letter from Airey Neave to Frank Falla, 18 June 1964, Frank Falla Archive.
44 'After Sachsenhausen, Victims Still' by Helen Mason, *The Sunday Telegraph*, 26 February 1968.
45 Letter from Frank Falla to Richard Butler, Foreign Secretary, 6 July 1964, Frank Falla Archive.
46 Letter from Frank Falla to the Under-Secretary of State, 26 July 1964, Frank Falla Archive.
47 Letter from Frank Falla to Mr Littler, Foreign Office, 30 November 1966; letter from Frank Falla to Harold Le Druillenec, 27 October 1964, Frank Falla Archive.
48 For example, Frank Falla's diary entry, 28 October 1964.
49 'I … popped in on Duque … re compensation which I typed later'. Frank Falla diary entry for 24 October 1964.
50 Rough notes written by William Symes, Frank Falla Archive.

51 Letter to Eileen Tierney from A. Koch, 1945.
52 Testimony dated 29 August 1964, handwritten by Norman Dexter. Papers of Norman Dexter.
53 Form A, Frank Falla Archive.
54 Letter from Frank Falla to Foreign Office, 28 October 1964, Frank Falla Archive.
55 Letter from Frank Falla to Foreign Office, 11 November 1964, Frank Falla Archive.
56 Letter from G. C. Littler at the Foreign Office to Dr N Burckhardt at the International Tracing Service, 4 November 1964. TNA ref. FO 950/740.
57 Falla, *The Silent War*, pp. 161-2.
58 Letter from G. C. Littler, Foreign Office, to Frank Falla, 10 December 1964, Frank Falla Archive.
59 For example, letter from Foreign Office to Frank Falla, 6 May 1965, and from Frank Falla to Foreign Office, 13 May 1965 concerning the case of Emile Paisnel, Frank Falla Archive.
60 Letter from Frank Falla to G. C. Littler, Foreign Office, 13 April 1965, Frank Falla Archive.
61 Letter from Frank Falla to Airey Neave, 5 March 1966, Frank Falla Archive.
62 Letter from Frank Falla to Airey Neave, 19 November 1966, Frank Falla Archive.
63 Notes for Guidance, copy in Frank Falla Archive.
64 Annex B, explanatory memorandum. TNA ref. FO 950/766.
65 'Nazi Persecution: Machinery within the Foreign Office'. TNA ref. FO 64/100.
66 Carr, G. 2014. 'The V-sign campaign and the fear of reprisals', pp. 43-64 in G. Carr, P. Sanders and L.Willmot (eds), *Protest, Defiance and Resistance in the Channel Islands: German Occupation 1940-1945*. London: Bloomsbury Academic, pp. 50-2.
67 Foreign Office case file TNA ref. HNP 734, testimony of Roy Machon.
68 Foreign Office case file TNA ref. HNP 735, testimony of Roy Machon.
69 Letter from G. C. Littler to Frank Falla, 10 June 1966, TNA ref. HNP file 734.
70 Letter from N. Burckhardt, Director of ITS, to Foreign Office, 14 July 1945. TNA ref. HNP file 734.
71 Letter from Miss A Windham, Foreign Office, to Roy Machon, 28 July 1965, TNA ref. HNP file 734.
72 Letter from Roy Machon to Foreign Office, 20 September 1965, TNA ref. HNP file 734.
73 Letter from CWM Wilson in the Claims Department, 21 October 195, to Roy Machon. TNA ref. HNP file 734.
74 Letter from Roy Machon to Foreign Office, 20 March 1966, TNA ref. HNP file 734.
75 Letter from Miss A Windham, Claims Department, Foreign Office, 18 April 1966, TNA ref. HNP file 734.
76 Guernsey police records of German Military Tribunal (unarchived).
77 Letter from Roy Machon to Miss A Windham, Claims Department, Foreign Office, 23 April 1966, TNA ref. HNP file 734.
78 Letter from Miss A Windham, Claims Department, Foreign Office, to Roy Machon, 12 May 1966, TNA ref. HNP file 734. Original emphasis preserved.
79 Letter from Frank Falla to G. C. Littler, 25 May 1966, TNA ref. HNP file 734.
80 Letter from G. C. Littler to Frank Falla, 2 June 1966, TNA ref. HNP file 734.
81 Letter from Frank Falla to G. C. Littler, 5 June 1966, TNA ref. HNP file 734.
82 Letter from G. C. Littler to Frank Falla, 10 June 1966, TNA ref. HNP file 734.
83 For example, 1967-68(350), Second report from the Select Committee on the parliamentary commissioner for administration together with the proceedings of the

committee relating to the report and minutes of evidence, Session 1967–68; 1967–68(54), Third report of the parliamentary commissioner for administration, Session 1967–68, presented to Parliament pursuant to Section 10 (4) of the Parliamentary Commissioner Act, 1967.

84 Letter from Frank Falla to GC Littler, Claims Department, Foreign Office, 30 November 1966, Frank Falla Archive.
85 Letter from Frank Falla to Mr W Marsh, 31 August 1965, Frank Falla Archive.
86 Letter from Frank Falla to Airey Neave, 23 July 1965, Frank Falla Archive.
87 Hansard, 26 October 1965, vol. 718, c.19.
88 Letter from Frank Falla to Airey Neave, 31 October 1965, Frank Falla Archive.
89 Letter from J Russell, Private Secretary of Airey Neave, to Frank Falla, 29 October 1965, Frank Falla Archive.
90 There is some indication that the Foreign Office considered some French prisons as comparable to a concentration camp: 'Institutions comparable to a concentration camp'. TNA ref. FO 64/100.
91 Letter from Frank Falla to EJ Lawrence, 1 March 1966, Frank Falla Archive.
92 Letter from Hubert Lanyon to Frank Falla, 3 November 1965, Frank Falla Archive.
93 Diary of Frank Falla, entry for 20 November 1965 (in private ownership).
94 Letter from Frank Falla to Airey Neave, 5 March 1966, Frank Falla Archive.
95 For example, Hansard 25 April 1966, vol. 727, cc.348–9.
96 Hansard, 23 January 1967, vol. 739, cc.188–190.
97 Schrafstetter, S. 2008. '"Gentlemen, the Cheese is All Gone!" British POWs, the "Great Escape" and the Anglo-German Agreement for compensation to victims of Nazism', *Contemporary European History* 17(1): 23–43.
98 *Daily Telegraph*, 22 December 1967.
99 Kushner, T. 2017. 'The Holocaust in the British imagination: The official mind and beyond, 1945 to the present', *Holocaust Studies* 23(3): 376.
100 Schrafstetter, 'Gentlemen, the Cheese is All Gone!' p. 42.

Chapter 7

1 Etkind, A. 2010. 'Mapping Memory Events in the East European Space', *East European Memory Studies* 1: 4–5.
2 Etkind, 'Mapping Memory Events in the East European Space', pp. 4–5.
3 Winter, J. 1999. 'Forms of Kinship and Remembrance in the Aftermath of the Great War', pp. 40–60 in J. Winter and E. Sivan (eds), *War and Remembrance in the Twentieth Century*. Cambridge: Cambridge University Press, p. 40.
4 Carr, G. 2015. 'Islands of war, guardians of memory: The afterlife of the German Occupation in the British Channel Islands', pp. 75–91 in G. Carr and K. Reeves (eds), *Heritage and Memory of War: Responses from Small Islands*. London: Routledge, p. 79.
5 Falla, *The Silent War*, p. 167.
6 Wieviorka, A. 2006. *The Era of the Witness*. Ithaca and London: Cornell University Press, p. 88.
7 Wieviorka, *The Era of the Witness*, pp. 57, 87.
8 The history of the Joe Mière collection, written by Joe Mière. Research files, JWT.
9 Obituary and tributes to Joe Mière, *Jersey Evening Post*, 22 June 2006.
10 Letter from David Lance, Keeper of the Department of Sound Records, IWM, to Frank Falla, 28 March 1980. Island Archives, Guernsey, Frank Falla Archive.

11 Interview with Joe Mière, IWM sound archive ref. 10683.
12 Letter from Frank Falla to Joe Mière, undated but replied to on 20 February 1980. Joe Mière collection, JWT. This is likely to have been the first time that the men exchanged letters, because this one in early 1980 was addressed to 'Mr Mière' and signed 'yours sincerely, Frank Falla'. The next letter, dated April 1980, was addressed to 'Dear Joe', and the third, dated 1981, was signed 'As ever, Frank Falla', indicating men now on first name terms.
13 Carr, 'Heritage, memory and resistance', p. 327.
14 Speech given by Philip Bailhache, 27 April 1995. I thank Sir Philip for sharing this speech with me.
15 Interview with Philip Bailhache, 22 June 2009.
16 Luckhurst, M. 2001. 'The Case of Theresa: Guernsey, the Holocaust, and Theatre Censorship in the 1990s', *European Studies* 17: 255, 262.
17 Etkind, 'Mapping Memory Events in the East European Space', p. 5.
18 Interview with Michael Day, 11 February 2016.
19 Ibid.
20 Paul Sanders was originally commissioned by the Liberation 50 committee; various sponsors then made the work possible.
21 https://www.bbc.co.uk/news/world-europe-jersey-24523007 [accessed 5 July 2018].
22 Sanders, *The Ultimate Sacrifice* (3rd edition), pp. xiii–xiv.
23 Telephone interview with Freddie Cohen, 5 February 2015.
24 Cohen, *The Jews in the Channel Islands*, p. 11.
25 Telephone interview with Freddie Cohen, 5 February 2015.
26 Ibid.
27 Interview with Michael Day, 11 February 2016.
28 Fraser, *The Jews of the Channel Islands and the Rule of Law*.
29 Carr, *Legacies of Occupation*, pp. 108–9.
30 Pearce, A. 2014. *Holocaust Consciousness in Contemporary Britain*. New York and Abingdon: Routledge, p. 148.
31 Interview with Paula Thelwell, member of HMD committee, Jersey, 16 August 2015.
32 The Constable (or Connétable) is the elected head of a parish in the Channel Islands.
33 People of note here, although not an exclusive list, include Doug Ford and Jon Carter who worked for Jersey Heritage Trust under Michael Day in this period; Gary Font, whose father, Francisco Font, was a Spanish Republican forced and slave worker, who remained in the Island after the Occupation and organized the annual ceremonies at the Slave Worker Memorial at Westmount; Simon Crowcroft, Angela Trigg (now Francey), and Michael Ginns, who promoted the memory of deportees, and Paula Thelwell, part of the HMD committee in Jersey and a reporter on the *Jersey Evening Post*.
34 http://elisbebb.com/myViews/index.html, January 2015 archive [accessed 5 July 2018].
35 19 January 2015, Facebook comment.
36 States of Guernsey. 'Code of Conduct for States Members'. http://www.gov.gg/codeofconductforstatesmembers [accessed 10 July 2018].
37 For example, comments on Facebook group 'Save the Guernseyman' for 20 January 2015: https://www.facebook.com/savetheguernseyman/?hc_ref=ARQcYkgix0szAPsbLOnlK90ujtI6xxMpaCNPrIr7dbbYTgH9kWqIySpL39tDn09lny4&fref=nf [accessed 21 January 2015].
38 https://www.gov.gg/CHttpHandler.ashx?id=100769&p=0, pp. 17–18 [accessed 5 July 2018].

39 'A 'States resolution' is an important part of the democratic process in Guernsey. It is a decision made by the elected representatives who comprise the States of Deliberation. A States resolution is an expression of the political will of the States. States resolutions can therefore be used to hold departments to account' (text taken from executive summary of 'Monitoring States resolutions: April 2012 discussion document'), Scrutiny Committee of the States of Guernsey, https://www.gov.gg/CHttpHandler.ashx?id=74648&p=0 [accessed 10 July 2018].
40 Carr, *Legacies of Occupation*.
41 http://www.bbc.co.uk/news/world-europe-guernsey-38136385, published online 29 November 2016 [accessed 29 November 2016].
42 Keate, G. 'Guernsey finally opens up about Nazi past', *The Times* 10 December 2016, p. 41.
43 'Holocaust Education – what the islands' pupils can learn', *Guernsey Press*, 2 January 2017.
44 Information from Elis Bebb, 9 December 2017.
45 Words spoken by the Dean of Guernsey, the Very Reverend Tim Barker, 27 January 2018.
46 http://news.bbc.co.uk/1/hi/uk/8558739.stm [accessed 5 July 2018].
47 https://www.bbc.co.uk/news/world-europe-jersey-42795152 [accessed 5 July 2018].

Chapter 8

1 This diagram was first published in Carr, *Legacies of Occupation*, p. 14.
2 Carr, Sanders and Willmot, *Protest, Defiance and Resistance*.
3 Hirsch, M. and Spitzer, L. 2015. 'Small acts of repair: The unclaimed legacy of the Romanian Holocaust', *Journal of Literature and Trauma Studies* 4(1–2): 13–43.
4 Meskell, L. and Scheermeyer, C. 2008. 'Heritage as therapy: Set pieces from the new South Africa', *Journal of Material Culture* 13(2): 156, 168.
5 Tunbridge, J.E. and Ashworth, G.J., 1996. *Dissonant Heritage: The Management of the Past as a Resource in Conflict*. Chichester: John Wiley & Sons, p. 6.
6 Tunbridge and Ashworth, *Dissonant Heritage*, p. 190.
7 Ibid., p. 237.
8 Viejo-Rose, D. 2011. '"Memorial functions": Intent, impact and the right to remember', *Memory Studies* 4(4): 477.
9 For example, Viejo-Rose, 'Memorial functions'.
10 For example, Meskell and Scheermeyer, 'Heritage as therapy'; Lehrer, E., 2010. 'Can there be a conciliatory heritage?' *International Journal of Heritage Studies* 16(4–5): 269–88.
11 While the Channel Islands cannot be described as a post-conflict society today, they are still in a post-conflict phase whereby they are still reverberating with the legacies of the German Occupation.
12 Giblin, J.D. 2014. 'Post-conflict heritage: Symbolic healing and cultural renewal', *International Journal of Heritage Studies* 20(5): 500–1.
13 Giblin, 'Post-conflict heritage', p. 513.
14 Hirsch and Spitzer, 'Small acts of repair', pp. 19, 31.
15 Letter from Henrietta Gillingham to the Bailiff, 11 December 1949; letter from Bailiff to Henrietta Gillingham, 13 December 1949. IA, Guernsey, ref. BF 26-09.
16 Emails from director of Guernsey Museum to author, 11 and 6 June, 2014.

17 Letter from Lieutenant-Governor Air Marshall Peter Walker to author, 29 May 2014.
18 A *Vin d'Honneur* in the Channel Islands is a wine reception following a ceremony and is held in honour of a person or group.
19 Letter from Bailiff to author, 5 June 2014.
20 Letter from author to Bailiff, 13 June 2014.
21 Letter from Bailiff to author, 24 June 2014.
22 Carr, Sanders and Willmot, *Protest, Defiance and Resistance*.
23 Paul Sanders has recently re-analysed the case; see 'Economic resistance and sabotage'.
24 Notes taken from Resistance Memorial committee meeting, 28 July 2014.
25 Hirsch and Spitzer, 'Small acts of repair', p. 39.
26 Ingrouille miraculously survived five years in Nazi prisons only to die of TB while in a displaced persons camp at the end of the war. His body was repatriated to Guernsey.
27 Building up the story of Sidney Ashcroft and tracking down his relatives would not have been possible without the help of family historians Brian Dobson (Tunbridge Wells) and Margaret Crosbie (St Helens).
28 The story of Sidney Ashcroft can be read here: https://www.frankfallaarchive.org/people/sidney-ashcroft/ [accessed 22 August 2018].
29 https://www.youtube.com/watch?v=OCKGYIEeI28&t=5s, BBC Inside Out South West, filmed in November 2015 [accessed 1 June 2018].
30 Quote from speech given by Bailiff, 4 May 2015.
31 My sincere thanks to Pavel Vařeka of the University of West Bohemia for finding records relating to Tierney's last resting place.
32 Email from Michael Viebig to author, 4 March 2016. The honour of finding Joseph Gillingham's records go to Michael Viebig, head of the Roter Ochse prison (Halle) memory foundation, and an activist for local victims of Nazi persecution.
33 The documentary *Finding our fathers: Lost heroes of WWII*, first screened on 6 May 2016, can be viewed here: https://vimeo.com/229688437 [accessed 1 June 2018].
34 https://www.bbc.co.uk/news/world-europe-guernsey-36039498, https://jerseyeveningpost.com/news/2016/05/06/lost-heroes-of-the-occupation-found/, https://www.mirror.co.uk/news/real-life-stories/women-drawn-together-second-world-7908039 [accessed 1 June 2018].
35 http://www.geschichte-hameln.de/verein/interessenziele.php [accessed 1 August 2018].
36 The Frank Falla Archive, www.frankfallaarchive.org, was sponsored by the *Erinnerung, Verantwortung, Zukunft Stiftung*, Berlin.
37 Carr, Sanders and Willmot, 'Conclusion'.
38 Number accurate as of 21 June 2018.
39 https://www.bbc.co.uk/news/world-europe-jersey-44424122 [accessed 12 July 2018].
40 https://jerseyeveningpost.com/news/2018/06/25/holocaust-memorial-claim-is-nothing-other-than-a-theory/ [accessed 25 June 2018].
41 Carr, G. and Sturdy Colls, C. 2016. 'Taboo and Sensitive Heritage: Labour camps, burials and the role of activism in the Channel Islands', *International Journal of Heritage Studies* 22(9): 702–15.
42 https://www.jerseyheritage.org/walks-trails-and-tours/resistance-trail [accessed 1 August 2018].
43 Sturdy Colls, C. 2015. 'Uncovering a painful past: Archaeology and the Holocaust', *Conservation and the Management of Archaeological Sites* 17(1): 38–55; Sturdy Colls, C. 2015. *Holocaust Archaeologies*. Switzerland: Springer International (Chapter 12).

44 June 2018.
45 https://www.frankfallaarchive.org/further-information/resistance-trail-guernsey/ [accessed 1 June 2018].
46 Billig, M. 1995. *Banal Nationalism*. London: Sage.
47 See Carr, G. 2012. 'Examining the memorialscape of occupation and liberation: A case study from the Channel Islands', *International Journal of Heritage Studies* 18(2): 174–93, for discussions of how narratives can be read from memorialscapes.

Chapter 9

1 Captain JR Dening files, JRD 9, History of the GFP in the Channel Islands. IWM ref. 13409.
2 Pearce, *Holocaust Consciousness*, p. 47.
3 'Soviet delegation flies in', *Jersey Evening Post*, 28 March 1966; 'Russian gold watches for 20 Occupation Islanders', *Jersey Evening Post*, 29 March 1966.
4 Letters from Lieutenant-Governor to Bailiff, 14 September 1965 and 26 January 1966. JA ref. B/A/L31/10.
5 Ivy Forster, another of Le Druillenec's sisters, had been awarded a gold watch. Although she, too, had been caught and imprisoned with her siblings, she was not deported after a local doctor helped to pretend to the Germans that she had TB.
6 Sanders, *The Ultimate Sacrifice* (3rd edition), p. 64.
7 Women who had relationships with German soldiers.
8 Young, J. 1993. *The Texture of Memory: Holocaust Memorials and Meanings*. New Haven and London: Yale University Press.
9 Geyer, M. 1997. 'The place of the Second World War in German memory and history', *New German Critique* 71: 5–40.
10 Wallis, R. 2017. *British POWs and the Holocaust: Witnessing the Nazi Atrocities*. London and New York: I.B. Tauris.
11 Harold Le Druillenec, Stanley Green and Julia Barry.
12 Julia Barry was deported for black market offences; she was sent to Ravensbrück and her Jewish identity was only conclusively proved by the author in 2017. Although we have no independent verification, Maurice Green stated that his father, Stanley Green, deported to Buchenwald, was from a Jewish family even though he had converted to Christianity (Imperial War Museum ref 10716). John Draper, too, stated in his compensation testimony that his mother was Jewish (TNA ref FO 950/1732). None of these three were registered as Jewish, and Green and Draper appeared not to self-identify as Jewish.
13 See www.frankfallaarchive.org [accessed 1 August 2018].
14 Kushner, T. 2013. 'Loose connections? Britain and the "Final Solution"', pp. 51–67 in C. Sharples and O. Jensen (eds), *Britain and the Holocaust: Remembering and Representing War and Genocide*. Basingstoke: Palgrave Macmillan, p. 55.
15 Kushner, 'Loose connections?' p. 63.
16 Berger, S. 2010. 'Remembering the Second World War in Western Europe, 1945–2005', pp. 119–36 in M. Pakier and B. Stråth (eds), *A European Memory? Contested Histories and Politics of Remembrance*. New York and Oxford: Berghahn Books, pp. 128–9.
17 Donnelly, M. 2013. '"We should do something for the fiftieth": Remembering Auschwitz, Belsen and the Holocaust in Britain in 1995', pp. 171–89 in C. Sharples and O. Jensen (eds), *Britain and the Holocaust: Remembering and Rrepresenting War and Genocide*. Basingstoke: Palgrave Macmillan, p. 173.

18 Kushner, 'The Holocaust in the British imagination', p. 374.
19 Ibid., p. 375.
20 Ibid., p. 376.
21 Sanders, *The Ultimate Sacrifice* (3rd edition), p. xiv.
22 Sharples, C. and Jensen, O. 2013. 'Introduction', pp. 1–10 in C. Sharples and O. Jensen (eds), *Britain and the Holocaust: Remembering and Representing War and Genocide*. Basingstoke: Palgrave Macmillan, p. 2.
23 Ibid., p. 3.

Bibliography

Key for archival sources listed in chapter endnotes

CFU   *Crown Film Unit*
CIOS   *Channel Islands Occupation Society*
GMAG   *Guernsey Museum and Art Gallery*
IA   *Island Archives (Guernsey)*
IWM   *Imperial War Museum*
JA   *Jersey Archives*
JH   *Jersey Heritage*
JWT   *Jersey War Tunnels*
SJ   *Société Jersiaise (Lord Coutanche Library)*
TNA   *The National Archives*

Published sources

American Psychiatric Association. 1987. *The Diagnostic and Statistical Manual of Mental Disorders*. 3rd edn. (DSM-III). Washington DC: APA.

Bailey, K.0047. 1979 [1958]. *Dachau*. Guernsey: CI Marine Ltd.

Bar-On, D. 1995. *Fear and Hope: Three Generations of the Holocaust*. Cambridge, MA: Harvard University Press.

Barry, J. 1945a. 'I Was Condemned to Death'. *Guernsey Evening Press*, 18 July.

Barry, J. 1945b. 'The War Disclosures of Mrs Julia Barry'. *Guernsey Evening Press*, 20 July.

Barry, J. 1945c. 'From Ravensbruch [sic] to Guernsey'. *Guernsey Evening Press*, 17 August.

Berger, S. 2010. 'Remembering the Second World War in Western Europe, 1945–2005', pp. 119–36 in M. Pakier and B. Stråth (eds), *A European Memory? Contested Histories and Politics of Remembrance*. New York and Oxford: Berghahn Books.

Billig, M. 1995. *Banal Nationalism*. London: Sage.

Bunting, M. 1995. *The Model Occupation*. London and New York: HarperCollins Publishing/BCA.

Butler, J. 2010. *Frames of War: When Is Life Grievable?* London and New York: Verso.

Carr, G. 2012. 'Examining the Memorialscape of Occupation and Liberation: A Case Study from the Channel Islands'. *International Journal of Heritage Studies* 18(2): 174–93.

Carr, G. 2013. 'Stories of Suffering under the Nazis'. *Jersey Evening Post*, 11 July.

Carr, G. 2014a. *Legacies of Occupation: Heritage, Memory and Archaeology in the Channel Islands*. Switzerland: Springer International Publishing.

Carr, G. 2014b. 'Defiance and Deportations', pp. 127–52 in G. Carr, P. Sanders and L. Willmot, *Protest, Defiance and Resistance in the Channel Islands: German Occupation 1940-1945*. London: Bloomsbury Academic.
Carr, G. 2014c. 'Heritage, Memory and Resistance in the Channel Islands', pp. 307–37 in G. Carr, P. Sanders and L. Willmot, *Protest, Defiance and Resistance in the Channel Islands: German Occupation 1940-1945*. London: Bloomsbury Academic.
Carr, G. 2014d. 'The V-Sign Campaign and the Fear of Reprisals', pp. 43–64 in G. Carr, P. Sanders and L. Willmot, *Protest, Defiance and Resistance in the Channel Islands: German Occupation 1940-1945*. London: Bloomsbury Academic.
Carr, G. 2014e. 'Help Me Tell Brave Islanders' Stories'. *Guernsey Press*, 15 August.
Carr, G. 2015a. 'Islands of War, Guardians of Memory: The Afterlife of the German Occupation in the British Channel Islands', pp. 75–91 in G. Carr and K. Reeves (eds), *Heritage and Memory of War: Responses from Small Islands*. London: Routledge.
Carr, G. 2015b. 'Mum of a Nazi Victim: Did You Know Charlotte Ashcroft?' *Guernsey Press*, 17 January.
Carr, G. 2015c. 'Remembering Those Absent Friends'. *Guernsey Press*, 21 May.
Carr, G., Sanders, P. and Willmot, L. 2014a. 'Conclusion', pp. 329–54 in G. Carr, P. Sanders and L. Willmot, *Protest, Defiance and Resistance in the Channel Islands: German Occupation 1940-1945*. London: Bloomsbury Academic.
Carr, G., Sanders, P. and Willmot, L. 2014b. *Protest, Defiance and Resistance in the Channel Islands: German Occupation 1940-1945*. London: Bloomsbury Academic.
Carr, G. and Sturdy Colls, C. 2016. 'Taboo and Sensitive Heritage: Labour Camps, Burials and the Role of Activism in the Channel Islands'. *International Journal of Heritage Studies* 22(9): 702–15.
Cesarani, D. and Sundquist, E.J. 2012. *After the Holocaust: Challenging the Myth of Silence*. London and New York: Routledge.
Chapman, E. 1966. *The Real Eddie Chapman Story*. London: Tandem Books Ltd.
Cohen, F. 2000. *The Jews in the Channel Islands during the German Occupation 1940-1945*. Jersey: Jersey Heritage Trust.
Connelly, M. 2010. 'We Can Take It! Britain and the Memory of the Home Front in the Second World War', pp. 53–69 in J. Echternkamp and S. Martens (eds), *Experience and Memory: The Second World War in Europe*. New York and Oxford: Berghahn Books.
Cottrell, L. 1950. 'The Man from Belsen', pp. 97–110 in L. Gilliam (ed.), *BBC Features*. London: Evans Brothers Ltd.
Crocq, M. and Crocq, L. 2000. 'From Shell Shock and War Neurosis to Posttraumatic Stress Disorder: A History of Psychotraumatology'. *Dialogues in Clinical Neuroscience* 2(1): 47–55.
Cruikshank, C. 2010 [1975]. *The German Occupation of the Channel Islands*. Oxford: Oxford University Press & Guernsey: The Guernsey Press. [Reprint, Stroud: Sutton Publishing.]
Davidson, S. 1984. 'Human Reciprocity among the Jewish Prisoners in the Nazi Concentration Camps', in pp. 555–72 *The Nazi Concentration Camps*. Yad Vashem. http://www.yadvashem.org/odot_pdf/Microsoft%20Word%20-%203554.pdf [accessed 8 June 2018].
Donnelly, M. 2013. '"We Should Do Something for the Fiftieth": Remembering Auschwitz, Belsen and the Holocaust in Britain in 1995', pp. 171–89 in C. Sharples and O. Jensen (eds), *Britain and the Holocaust: Remembering and Representing War and Genocide*. Basingstoke: Palgrave Macmillan.
Durand, R. 1946. *Guernsey under German Rule*. London: The Guernsey Society.

Dutot. L. 1974. *Bread between the Rails*. Liverpool: F.H. Tuck.
Eitinger, L. 1961. 'Pathology of the Concentration Camp Syndrome'. *Archives of General Psychiatry* 5(4): 371–379.
Etkind, A. 2010. 'Mapping Memory Events in the East European Space'. *East European Memory Studies* 1: 4–5.
Falla, F. 1945a. 'Revelations of Prison Life in Germany'. *Guernsey Evening Press*, 2 July, front page.
Falla, F. 1945b. 'Revelations of German Prison Life'. *Guernsey Evening Press*, 4 July, front page.
Falla, F. 1967. *The Silent War*. London: Leslie Frewin Ltd.
Faramus, A. 1954. *The Faramus Story*. London: Brown Watson Ltd.
Faramus, A. 1990. *Journey into Darkness*. London: Grafton Books.
Fraser, D. 2000. *The Jews of the Channel Islands and the Rule of Law, 1940–1945*. Brighton: Sussex Academic Press.
Gersons, B.P.R. and Carlier, I.V.E. 1992. 'Post-Traumatic Stress Disorder: The History of a Recent Concept'. *British Journal of Psychiatry* 161: 742–8.
Geyer, M. 1997. 'The Place of the Second World War in German Memory and History'. *New German Critique* 71: 5–40.
Giblin, J.D. 2014. 'Post-Conflict Heritage: Symbolic Healing and Cultural Renewal'. *International Journal of Heritage Studies* 20(5): 500–18.
Ginns, M. 2006. *The Organisation Todt and the Fortress Engineers in the Channel Islands*. Jersey: Channel Islands Occupation Society Archive Book No. 8.
Harris, R.E. 1979. *Islanders Deported*. Ilford, Essex: CISS Publishing.
Helm, S. 2015. *If This Is a Woman*. London: Little, Brown Book Group.
Hirsch, M. and Spitzer, L. 2015. 'Small Acts of Repair: The Unclaimed Legacy of the Romanian Holocaust'. *Journal of Literature and Trauma Studies* 4(1–2): 13–43.
Hovinga, H. 2010. *The Sumatra Railroad: Final Destination Pakan Baroe, 1943–1945*. Trans. Bernard J. Wolters. 5th edn. Leiden: KITLV Press.
Jorgensen-Earp, C. 2013. *Discourse and Defiance under Nazi Occupation: Guernsey, Channel Islands, 1940–1945*. East Lansing: Michigan State University Press.
King, P. 1991. *The Channel Islands War 1940–1945*. London: Robert Hale.
Kuch, K. and Cox, B. 1992. 'Symptoms of PTSD in 124 Survivors of the Holocaust'. *American Journal of Psychiatry* 149(3): 337–40.
Kushner, T. 2013. 'Loose Connections? Britain and the "Final Solution"', pp. 51–67 in C. Sharples and O. Jensen (eds), *Britain and the Holocaust: Remembering and Representing War and Genocide*. Basingstoke: Palgrave Macmillan.
Kushner, T. 2017. 'The Holocaust in the British Imagination: The Official Mind and Beyond, 1945 to the Present'. *Holocaust Studies* 23(3): 364–84.
Leale, J. 1945. *Report of Five Years of German Occupation*. Guernsey: Guernsey Press.
Lehrer, E. 2010. 'Can There Be a Conciliatory Heritage?' *International Journal of Heritage Studies* 16(4–5): 269–88.
Luckhurst, M. 2001. 'The Case of Theresa: Guernsey, the Holocaust, and Theatre Censorship in the 1990s'. *European Studies* 17: 255–67.
Major, E. 1996. 'The Impact of the Holocaust on the Second Generation: Norwegian Jewish Holocaust Survivors and Their Children'. *Journal of Traumatic Stress* 9: 441–54.
Major, E. 2003. 'Health Effects of War Stress on Norwegian World War II Resistance Groups'. *Journal of Traumatic Stress* 16(6): 595–9.
Mayne, R. 1974. 'Forgotten Islanders'. *Channel Islands Occupation Review*, 15–18.
Meskell, L. and Scheermeyer, C. 2008. 'Heritage as Therapy: Set Pieces from the New South Africa'. *Journal of Material Culture* 13(2): 153–73.

Mière, J. 2004. *Never to Be Forgotten*. Jersey: Channel Island Publishing.
Op den Velde, W., Frey-Wouters, E. and Pelser, H.E. 1994. 'The Price of Heroism: Veterans of the Dutch Resistance to the Nazi Occupation and the Holocaust in World War II'. *Holocaust and Genocide Studies* 8(3): 335–48.
Pearce, A. 2014. *Holocaust Consciousness in Contemporary Britain*. New York and Abingdon: Routledge.
Persson, S. 2009. *Escape from the Third Reich: Folke Bernadotte and the White Buses*. London: Frontline Books.
Pocock, H.R.S. 1975. *The Memoirs of Lord Coutanche*. Chichester: Phillimore.
Ramsden, J. 2010. 'Myths and Realities of the "People's War" in Britain', pp. 40–52 in J. Echternkamp and S. Martens (eds), *Experience and Memory: The Second World War in Europe*. New York and Oxford: Berghahn Books.
Rousso, H. 2007. 'History of Memory, Policies of the Past: What For?' pp. 23–77 in K. Jarausch and T. Lindenberger (eds), *Conflicted Memories: Europeanizing Contemporary Histories*. New York: Berghahn Books.
Routledge, P. 2002. *Public Servant, Secret Agent: The Elusive Life and Violent Death of Airey Neave*. London: Fourth Estate.
Sanders, P. 2004. *The Ultimate Sacrifice*. 2nd edn. Jersey: Jersey Heritage Trust.
Sanders, P. 2005. *The British Channel Islands under German Occupation, 1940–1945*. Jersey: Jersey Heritage Trust.
Sanders, P. 2012. 'Narratives of Britishness: UK War Memory and Channel Islands Occupation Memory', pp. 24–39 in J. Matthews and D. Travers (eds), *Islands and Britishness: A Global Perspective*. Newcastle upon Tyne: Cambridge Scholars Publishing.
Sanders, P. 2014a. 'Radio Days', pp. 65–96 in G. Carr, P. Sanders and L. Willmot, *Protest, Defiance and Resistance in the Channel Islands: German Occupation 1940–1945*. London: Bloomsbury Academic.
Sanders, P. 2014b. 'Economic Resistance and Sabotage', pp. 277–306 in G. Carr, P. Sanders and L. Willmot, *Protest, Defiance and Resistance in the Channel Islands: German Occupation 1940–1945*. London: Bloomsbury Academic.
Sanders, P. 2018. *The Ultimate Sacrifice*. 3rd edn. Jersey: Jersey Heritage.
Saunders, N.J. 2001. 'Apprehending Memory: Material Culture and War', pp. 476–88 in P. Liddle, J. Bourne and I. Whitehead (eds), *The Great World War, 1914–45*. London: HarperCollins.
Saunders, N.J. 2003. *Trench Art: Materialities and Memories of War*. Oxford and New York: Berg.
Schrafstetter, S. 2008. '"Gentlemen, the Cheese Is All Gone!" British POWs, the "Great Escape" and the Anglo-German Agreement for Compensation to Victims of Nazism'. *Contemporary European History* 17(1): 23–43.
Sharples, C. and Jensen, O. 2013. 'Introduction', pp. 1–10 in C. Sharples and O. Jensen (eds), *Britain and the Holocaust: Remembering and Representing War and Genocide*. Basingstoke: Palgrave Macmillan.
Sherwill, A. 2006. *A Fair and Honest Book*. Lulu.com.
Sturdy Colls, C. 2015a. 'Uncovering a Painful Past: Archaeology and the Holocaust'. *Conservation and the Management of Archaeological Sites* 17(1): 38–55.
Sturdy Colls, C. 2015b. *Holocaust Archaeologies*. Switzerland: Springer International.
Tunbridge, J.E. and Ashworth, G.J. 1996. *Dissonant Heritage: The Management of the Past as a Resource in Conflict*. Chichester: John Wiley & Sons.
Turner, B. 2010. *Outpost of Occupation*. London: Aurum Press Ltd.

Uzzell, D. and Ballantyne, R. 1998. 'Heritage That Hurts: Interpretation in a Post-Modern World', pp. 152–71 in D.L. Uzzell and R. Ballantyne (eds), *Contemporary Issus in Heritage and Environmental Interpretation: Problems and Prospects*. London: The Stationery Office.

Viejo-Rose, D. 2011. '"Memorial Functions": Intent, Impact and the Right to Remember'. *Memory Studies* 4(4): 465–80.

Wallis, R. 2017. *British POWs and the Holocaust: Witnessing the Nazi Atrocities*. London and New York: I.B. Tauris.

Weisberg, R.H. 2014. *In Praise of Intransigence: The Perils of Flexibility*. Oxford: Oxford University Press.

Wieviorka, A. 2006. *The Era of the Witness*. Ithaca and London: Cornell University Press.

Willmot, L. 2014a. 'Humanitarian Resistance: Help to Jews and OT Workers', pp. 97–126 in G. Carr, P. Sanders and L. Willmot, *Protest, Defiance and Resistance in the Channel Islands: German Occupation 1940–1945*. London: Bloomsbury Academic.

Willmot, L. 2014b. 'Sabotage, Intelligence-Gathering and Escape', pp. 213–42 in G. Carr, P. Sanders and L. Willmot, *Protest, Defiance and Resistance in the Channel Islands: German Occupation 1940–1945*. London: Bloomsbury Academic.

Winter, J. 1999. 'Forms of Kinship and Remembrance in the Aftermath of the Great War', pp. 40–60 in J. Winter and E. Sivan (eds), *War and Remembrance in the Twentieth Century*. Cambridge: Cambridge University Press.

Withuis, J. 2010. 'The Management of Victimhood-Long Term Health Damage from Asthenia to PTSD', in J. Withuis and A. Mooij (eds), *The Politics of War Trauma*. Studies of the Netherlands Institute for War Documentation. Amsterdam: Aksant.

Wood, A. and Wood, M. 1955. *Islands in Danger*. New York: Macmillan.

Yehuda, R., Kahana, B., Southwick, S.M. and Giller, E.L. 1994. 'Depressive Features in Holocaust Survivors with Post-Traumatic Stress Disorder'. *Journal of Traumatic Stress* 7(4): 699–704.

Young, J. 1993. *The Texture of Memory: Holocaust Memorials and Meanings*. New Haven and London: Yale University Press.

Unpublished sources

Domaille, Gerald. Unpublished memoirs. https://www.frankfallaarchive.org/wp-content/uploads/2016/10/Gerald-Domaille-memoirs.pdf [accessed 23 August 2018].

Duquemin, C. Unpublished memoirs. https://www.frankfallaarchive.org/wp-content/uploads/2016/10/Cecil-Duquemin-Memoir-edited-RM-GC.pdf [accessed 23 August 2018].

Falla, F. Unpublished. *Guernsey Ink in My Veins*. Unpublished manuscript in author's possession.

Hassall, P. 1997. *Night and Fog Prisoners*. Unpublished memoir, Jersey Archives. See also: https://www.frankfallaarchive.org/wp-content/uploads/2016/08/Peter-Hassalls-memoirs.pdf [accessed 1 August 2018].

L'Amy, J.H. *The German Occupation of Jersey*. Société Jersiaise Library ref. MIL/GO/D/12.

Oliver, E. 2014. *Interpreting Memories of a Forgotten Army: Prisoner of War Narratives from the Sumatra Railway, May 1944–August 1945*. Unpublished PhD thesis, University of Leeds.

Newspapers

Daily Herald
Daily Telegraph
Daily Worker
Liverpool Post
The Guernsey Press
The Jersey Evening Post
The Times

Index

acts of repair   170, 173, 175, 177, 181, 199
acts of rescue   xi, 21, 169, 171, 173, 181, 184, 187–8, 193, 199
Anglo-German (bilateral) compensation agreement   6, 7, 120, 123–4, 130, 197
antisemitic legislation   13, 159, 165, 208
Ashcroft, Sidney   xi, 9, 12, 28–30, 38, 41, 44, 89, 178–84

Bailey, Kingston   28–32, 34, 35–6, 40, 47, 76–7, 87, 91, 100, 102
Bailhache, Philip   x, 151–8, 169, 208
Bailhache effect   xi, 153
Barry, Julia. *See* Brichta, Julia
BBC   5–6, 8, 45, 51, 53, 68, 75, 84, 88, 103, 107, 125, 133, 165, 177, 179, 182–3, 188–9, 193
Bebb, Elis   159–60, 162, 165–7
Bedane, Albert   189–90, 208
Bergen Belsen concentration camp   5, 27, 36, 40–1, 49, 60, 66, 83–5, 104, 124, 140–1, 143
Brichta, Julia   7, 10, 24, 41
British Hero(es) of the Holocaust   5, 169, 208
Buchenwald concentration camp   7, 9, 14, 24–5, 27–8, 33, 36, 39, 46, 67, 77, 82–3, 86, 90–2, 97–8, 100, 104–5, 111, 126–7, 140–1, 143, 161, 206

Carey, de Vic   153, 161, 168
Carey, Victor   13, 51, 65, 68, 108, 110, 153, 160, 168, 169, 196
Carey effect   153, 160, 165, 191
Channel Islands Occupation Society (CIOS)   154, 165–7, 169, 191–2
Channel Islands war memory   4, 19, 50, 74, 153, 170
Churchillian narrative or paradigm   4–6, 74, 117, 197–8

civilian internees   67, 112, 127, 157, 166, 176, 178
Cohen, Frederick   17, 155, 156, 158, 160
Coutanche, Alexander   51, 62–3, 65–6, 69–70, 110–12, 153, 200
Crown Film Unit (CFU)   49–53, 58, 68

Day, Michael   16, 154, 156–7, 159
deportations, February 1943   15, 56, 112
deportations, (of Jews)   8
deportations, (of political prisoners)   76, 111–12, 114–15, 148, 153, 176, 180
deportations, September 1942   15, 56, 112, 189–90
deportees. *See* civilian internees
Deportees Memorial   166, 176, 178
Dexter, Norman   32, 37–8, 41–2, 44, 47, 128–30
digital heritage   6, 9, 20–1, 169, 171, 173, 188, 190, 192–3, 199
Domaille, Gerald   33, 36–8, 41–2, 47, 97–8, 101, 128, 130, 161
Duquemin, Cecil   29, 37, 53, 128, 130
Duquemin, Frederick   90, 97–8, 101

Falla, Frank   6, 9, 12–19, 21, 25, 31–32, 36–40, 42–4, 46, 49, 53, 59, 61, 81, 83, 88, 92, 96, 102, 104–5, 107–8, 110–11, 113–43, 147–51, 159, 172, 181–3, 185, 186–8, 190, 193–4, 197–9, 206, 208
Faramus, Anthony   25, 32, 34, 39–41, 67, 77, 86, 87, 90–2
Finkelstein, John Max   7
forced labour   5, 23, 27, 30, 32, 35, 76–7, 97, 112, 125, 134–5, 138
forced labourers   5, 7, 10, 35, 112, 155, 167–8, 178, 180, 200
Frank Falla Archive   17, 181, 186–8, 190, 193–4, 206, 208

Frankfurt (Main) Prison   25, 27, 31–2, 36–8, 42, 44, 46, 88, 104–5, 124–5, 127–30, 135–6, 138–41, 143, 158, 178, 182–3
friendship groups   20, 23, 29–31, 34–6, 42, 45–7, 68, 103, 105, 195, 197

game-changers   21, 22, 143, 147, 152, 154, 158, 159, 169, 198, 200, 208
Geheime Feldpolizei (Secret Field Police)   16, 32, 59, 149, 189–90, 192, 195, 204
Gelderblom, Bernhard   184
Gillingham, Joseph   12, 47, 53, 88, 130, 140, 175, 177, 182–5
Gould, Louisa   5, 15, 18, 60, 61, 77, 84, 143, 189–90, 204
Gould, Maurice   11, 30, 36, 42, 112, 189–90, 200–1
guardians of memory   21–2, 69, 74, 103, 143, 147–8, 153, 157, 159, 171, 195, 197–8
Guernsey prison   10, 18, 106, 114
Guernsey Underground News Service (GUNS)   15, 53, 58–9, 82, 88, 104, 106, 114, 124, 128, 130, 133–4, 140, 142, 150, 175, 182, 184, 192

Hague Convention   55–8, 66, 68, 195
Halle Prison   182–4
Hamelin Prison   184–6
Hassall, Peter   11, 29–30, 36, 42, 74, 200, 201
Holocaust   3–4, 21, 79, 80, 96–7, 142, 149, 154, 157–60, 162–3, 166–7, 169, 173, 178, 206–8
Holocaust, witnesses to the   162, 206
Holocaust education   162–3, 165–6, 168–9, 198, 207–8
Holocaust Educational Trust   208
Holocaust gallery. *See* Imperial War Museum
Holocaust Memorial Day (HMD)   21, 147, 154, 156–70, 181, 188, 198–9, 205, 206, 208
Holocaust Memorial Day Trust (HMDT)   167–8
Holocaust narratives   206–8

Holocaust Requête/Resolution   162–3, 166–9, 198
Holocaust survivors   79–80, 97
Holocaust victims   173

Imperial War Museum Holocaust gallery   207
incremental memory event   21, 143, 147, 152–4, 156–60, 167–9, 171, 180, 193, 198–200, 208
informers   15, 21, 49–50, 53, 58–70, 196, 203–5
Ingrouille, John   13, 69, 88, 130, 140, 178, 201–4

Jersey Loyalists   50, 58–63, 65–8, 148, 197
Jersey prison   18, 53, 80, 91, 106
Jewish community, Jersey   17, 155–7, 190
Jewish memorial, Guernsey   157, 158, 162, 164, 166–7, 178, 206
Jewish refugees   7, 55, 123, 153, 159, 162, 166, 207
Jews   7, 10, 14, 17, 52, 55, 57–8, 79–80, 89, 106, 120–1, 123–4, 147, 149, 153–7, 159–60, 162, 163, 166, 173, 178, 189, 198, 205–8
Johnson, Peter Bruce   188

Kaštice (*formerly* Kaschitz)   45, 88, 182, 183

Lainé, Walter   37–8, 41–2, 44, 46–7, 89, 97, 128, 130, 179
L'Amy, John Hamptonne   14, 60, 66
Leale, John   53–8, 65, 69–70
Le Druillenec, Harold   5, 12, 15, 18, 23, 36, 40, 46, 49, 60, 83–7, 92, 93, 104, 124–5, 140, 143, 157, 198, 200, 206, 208
Legg, Ernest   37, 38, 40, 53, 128, 130, 182
legitimacy   6, 9–12, 15–16, 20–1, 51, 69–70, 94–6, 105, 116–18, 128–9, 142, 148, 169, 174–5, 179, 184, 189, 193, 196–9
Lighthouse Memorial, Jersey   16, 42, 47, 67, 81, 153, 155–7, 188–90

Machon, Charles   12, 53, 143, 184–6
Machon, Roy   130, 132–8
Mière, Joe   8–9, 16–17, 67, 69, 103, 147, 149–51, 155, 157–9, 186–9, 204
Miller, Percy   32, 130, 140, 178

Naumburg Prison   14, 25, 27, 31–2, 36–8, 40, 43–6, 81, 88, 103–5, 112, 124–5, 127–8, 130–1, 135–6, 138–41, 143, 159, 175, 182–3
Neave, Airey   19, 110–11, 121–2, 124, 126, 139–41
Nelson, Thomas   188
Neuoffingen labour camp   9, 27, 29, 34, 76–7, 82, 86, 98, 101–2, 108, 177

Occupation Tapestry   154–5, 157, 190
O'Meara, Brian   9, 92, 97, 100–2
Ozanne, Marie   3, 10–11, 178–9, 192

policemen, Guernsey   32, 36, 75–6, 89, 90, 92, 98, 103, 106–8, 113–14, 116, 125, 148, 164–5, 167, 177, 192, 198, 202
political prisoner memorial, Jersey   153, 189–90
post-traumatic stress disorder (PTSD)   5, 10–11, 20, 42, 59, 73–5, 77–81, 83, 85–7, 91–2, 102, 105, 196–7
prisoners of war (POWs)   35, 107, 121, 131, 133, 206–7
Pšov   46, 182–3, 185
PTSD. *See* post-traumatic stress disorder

Quin, William   33, 75–6, 83, 86

reparative heritage   21, 169, 171, 174–5, 177–9, 193, 199

resistance memorial, Guernsey   3, 19, 47, 164, 166–8, 171, 175–7, 179–82, 184, 191–4, 198, 206, 208
resistance trail, Guernsey   165, 171, 188, 192–3
resistance trail, Jersey   171, 188–91
Righteous Among the Nations   189–90
Romainville Prison   25–7, 34, 91
Russian gold watches   200

St Saviour's wireless case   106
Sanders, Paul   4, 8–9, 14, 16, 51, 58, 60, 64–5, 67–70, 106–8, 125, 155–6, 158, 208
Sherwill, Ambrose   34, 35, 49, 53–4, 58, 69, 90, 103–4, 107, 110–11, 114–15, 135, 151
Smith, Herbert   9, 12, 44–5, 75–6, 90, 108, 177–8

taboo heritage   189
Tierney, Joseph   37, 44–6, 61–2, 88, 128, 130, 182–5
Tuck, Frank   29, 34–6, 44, 58, 76, 86–7, 92–3, 98–101, 103, 108, 115–16, 164, 197

UK Holocaust Memorial Foundation (UKHMF)   207

Vielsalm gathering   103
Villeneuve-Saint-Georges Prison   27, 29, 31, 34, 36, 76, 81–2, 155
V-sign badges   132–3
V-signs   57, 68, 106–7, 190

Weber, Dorothea (née Le Brocq)   208

Zöschen labour camp   10, 33, 45, 182–3, 189

Milton Keynes UK
Ingram Content Group UK Ltd.
UKHW022148290324
440228UK00005B/60